Almost British

By

Olivea Ebanks

ALMOST BRITISH

Copyright © Olivea Ebanks September 2010

All Rights Reserved

No part of this book may be reproduced in any form,

by photocopying or by any electronic or mechanical means,

including information storage or retrieval systems,

without permission in writing from both the copyright

owner and the publisher of this book.

978-0-95665 19-7-6

First Published September 2010 by

Direct POD

www.direct-pod.com

Printed in Great Britain by

The Direct Printing Company Ltd

Acknowledgements

I am grateful to God through faith in Jesus Christ for his constant presence and guidance. I love the Lord.

My darling husband Rudy and my wonderful mother Rubertha, thank you for your love and care of me during this especially difficult episode in my life. I love you both.

To Doreen Lawrence, Proverbs 22:1 says 'A good name is to be chosen rather than great riches, [and] loving favour, rather than silver or gold.' Thank you for lending me your good name.

It is a privilege to be supported by the core ministerial team in Emmanuel Ministries and the saints – you are all a gift to Rudy and me, and we appreciate you. I am also thankful for Apostle H C McFarlane, my Bishop and father in the Lord – you are a positive and needful influence in my life. I thank God for your anointing, wisdom and love.

To all the friends who knew that God would perform this miracle and who blessed my household with prayer and kindness – I thank and love you too.

PART ONE

Five Score Years Ago...

'Here (scientific confirmation) is proof of the necessity of slavery. The African is incapable of self-care and sinks into lunacy under the burden of freedom. It is a mercy to give him the guardianship and protection from mental death.'

John C. Calhoun (1844), Secretary of State, arguing for the extension of slavery

'(Black and other ethnic minority children) are uneducable beyond the nearest rudiments of training. No amount of school instruction will ever make them intelligent voters or capable citizens in the sense of the world...their dullness seems to be racial, or at least inherent in the family stock from which they come...Children of this group should be segregated in special classes and be given instruction which is concrete and practical. They cannot master abstractions, but they can be made efficient workers...There is no possibility at present of convincing society that they should not be allowed to reproduce, although from a eugenic point of view they constitute a grave problem because of their unusual prolific breeding.'

Lewis Terman (1916), *The Measurement of Intelligence*

'...Instability of character is ascribed to the Negro, involving a lack of foresight, an improvidence, a lack of persistence, small power of serious initiative, a tendency to be content with immediate satisfactions, deficient ambition...along with high emotionality and instability of character, defective morality is held to be a Negro characteristic.'

G. O. Ferguson (1916), *The Psychology of the Negro*

'His lips are thick, his zygomatic muscles, large and full* (* "These muscles are always in action during laughter and the extreme enlargement of them indicates a low mind." Lavater)...his jaws large and projecting,...his chin retreating...his forehead low, flat and slanting, and (as a consequence of this latter character) his eyeballs are very prominent,...apparently larger than those of white men;...all of these peculiarities at the same time contributing to reduce his facial angle almost to a level with that of the brute...Can any such man become great or elevated?'

Richard H. Colfax (1833), An Excerpt from: Evidence Against the Views of the Abolitionists, Consisting of Physical and Moral Proofs of the Natural Inferiority of the Negroes

'A merrier being does not exist on the face of the globe, than the negro slave... Why then, since the slave is happy, and happiness is the great object of all animated creation, should we endeavour to disturb his contentment by infusing into his mind a vain and indefinite desire for liberty—a something which he cannot comprehend, and which must inevitably dry up the very sources of his happiness.'

Thomas Dew (1832), *An Essay in Favor of Slavery*

One Score Years Ago…

I don't ever remember wanting to be white as a child; I do however remember wanting to be distinctive. In my formative years, I had no clear sense that my blackness was a problem to anyone. Whatever change I envisaged, whether that meant being darker or lighter, didn't matter much to me, as long as I was striking and exotic. I loved the many shades of black—there was far more to choose from. What I wanted was to be pretty! Prejudice was not something that I understood per se; yet I understood favouritism. As I grew up, I could see that others were preferred to me, although I have very little recollection of putting it down to colour. If there was any discontent it was never remedied by thoughts about a distant homeland, because I was home and didn't know any different. Instead, I remember wondering if I were more talented, more beautiful, would that have made the difference.

My first memorable experience of racism in adulthood was when I went for my first interview after leaving college. I was 19 years old. It was a junior researcher job and as I had just finished my 'A' levels I felt it would be perfect. I had enjoyed pouring over theory books for psychology and sociology and finding links to answer assignment and exam questions. I figured a research job would draw on the same set of skills. Having filled in the application form I got a call from the company and spoke to the director over the phone. The conversation was a good 30 minutes and it was fun. He explained the company researched thoroughbred horses. Naturally, I disclosed that I had not had any exposure to horses. Thankfully, he told me that would not be a problem: it was my skill as a researcher that was of interest. We talked at length about a great many things. It didn't feel like an interview at all, it felt like a conversation with someone whom I had just met with mutual interests, and together we were happy to find out more about each other.

The telephone interview ended with what he called 'a formality': the invitation to come in and meet face to face. I was surprised when he asked if I could come in the very next day.

I enthusiastically said, 'Yes'.

He said I would be given a tour of the premises and be introduced to the staff. Then I would meet with him and he would make a decision.

The next day I was eager and excited. He seemed so nice on the phone. We really hit-it-off and I was especially motivated as I considered that by the end of the day I could have my first job. On arrival I was met by the office manager. She showed me around and introduced me to the staff. I had a quick chat with a couple of them. The offices were spacious and the people looked happy. I could see myself fitting in and working there. I didn't notice throughout the tour that I was the only black person anywhere. But then, what was there to notice, when to date that had largely been my life's experience? It was normal to be the only one.

After the tour, the office manager handed me over to the director's secretary who made me aware that the director was on the phone. I waited. A few minutes passed and she ushered me into his office. On entry, I saw him sitting at his large desk writing furiously. His secretary politely announced, 'This is Olivea.'

Without looking up and whilst continuing to scribble, he said quite lightly, 'Hello Olivea. Won't keep you a moment.'

His secretary smiled at me reassuringly and left the office. As she drew the door softly shut the director cleared his throat and elongated the word 'o-o-ok-a-ay' as if stretching out the vowels gave him a few extra seconds to finish what he was doing. As he spoke, he began to stand whilst pushing his chair back with his knees. He dropped the pen onto his desk blotter and stretched out his hand to greet me. With his hand outstretched, he lifted his head with a smile that simply froze on his face when he saw me. Almost instantly the hand I was about to grasp in the firm handshake that I had always been taught was an essential part of creating a good first impression, was being withdrawn. Instead, it became an icy indication to take a seat.

His whole demeanour changed. The smile was gone and the chatty, informal person I had spoken to the day before was replaced by this officious, no-nonsense man. I suddenly felt much smaller than my 5'1" stature standing in front of this man who was no more than 5'7" but now seemed unnaturally lofty. When I had entered his office, the room was large and impressive with modern furniture and colour-co-ordinated fixtures. It was light and airy with two big windows. But as I walked towards the chair, the room grew dark and claustrophobic. It became oppressive and the air was thinning. With the anxiety rising in my throat, I sat down as non-verbally directed.

'Thanks for coming along,' he said coldly. 'Presumably you've had a look round and had a chat with some of the staff.'

It was not a question. There was no customary speech inflection at the end of the sentence. He was not looking at me anymore. He was not inviting me to respond.

I couldn't help myself and said 'yes' anyway. My response was followed by a silence that gave me no indication as to what was going to happen next and offered no comfort or assurance that the situation was about to thaw out. I became rigid in my seat. I clasped my hands and pressed my feet into the floor to stop myself from fidgeting or tapping my heels. I was very nervous now.

When he eventually spoke, it was not to ease the tension deliberately hanging in the air. He said, 'Most of the people out there,' he motioned with his eyes to the office behind me, '—either own a horse or have access to a horse. It's a very important part of the job.'

I was confused and began to say, 'But yesterday when we spoke you said…'

He interrupted me. 'Owning a horse and understanding horse owners is integral to the role.' His words had an incontrovertible finality to them.

He looked at me with expressionless eyes. I had been disarmed and conquered and I had not even realised I had gone to war. Before I could consider retreating, advancing or terms for surrender, he was already standing and holding his office door open. Somewhat dazed I stood up and walked towards the door he was holding open with a feigned courtesy that barely masked his contempt for me. Then with the most animation I had seen in him since my arrival he smiled, thanked me very much for coming and he wished me luck in my hunt for a job. This was quickly followed by an almost apologetic reiteration, as if his hands were tied by some invisible cords of modus operandi that he really needed to offer the job to someone with knowledge of horses.

Before I knew it, I was in the car park waiting for a taxi home.

As the years have gone on, I have made a conscious effort to make myself more appealing–at least as appealing as my voice, which has consistently fuelled a perception of height and shade that is immediately contradicted by my actual appearance on arrival. I have looked at my personality traits and learnt new behaviours to counterbalance personality preferences. I have adjusted my attitude. I have upgraded my skills and education and put myself 'out there.' When required, I have been the quiet, unassuming one; at other times the forthright, assertive one. Yet still today, I find myself asking: if my face was white, even for a moment and I re-lived a particular episode, would it have made a difference?

Present Day...

BLACK PEOPLE 'LESS INTELLIGENT' SCIENTIST CLAIMS

'One of the world's most respected scientists is embroiled in an extraordinary row after claiming that black people are less intelligent than white people.

Dr Watson, who runs one of America's leading scientific research institutions, made the controversial remarks in an interview in The Sunday Times.

The 79-year-old geneticist said he was "inherently gloomy about the prospect of Africa" because "all our social policies are based on the fact that their intelligence is the same as ours—whereas all the testing says not really". He said he hoped that everyone was equal, but countered that "people who have to deal with black employees find [that] *this* [is] *not true*".

He says that you should not discriminate on the basis of colour, because "there are many people of colour who are very talented, but don't promote them when they haven't succeeded at the lower level". He writes that "there is no firm reason to anticipate that the intellectual capacities of peoples geographically separated in their evolution should prove to have evolved identically. Our wanting to reserve equal powers of reason as some universal heritage of humanity will not be enough to make it so."

Dr Watson was hailed as achieving one of the greatest single scientific breakthroughs of the 20th century when he worked at the University of Cambridge in the 1950s and 1960s, forming part of the team which discovered the structure of DNA.

He shared the 1962 Nobel Prize for medicine with his British colleague Francis Crick and New Zealand-born Maurice Wilkins.'

From *Times* Online October 17, 2007
http://www.timesonline.co.uk/tol/news/uk/article2677098.ece

Preface

Defying the Odds

This is a story of triumph. In January 2008, I took the Prison Service to court for direct racial discrimination, harassment and victimisation. My journey was arduous, terrifying, and painful. I endured racial comments and ostracism. Then I was deliberately forgotten, and put on 'garden leave' for 19 months whilst simultaneously being accused of aggressive and anti-social behaviour as a poor performer. I was unsupported by a national institution that was not only flush with money from the public purse but was fortified by its familiarity with the law. Nevertheless, I stood alone; I represented myself in a 15-day hearing and won!

I came across the aforementioned pro-slavery arguments when I was looking for legal discourse to support myself through the court case. Aside from the shock that a simple search could throw up such incendiary 'finds', when looking for information about the devastating effects of stereotyping black people in the workplace, I was immediately struck by horror and offence. The statements perfectly crystallised what I was up against: fearful, misinformed, archaic thinking. I found it incomprehensible that anyone could make such damning indictments about me and mine, for no other reason than the colour of my skin. Having only ever been confronted and repulsed by slavery in my early teens as a result of watching Alex Hayley's *Roots*, I had never made my own personal journey of discovery in relation to who I am or how others see me. Growing up, my mind had not been furnished with balanced views and a sense of self, gained by studying my history. Even though watching *Roots* generated complex emotions, they were never explored with our parents and we were too young to unravel and challenge them for ourselves. Shortly after the screening, the storyline and messages were archived in vaulted memory and surfaced only in indefinable form whenever we were wronged by white people. Yet now my eyes were being forced to undress every sentence of these obsolete arguments with a strange mix of incredulity and sickness, hoping to find the top layers of the messages deliberately misleading. My heart prayed that they were written only for shock value to grab attention, like a protester running naked across a playing field in the middle of a game–the nakedness being the vehicle, not the purpose. As my brain struggled to process the information and my heart wrestled with whether picking at such ancient wounds would distract me from making my points, I found no such reprieve. Neither could I excuse them as if they had been spoken in some back street by a drunken, disorderly and unlearned rabble. These words were carefully spoken with calculated intention by an organised people, parliaments and legislators. Somehow, I should be able to derive comfort from the fact that these words are nearly 200 years old, and say confidently that their potency and relevance is vilified by both the passing of time and common sense, if I were not able easily to find evidence that they are still being spoken in various forms as truth and argument today. Indeed, had I not found myself on the receiving end of the same sentiments, whilst working for the Prison Service? Had I not battled to dispel perceptions of me as black, therefore lazy and aggressive? Despite all the many years passing and the apparent progress made, there seems to be no escape from people who will take one look at me and decide that I do not belong–and the reasons why.

 I have lived my life in Britain consciously avoiding the crippling effects of mistrust brought on by being obsessed about which of the white people I meet everyday hold putrid views like these. Is it the train steward who, no matter how many white people board the train at the same time as me and join the same carriage, will only ask *me* if *I* have a ticket? Is it the white person I consider a friend, who will not come to the get-together I have invited them to because they think they will be the only white person there and it would be 'awkward' for them or they would 'feel funny about being the only one'? And whilst they are conveying their concern, the irony is completely lost on them that I am the only black person in the room, or on the board or in the company. Yet I am still expected to function and automatically feel that I belong, without any special effort to include me being made on their part. I have learnt to dismiss these indiscretions, to lay no charge against a people who seem unable to help themselves, who seem oblivious to their fault. To a large extent, I have been successful in my endeavours—until now.

What follows is a detailed story of how I got my victory, how I flew in the face of these pro-slavery assertions. My account is not one of smooth sailing, or catlike responses to danger. This is a very human story, one of discovery and the many trials inherent in moving from one state of realisation to another. When I started this journey, I was a strong black woman who was full of faith, with dreams of affecting broken lives and successfully enhancing her career, a woman who was a motivated, well-qualified training and development professional. Then I became a shadow of a person whose circumstances forced her to sit in a tribunal hearing a mere 141 weeks after joining the Prison Service College. Here I was forced to outline the humiliation of racist comments, forced to admit that my strategies, armour and strength failed to protect me as they had formerly done.

Excerpts from my personal diary and the witness statement I read to the court, letters and emails that were presented as evidence, have been used extensively to chronicle the passage to what felt like the darkest place on earth. I have done this so that my family and friends can fully appreciate how the transition was made. I have recorded the individual players, their actions, comments and behaviours, from single-line emails to racist remarks, all of which combined to set in motion a series of events that caused me to question if I belong here and, if not here, then where? In these pages I have shared how I found it nigh impossible to reconcile my role as a Christian Pastor—who needed to be strong for others, who needed to be an example of courage and fortitude—with the woman who ended up taking anti-depressants and feeling like a basket-case and, worst of all, a fraud. King Solomon said, 'They made me the keeper of the vineyards, but my own vineyard I have not kept.' [1] And that is how I was; my focus was ever other people and their needs whilst I missed the changes in myself, and the onset of insanity's cousin–depression.

This exposure to racism in the Prison Service catapulted me into a new world that was fraught with flashes of intense anger and overwhelming sadness. It held me captive and subsequently changed me on a most profound and fundamental level. I bore repeated assaults on my spirit with each blow draining my inner well of peace, optimism and identity. It gave me a basis to wonder what it was that made me so compliant, even in the face of brazen disregard. Was it my faith, was it my culture, or was it both? The answers were in my journey.

As such, I have endeavoured to present the raw escalation of events and emotions, hoping that sharing will help others suffer less anxiety. I would feel that I have accomplished much if my story helps to educate and enlighten my family to the fact that, although we live in an unfair society, we can excel if we stop listening to what those who oppose us have to say about us and strive on regardless. Rudy my husband is always saying, 'Don't believe the lie!' I knew the truth about myself. I knew that I was capable, smart and funny, yet I allowed a few individuals to impose their limiting belief systems on me. I lost my focus and my joy–this cannot keep happening to us. We must be under no illusions that there are times when the strong become weak and when the shepherd becomes as lost as a sheep bleating on a lonely hill. If anyone has gone through or is going through a similar trial my counsel is–know that disorientation is normal. You have not failed. Cry if you must and moan if you need to, but always know that you can make it. Be clear about what is happening to you and make it work for you. Recognise the tricks of the enemy and his many guises. It is the little foxes that destroy the vine. [2]

I feel confident that many organisations are fairly attuned to resolving blatant displays of hate. They have done this in part because of the need to embrace diversity as a mode to remain competitive in a delicate global economy. But all too often, the year-on-year moving around of incompetent white managers who are known to have 'issues', instead of confronting them, erodes attempts at building inclusive businesses reflective of our communities. For example, people from Black and Asian backgrounds make up 10% of the total population in Britain, yet when it comes to making it into senior and general management positions in the workforce, the numbers are not representative of our overall presence. The white workforce, which stood at 90% at the end of 2007, still holds nearly all of the management positions in the country at 93.2%.[3] As organisations recycle, rotate and relocate their managers, such reluctance to stamp out anything that perpetuates dysfunction and prejudice in white people tells us uncompromisingly that, no matter how competent we are, to them we still matter less than the bungling and the ineffectual white manager. Therefore, when we have dried our tears, we must commit ourselves to constructing our own reality and become authors of our own destiny, for the ones built for us have structural flaws and we cannot hope for others to have the same passion for our advancement as we need to have for ourselves. Ask not what they can do for you but ask what you can do for yourself!

In the process of talking about who is for us and who is against, I am careful not to speak out arbitrarily opposing all white people or else I would become as guilty as those who would brand us all the same. I have not experienced treachery at the hand of every white person nor have I known love to flow from the heart of every black person. My sister always says, 'If the cap fits, wear it.' In talking about white people, my complaint sits mainly with two groups. The first group are those who occupy the seats of power, the ones who control the institutions, education and legislation. The order and form that they have fashioned has been inflicted on us; it is longstanding and resistant to significant reform because they have willed it so and because we have offered little by way of challenge from a strong economic or political base. We choose not to vote because we feel there is no point! Yet for every one of us who doesn't vote (and I include myself in this, for I am not without blame), we maintain the status quo, inadvertently supporting the ones who live only to preserve and replicate themselves. They are master puppeteers, opinion-formers who craft what appear to be plausible arguments, generating fear and unrest to the other group in question–the Led–who are the puppeteers' malleable instruments of prejudice. The Led are those who are ignorant, misguided, misinformed and easily manipulated. The master puppeteers collate and analyse demographic trends for the simple-minded Led, provocatively claiming that white British people will be overrun and become an ethnic minority in their own country within a few decades.[4, 5] They incite white British people, urging them to retain their homeland and identity by calling for immediate halts to immigration, the deportation of criminal and illegal immigrants, along with the introduction of a system of voluntary—no doubt for now—resettlement programmes of assistance[6] so that we can return to our lands of ethnic origin. They call for the government to abolish positive-action schemes that actually do no more than encourage and develop under-represented and actively contributing groups. Yet they call for a curtailing of such schemes, alleging that positive action has made white Britons second-class citizens in their own country.[7] They emotively call asylum seekers a 'flood'[8] and deem them 'bogus'[9] and harmful to the economic infrastructure and the British way of life. Serious diseases like AIDS and TB have become 'immigrant plagues' brought in to Britain unchecked.[10, 11] The master puppeteers' inflammatory opinions and suggestions spill over into our mainstream newspapers,[12, 13] and their bloggers clog up cyberspace.[14] And their pages are read by the Led who, by the very nature of their construction, lack the discernment and backbone to challenge. The Led offer no resistance to having their minds poisoned, as we are branded a drain on resources. These unlearned and hapless victims are constantly bombarded by stories about guns and gangs, criminals and crackheads, and genuinely believe that we are the source of their entire malcontent.[15] This is the world that has been constructed for us. This is the world that we have to change, together. These people exist, and they do not mean us well and when we meet them, we must not allow them to break us. Nor must we treat them as they have treated us—we must not trade one form of madness for another. Even though they cannot see themselves in us, we must always see ourselves in them. The air I breathe out is the air they breathe in and vice versa. Their ignorance keeps them poor in spirit—our knowledge must make us rich. We are all interconnected[16] and, if anything, it is denying this that makes them unstable—for where they would be rid of us, on some level they know that they cannot survive without us. Hence, this is not an attempt at demonising white people and brandishing their crimes in front of their faces so that they are consumed with guilt. For that is of no benefit to the work of progression, and simply to trade places with our oppressors will leave humanity in a quagmire of inequality and despicable treatment of each other.

As I write this book, I long for meaningful discussions and action to shape a future where we all fit. This future must follow an intricate design of which I have only seen glimpses. Hence, I do not dare to think that I have all the answers or that this single journey has allowed me to offer a solution that, for whatever reason, has been overlooked by minds greater than mine. I have experienced racism all my life, yet I have not thought what to do about it for the same length of time. A good portion of my views are newly formed and untested, having never lived through such a sustained attack on my person before now. Up until this point, like many of my friends, I hardly ever talked about personally experienced racism. Like dog muck on a pavement, it is instantly abhorrent. There is an urgency to step over it or skilfully negotiate through a trail of it as we take care to make sure none of it touches us. If we step in it, there is anger at the owners who failed to scoop the poop, followed by a compulsion to get rid of it with maniacal fervour, sometimes resulting in the throwing out of the spoilt shoes even if they are a favourite pair. Thus, racism is so ordinary a thing that, unless it blatantly inconveniences us, we work around it to the extent we might even walk away from a really good job. We do this because, no matter the threat of legislative penalty for those who discriminate, we have made peace with the knowledge that there will always be an irreverent dollop of racism in our path and the best thing to do is to skip past it and get on with our lives.

But now, it is time for a different approach, because walking away isn't the only option available to us. We have experienced racism like being one of two children who are told that they are loved equally. The slighted child might not necessarily be able to articulate the nuances of differential treatment, yet he or she will always know that they are the second preferred child. And the colonial parents in denial (because they would never admit the truth) explain that the fault for the difference in treatment, if any, lies with the personality of the children. For where one is amenable, intelligent and the image of a beloved patriarch, the other is disagreeable, has 'special needs' and looks nothing like any other member of the family. And that is who we are, those who share my story—the second preferred child. With this awareness might come tears and anger, but they are not a sign of weakness, for it is what we do with the hurt that counts. Things will change when we stop expecting people to do things for us, and we start to do things for ourselves, no matter the rejection or opposition, because the second preferred child may never win what should have been from the outset, the unconditional love of the parent.

I am grateful that this story ends in victory. I tasted bitterness and resentment and, although they were constant companions for a time, conquering them translated me to a place where pain has function and a great work awaits me. For all my conflicting emotions, my dalliance with demons and aspiring with angels, I am a better person. I am wiser, more engaged and more vigilant. Though hurt, I hate no one and I am healing. This is not just because I took on a major institution and won judgements against them using their rules and their tools—it's because I stayed the course. I was uncertain about a great many things, yet I firmly believed that poor treatment of staff becomes poor treatment of prisoners and vice versa. Someone had to state the obvious: racism doesn't respect boundaries. It won't blight the lives of employees like me and then ignore the prisoners. Pursuing my cause was important for me and others like me in order to herald change for the vulnerable, the disaffected and the ignored. And now it is a record that cannot be erased. Racism exists within the senior management grades of the Prison Service! My win is proof. As a single step, it is no longer the beginning of a journey from a place of easily disputed and readily dismissed feelings and perceptions: the starting point is fact and judgement. It is because of this I can say that it was worth it and I don't have to apologise for who I am or make excuses because I think differently from the dominant social groups within the Prison Service, or indeed anywhere. Today I can say without shame or regret that, accepted or not, I have a right to be here and to be me. I have a right to draw on everything that makes me Olivea—my God, my history, my skin, my people, all of which enable me to make rich deposits and impartation in any place I dare to tread. And I am not alone in this. As I tap into my past, seize the day and lay hold on my future, I know that I am a part of something glorious. It is a shame that for some my blackness means that I will never be British enough, but the limitation and shortness of sight is theirs to own, for it is not the colour of a balloon that makes it rise—it is the air inside it! [17] Thus I am persuaded that the prejudice of others won't ever stop me from aiming high, pressing forward, gaining ground and achieving my purpose.

Endnotes

1 Song of Solomon 1:6
2 Song of Solomon 2:15

3 Race for Opportunity (2008) *Race to the Top*: The place of ethnic minority groups within the UK workforce. This report is based on new research carried out by Race for Opportunity who used data from the Office of National Statistics (ONS) in order to analyse the changes in ethnic minority populations, both in terms of total numbers and in the number achieving management positions and particularly senior-level jobs. It then broke the data down by region, gender, ethnic group and occupation to give an overall picture of the successes—and obstacles—on the path to management. It highlights four key areas of concern: 1) On current trends, ethnic minorities in management will never be in line with their representation in the overall population; 2) The number of black and ethnic minority workers making it to the highest levels of management—the boardroom—is very small and in some cases too small to analyse; 3) In an increasingly diverse society this shortfall is not only morally wrong but a self-inflicted wound by companies that waste management potential; 4) Policymakers and employers must be on guard to ensure that the current recession does not lead to a reversal of the progress that has been made. The last time the UK came close to recession, there was a noticeable slowdown in the growth in BAME managers. Available online: http://www.bitc.org.uk/workplace/diversity_and_inclusion/race/index.html

⁴   *The Guardian*, September, 3, 2000. 'UK WHITES WILL BE MINORITY BY 2100' by Antony Browne. 'Whites will be an ethnic minority in Britain by the end of the century. Analysis of official figures indicate that, at current fertility rates and levels of immigration, there will be more non-whites than whites by 2100. It would be the first time in history that a major indigenous population has voluntarily become a minority, rather than through war, famine or disease. Whites will be a minority in London by 2010. In the early 1950s there were only a few tens of thousands of non-whites in the UK. By 1991 that had risen to 3 million–6 per cent of the population. The population of ethnic minorities has been growing at between 2 and 4 per cent a year. Net immigration has been running at record levels, with 185,000 newcomers last year.

New immigrants, who are on average younger than the population at large, also tend to have higher fertility rates. In contrast, the population of white British citizens is static. Their fertility rate is very low–at under 2 children per woman–and there is overall emigration of British citizens… The analysis of the figures showed that if the population of ethnic minorities grows at 4 per cent a year, whites will become a minority before 2100. The demographer who made the calculation wished to remain anonymous for fear of accusations of racism.' Available online http://www.guardian.co.uk/uk/2000/sep/03/race.world1

⁵   Telegraph.co.uk, Friday August, 31 2007. 'WHITE PEOPLE A MINORITY BY 2027' By Christopher Hope, Home Affairs Correspondent. 'White people living in the UK's second biggest city are likely to find themselves in a minority in 20 years' time, according to researchers. A team of demographers from Manchester University has claimed that the number of white people living in Birmingham will be overtaken by the number of those with other ethnic origins by 2027. The news came as it emerged that 35 towns and cities in Britain have at least one ward which is "minority white". And experts have already forecast that Leicester could become the first city in which white people are a minority in four years' time.' Available online www.telegraph.co.uk/news/uknews/1561758/White-people-a-minority-by-2027.html

⁶   *Daily Express*, Friday October 10, 2008. 'HUGE EU CASH 'BRIBES' TO SEND MIGRANTS HOME' by **Nick Fagge in Mali.** 'HUGE cash bribes are being offered to African migrants to return home from Europe, the *Daily Express* can reveal. Handouts, of more than £5,500, funded by taxpayers, are being dangled in front of thousands of immigrants–some working illegally–in EU states. The aim is to persuade them to return to Mali and other poverty-stricken countries in Africa…The project…encourages migrants working both legally and illegally to apply for grants for business in their home countries.' Available online http://www.express.co.uk/posts/view/65477/Huge-EU-cash-bribes-to-send-migrants-home

⁷   BNP Immigration Policy

⁸ *The Independent UK, Monday May 1, 2000.* 'ASYLUM FLOOD MAY BRING BACK FASCISTS, SAYS HAGUE,' by Paul Waugh, Political Correspondent. 'William Hague was accused of pandering to neo-Nazis last night after he warned that the National Front would become more popular unless the Government clamped down on asylum seekers. The Conservative leader faced a barrage of criticism after he predicted there would be more NF marches if the "flood" of people seeking entry to Britain was not halted. Jack Straw, the Home Secretary, claimed Mr Hague was "pandering" to the far-right.' Available online: http://www.independent.co.uk/news/uk/this-britain/asylum-flood-may-bring-back-fascists-says-hague-718403.html

⁹ Continued from citation 8 '…Mr Hague also refused to back away from his claim that Britain was being "flooded" with "bogus asylum-seekers". [He said] "The dictionary definition of a flood is a flow that is out of control…There is no question when we have more than 100,000 asylum seekers in the queue for processing their application that we have a flow that is out of control."'

¹⁰ *The Mail on Sunday*, Sunday January 26, 2003. 'MADNESS OF BLAIR'S IMPORTED PLAGUES' by Anthony Browne. 'We live in fear of foreigners bringing death to our land… But… it is not by allowing in terrorists that the Government's policy of mass immigration, especially from the Third World, will claim most lives. It is through letting in too many germs.' Available online: http://www.irr.org.uk/2003/march/ak000003.html

¹¹ *The Sun*, Monday September 8, 2008 'AT LAST WE CAN ALL BE FRANK ON IMMIGRATION' by Trevor Kavanagh, Political Editor. 'Killer diseases such as Aids, hepatitis and incurable strains of TB are accelerating among migrant communities. Brutal drug gangs, people traffickers and money launderers have turned London into the organised crime capital of the world. Our jails are stuffed with foreign prisoners…' Available online:
http://www.thesun.co.uk/sol/homepage/news/columnists/kavanagh/article1659657.ece

¹² *The Times* Online, Wednesday August 27, 2008 'IMMIGRATION TO MAKE BRITAIN EUROPE'S MOST CROWDED NATION. Britain is set to become Europe's most highly populated nation within two generations, driven by immigration. Forecasts published by the European Commission suggest that Britain will overtake Germany within 50 years as the population rises from 60.9 million today to 77 million. The projected 25 per cent increase triggered renewed calls for the Government to stem the flow of immigration, which has surged since Labour came to power 11 years ago. Increasing population, together with a rise in the number of elderly people, will heap further pressure on public services, particular the NHS.' Available online http://www.timesonline.co.uk/tol/news/politics/article4615213.ece

¹³ *'Confluence' Magazine*, Tuesday December 2, 2008. 'MANAGED MIGRATION: HISTORY AND DEVELOPMENTS-A REJOINDER' by Eddie D' Sa. "Some supposed asylum seekers repay our generosity by cheating the benefit system…begging and thieving in town & city centres; and even setting up criminal networks" (*Daily Mail*, Mar 00) "Handouts to refugees are robbing the British poor" (*Evening Standard*, April 00) "We need deportations on a huge scale" (*Sun*, 9 Mar 00) "Beggars build mansions with OUR handouts" (*Sun*, 14 Mar 00) "Time to kick the scroungers out" (*Sun*, 17 Mar 00) "Refugees get flats with Jacuzzi, sunbeds and…a sauna" (*Daily Star*, 25 March 00) "Asylum seekers eat our donkeys" (*Daily Star*, 21Aug 03) "Asylum seekers steal the Queen's birds for barbecues" (*Sun* 4 July 03). Available online: http://www.confluence.org.uk/2008/12/02/managed-migration-history-and-developments/

¹⁴ *Telegraph.co.uk*, Monday December 7, 2009 'ROD LIDDLE ACCUSED OF RACISM FOR BLOG' by Chris Irvine. 'Rod Liddle, the journalist and magazine columnist, has been accused of racism after suggesting in a blog that young African-Caribbean men were responsible for most of the crime in London.

Mr Liddle, referring to the case where two teenage rappers tried to murder a pregnant 15-year-old, described the perpetrators as "human filth" before adding "It could be an anomaly, of course. But it isn't."

In the blog for *The Spectator*, he then says: "The overwhelming majority of street crime, knife crime, gun crime, robbery and crimes of sexual violence in London is carried out by young men from the African-Caribbean community. Of course, in return, we have rap music, goat curry and a far more vibrant and diverse understanding of cultures which were once alien to us. For which, many thanks."' Available online: http://www.telegraph.co.uk/finance/newsbysector/mediatechnologyandtelecoms/digital-media/7536940/Rod-Liddles-blog-becomes-first-to-be-censured-by-PCC.html

¹⁵ *London Evening Standard*, Tuesday March 30, 2010 'ROD LIDDLE CENSURED OVER "RACIST" BLOG ON BLACK CRIME' **by Peter Dominiczak.** Censorship article followed by unedited comments from the public. Available online at: http://www.thisislondon.co.uk/standard/article-23820210-rod-liddles-blog-censured-in-landmark-move.do

I saw Rod's blog. He was stating the blindingly obvious. My son was mugged twice by Afro-Caribeans in 2008. The PC fascists are trying to suppress free speech'–**Keith, London**

Wait a minute I am confused. So Black teenagers are not responsible for the majority of street crime in London or they are but we just cannot say they are even if they are…Does this mean it is now safe and I should not worry about my relatives being mugged by black kids now and worry more about the white kids because if that is the case my granny would no doubt be a lot safer or can I not say that....I'm confused...– **Gary, London**

Liddle is right, of course-but as Geert Wilders was told by the judge in the Netherlands–" What you say may well be true but it is illegal to say it." BNP leader Nick Griffin was also informed by the judge at his trial in Leeds that "The truth is no defence". The powers that be are so afraid of upsetting minority groups that they will quite happily stamp on freedom of speech. Bring on the revolution!–**Dave N, Lancaster UK**

All he's did is point out the blindingly obvious. Wheres the crime in that. The black community actively encourage the discrimination the hate so much. I remember reading an article years ago, one point was "whites have an inherrent fear of blacks, however blacks do absolutely nothing to allay those fears". The black community like the power the fear gives them but when that fear provokes discrimination its a totally different story.–**George, London**

Why are people so surprised that whites are racist? Given that most violent crime, rape, theft, muggings etc are committed by non-whites, then racism is a perfectly logical response. The truth is, that if there were fewer black people in this country, then there would be less crime. Everyone knows that!–**Conspiracy Factualist, London UK**

I viewed Crimewatch last night. They have a feature where the faces of ten wanted poster boys are pictured. Even filtered through the BBCs' notorious PC stand point, it was immediately obvious, as it is on every programme, that proportionately our Ethnic friends are well ahead in the criminal stakes.–**Fred, Horsham**

So he has to prove what daily experience, common sense and press reports confirm is the truth? Most violent crime in London is committed by Afro-Caribbeans and Somalis. Live it. See it.–**David, Ramsey, Isle of Man'**

[16] *BBC News*, Friday May 1, 2009. A GENETIC MAP OF AFRICA by Victoria Gill 'the continent from which all modern humans originate-has provided information about its huge diversity of language and culture. It is the result of the largest African genetic study ever undertaken. The work revealed the continent to be the most genetically diverse place on Earth, and identified descendents of our earliest human ancestors...'
[17] Mattie T. Lawson

PART TWO

Chapter One

Joining the Service

There are times when I am convinced that I have tasted heaven. Every so often I wake up between 4.00am or 5.00am to find Rudy's protective arms wrapped around my body, pulling me into him—my back against his chest—until I fit neatly into his 6' 1" frame. I know I am safe. I listen to his rhythmic breathing and I am comforted by it. I feel the strong, steady beat of my own heart confirming that I live and life is a gift. I am happy and contented. Although my life is not perfect, I am not overly troubled by any one thing in particular. I whisper 'thank you' into the still air because I know I am blessed and my heart swells with gratitude for the security I feel. As I lay in my warm bed, loved by God and loved by my husband I have a precious hope, and alacrity and courage to embrace change, without the deep and abiding fear that I have witnessed in so many. How wonderful to know peace like this; to have such assurance that I am loved and wanted; to have the belief that I can achieve anything I set my mind to.

It is Saturday and we don't have to do anything when we get up. Bliss! I finished working for my old company yesterday and on Monday I start a new role in the Prison Service. I am excited and tired as it was a long, long week. I worked hard tying up loose ends and making things easy for my successor's first few days.

I tell myself that I need to get back to sleep, except Rudy has just started to snore. He is not a horrendous snorer but his mouth is just above my ear. As such, the proximity of the sound of his relaxed and low vibrating soft palate is sufficient to keep me awake. Still, it is easily remedied, as I consider that all I have to say is, 'Baby, you're snoring', and without waking he simply turns over onto his left side, bends his knees and sticks out his bottom. Then I turn over and fit around the shape he has made like human Tetris. Another flush of contentment sweeps over me as I wallow in the gorgeousness of the moment! Skin to skin and limb to limb, our breathing in deepening, alternating rhythm heralds the sleep reclaiming my mind. I begin to drift without resistance. Miraculously Rudy is no longer snoring. Maybe he is tasting heaven too.

In April 2003, I was working for a recently sold blue-chip company. As a European training manager, I travelled extensively throughout Europe, which had high and low moments. The main high was the travel to many of Europe's finest cities; the main low was mostly never getting a chance to leave the hotel room to see anything of note. Yet the work was sufficiently challenging and my basic salary was very good, coupled with bonuses that increased my earning capacity by approximately thirty percent. Life overall was good and my husband, Rudy, and I were excited about our future.

Having been with the company for nearly five years, I found that the last eighteen months had become particularly gruelling, as it went through the merger and acquisition process. The travel had increased and was taking its toll on me: I was now out of the country approximately three or four days per week. I hardly saw Rudy or my Mum and I missed them. They are the cornerstones of my life. Rudy is a beautiful and strong man. He is tall, well toned and proportioned. His golden skin contrasts prominently with his jet-black hair, long eyelashes, thick eyebrows and goatee beard. He has big, brown, heavy-lidded, smile-a-lot eyes that tell you everything in a moment. They speak long before his brain processes any signal his senses send. And long before his mouth tells you what is going on in his head or his heart, his eyes embrace or distance you. Oftentimes when I tell him what his face is saying, he denies the emotion or conclusion. But I know what I have seen and only need to wait a short while for his brain to catch up with his eyes and then he agrees with me. It's not that I'm clever. His eyes, his face, his soul are always talking. All you have to do is listen, and you know where Rudy is. Before I met him, Suzie my sister described him as a serious and purposeful, gentle and genuine man. She said that whoever married him would be the envy of everyone because Rudy would treat his wife like a queen. She was right. At seven years into our marriage, I had been blessed by a man who I could rely on to love and care for me in a way that made romantic novels read like true stories—mostly! Whenever I talk about him, the things I have to say always sound a little clichéd. Yet I make no apologies, because he is a good man and they are hard to find. He is my best friend and he knows more about me than anyone and loves me more deeply than anyone I have known before him.

And my Mum is another blessing that I treasure. She has eyes that sparkle and high cheekbones. She is full of face and wide of smile. Although ill for most of her life, I have never known her to be thin. There is weakness of heart, though not frame, as her figure has always been curvy and womanly. Mum can be shy at times yet she is a very sociable person at her core, loving to cook, bake, and share with others. For her, good food answers all things and makes everything better. As children, we never had a bad or bland meal. She always poured her love and creativity into every Jamaican dish. With each mouthful, we could taste the sun and knew how cherished and important we were to her.

As we grew we lived in constant fear of Mum dying, yet she is miraculously still with us and now she is living with Rudy and me in our home and, much to Rudy's delight, still cooking! Spending quality time with these two people is important to me. The constant travel meant I was unable to do this. It also meant that as a Pastor I was less available to the Church and the needs of our members. People would ring me for help and guidance and I would be in Italy or Switzerland and unable to talk at length. This would be because of the expense or, worse, I was unreachable because of poor network coverage. I took my pastoral care responsibilities seriously and recognised the need to be more accessible. What is more, Rudy and I were partners in the gospel. He was doing most of the work when we had agreed to minister together. When the resultant restructure brought with it a threat of redundancy, this prompted a critical rethink of my career plans and personal goals.

Then there was the job itself. Over the years, I had moved from directly helping people secure their first job to European corporate management and endless board meetings. It was okay designing training packages to facilitate the harmonisation of product ranges (I often watched people's eyes glaze over whenever I said anything like this because it meant little unless you came from the industry). Yet I longed for the human interaction that accompanied dealing with matters of personal development for people. I loved being involved in learning that touched and changed lives. I was nearly 40 years old. I had reached a point in my life where I was clear about what was important to me and I needed to be true to the pull that consciousness was having on me. I had left school with very few qualifications and fewer options. It had taken me a good while to regain the educational ground I had lost. But in the last 20 years I had pushed myself hard and believed that I was close to where I would have been had my beginning been more productive. I had done well: married with career, house and car. I was Pastoring, working in the community, writing songs and singing in a group. I was now in a position where I could choose the next job I wanted. So I started to look for a way that would enable me to progress my life and the lives of others.

Once I had made the decision to move on, within a month I saw and applied for a Head of Learning and Skills role in the Prison Service. It seemed to tick all the right boxes in terms of a good career choice. It involved working with prisoners and dealing with issues relating to rehabilitation and social inclusion, curriculum development which would play to my strengths in design. Although the top band of pay was less than what I was earning, I considered the sense of purpose the role would give me, the alignment to my work in ministry and the opportunity to be based locally were acceptable trade-offs—at least for a couple of years until I progressed.

As motivated as I was by the prospect of working with prisoners, initially I was not completely convinced about working for the Prison Service as an organisation. For one thing, it was shrouded in mystery—a closed shop. Any approach to the unknown was to be made with caution. There was a time when crime and resultant punishment were readily understood and highly visible, as criminals were put in stocks in the market square or hanged in public after a reading of their crimes or transported to another country for hard labour. Sanctions were designed to shame and deter. Prison used to be a place where you were held until your punishment was decided. A few centuries later and punishment has become internalised, away from the public eye, and the structures and mechanisms used to maintain discipline have become unfamiliar to the average person. Ordinary folk like me had no idea what went on behind those fortressed walls. The official information on the internet seemed fairly informative and innocuous, talking generally about goals to educate and rehabilitate prisoners and the different types of prisons that helped the Service discharge its responsibilities to keep the public safe. Yet there were some things that belied the apparent transparency. Firstly, public opinion of the Prison Service was low. There were constant questions about how prisoners were treated and whether public money was being spent well on initiatives to rehabilitate prisoners. Most disturbing, however, was the long-held view across the ethnic communities that the Prison Service, the police force and many other government sectors in Britain were racist and did little to eradicate racism. There was an arrogance about these agencies that seemed to permeate everything they did. It defined what they considered important and worthy of their time and resources. It determined whether they would spring to action or drag their feet, and black people regularly seemed to be on the receiving end of their contempt, indifference and superior attitudes. There were always stories circulating throughout the communities about unfair treatment, negligence and a lack of care, which never made the headlines. And the stories that did, served only to reinforce and justify the mistrust that slowly simmered across community groups. Although the Prison Service and the police were different organisations in the Criminal Justice System, when it came to matters of race, to us their uniforms were cut from the same cloth. As I considered what to do with my application, I realised that it was some ten years since Stephen Lawrence, an 18-year-old 'A' level student was murdered on 22nd April 1993. He was stabbed to death whilst waiting for a bus, by white youths who called out to him, 'what what nigger'. Even though there were arrests and everyone knew who the murderers were, no one was convicted, as the police failed to initially recognise and pursue the racial element in the case. This led to vital clues and evidence being missed. Stephen's parents Neville and Doreen refused to accept that the matter was over, and their dedication to their son paid off, as a public enquiry into how the police had handled the murder was ordered. In 1999, the Macpherson Report found that the police investigation was incompetent and it labelled the Metropolitan Police Service–the

Met—as 'institutionally racist.' Even with this there seemed to be little change, and we had not forgotten that Stephen's killers were known, yet still walked freely among us. One year on from the report, the Prison Service seemed to be repeating the same sort of mistakes. On 21st March 2000, Zahid Mubarek, a 19-year-old Asian man was murdered in his cell by a known racist. For six weeks, Zahid was made to share the same cell as Robert Stewart, even though the officers knew that Stewart was a violent and racist psychopath. Stewart, also 19 years old, had a prison career which, despite his youth, spanned six prison sentences. His previous convictions included the attempted murder of another prisoner, stabbing a prisoner below the eye and racial harassment. His prison records also suggested that he had a long history of mental illness and extreme racist views. Zahid's cries to be moved to another cell were ignored. Stewart bludgeoned Zahid to death with a table leg on the day that Zahid was due to be released. Three years later, this had not been forgotten and there were still cries from Zahid's family and the Asian community for a public inquiry amid deeply held views that the Prison Service was as institutionally racist as the police.

Yet over a number of days and much prayer, I found myself overriding but not dismissing these concerns, with visions of helping at least one small corner of the public sector to learn from its mistakes. After reading all of the supporting information, I felt the Prison Service seemed genuine about wanting to change the way it treated prisoners and staff. I felt this was at least partially evident by the very existence of this newly created role that was designed to help prisoners develop new skills. When I saw the job advertised and read about a career in an organisation that said it cared about changing lives for the better—that appealed to me. Some of us had to work on these problems from the inside out, I reasoned, whilst some of us worked from the outside in. I was prepared to make that leap of faith. I was sure that there would be some difficulties and maybe even real hardship for me as an assertive and intelligent black woman working in an organisation that was steeped in tradition, yet that was the price for change. If change resulted then it would be worth it and I was willing to pay.

The Prison Service was conducting a national recruitment campaign looking for education staff for over 100 prisons. I felt fairly confident that, with my experience and qualifications, I would be able to secure a role in any one of six prisons that were reasonable distances from my home. However, when I applied I particularly expressed an interest for HMP Wellingborough and HMP Bedford because they were the closest. As a local minister, I was used to working with ex-offenders in the community and wanted to work in a prison where I would be able to maintain links with the local prisoners when they were discharged.

After a number of weeks, I was invited to an interview.

The summer had not been great thus far but this day was markedly different. The sun was strong and deliberate. I always feel so much better in the sun about everything. There were wisps of white cloud perfectly positioned across the bluest sky. Streaks of cotton wool and puffs of white flour finished the picture. Flowers came to life and trees swayed to music only they could hear in a gentle and welcomed breeze. I loved the wonder. I was glad I had taken the whole day off as annual leave. After the interview I would go to the park near our house and lap up the gifts for the day for there was no telling what the morrow would bring–this being England.

The interview was to be conducted by panel some 30 minutes drive from my house, at HMP Glen Parva's learning centre in Market Harborough. I put a little make up on. I tend not to wear much anyway and most days I don't wear any. I have good skin, although that has not always been the case. I had spotty skin until I was nearly 30 and that made me a little self-conscious. Yet now my skin is lovely, even toned and radiantly black. I dressed professionally and conservatively in a simple, grey skirt suit, which was virtually touching the floor. Any outfit that is designed to be calf length is nearer maxi length on me because I am so short. This means that I wear high heels most of the time. And I love shoes! I am quite petite and even though I am getting older and wider, I am hiding the extra bumps well. I broke up the grey jacket and skirt with a vibrant cerise fitted top, with a high tie-neck finish to the side. I could only do conservatism so far. If ever there is a need to dress simply one will always find the real me defiantly announcing myself with a distinctive pair of shoes, a top or shawl or jewellery. I make sure there is something that says 'the real me is escaping the grey'. I tied my jet-black hair back into a neat bun. There is the odd silver hair making an appearance and I am thankful for two things: firstly that I have lived long enough to see them and, secondly, where they were once wiry and insistent that the perm has made them graceful and yielding. Thus, I continue to defy the years. This is something my family is blessed with, though looking young does have a downside, as sometimes people struggle to accept that I am old enough to know what I am talking about or believe that I can hold my own when challenged. They rarely hold these views for long though as, in the main, asserting myself is not something I find difficult!

As I drove, I rehearsed issues around social inclusion as prompted by the information pack I had received as part of the application. I asked myself questions and answered them audibly even though I was alone in my car. I wanted to hear how my answers sounded and challenged myself if I took too long to answer a question. When I arrived, I was greeted and asked to wait by a diminutive woman called Val Perry. It was rare to meet someone shorter than myself. She had classically styled, well-cut, short blond hair and a smile that was welcoming and put me at ease. She said that they were running a little behind schedule but assured me that I wouldn't be kept waiting long. As she walked away I sat down and quickly got my materials together for the presentation that I would have to deliver as the first part of the interview process. It wasn't long before I was led into a room with a panel comprised of two women, one of whom was Val Perry and one man sitting in front of me. The other woman worked for the Offender Learning and Skills Unit (OLSU) as they were part-funding the Head of Learning and Skills role. The man was a governor from the East Midlands region. I was quite calm because I knew I had a shot at the job. I had the skills they said they wanted and this bolstered my self-belief. It was time to make my pitch.

Twenty minutes later I had finished and I had answered the questions posed. I was moderately comfortable and felt that the session went very well. Then it was time to go through my Curriculum Vitae.

Val Perry looked at my documents and queried my salary expectations. 'Looking at your experience and current salary,' she enquired, 'can you tell me what you're hoping to earn?'

'I was looking to earn the top of the grade as advertised, as that would facilitate my staying within the range of what I am used to earning.' I confirmed my basic salary as detailed on the application form she was now reading intently, whilst I was speaking. I went on to explain how and when I got my bonuses. Then she looked across to the other two panel members with raised eyebrows almost as if to seek approval to continue.

'Well,' she replied, looking back at me 'there was only one post that attracted the top salary in the region and that post was a Manager D grade and it's already gone. This role will be at the next band down, as a Manager E.'

I sat motionless as she explained the salary gradations.

'We should, however, be able to match your basic salary. All you would need to do is send us a recent payslip as proof,' she encouraged. But this confused me because, based on what she had just explained, matching my basic would take me over the top salary band of the E grade to earning within the salary band of a D grade.

'Are you still interested in the role at this grade?' she asked.

At some £18,000 less than what I was used to and with no biannual bonus, the salary was so much lower than what I expected. I was prepared to take a slight drop but this would be a dramatic cut in pay. My mind was bombarded with even more questions whilst the panel waited for a decision. Questions like: Why are they still advertising at a rate they know is gone? Why have they knowingly waited until the interview to tell me this? I reasoned that a good two months had passed since I had sent my application to them. They could have easily let me know which prison jobs were still available, and the salaries they each attracted. Instead, they put me on the spot. My internal dialogue continued. What am I supposed to say: 'No I've changed my mind!'? But I couldn't, because I wanted this job. I had already convinced myself that the Prison Service was going to be a good place to be. I was incredibly optimistic and excited. I had not been this excited about a new role for years. I couldn't quite explain what it was about the prospect of joining the Prison Service that had me champing at the bit to start. Something about it had gotten my ideals all fired up and the longer I had to wait for it, the harder I had to work for it, the more I wanted it. I regained my composure and I thought to myself 'Don't be negative, just get your foot in the door, woman, and give them a chance to see how much value you can add–let them sort out their logistical issues and internal politics about pay and grades. Don't worry, they'll do right by you.'

I said 'Yes'.

Through the months that followed, I formally accepted the Manager E post and by the time they had secured references and done their security checks, my start date was five months down the line at 8th September 2003. Yet in spite of the time taken, I was so keen to join 'the Service' (as it is colloquially known) that even when they failed to match my basic salary as promised by £4,500 or offer me either of the prisons I had asked for, it did not phase me. Instead of thinking, 'this has taken too long' or 'this is the second let down and you haven't even started yet, maybe this isn't the place for you,' I chose to think, 'they were slow because they were being thorough: remember you're going to work with the vulnerable and disenfranchised'. I said to myself, 'Don't worry about how you're going to cope with such a drop in salary, focus on getting through the door, it's a good place to be. You can add value here and change lives.'

I had to remember what was attractive to me about the role. I would be managing prisoner education. I could be instrumental in bringing about positive change for offenders. Although I had little idea as to what changes were necessary or what role I would specifically play in these changes, I was committed to the prospect of being active in the Service's bid for transformation. With my skills and experience and the Service's desire to change, something good was bound to happen. I focused on these thoughts repeatedly and silenced my nagging insecurities.

After joining the Service and working at HMP Leicester, it very quickly became apparent that there were a number of factors affecting the capacity of the Service to deliver their agenda of change. Although the prisons varied across the country, there were common themes surfacing as I got to know the staff at HMP Leicester and the other Heads of Learning and Skills (HoLS) across the region. Within months we realised the role carried little weight. There was no significant opportunity to shape the prisoner experience (with a few exceptions). There was no real desire to help the prisoners learn anything of substance or challenge their behaviour with new initiatives. The focus was to meet the government targets for Basic Skills even if there were no quality learning experiences for the prisoner. Certainly, at HMP Leicester I found that the teaching staff were counting Basic Skills awards more than once in order to do this. It was a practice I immediately put a stop to, which resulted in us missing our targets for the following year. At the centre of all prisoner activity was the need to occupy prisoners so that 'time out of cell' figures looked good for the prison. Despite our senior grades as Manager Ds and Es, as HoLS we found that an air of indifference was levelled at civilian staff by uniformed staff. You were rarely taken seriously if you had never worn a uniform.

Additional complications related to gender and race issues. The Service is a white male-dominated, testosterone-fuelled, golf-playing environment. When I arrived I found it was set in its ways and happy to be so. 'If it ain't broke—don't fix it' was a phrase I heard often, along with the terms 'robust management' and 'command and control.'

Women were an imposition. If they were too feminine, the male officers were uncomfortable. If you wanted to be tolerated you had to be 'butch', as one female officer once put it. Even though the uniforms were the same, she felt strongly that it was the way you carried yourself that made the difference. She believed that the way she interacted with the prisoners drew criticism from fellow officers. If you spoke calmly and intently in order to build rapport and trust you were seen as either mothering or flirting. There couldn't be any kindness in your eyes or gentle smiles or you'd be accused of eroding the boundaries. To get on, you had to disguise all sense of femininity. Speaking firmly and always maintaining a no-nonsense attitude was the preferred approach. If a prisoner was difficult, she was told to ask him to comply twice and if he didn't she was to 'drop 'im (use force) and put him on report'. Anything else was just weak and dangerous. She reckoned the male officers were jealous because they couldn't get 'the biggest and baddest to obey a simple instruction without using force' and she could. I myself was not safe from leering looks and inappropriate comments and by that, I mean from the senior management team. Prisoners always treated me courteously. They were ever polite and very quickly dispelled my initial apprehensions about what it would be like to work in an environment where people had committed crime and were being punished. From my first day talking with the prisoners, I felt safe and respected. But the behaviour of some of the management team was unexpected. There was one manager in particular who would tell me which of my outfits and shoes he liked best and why. His preoccupation with my 'kinky boots' and 'saucy shoes' took the admiration of footwear to a whole new distasteful level, as he would ask other officers from time to time if they had seen what footwear I was wearing. Then they would stare and make improper comments about me being 'Madam Whiplash!'

Black and Asian people were seen as political correctness gone mad! No one understood why there needed to be a focus on race. Apparently, it wasn't the Service's fault that they couldn't attract or retain enough Black and Minority Ethnic (BME) candidates. What could they do after all if we just didn't want to work for Her Majesty? Therefore, a black woman was an anomaly and a black, female senior manager—well that was just asking for trouble! There was much to contend with. I often wondered if I would have even gotten the job, had the selection and appointment of the Head of Learning and Skills role not been a *joint* initiative between the Offender Learning and Skills Unit and the Prison Service.

Then there was the terminology 'BME'. It was not a term that I was used to hearing or using. But on arrival in the Service, I heard virtually nothing else. It was used without restraint and with great proliferation in conversations, meetings and phone calls, emails, reports, statistical forecasts and analyses. Its use everywhere made me uncomfortable: BME staff, BME prisoners, BME males, BME females, BME nationals, BME communities, BME youth offenders, BME visitors, BME learners, BME service users and BMEs. With each use, I felt more and more like a non-person—part of a homogeneous brown sticky mess—and a problem to be solved. It is impossible to communicate in the Service without using the terminology, something that I had previously done without any difficulty before I joined. Even if I said 'black', 'ethnic' or 'historically excluded groups' when referring to staff, I would be corrected as if I didn't know what I wanted to be called. I didn't like the ease with which I was downgraded to be part of a minority and simultaneously associated with everything that was apparently wrong about being anything other than white. The terminology made me feel like cattle. I was branded. I could have been part African, part Asian and part Irish; no matter my name, my colouring, or achievements, all anyone needed to know was that I was a BME. This isn't a badge of honour. It isn't a way of recognising how rich my culture and heritage are. It certainly is not used in the same way that white people from different countries are called European or simply retain their national heritage as, for example, Canadian or Australian. It is a way of grouping the same, unvarying issues of immigration pressures and over population together. It is only used when talking about overcrowding in prisons, prolific repeat-offenders, or prisoners who are causing some form of disruption or dealing in drugs. It is only used when talking about community groups who are dissatisfied or complaining. Funnily enough, in the Service the term BME is never used to talk about jazz or football. I have never heard anyone say they were going on holiday to a BME country–BME Singapore, BME Jamaica or BME Hawaii. You really only hear the term in British government agencies when talking about us, no matter our national heritage or ethnic origin. And if any sub-groups are identified within the BME classification, it is only in relation to the specific problems that the Service and other agencies associate with particular groups–like drugs and Jamaicans, scams and Nigerians, terror and Muslims or teen violence and Congolese. So as soon as you mentioned Muslims or Nigerians for example, contributions in a meeting would soon be peppered with language about radicalisation or dishonesty. These labels stuck to us and defined us in the minds of the users as problematic first with the exception of a few (like me) who were not like 'the others'. I hate the terminology and, even now, every time I use it, I am rankled by it and feel like a traitor. Like a double agent, I am collaborating with the conspiracy to de-nationalise and alienate us. Yet challenging it made me look as if I was some sort of political activist. I didn't want to be seen in this way–I had just arrived and didn't want any trouble. I found there was not a single manager that I could talk to about this. There was no one to ask why we were using it, where it came from and what we could use in its place. It was accepted. Ironically, its presence in the English language seemed far more readily integrated than the black faces in the Service it referred to!

The clever marketing information I read before I joined had created a very different world from the one that I was experiencing. In April, I had seen images of multi-ethnic staff who looked motivated and energised about providing an essential service to the public. The first thing I found was that the staff were predominantly white, and not by a small margin. The approximate make-up across the organisation of over 45,000 [1] employees (enough people to populate a city), was 95% white.[2] With all my research before joining, I never thought to check what the actual ethnicity ratios were. I never thought about just how outnumbered I would be. But then, who does? It had been many years since I worked in such an overwhelmingly white environment.

At HMP Leicester, the ratios were even worse. The prison was not at all representative of the community in which it stood. Leicester City's cultural mix was vibrant and evident. The city had been described as likely to be the first in Europe to have a majority non-white population by the next summer Olympics in 2012.[3] Britain would be bidding again to host the Games and would most likely cite diversity, integration and legacy as positives to secure the privilege. The Olympics are known for their celebration of unity, embodying pride and multiplicity, yet this spirit of perpetual hope and variety was starkly contrasted by the sea of same-gender white faces that met me when I entered the prison. Out of over 200 staff, there were only six from a Black or Asian background: two officers, one officer support guard, two administrators and me. It dawned on me very quickly that the sad reality for many of the officers was that the only black people they had anything to do with were the ones they were locking up each day, reinforcing negative stereotypes. Unless officers were individually prepared to look beyond the immediate Neanderthal dynamics of 'me, officer–you prisoner!', many officers were destined to fail to realise that they were interacting with intelligent black people with goals, aspirations and skills. For the prisoners, with only two black uniformed staff, the capacity to communicate with someone who understood their issues was virtually nonexistent.

The other issue was how tired and worn out the staff were.[4] They were barely getting through a working day. The pressures of the role and the constantly changing demands that were being made of them, burdened them. This included the changes that I, as a fresh-faced idealist wanted to make. I found that de-motivated and distracted staff made for people with little time to get excited about change. Change simply meant more work for the same pay. This was extremely disappointing to me especially since I had had such high hopes for the role. The realisation that I could not appreciably influence the quality of life of the prisoners was a real letdown.

I am not sure what I was expecting. Maybe I was romantically looking for some kind of *To Sir with Love* experience—after all, I shared my maiden name with the author, E. R. Braithwaite. A tenuous link no doubt, but I felt that one could not read a story like that and remain unaffected about the part one could play, if ever the opportunity to mend broken lives presented itself. I was a dreamer and my dreams of helping others, however outdated and old fashioned, kept me happy and aspiring to one day be a part of something great. It has been with me since childhood. However, with my arrival in the Service came a rude awakening to archaic officialdom, civilian phobia, and almost anaphylactic-shock responses to change.

In terms of career progression for me, I found that the role would not lead anywhere at all simply because I was a non-uniformed employee. There were routes for moving forward like secondment, exams, and fast-track intensive development programmes—but only if you were an officer. The organisation had few progression routes for people who did not start their career by physically locking up and unlocking prisoners.

After nearly two years as the Head of Learning and Skills, I applied to be an advisor at the Prison Service College based in Newbold Revel, Rugby. I had applied there because I felt the college seemed less reliant on operational protocols in relation to new ideas and advancement, than the prisons. In other words, I knew that if I made suggestions for improvement of services rendered, thoughts would not automatically run to matters of security or prisoner escapes. My thinking was I could challenge the status quo as well as advance on merit as a learning specialist, without the disadvantage of never having worn a prison officer uniform.

It was amazing that, after everything I had experienced by this time, I was still motivated about being party to transformation and positively affecting the prisoner experience. I felt I still had a lot to offer if I could find the right position to make a difference. My work with the Service still had the potential to be a highly and mutually effective partnership. In this new role, I would no longer be managing the prisoners' education but I would be managing the development of the officers and governors. I would be tackling problems from a different perspective.

Hope alive, I thought, I could still contribute to change in the Service. I gave myself new arguments to keep trying. Arguments like: prisoners do not govern themselves—fact. They are governed by staff—another fact. And the staff who governed them are trained at the Prison Service College. All of these facts meant I would be in a position to influence the way officers and governors thought, the way they approached problems and, ultimately, *the way they treated prisoners*. I determined this had to be a good place to be. I would be at the beginning and at different stages of management development. I would have regional and national access to the minds of the men and women who touched prisoners' lives every day. This had to be more strategically relevant than being based in a single prison where some were happy for the prisoners to count beads all day!

I was interviewed by Chris Croombes, the Head of the Leadership Management and Development unit (LMD). She immediately got me energised about prospects and the future of the college. She was a stunning and passionate woman, with elegantly coiffed blond hair and pink Chanel lipstick. She wore a silk scarf tied around her neck like an air stewardess, only she was clearly the pilot. Chris was designer-dressed and business-savvy, all wrapped up in a neat little size-twelve package. She exuded confidence and we had instant and excellent rapport. For the first time since joining the Service, I felt I had met someone I could trust with my dreams and my future. I had finally found someone who both wanted to and had the capacity to help me reach my potential. She was someone who genuinely wanted to improve the services we offered staff and she was aware of the links to prisoner treatment.

Chris explained where the leadership and management department (LMD) sat in relation to the other activities within the college. She told me that the college was responsible for training the entry-level prison officers and managed their on-going operational, management and leadership development. The college designed learning programmes and delivered most of the work and also used outside consultants. The courses that were delivered were many and varied, from dog-handling techniques to presentation skills. Chris was responsible for both governor development and the Fast-Track programmes. Her vision for the leadership advisor role was to help governors to make the transition from a command-and-control style of leadership to one that was more transformational. If successful at interview, I would be responsible for designing programmes both nationally with the other advisors and locally for my region. I would be consulting with various governors and heads of departments to determine the level of development they needed for themselves and their staff. I would also be responsible for delivering individual performance coaching and feedback to aid the career development of governors, non-operational managers and officers. The role sounded exciting and I very much felt that it was the career move I had been waiting for.

The college itself was huge and looked like an aesthetically great place to work. I loved period buildings. The main building called 'the Mansion' was a converted eighteenth-century stately residence with offices, bedrooms, meeting rooms, a bar and dining room. The complex was also home to a library, conference theatre and additional modern buildings used as learning centres, more offices, lounge or common room areas and more bedrooms in sprawling grounds. There was a gym and sauna. The winding approach to the college was lined on either side of the driveway by around sixty trees. When I drove up that morning, I passed horses and cows in the paddocks and saw various types of game. There was even a fountain and a lake with swans a-swimming. I had never been interviewed in such grand surroundings. I imagined myself eating lunch whilst sitting on one of the many benches I saw, taking in the beauty and feeding the ducks. I was looking forward to being offered the job.

After my successful interview, I was happy to join the college with nearly two years' relevant Prison Service experience, transferable skills and over 20 years in learning and development. I was keyed up by the prospect of being able to cultivate an all-round Prison Service experience and gaining hands-on knowledge of both prisoner and staff development needs. I was offered the East Midlands area, after being told by phone by Sue Brookes that she had just been promoted to become Chris's deputy and was subsequently handing the East Midlands over to me.

On the morning of 9th May 2005, I met Sue for the first time. As she was Chris's deputy, I was to report to her. She was completely different from Chris in appearance. She was taller and much heavier, and didn't seem too fussed about executive dress. She wore a brown tweed jacket with patches at the elbows, with a pink blouse that struggled to button over her very full bosom, a floral skirt and black shoes that were old and scuffed. Her hands were chubby and un-manicured and her skin was dry and blotchy. Sue's hair was short, thick and mousey. And she didn't have on any make-up. Unlike Chris, there was no light in her eyes when she spoke and she said nothing of vision or purpose. Chris and Sue looked very different from each other and early indications were that they were very different. That in itself didn't bother me as Sue seemed nice enough. I had no idea how much deeper the differences between these two women ran and how, as a result of this, my life was about to plummet to depths of despair I had never before experienced.

My induction started with the normal departmental introductions, which included another good encounter with Chris. She was just as stunning as before, with another silk scarf around her neck. (I later learned the scarves were her signature look and I never saw her without them.) She shared her vision again in more detail. Every time I met her, I was inspired and motivated. I had spoken to her a few times on the phone before joining the college and, each time, she exuded the kind of confidence and care that made me feel as if she had been waiting for someone like me to help her take her vision forward. And when she finished speaking, I always felt as if I was already an actively contributing member of her team. Now that I was here, she still had the capacity to make me feel the same. I was sure she had the same impact on everyone: it was a rare gift indeed to be able to make each person feel so special. I was confident that I was going to enjoy working at the college.

As we continued to talk about how Chris wanted each advisor to engage with the prison governors in particular, she also took the time to explain how she expected me to work. She told me things like, 'Don't feel guilty about going home early when the opportunity to do so presents itself, because it'll be more than offset by the times you will have to set out before 7.00am and return home after 7.00pm.'

She asked if I had had psychometrics training, in particular Myers Briggs Type Indicator training (MBTI). I said I had not and she said that she would arrange it for me. She jokingly said that now I couldn't leave LMD because the training was expensive. I was just grateful for the investment, as I hadn't received any since joining the Service.

Our meeting ended with Chris asking if I had anything else I would like to discuss. I mentioned that I had spoken with Zoe, the Head of Finance that morning about expenses and told her that indications were that the journey to the college at Newbold as my base, was taking longer than expected and might be more expensive to travel to than I first thought. Even though I would claim my expenses back, the initial outlay was still quite an inconvenience and waiting for reimbursement was widely known to take a long time. (As the move to the college was not a promotion, my salary was still much lower than I was used to so it was important that I was not out of pocket unnecessarily.) Chris encouraged me to continue with the journeys for the month under the proviso that if I encountered real difficulty we would be able to work something out.

I continued to follow the induction programme, which also included keeping some of Sue's diary commitments along with visits to various prison types across the country. Not every prison is the same; some hold dangerous prisoners in high security–Category A prisons. Prisoners who do not require maximum security, but for whom escape needs to be made very difficult, are held in Category B prisons. The Category C prison is for those who cannot be trusted in open conditions but who are unlikely to try to escape, and then there are the Category D, or open prisons, that allowed the prisoners the freedom to go out to work in the community during the day. It was important that I got a feel for the different types and the different needs of the managers. I appreciated this even though I had visited other prisons in my previous role; my responsibilities were now different, and I needed to foster new perspectives. By the second week, however, I started to feel that the induction was not tailored to consider my previous operational experience. The visits that had been arranged were not designed to give me alternative views to the ones I already had. For example, I was arriving on site at various prisons and being met by staff who were at a loss to know what to show me because I already had experience working as a manager in a prison and already had a good understanding of the needs and concerns of uniformed staff and governors.

I was being asked questions like, 'Have you seen a SEG before?' The SEG, or segregation unit, contained cells away from the main prison population. Prisoners would be placed there sometimes for their own protection because they were high-profile prisoners at risk of harm from other prisoners. At other times prisoners were placed in a segregation cell because they had misbehaved and being separated from their cellmates was deemed punishment for their misdeeds. Naturally, I answered 'Yes,' and told them about my experience in a local Category B prison. This was usually followed by a bewildered, 'Oh, well, I don't know what else to show you if you've seen how a prison works and I think I can only spend a couple of hours with you as we're very short-staffed.' The officers' display of discomfort and uncertainty was all too familiar to me as I often witnessed such pained expression when uniformed staff met with civilians. There always seemed to be a nervousness around us as if we were about to expose them for some wrongdoing. It was an understandable response, inasmuch as the Service was constantly under scrutiny from many organisations eager to prove that the principle of incarceration is ineffective for a myriad of reasons. However, even though I had never worn a uniform, I was not the enemy and I needed to build trust and confidence that I was there to help. As such, I tended to suggest that the time would be better spent if I could talk to them about *their* development needs in relation to the type of prison they were managing. The officers then often relaxed and provided useful insight into the culture of the prison and things they mostly wanted to see changed. Although a good exercise, it only kept me busy for half a day from around 10.00am until maybe 2.00pm or 3.00pm. I tried not to be at a loose end and, depending where I was, I would go back to base at Newbold or home to catch up on the reading for the role.

By the end of the third week, I really wanted to get involved in the East Midlands as my region, but I had noticed this prevailing attitude in LMD that every advisor needed a long time to get to grips with the role. Apparently, some of the governors could be quite formidable and you needed to be very familiar with the working of a prison before you approached them. And there were others who had little patience for management and competency development, and were not afraid to tell you so. I did not doubt that I would need some time to understand who the movers, shakers and blockers were, but this hands-off approach was making me a bit fidgety as sitting still on the by-lines is hard for me to do.

I wasn't sure what I should do. I wondered if I should tell Sue that the induction was not stretching me enough and that I felt able to actively manage my region, especially having worked in a prison for nearly two years already. I thought perhaps I could remind her that in my previous role as Head of Learning and Skills, I had already met several of the governors in the region. I could propose I make my initial consultation appointments with them. In the end, I was fairly sure my induction was not going to extend much beyond the month and, even though at three weeks it was already the longest induction I had ever experienced, I decided it was probably better for me not to say anything and let Sue draw the programme to a convenient close.

Endnote

[1] The Management of Sickness Absence in the Prison Service. REPORT BY THE COMPTROLLER AND AUDITOR GENERAL HC 533 Session 2003-2004: 19 May 2004. The Prison Service employed some 45,400 staff1 in 2002-03, including 23,300 prison officers, 1,200 nursing staff and 1,200 senior operational managers, at a cost of £1,214 million-some 46 per cent of gross operating costs. Available online: http://www.nao.org.uk/publications/0304/sickness_absence_in_the_prison.aspx

[2] Prison Reform Trust. Experiences of Minority Ethnic Employees in Prison: A briefing on a PRT survey of the views of black and minority ethnic prison staff. People from BME groups make up about 9% of the general population, 25% of the prison population, and less than 6% of those employed in prisons. Available online: http://www.prisonreformtrust.org.uk/subsection.asp?id=640

[3] Commission for Race and Equality Website (2007) Available online: http://83.137.212.42/sitearchive/cre/diversity/map/eastmidlands/leicester.html

[4] The Management of Sickness Absence in the Prison Service. REPORT BY THE COMPTROLLER AND AUDITOR GENERAL HC 533 Session 2003-2004: 19 May 2004. The Service recorded 668,337 working days lost due to staff sickness absence in 2002-03, representing a year's work for around 3,000 full time staff. The main causes of illness included psychological conditions, such as anxiety, stress or depression, and musculoskeletal problems, such as back or neck problems. Time lost due to sickness absence cost the Prison Service some £80 million in lost staff time in 2002-03 (6.6 per cent of staff costs), although this figure excludes indirect costs, such as having to bring in additional staff to fill staff shortages. Available online:

http://www.nao.org.uk/publications/0304/sickness_absence_in_the_prison.aspx

Chapter Two

Lasting Impressions

I was due to meet Sue at Stirling house, a prison training centre in Suffolk. She had suggested that I observe her deliver a few one-to-one personal development sessions with staff who were approaching their exams. I was looking forward to this because it was my first chance to see an advisor in action. I had not yet had a handover from Sue; however, I was hoping that as I watched her in full flow I would quickly pick up any lessons she wanted me to learn. Although Sue had been temporarily promoted to be Chris's deputy, she was still carrying out some of her regional responsibilities as an advisor. This was only going to be until another advisor joined the team in the next few months. The new starter would release Sue to concentrate fully on being Chris's second-in-command.

I arrived a good half an hour before Sue, so I had a wander round the premises. I spoke with a couple of officers who arrived shortly after me: they were scheduled to be on a course in the conference room for the whole day and were not sure about the arrangements for their one-to-one sessions. Keen to respond to their query and build some credibility as a responsive new member of the team, I made a point to ask Sue as soon as she arrived what she had planned for the day. In response, she explained that the delegates would actually be 'nipping out' one by one from their scheduled team building session in the conference room. They were to meet with her in one of the meeting rooms upstairs for approximately 20 minutes each and then return to their full-day meeting. Even after she explained her two-birds-with-one-stone approach, I couldn't understand how that would be a quality experience for the delegates, who were on the verge of taking their exams–however it was not my call. I was only there to observe and learn, so I quickly silenced my curiosity.

Sue and I went upstairs to a small room. It had a single desk in the centre and a number of chairs around the side of the room. I took one chair and sat in the corner attempting to be as unobtrusive as possible. This was quite difficult considering the size of the room. Sue took two chairs, positioned them so that they were on opposite sides of the table, and sat on one of them. We waited for the delegates.

As an observer, I was armed with a notepad and pen. I had expected Sue perhaps to have a file with the delegate details, personal development plans and outstanding actions per person, and so on. But the only thing she had was a small box that she had carried into the room under her arm. When she had put the box on the desk I could see that it contained what looked like professionally produced blue A5 ring binders. They were entitled *Personal Development Pack*. I was intrigued. Sue had sensed this and offered me one of them to look at. As we waited, I flicked through the pages. I found generic guidance on communication skills, problem analysis, and adopting a systematic approach to working practice. The content was laid out like a workbook with templates and forms about development activity, to be filled in by the reader. It looked like a useful support pack, referring the reader on to other books and resources for self-development. My experience was that these kinds of tools worked really well for people who were self-starters and who were disciplined enough to work on their own. However, for people who needed to interact with others in order to be motivated and be accountable to aid their development, it was the kind of resource that would end up on a shelf and grow an inch of dust. As I thumbed through the templates, I wondered if Sue had already set targets using the binders and was here today to monitor progress and review the forms and templates that had previously been filled in as evidence of learning activity by the officers.

I was about to test my theory and ask how the blue binders were being used when there was a gentle knock on the door. The first delegate had arrived. He was of medium height and build with dark hair, dressed in jeans and a polo shirt. He came in and as he sat, Sue explained that I was just observing because I was on induction and that he was not to worry about my being there. He turned to me and extended his hand for me to shake. I stood up and stepped forward to take his hand.

'Hi, I'm Graham,' he said shaking my hand warmly.

'Hi, I'm Olivea.' I retook my seat. From that point on I was as invisible as one could be in a tiny room with two other people in it. With the pleasantries done, Sue got straight on with the session.

'What have you done since we last met to prepare for your exams?' she asked.

Graham said he had not done very much due to the increased pressures of the job. He seemed relatively sincere.

Abruptly Sue said, 'Well, you're gonna have to do more if you're hoping to pass.'

Graham readily acknowledged this. I waited for her to identify his needs or find out what was eating away at his study time or give him some specific direction in relation to perhaps previously discussed initiatives, but there was nothing forthcoming.

Instead, Graham went on to explain in detail how much more work he had taken on and the difficulties of finding time to study and get support. He sounded desperate and frustrated. He explained his eagerness to prepare for his exams and the irritation of being given extra work that was neither stretching him nor giving him insight into the world of prison management, which was what he felt he needed so that he could successfully move up to the next level.

Almost as if she had not heard what Graham had to say, Sue said, 'Do you have one of these binders?' as she held up one of the little blue files. He simply said, 'No'. Graham looked a little nonplussed, as did I. Sue had not responded at all to anything he had said regarding his inability to prepare for his exams. She reached across the table and gave him a file.

'It's filled with useful tips that should help. They're quite new. We're trying to give them out to as many as need them,' she said as she made her sales pitch. As he started to look through the pack, she smiled and asked, 'Do you know who's coming up next?'

And then his session was over. I was stunned. He had not been given any help. No direction, no guidance, just the little blue binder. No follow-up meetings had been set and no specific actions had been given other than consulting the little blue book. She didn't even direct him to a specific section in the blue book to get him started. When he left she said indifferently 'He'll fail again this year, he hasn't done enough to pass. He's what we call a serial fail!'

We saw around eight people that day and each session was the same: no one left with any actions other than a cursory, 'Find someone to shadow, do more and find the time!' I was speechless which was a rarity in itself. I was genuinely taken aback by this hit-and-miss approach to staff personal and career development. As I made my way to the car I thought that there had to be more to the role than this, and if there wasn't I had to raise the bar or I would not be able to sleep at night, Horlicks or no Horlicks. Doing a good job is of paramount importance to me.

During the drive home, I pondered if I had perhaps been a bit too harsh. After all, people work in different ways, I rationalised. However, the images of all the bemused faces at the end of each 20-minute session reasserted themselves in between each plausible argument I tried to make. It was clear from each expression that the delegates really didn't know what they were supposed to do next, in terms of their own development. Not one person left the sessions saying 'thanks, that was really helpful,' or something similar. I decided I would run the whole episode by Rudy, my husband. He was always objective whenever I started obsessing about anything. He would put me right.

When I got home I told Rudy how my day had gone and about the one-to-ones. He said, 'Are you kidding me? Can you get me a job there, I could do with a rest!'

The next day Sue and I were scheduled to meet at the Bobsleigh pub in Hemel Hempstead for the HMP Mount's management 'awayday'. Sue had been given a one-and-a-half hour slot to do an interactive presentation. I arrived early and waited in the reception area. Sue arrived just five minutes before her session was supposed to start. Fortunately, the management team was behind schedule. By her own admission, Sue was unprepared for this event, having only made decisions about what to cover in the session en route that afternoon. She had decided to do a game and have a discussion afterwards. She opened her document bag and pulled out wads of papers. She thrust a bundle of them in my hands. I leafed through papers about team dynamics, unsure of what it was she wanted me to do. I noticed that some of the sheets were barely legible, as they had been photocopied to death. Having seemingly emptied her TARDIS-like bag, Sue said that the papers hadn't been stapled in the correct order, so we spent the next 15 minutes splitting the sheets up and re-stapling them.

Keen to get involved I asked, 'Is there anything in particular you want me to do in the session to help?'

'Oh, um, I haven't really given it much thought,' she shrugged.

'Not a problem,' I said. 'Just give me a shout if you need anything.'

Not long afterwards, the management team had a 10-minute break and Sue used the time to set up the *Murder Mystery* game, a team-building and problem-solving exercise where each delegate is given a certain number of clues that relate to a murder and, as a team, they are expected to solve the murder by communicating well and piecing the clues together. I tried to make myself useful and got her some coffee and biscuits. The ten minutes seemed to go very quickly and the managers filtered back in. The governor running the day introduced Sue. Sue outlined the rules of the game, which were simply to listen to the clues each delegate had been given, not to write anything down and to agree as a team who the murderer was, the weapon used and time of death. Then she allowed the team of approximately twenty managers to discuss and make their deductions.

I thought the exercise would take around 20 to 25 minutes because I had seen it before, but Sue let the game run for nearly an hour. To begin with, the room was filled with high energy as the delegates were eager to hear all the clues but, as the minutes lapsed, there were times of utter silence as the delegates practically gave up taking part in the *who dunnit* exercise. With no more guidance or input from Sue, the delegates agreed and disagreed, solved and then unsolved the murder. It was only after the delegates had become irritable and the confusion and exasperation could be seen plainly on their faces and their body language—as some slumped back in their chairs whilst a couple held their heads in their hands saying nothing for at least ten minutes—that Sue stopped the exercise and gave them the answer. All the energy had been sucked out of the room and, on hearing the answer, a few individuals protested that they had got it right at the very beginning but because they were overruled by the other team members they had to concede. I held my breath waiting to see how she was going to lift the learning for the exercise, justify the approach and outcomes, and re-energise the group. But Sue didn't do anything like what I was expecting. Instead, she spent the next 20 minutes going through the handout we had previously re-stapled. She didn't link the activity to the handout. She didn't link the handout to anything they had covered for the day. Then the session was over.

The governor quickly thanked her for her input and we left the room. As I followed behind her, I thought perhaps we were heading for the reception area for a debriefing session about the last two days, but Sue didn't stop; she walked straight through and made for the pub car park. I struggled to keep up with her hurried stride as we negotiated our way through the randomly parked cars. Desperate for some clarity, I asked, 'Is the murder game a standard tool for management 'awaydays' or did you choose it because it was the best fit to underpin their activities for the day?' I was thinking that maybe there was a link and I had perhaps missed it.

She responded with a shrug of her shoulders as she scanned the car park for the exact spot she had left her car in, 'Oh I don't know what they covered today. I was only asked to do something to lighten the mood for the day.'

Lighten the mood for the day? Were we learning and development specialists or the entertainment? What a waste, I mused to myself. If it had been me, I would have enquired from the governor what he was hoping to achieve for the day, what strategies they were working with and how he felt I could help to underpin or connect with their leadership team plans. Sue had not done any of this. I couldn't see how, as a leadership development team, we could be viewed as adding value if this was indeed the standard.

We said our goodbyes and I made my way to my car. As I walked, I continued to think about how unproductive the day had been. I arrived at my car and whilst rumbling in my bag for my keys I realised that I was judging again. 'Oh Olivea, you've got to stop doing this!' I scolded myself. It was hard for me to switch this part of myself off. I had spent years assessing others and making judgements; however, I reminded myself that I had just started at the college and shouldn't be criticising my boss. Yet still I pondered, how does one observe without making a judgement about what one is seeing, especially when it's what one is being paid to do? If I had watched any other staff member do what Sue did, I would have come to the same conclusions. Of course, I knew I wasn't being paid to evaluate Sue, yet it was really difficult to watch her disappoint and confuse clients and not see it through professionally assessing eyes. Nevertheless, this was not my problem, I stressed to myself. All I had to do was make sure that I didn't behave in the same way. Then, if there was any backlash about the quality of our service, it wouldn't be levelled at me.

At the end of the month, another outline of activities was sent to me via email for the whole month of June. In my last one-to-one with Sue she didn't say that I would still be on induction, and my assumption that I wouldn't be prevented me from raising the duration of the programme for discussion. This meant that contrary to my assessment of how I would develop in the role, I was still going to be on induction. I wasn't sure what another month following the same pattern would yield and I became torn about whether or not I should say something to Sue about when I would be free to manage my region as a fully fledged member of staff. I didn't understand the reluctance to formally hand the region over to me.

On Friday 3rd June, I met with Sue in her office where she informed me that due to her new responsibilities she was unable to deliver training that was promised to HMP Foston Hall staff, on site at HMP Sudbury's training room, for Tuesday the following week. Apparently, both prisons were in close proximity and HMP Foston Hall staff often used HMP Sudbury's training room and restaurant. Even though I had not been to either prison before, or met any of the staff, Sue asked me to deliver training that was part of a series involving a number of groups and modules she had been rolling-out there. I agreed because I was keen to get on, so I asked for an outline of what had already been delivered, names of who had had what training, along with a request for the course content, notes and activities she wanted me to use. I was both surprised and bewildered when in response to my very specific request for vital information Sue gave me two games. The first was a communications game called 'Colourblind'. In it, the delegates are blindfolded, given a number of different coloured shapes that they have to describe to each other whilst relying on the facilitator when asked, to disclose the colour of each shape, the goal being to work out how many shapes are the same and what colour they are. The other game was the 'Murder Mystery' game she had used at HMP Mount's management 'awayday'. Sue explained that, prior to this she had actually delivered three or four half-day programmes on Team Building, but this was to be the first full-day programme in the series that she had designed and was rolling-out. I asked if there was anything else she could give me in terms of what she had previously designed as the full-day programme, and she simply said 'No'.

As an afterthought, Sue suggested that if I had done 'Belbins' before, I could use that. The Belbin Team Inventory is an assessment tool that is used to gain insight into how individuals tend to behave in a team environment. I said that I had used it before and she said, 'okay, good'.

I realised I was not going to get any more help than that, so I took the games and left her office. When I got to my desk, I sent an email to Liz, the Head of Personnel at HMP Foston Hall and informed her that Sue would not be delivering the programme as planned. I asked her for the delegate names, their grades, roles and her understanding of the rationale behind the series. Trying not to raise the alarm, I said that the information would help me to 'tailor' what Sue had given me, because I didn't want her to know that a mere two working days before the event nothing had been done for her staff, except for the proposed use of a couple of games. She responded to my questions later on that day, conveying some apprehension that I needed to ask those questions so close to the event, and she also expressed some disappointment that changes were being made just days before delivery. Had I been in her shoes I would have felt exactly the same, yet I was sure that to offer her further explanation and assurance would have only served to fuel her anxiety that there was a problem with the programme and, possibly, the quality of its delivery. All I could do was turn up and do the best job I could without the slightest suggestion that the whole thing had just been put together.

For the rest of the day I got down to the real work of designing the programme. As much as I appreciated that the games were legitimate tools for learning, by themselves they gave no indication to content already delivered nor were they sufficient to do a full day's training starting at 9.30am and concluding at 5.00pm. As a consequence, I additionally worked most of the weekend, including Sunday, after honouring my church commitments and late at Newbold on Monday, to design a full day's programme incorporating the games. My hope was to design something that the delegates had not already seen in the previous sessions that Sue had delivered as part of the series. Although I had never experienced delegates telling me en masse that they had already done a piece of work, because I had never designed 'blind' before, this was now a genuine risk. If Sue had already delivered three or four sessions to the same group on the same subject, that level of activity increased the chances of my presenting something they had already seen. I was not looking forward to this and even though it did not make any logical sense, I felt as if I was being set up to fail.

In all the years I had worked in learning and development, I had never been expected to perform with so little information and support. It is crucial, as a design consultant, to have a degree of client information to enable creation of a tailored response to client needs. This is an essential component to effective design and delivery! I couldn't believe that Sue only gave me two games without expressing what the needs of the learners were. However, as I was still on induction, I didn't want to complain about what I felt was inadequate support.

I set out for HMP Sudbury on Tuesday. I was quite nervous and my stomach churned for the entire journey. This was to be my first management development delivery for nearly two years and, even though I had worked some contingency activities into the programme, I found it impossible to shake off the feeling that at some stage during the day the whole group would chorus 'We did this the last time!'

Thankfully, my fears were not realised. The training was well received and I was told that I was an excellent trainer by the delegates and Liz, the Head of Personnel, who had decided, because I was new, to sit in the session for the whole day. On the way home I breathed several sighs of relief for what I felt was a narrow escape.

I didn't get a chance to see Sue until the end of the week when she returned my expenses forms unauthorised, saying that I couldn't claim expenses for travel from home to my base in Newbold. I felt sure I had been told I could, and I quoted the conversations I had had with the Zoe, the Head of Finance, as part of my induction, and with Chris. Sue dismissed this whilst waving the papers in the air and remained adamant saying, 'Well you can't claim from home to base.' She spoke in a much laboured way as if I was either dim or deaf.

And that was that. She thrust the forms back into my hands and bade me delete the offending entries and resubmit, otherwise none of my expenses would be paid. After our conversation ended, I sat alone in my office and was uncharacteristically upset. I couldn't decide if my upset was caused by my not being able to claim all of my expenses or if I was upset about the way she spoke to me—or both. After this conversation, there was an inexplicable sense that I had been shoved to one side as unimportant. There was nothing specific; the sense was more primal and intuitive than actual. Sue had not said anything offensive and she was perfectly entitled to tell me what I could and could not claim for. Yet there was something about the *way* she looked at me during this conversation, as if I wasn't worthy of her time, as if I was an annoyance. She was distracted and dismissive whilst barely making eye contact and this made me feel as if I didn't matter and my understanding of expense claims was irrelevant. I *could* have made a mistake about what I could claim for, but that should not have made me something undesirable underfoot. I could not account for where these feelings were coming from, but all things considered there was something wrong: it was hanging in the air. Building. Waiting for its moment. I just didn't know what it was, and not knowing was unnerving me further.

I realised that I wasn't settling in and that was unusual for me. The last time I had felt this uncomfortable was nearly 20 years ago. I had joined an equipment maintenance company as a sales controller. My friend Eugenie had recommended the role because, as the newly appointed sales manager, she needed someone to do the role she had just given up. It was to be the first time I had ever worked alongside another black person—what's more we were around the same age and this job would give us an opportunity to rekindle our friendship, having lost touch since college.

Although the move was mutually convenient, from day one I saw a side to her that I had never seen at college. She immediately alienated me from the rest of the group by staggering the lunches so that I manned the office alone whilst she went to the pub with everybody else. She loudly picked my work to pieces in the open-plan office and would sit at her desk and glower at me from time to time, which was most disconcerting. But, worst of all, I had never heard such foul language from an individual. Even though she knew how much I loved God, she profaned him continually. The environment was horribly oppressive and I felt compromised every single day. It was the shortest work experience of my life. I left after three months with no job to go to.

I was confused about how the same kind of discomfort and uneasiness could come to the surface, even though Sue had not done any of these particular things to me. That being said, however, like Eugenie, Sue wasn't treating me with respect and I didn't know why. Furthermore, the situation with Eugenie was slightly different in that she was black. As far as I was concerned, that experience turned out to be a classic case of a black person progressing and pulling the ladder up after them! There I was doing Eugenie's old job, and she certainly was not going to let another black woman come in and either show her up or take her new place. But Sue, what was her problem? Why did she feel the need to disrespect me?

On 10th June, there was an extraordinary turn of events. I had joined a few members of my team in Leadership and Management Development (LMD) in the conference building along with about sixty other people from across the organisation, to listen to a series of lectures about the purpose of prisons and the issues facing officers and offenders. During the break, as I mingled with the other attendees, in a flurry of activity all of my team members gathered by the fire exit in the coffee room. I watched them from the opposite side of the room and could see from their shocked facial expressions and how they waved their arms about, that something bad had happened. Then they all left the building without a word of explanation. I continued to drink my coffee and meet new people thinking that my team were bound to return soon. After the break, I returned to the conference room with the other delegates and listened to the various speakers. I found the lectures insightful and I was eager to learn anything that would help me to do my job well; however, I was distracted by the absence of my colleagues. By lunchtime I realised that they were not coming back. I had lunch with the other delegates and then I went back to my office.

After about an hour, Sue came in to find me sitting at my computer. She looked pensive. She sat down and took a deep breath.

'You must be wondering what was happening this morning?'

'Yes,' I said expectantly. 'Why didn't anyone come back to the lectures?'

'I have some bad news,' she paused.

I couldn't imagine what she was about to say. My emotions were all over the place. During the lectures I had been plagued by thoughts of losing my job based on the principles of 'last in, first out.' Why else would they have left me at the lectures alone, I reasoned, if not to explain that there were now fewer roles but theirs were safe?

Oblivious to my ruminations, Sue announced, 'Chris has been marched off the premises!'

'What?' I was confused. I was immediately relieved I still had a job but that relief was short-lived and instantaneously gave way to a mixture of irrational fear and panic.

'Why? What's happening? I don't understand.'

Sue started to explain. 'Well, there have been some issues. Er Stacey and…and Chris…um well, some things, er… how do I put this?'

Stacey Tasker was the Head of the college and I had not met her yet because of her busy schedule. Sue continued to babble. She wasn't looking at me as she talked. Instead she seemed fascinated with her hands as she waved them in front of her almost as if the clarity that she sought was written on each palm.

'—well…they have different views about the leadership team and they haven't er, seen eye to eye for a while, and so…well, some things have come to light, that had to be dealt with…'

What was she blathering on about? I had given up. I couldn't make sense of what she was saying. What did this all mean? How could they simply march Chris off the premises? What could she have possibly done to warrant such an ignominious and dramatic exit?

Sue continued in a much lighter tone. 'Well Stacey has asked me to act up as the Head of Leadership. I was so surprised when she asked me.'

My attention snapped back into the room.

'—I don't know how I'm going to do this, it's a pretty big role and there's so much to do,' she said excitedly. All traces of the sombreness associated with Chris's exit had left her voice. 'Some of the girls are really affected. They were very close to Chris, which is why we left the lectures. In fact, some of them are a little angry about how the whole thing was carried out. Rachel's in tears. This is going to take some time to get over.'

Sue was in charge, I questioned in my head? Sue was in charge! The realisation hit me like a brick in the face. No matter how I said it in my head, I could not shake the increasing sense of vulnerability I started to feel. There was no comfort in what she was saying. For the last month, Sue had not left me feeling confident that she respected me or cared about me. I already felt let down by her about my induction, the delayed East Midlands handover, HMP Sudbury *and* we had already had disagreements about my expense claims. All of this was barely one month into the role. And unfortunately the one person that I could have talked to, and trusted, was no longer available; only God knew what crazy scheme led to her demise that day. I was horrified by the thought that if they could march that amazing woman off the premises, they could do anything to anyone!

I left the office that day about to commence my annual holiday abroad. Sue said that on my return I might be expected to go back to HMP Sudbury on 27th June on her behalf. She wanted to know if I had used a tool called Team Effectiveness Profile (TEP). I later found out that it was a research and development tool designed to determine team dynamics and identify blockages in team productivity. As I had not used the tool before, this meant she would have to deliver the session herself and I would have to watch and take notes to enable me to deliver it the next time. Sue toyed with the idea of cancelling the event. But as I had planned to be back in the country by 25th June, she agreed to confirm by phone whether or not the training would take place on my return. I would need to know if I was to make my way to HMP Sudbury or go in to the office at Newbold.

My holiday was fabulous. It started with a surprise 40th birthday party for Rudy. I invited his family from London, packed our suitcases for the surprise holiday and hid them in Mum's bedroom. I booked two weeks' annual leave for Rudy directly with his manager, Yvonne, who was happy to play along because, unbelievably, she was due to spend a week in the same hotel with her husband for our first week. She got on so well with Rudy and relished the thought of bumping into us at breakfast by the pool. The party ended with a slide show of the five-star hotel we would be staying at in Egypt alongside the Red Sea. On the flight, the captain announced Rudy's birthday to the passengers and crew and we had champagne and chocolates. The hotel was beautiful, the staff were courteous, the food was marvellous and the weather was perfect. The whole thing went without a hitch. Rudy loved the attention. He enjoyed the sun and massages. He raved about the scuba diving, the variety of fish and coral. He was in his element. I wanted to do this for him because he is such a great guy. I had a wonderful time too. The only problem was keeping my levels of apprehension in check. I kept asking myself if I was reading too much into the encounters I had with Sue. With Chris gone, I wondered if Sue would make changes to the team, and what I would be returning to. It was unusual for me to have this kind of anxiety but something was gnawing away at me, warning me not to be my usual trusting self. But why? Even though I had no evidence that anything was wrong, the feeling was difficult to shake off.

On return from my holiday, I didn't receive a call from Sue as expected nor had she left any messages. Her not confirming where she wanted me to be on my return, only amplified the discomfort that now seemed to be with me more often than not.

The next morning I woke up just after 5.00am. As I opened my eyes, it dawned on me that *I* could have called Sue to check where I was to be that day. Why hadn't I thought of that before? Instead of waiting for her to call, I could have called. I know it wasn't rocket science yet it never occurred to me once. It scared me to think I was feeling so compromised that even the simplest solutions were beginning to elude me. I needed to stop obsessing about what was most probably nothing. I needed to free my mind up to be its normal, proactive and creative self. I needed to relax. This fear was beginning to curtail my freedom to enjoy my life and my work. I decided that I had to stop this now.

Even though I had not heard anything from Sue about the plans for the day, I accepted my part for where there was a lack of clarity and travelled to HMP Sudbury. I left the house at approximately 6.30am. En route, I played my music, and gave God thanks. This got me to a much better place emotionally. When I arrived a little before 8.30am, I found Sue there setting up the room. I said 'Hello' and immediately got involved by moving chairs and filling jugs with water for the tables.

The day was to be comprised of a half-day session with Sue and a half-day session for a stress management presentation by a staff care and welfare official. During Sue's session, I took copious notes so I could use the TEP tool next time. There was a lot to remember.

We broke for lunch at 12.30pm. Sue said she needed to return to Newbold and I went to the staff restaurant with the delegates. I had met some of them before at the session I ran earlier in the month, and a couple of them wanted to know how the surprise birthday arrangements for Rudy had gone. I enjoyed going over the details as we waited for our food. They were amazed that Rudy didn't have a clue about what was going on until the party. I told them how he wouldn't believe that we were going on holiday because his boss had outlined work for him for the next week whilst *she* was away on holiday. They commended me for having the foresight to get an email from Yvonne agreeing annual leave for Rudy and thought it hysterical that Rudy didn't believe me until we were sitting on the plane and no one had asked us to get off! I explained every tiny detail with great joy and accomplishment.

Whilst I was eating my lunch, Sue reappeared and presented me with a Staff Performance Development Record (SPDR) to sign. The SPDR form is used to record individual performance objectives and development activity as part of the Prison Service appraisal system. Hurriedly she said, 'I don't have time to stay for lunch or wait for you to read this, but could you sign it please?'

'Oh,' I said a little taken aback. 'Will you take me through the form another time then?' I asked, poised to sign.

'I'll do it at the next one-to-one,' she said impatiently.

The form she handed to me didn't have my name on it and the generic objectives for the LMD team had been cut and pasted into the space where my personal targets should have been. As much as I didn't want to sign the form without going through the process of a proper appraisal, I was well aware of how these things worked in the Service. Meeting the deadlines and targets was more important than the content and quality of the appraisal. I felt a little under pressure–the deadline for opening my appraisal and setting targets for my new role was just two days hence and I knew there would not be another opportunity for me to sign before the end of the month.

'Why did she leave it so late?,' I thought. We had worked together since the beginning of May. We had been in the office simultaneously many times. She could have had an initial appraisal meeting with me on any of those occasions and avoided this last-minute rush. However, I knew if I did not sign the form, I could quite possibly be contributing to the college missing the required 95% target for signed forms. So I signed it, even though everything I knew about contracts was screaming at me not to do so. I could not afford to be out of favour over something so simple. In any case, Sue did say she would go over the form with me when we had more time. I signed in all the required spaces. She rustled the paperwork together and left for Newbold.

I left the restaurant 25 minutes later because I wanted to use the desktop computer in the training room to check my emails. After nearly two months, I was still without a college laptop configured to allow access to the Prison Service intranet from home, so I decided to take this opportunity to get up to date quickly with what had been happening since my holiday. I logged on and whizzed through the emails. I didn't see anything that required immediate action. I wrote an email to Zoë, the Head of Finance for Newbold, with the query about my expenses and asked her to confirm where else my base could be instead of the college. I hoped she would respond quickly enabling Sue and me to come to a speedy agreement about my expenses.

Amongst the emails, I found an induction schedule for July *and* August. Dismally, this meant that not only would I be on induction for another two months, but Sue had not communicated when the induction programme was going to end. I exhaled. No matter, I thought, they're just being thorough and giving me the best possible start.

As everyone started to filter back into the training room, I closed down the computer so that I could take my seat.

'Checking emails?' said Martin, a member of the group who was one of the first officers back into the room. Having observed me shut the computer down he said, 'You'd better make the best of it 'cos they're unplugging that soon.'

'Oh right. I suppose it is unusual to have a single desktop in a room like this,' I queried without really asking the question. I took my seat.

'Yeah, it was only a temporary thing anyway for someone next door 'cos they needed an extra terminal, but I think they've sorted it now,' he said as he took his seat next to me.

I had decided to stay for the stress management session that followed so I could continue to bond with the staff and perhaps build on whatever was about to be delivered; however, the session was very basic and after nearly an hour I decided to head home.

At around 4.15pm when I arrived home, my phone rang and it was Sue.

'Hello,' I said brightly.

'Oh,' she sounded startled. 'I didn't expect you to pick up the phone. I thought you said you were going to stay at Sudbury,' she said, as if to test me.

'I did stay,'– I became guarded. 'But after about an hour I decided the session was really basic and that it wouldn't necessarily further my understanding of stress management.'

'Well I'm *very* disappointed that you didn't stop off at Newbold, if you were leaving early. There are a lot of emails that you need to pick up since coming back from holiday! You should have come back here.'

I was quite shaken by her immediate launch into criticism. I felt she was being unreasonable for three reasons. Firstly, including the travel (which was part of my working day) I had already done a nine-hour day, give or take 15 minutes, but she was expecting me to go back to Newbold and add a further hour and fifteen to thirty minutes to my day, depending on rush hour traffic. Secondly, the admin department regularly sent copies of minutes etc. to the advisors' home addresses, so I had two weeks of mail waiting for me, which would enable me to catch up. And, of course, I had already checked my email account and hadn't found anything that urgently required my attention.

The call ended without her telling me why she had even called, which left me with a niggling suspicion that it was simply a call to check up on me. My bid to remain positive had grown wings and flown out of the window.

Chapter Three

Metamorphosis

As June drew to a close, there were further problems coming to the surface in this new role and with my relationship with Sue. On 29th June, I got an email from Louise in the LMD administration department saying that she had been *'given some outstanding operational managers' feedback from Sue for* [me] *to collect'*. I queried if these feedbacks were for me to use as case studies as part of my induction, however Louise thought they were to be delivered by me to the officers and managers in question during one-to-one sessions that I now needed to plan. I didn't mind inheriting workload except that these were 360-degree feedbacks and J-SAC (Job Simulation Assessment Centre) feedbacks that I had not been trained to deliver and, to compound things further, they were overdue by nearly a year.

The J-SACs are part of the exams that officers sit at respective levels. The officer attends an assessment centre where they are filmed handling a number of scenarios. The Prison Service core competencies are measured during each performance and DVDs are produced for the advisors, along with moderator or feedback packs to enable coaching on performance for those who passed or failed the assessment. Yet here I was without the moderator packs and without the training, expected to deliver a service in the same way and to the same standard as the other advisors. The other complication of course was that the J-SAC feedbacks were so overdue that these particular officers were about to sit their exams again. I was not looking forward to having to calm disgruntled candidates or explain why this service had not been provided before now. I knew that if I was one of the officers affected, I would be concerned that I wasn't getting my feedback in enough time to fully implement the observations and recommendations. But then not everyone is like me.

The outstanding 360-degree feedbacks posed a slightly less antagonistic problem, in that the managers were awaiting feedback for personal development and not necessarily preparing for internal exams. 360 refers to degrees in a circle with an individual figuratively placed in the centre. Feedback is provided after a participant self-assessment and assessments by subordinates, peers and supervisors, using the same criteria. It was also nearly a year since these assessments had been done and collated ready for feedback. It was at this point that, after thinking about the duration of my induction, the levels of support I felt I needed and my relationship with Sue, I decided that I would raise these issues with her at my next one-to-one session. It made sense. I didn't want a repeat performance of HMP Sudbury in terms of the uncertainty and stress, and I needed to make sure there was no more overdue work waiting in the wings. I always preferred to know exactly what I was expected to do from the outset, no matter how much, so that I could prioritise accordingly.

A week later I had a one-to-one meeting with Sue to check my progress. Prior to the meeting, I forwarded the response to my queries about my expenses and my base that I had received in the week from Zoë, the Head of Finance. I was so glad when I received her email because it outlined a simple remedy to the problem of where I could be based. In it, Zoë confirmed I could be based at a prison closer to my home, like HMP Wellingborough, and she even outlined a 'no base' option which essentially meant I would be paid expenses wherever I travelled from. For me the only downside was that the decision was solely at Sue's discretion and our relationship was fragile. I very much wanted to believe she would see that my request was reasonable and not unlike anything that had already been done for others.

Sue and I settled into the usual format of the meeting promptly. She looked at the priorities that had been set for the month of June, asked me for an update in relation to them and asked if I had experienced any problems. After answering her questions and demonstrating that I had met the objectives, I decided to tackle the issue of my prolonged induction. It felt like a good time, as she could see that I was doing well with the tasks set and she had not brought any concerns to the fore.

'Sue, I was wondering, is it normal to be on induction for an indefinite period of time?'

I paused to get a quick assessment of how my question had landed. Sue's face was like stone. I couldn't tell if I should continue, yet knew I couldn't wait for a schedule to arrive for September and October.

'So far,' I tentatively continued, 'I am getting a new schedule for each month and when I complete the next schedule I will have been on induction for four months. Is there anything in particular you want me to see that I haven't seen yet? I mean…is it *normal* to be on an open-ended induction?'

Sue didn't answer any of the questions. Instead, after perusing the hard copy of the induction she said, 'Well let's agree that the current schedule which has dates up to the end of August will be the last schedule.'

'Okay. Thanks.' 'And now onto the next thorny issue,' I thought. 'Also, I forwarded an email from Zoë. Did you get a chance to read it?' I asked tentatively.

'I had a quick look, but didn't you travel to Leicester every day without difficulty?' she queried.

'Actually,' I explained, 'travelling to Leicester daily created financial difficulty for me as I had been assured before joining that there was a way of helping me with the cost. But once I arrived, I found that there wasn't.' I went on, 'When I worked in the private sector I was used to getting help with travel by way of a car allowance and when I was told that I could get help when I joined the Service, I was expecting something similar.'

'Mmm. We don't have anything like that here,' she said.

'Yes, I know that now. But this email does say that you can be flexible about where I could be based. So it doesn't really matter about getting a special allowance or not being able to claim from home to base, if you can vary my base to HMP Wellingborough, for example.'

Ready with a response, Sue said, 'There are no spare desks or offices at Wellingborough Prison.'

Not to be put off, I replied, 'I have been there and the Governor's secretary is happy to find me a space to work.'

Sue capitulated and ended our game of verbal tennis. She agreed to look at my issues around where I could be based in relation to what I could claim for. Moving the conversation forward, I addressed the matter of the outstanding feedbacks.

'Louise has asked me to do some outstanding feedbacks,' I said handing over the emailed request, 'only I haven't done either 360s or J-SACs before. Can you help me with these?'

'I'll help with the 360-degree feedbacks, but you need to ask a member of the team to help with regards to the J-SACs.'

'Okay, great! Thanks.'

Once the meeting ended, I was quite pleased. I had raised the issues, made my case reasonably well and there didn't seem to be any great fallout from it. I had been given some direction and I was happy with her offer of support and the instruction to ask the other advisors for help. I remained hopeful that progress had been made.

I decided to use the next team meeting at Newbold on 13th July as a platform to ask the team for help with the outstanding J-SAC feedback. Straight after my meeting with Sue, I had sent an email asking for help and, as no one responded, the team meeting seemed like a good place to ask for help again.

When the day arrived, I asked the team members during the break for help with the J-SACs and guidance on how to provide feedback. It turned out no one had a formal pack outlining protocols for interpreting the DVDs from the last round of exams. Instead, they advised me to simply watch the DVDs and become familiar with the format in that way. I took their advice and collected the outstanding feedbacks from the admin department.

On 19th July, I began to watch the DVDs at home in my office. I decided to do the same any day I wasn't scheduled to be at a prison or a meeting elsewhere. Without the moderator packs it was difficult to determine the rationale and desired outcome for each simulated exercise. This meant I needed to watch the DVDs several times, in order to produce a consistent approach to understanding the scenarios and giving the feedback to each candidate. There were six 26-minute scenarios per candidate, with three to four marking sheets per scenario per candidate. As all the candidates I had inherited failed to pass the J-SAC, I decided to write a detailed profile for each person once I understood what they should have done per scenario. I then planned to give feedback and coach them using the profiles I had written.

During the day, I sent an email to Sue from my home desktop regarding continuation of training for HMP Foston middle managers. The training in June had gone well despite her lack of support; however Liz, the Head of Personnel, was now asking about 'Phase 3' of the project, which didn't mean anything to me. Unfortunately, she was unable to tell me what Phase 3 looked like when I asked because Sue, responsible for the design and collaboration on the project, never disclosed what this phase would contain. Neither did she agree the timescales for delivery. Eager to prevent a repeat of June, I wrote to Sue asking for her intentions and ideas. Based on my previous experience, which was admittedly quite short, I didn't expect a response that would take the query any farther forward, as Sue had already stated that she was very busy. However, I felt I should still ask just in case she had done some work on the project. If she had, it would save me some design time.

Watching the DVDs made for a very long day. It took me a good while to get into them and pick up on behavioural trends in relation to the expectations of each scenario. Nevertheless, I persevered and began to get a sense of what the candidates were doing in relation to what they were expected to do. I worked until about 7.00pm. I was quite drained by the end of the day, yet I was encouraged as I felt I had made good progress.

Just over a week later, on 27th July, another such gap in my induction lent itself to the opportunity to review the remaining DVDs. I was up fairly early and started watching them from around 7.30am. By 9.30am, I received a phone call from Sue on my mobile.

'Hello Sue,' I said cheerfully. Her call made for a welcomed distraction from the monotony of watching the DVDs. Her response to my upbeat greeting however left me reeling like a traffic cone that had just been struck by a car speeding off into the distance without a backward glance from the driver.

'Olivea!' she spat out my name. 'Where *are* you? And why doesn't anyone know where you are?'

Her raised tone drew my eyebrows into a deep frown that met my eyelashes and my bottom jaw jutted forwards like a three-year-old child that was being rebuked unfairly. There was silence. Sue was waiting for an answer. I placed my hand across my forehead and smoothed the frown back into my hairline. I took a deep breath to curtail engaging with Sue in a way that could only end in an outright free-for-all.

'I've spoken to Louise,' I said calmly. 'As soon as she got in I rang to tell her that I'm working from home today. I would have done it yesterday but, by the time I finished, everyone in admin had gone home, and so I called in first thing this morning.'

Sue was unconvinced and unimpressed. 'You shouldn't be spending *so* much time at home and you haven't updated your calendar.'

I didn't know what she meant by '*so* much time.' This was the second full day I had spent working from home since I had joined the team in May. And she knew very well that I couldn't update my calendar from home.

I protested. 'But you know I can't update my calendar remotely because you didn't order my RSA token, which means I can't use a college laptop to log into the system and make any changes. And, as I said, Louise does know where I am *and* my mobile is on.'

Apparently, Sue had forgotten to order my Remote System Access (RSA) token when my laptop was ordered. This meant that I couldn't remotely log into the Service intranet to update my diary entries to reflect any changes. There was the facility to log on at other prisons; however, this was only if there was a spare computer. As most officers had to share a computer–sometimes one computer between five or six users–it was nigh impossible to get online away from Newbold. Having to wait so long to be fully equipped to do my job was inconvenient; however, I had no idea that not being able to update my diary quickly was going to be so problematic.

'I told Louise that I was watching the DVDs so that I could give the outstanding feedbacks.'

Sue wasn't at all happy with my decision to work from home. 'You *don't* need to watch all the DVDs to give candidate feedback. After a couple of scenarios you can see what's going on,' she snapped.

Well, I figured I must be somewhat denser than most, because the last time I reviewed the DVDs it took me all day and part of the evening to get a semblance of what was going on. These particular candidates had failed, and in some cases their performances were so bad it was difficult in the absence of predetermined standards to know what they should have been doing. Furthermore, what Sue was now telling me was completely different from what I had been told by the team. And another thing—I had started to rant in my head—when I had spoken to her about the inherited workload at the beginning of the month, she had only offered to help with the 360-degree feedbacks whilst telling me to ask the team for support with the J-SACs. She hadn't given me any guidance about what to do with them and now that I was following the advice from the team, she was dismissing it as an illegitimate work practice. Her tone filled with anger and frustration as she got louder. I was at a loss as to where her heightened emotion was coming from and what I needed to do about it. There was a part of my brain that knew I needed to disengage, it knew that Sue was being irrational and there were no suitable arguments that I could build that would satisfy her enough to calm down. I was not going to win this one and I needed to keep quiet. I couldn't do it! I couldn't let the conversation end with her thinking I had done something wrong and that she had somehow found me out. So I kept up my fruitless endeavour to respond each time I thought she had finished, but as I did this she interrupted and talked over me some more.

She blustered on disapprovingly, 'You're just wasting time, Olivea! You should be at Newbold where you could get any assistance you need as the admin team is here to support you.'

'The admin team?' I thought, 'they don't give feedback to candidates, how could they help me with this?' Even the advisors whose job it was to give the feedback couldn't give me anymore of a steer than to watch the DVDs. What were the admin team going to do?

Ever determined to prove I had not wasted my time, I waited until I was absolutely sure she had finished reprimanding me. It was at least five or six agonising seconds of silence before I spoke again. 'I understand that you think simply watching the DVDs over and over again is unproductive, which is why I think you'll be pleased when you see that's not all I did. As well as watching the scenarios, I have also drafted a template that I feel sure the whole team will benefit from using. *And* watching the DVDs has really built my knowledge and given me confidence to give constructive feedback in a consistent way.' I was almost pleading by this point.

Sue wasn't interested. She sounded marginally calmer but she was still resolute. As if reading from a summarised list she said, 'I *don't* want you working from home. You need to be here where you can get help. Watching the DVDs in this way is a waste of time. I expect you to come in when you are not at a prison.' The call ended after Sue confirmed my whereabouts for the rest of the week.

When I put the phone down my head was spinning. I revisited everything leading up to this incident to try to work out what I had done wrong and how I had managed to provoke Sue so much. At the last team meeting, when I had asked for help with the DVDs, three prominent and long-standing members of the team–Rachel, Alison and Karen–had shared how and when they worked from home. They openly communicated that, when they first joined LMD, they spent quality time repeatedly watching the DVDs in an attempt to get a grounding in the style of assessment, the Service competencies, the marking sheets and the levels of candidate performance required. Having taken their comments on board, I could see that I was not doing anything different from them. They had outlined, with equal justification, that they had taken this approach to get a feel for what was going on, and I was doing the same. I moved on to consider if the frequency with which I had performed this exercise was the cause of the problem. I had only viewed the DVDs on two occasions when my induction left blank days with no direction, not forgetting that I was not yet at liberty to make my own appointments to pursue staff development initiatives, because the induction programme crafted by Sue had me mainly shadowing. This meant I couldn't look at my electronic calendar, see a gap and fill it with a consultation appointment, because she had determined the pace at which I was to be introduced into the region and who I would meet.

I was now very confused and nervous about what the accepted practice was, and when I would be allowed to show initiative. I was especially baffled because I had worked in a mobile role for several years before joining the Service and I was expected to make these kinds of decisions routinely. And then there was, of course, the fact that working from home was part of the flexibility of the role as endorsed by Chris, Sue's predecessor.

The feelings I buried in June resurfaced with overwhelming force. The illogical fear was back. The mystification and uncertainty was back. Why was she so angry with me? What had I done to provoke such contempt? She had raised her voice and scolded me! Why did she think it was okay to talk to me in that way?

'You're wasting time, *Olivea*!' echoed in my head. I felt her disdain, piercing hot, searing into my core. It was as if I had committed the most heinous of crimes. Yet what *had* I done? As a manager employed to be mobile, I had worked from home for a day. And that was it. There had been no previous discussion of the home-working policy as part of my overly long induction. At no time had Sue said, 'We are happy for you to work from home but only under 'x' conditions.' There was only this indistinct yet accepted practice that it was at advisor discretion, which I had exercised. I hadn't done anything illegal or immoral; I hadn't broken any codes of professional conduct to justify this outburst. Strangely, I felt shamed, powerless and stripped. I felt I had been reduced to a skulking, mangy dog that had displeased its master.

I wondered how it was that she had the power to do this. And why was I letting her do this? What was I afraid to discuss or possibly admit? That she didn't like me?—that was evident. But *why* she didn't like me was raising questions I was not able to answer. I knew I needed to talk to someone and, with Chris gone, I didn't know who I could go to for help.

The next day I was to shadow Val Woodcock, the advisor for Kent, Surrey, and Sussex at HMP Woodhill in Milton Keynes. I got to the prison's learning centre, situated outside the prison, shortly after 8.00am. I had a look around the premises, and when I saw a spare computer in one of the offices I asked at reception if I could use it to access my email. When I explained where the computer was, I was told that the person who normally sat there was on holiday so it was okay for me to use it. I logged on to find an email from Sue and when I read it my heart sank. She had cleverly entitled and summarised her angry outburst as 'our conversation'. Then she went on to suggest I shouldn't be having any difficulties because I had a clear induction programme. She reiterated that when I wasn't in an establishment I should go into Newbold, which effectively confirmed in writing that, unlike everyone else, I couldn't work from home any more.

During the day I worked well with Val. She was a thin, well-dressed woman with fine blond hair, cut in a short bob with a fringe. She was very pale, almost translucent, well spoken and seemed happy in her work. On first appearance, one would think her fragile almost as if she would break if you were to squeeze her too tightly, but when she spoke there was a confidence and intelligence that belied that initial impression.

After lunch, I tentatively checked with her about expenses, and how often she worked from home. I found out that, as far as she was aware, her contract classed her as being 'based at home', which meant she got her expenses paid from base (or home in her case) to any site. Val also confirmed that she regularly worked remotely from home like the rest of the team.

I plucked up enough courage to tell her I was having difficulties with Sue and told her about the email. Val was reassuringly confident that Sue and I had merely misunderstood each other and felt that we needed to have a good talk. She helpfully suggested I use her as an example of being based at home for the sake of expenses during my next conversation with Sue. Wow! It felt so good finally to talk about some of the things I was experiencing and what I was feeling. It felt as if a weight had been lifted. Until this point, I had not been able to talk to anyone at work about what was happening to me. And even though I hadn't gone into too much detail with Val, it was good to talk.

The following day, having responded to Sue's last email, I forwarded the whole communication exchange to Val. I wanted her to see that the tension between Sue and me was real, and I wanted to put her in an informed position so she could continue to advise me if I needed it. I especially wanted her to see that I was not exaggerating and to look at the tone of the email. Val responded by reiterating the need to talk with Sue and gave me some positive and congratulatory feedback about my performance the day before, because even though I was there to shadow her, I had got involved and had run a number of sessions with her.

On 5th August, I had my regular one-to-one meeting with Sue. I reported back as required, giving an account of what I had been doing with my time, what I had experienced and so on. I waited for any feedback about my performance from her. As usual there was none. When she was ready to conclude and asked if there was anything else I wanted to say, taking Val's advice, I broached the subject about the quality of our relationship.

'I think perhaps our relationship is not as good as it could be.'

Sue listened.

'I would like to know what *I* need to do to make it a better one, because it's clear that your mandate is very different from Chris's. And equally evident that I seem to be causing you problems.'

Diplomacy and ownership were paramount. I continued to wade tactfully into the deep end. It made sense to get everything out in the open. 'I think our communication needs work, as I find your emails to be quite dismissive. Now I'm not sure if perhaps I'm not using the right words, but when you respond it's as if you are responding to points I didn't make and the ones I did make remain unanswered.'

As if asking for death by firing squad, I then said, 'Also, since joining I haven't received any encouragement or positive feedback from you. I find this particularly unusual, especially with this being my induction—which is essentially a time for support and performance evaluation. I think there has been a lot of tension between us and I seem to be able to upset you,' I added. 'I want to clear the air.'

I additionally volunteered that all she needed to do was outline what she wanted me to do and I would do it because I really wanted to make this work. Then I breathed.

I noticed whilst I was talking she looked a little embarrassed and I felt that it could go either way. Either she would accept that what I was saying was true or she could deny there was a problem.

I was both grateful and relieved by her response. 'Well…I have been a bit snippy due to the pressures in my new role and the fact that the pay hardly makes the change worthwhile.'

She paused and reflected. I didn't say anything else on the matter. I had said enough, maybe even too much—only time would tell. Sue didn't say what she was going to do to make things better and I didn't want to press her; she needed time to think about what I had said.

We seemed to have stalled a little, so I moved on to remind her that she hadn't yet responded to my expense queries and that not being able to claim from home to base was affecting me financially. I continued to make my case by explaining that, having to come into Newbold when not at a prison as newly directed by her, increased my travel; however, it decreased my capacity to claim expenses. I concluded by telling her about Val's contract and how she was allowed to work from home.

Within an instant, we were back in the resistance zone. Sue was sure nothing could be done because I already signed my contract agreeing Newbold as my base. I persevered and clarified that my understanding was that my contract was reviewable. In any case, variation of the contract was possible, if deemed necessary by the manager—this was in line with the Prison Service Order (PSO) relating to the home-working policy. Sue conceded by saying she would look into it. Although she said that the last time, I let it lie. She was clearly very busy with her new role and maybe had forgotten to look into it as previously agreed. Now that I had reminded her, I was sure I'd get a response soon.

I left the meeting feeling a little fragile. I hadn't been in this kind of position before as a subordinate. As a manager I had, because sometimes when you inherit a team, members can come on board with all kinds of issues and you need to take some time to build team confidence. As a subordinate, though, I had never approached my manager to say the relationship wasn't good and I never had a manager suggest that one of the reasons he or she had been off-hand with me was because he or she was new in post and not earning enough money! I didn't quite know what to make of it, though I hoped that Sue and I had cleared the air sufficiently for our relationship to improve.

Throughout August, I continued with my induction and a few projects Sue had handed over to me. One such project was the design of an appraisal and poor-performance package to be delivered to Heads of Personnel. I attended full-day meetings, where I helped to guide discussions and reviewed materials put together by the team. I provided supplementary materials and worked on the speaker notes, facilitator packs and presentation materials. During such a meeting at HMP Littlehey, Val Perry, the Area Personnel Manager (who had interviewed me in 2003) asked if I would be available for the final meeting for the project. When she gave me the date of 12th September, I knew it was the LMD Team Meeting.

Immediately I said, 'Oh I'm sorry, I don't think I'll be able to make it because we have our advisor team meeting on that day.'

'I'm sure Sue can spare you for one meeting,' she said quite confidently.

I wished I shared her certainty. As I didn't, I said, 'Team meetings are pretty sacrosanct, I'm sure she won't go for it.'

Unconvinced she said, 'We could *really* do with your support to finalise the project. Once Sue is aware of your level of involvement, she'll let you go. Please try.'

I couldn't argue any longer: Val Perry was senior to me and it was a legitimate request. I knew that I shouldn't have felt so nervous about what any other advisor would have agreed to in a heartbeat. I also knew that I wasn't any other advisor. I was the one Sue regularly dismissed. I was the one she harangued with disdain. I was the one she was 'snippy' with.

'Okay, I'll ask her if I can attend,' I said.

Asking Sue was not something I was looking forward to doing. Even though not all the advisors turned up to all the meetings and even though individuals left early or arrived late, I knew that my asking to miss a day of the meeting would be an issue.

On 15th August, I forwarded good feedback from Val Perry to Sue about the *'first-rate work* [I] *was doing for the heads of personnel'*. On the back of that, I let her know Val had asked me to attend the last meeting for this project. I made sure I conveyed that I had told Val that I had a previous commitment to the LMD team meeting. Then I asked Sue which one she preferred me to do. Now all I had to do was wait.

As the week progressed, I had another appointment at HMP Sudbury and thoroughly enjoyed my day. I ended up designing Phase 3 without any support from Sue. I remembered how I asked her for help in relation to continuing the roll-out of the project in June, when she had only given me two games. I asked for help again in July, and this time there was no help forthcoming at all. In fact, she didn't even respond to the email. Although disappointed about the lack of help from her, I was very encouraged by the feedback I was receiving from Liz, the Head of Personnel at the prison and the people I had had the opportunity to train whilst on induction. I was itching to get on with making my own mark and developing the East Midlands in my own right. In the absence of a formal handover from Sue, it was impossible to know what had and had not been done by way of development activity in the respective prisons, but soon the region would be mine to build and furnish.

A week later, Sue had responded to my request to attend the last project meeting to design the Heads of Personnel programme. In it she outlined that,

> *'Team Meetings always take priority—but the Sept. core* [team] *meeting is on 13th enabling* [less pertinent] *work to take place pm on 12th—so you are able to attend* [the Heads of Personnel meeting].'

I was grateful, though reading between the lines, I felt a slight rebuke. I had personally not missed a single meeting since joining, yet I had never been in a team meeting with full attendance because there was always someone who was missing for reasons that were fully accepted. Yet for me, there needed to be a reminder about how *important* the team meetings were. I let it go because I was allowed to support the Heads of Personnel and that was what was important.

At the end of the month, I accompanied Sue to the Area Governors' meeting in Nottingham. I helped her set up to deliver the presentation that I had previously put together for her regarding the Leadership Development Programme (an accredited programme for first-line managers). Sue did the presentation, introduced me as the new advisor for the area, and presented course completion certificates to the candidates in attendance. It was a good meeting in that I got to meet some of the governors I would later be working with. I felt I made a good impression.

On 2nd September, I was free! I had tentatively started making appointments in August as it was my last month on induction. September started well. On 6th September, I delivered another workshop in HMP Sudbury and received rave reviews. Yet two days later my confidence was knocked out of the ball park! I had attended an area training meeting at HMP Gartree's learning centre, which concluded around midday. Instead of travelling to Newbold, I decided to stay at Gartree and work, as the computers in the IT training room were networked enabling me to email, make appointments and design. I was fortunate that there were no classes scheduled for that day, which meant that I could use a computer in the training suite for as long as I wanted. Also, staying at the learning centre to do my admin meant I would be able to claim expenses from Market Harborough to home; had I travelled into Newbold, based on what Sue had told me, I wouldn't have been able to claim. I switched on my phone and got on with my work.

Around 12.30pm Julie, the Area Training and Development Manager based at the centre, popped her head round the door with her mobile pressed to her ear. She said into the phone whilst looking at me, 'Yes…she's still here.'

Then she went back to her office. I waited for my phone to ring and, when it didn't, naturally intrigued I went to Julie's office to ask if someone was looking for me. She said Sue had rung her mobile to ask if I was still at Gartree. Julie then asked me why Sue was ringing *her*, to check where I was. I was so embarrassed. I had no explanation. My mobile was on since the meeting concluded so there was no reason why Sue couldn't have called me. I went back to the IT suite and waited to see if she would call. She didn't call.

After approximately ten unbearable minutes, I called Sue and got her voicemail. I left a message saying I understood she was looking for me. I told her where I was and that my mobile phone was on if she wanted to try again. She didn't return my call.

As the day progressed, I couldn't help feel that something was up. Maybe it was nothing, maybe she had been called away and she would ring back tomorrow. Then I thought, why didn't she just ring me in the first place? My phone was on and my number programmed into her phone. She probably had to look up Julie's number. She could have called me–why didn't she?

I had been honest and open about our relationship. It was clear we had problems, yet I couldn't fix them on my own. And Sue was only making things worse by prowling around and undermining me like this. In our last meeting, I had deliberately not complained about specifics in the way she was treating me and the way she was speaking to me. I merely pointed out that we needed a better relationship and I made some general observations. Then I thought, maybe that's the problem. Maybe I should have complained more pointedly. Maybe by not being explicit, I was fuelling her continued assault on our relationship.

As the month went on, I continued to do my job, hoping to make the right kind of impact in the region. It was the first month that I was left on my own to do my job. Whilst I was loving it, Sue was noticeably having difficulty letting go. Yet I believed that if I could get the next three months under my belt and keep the good results and feedback rolling in, I would be able to prove I was more than competent. It wasn't as if this role was particularly taxing–labour-intensive perhaps, due to outmoded training methods and equipment, however it was certainly less complex than previous roles I had held in the past.

On 13th September, I attended the second day of the LMD team meeting. We welcomed two new starters, Di Watkins and Rachel White. Their arrival meant a couple of things: firstly that Sue's workload was about to become much less and, secondly, that I had been promised Myres Briggs Type Indicator (MBTI) psychometric training (and the last time I had asked when I could have it, Sue had told me I needed to wait until the new starters arrived, so that we could all train together).

I settled down into the format of the meeting, which was usually made up of loud and unbridled contributions from most of the group. Their temperaments were so fiery, Sue could barely control them from meeting to meeting, and regularly added a point of view that fuelled their distemper. They would often talk across each other, swear and speak their minds so freely that it was on occasion unprofessional. It was the culture of the group to vent their feelings during meetings and complain about things they had little control over. They criticised people from Stacey Tasker as the Head of the college who, they maintained, as an ex-governor didn't understand the training mandate she had so comfortably been given, to the admin staff who didn't pick up the phone quickly enough when the advisors rang in. No one was safe from their insurgent rampages. Even though there was an agenda, someone would start a discussion about the bugbear of the month and we would be off point for at least fifteen minutes and sometimes more. I tended not to get involved in these extra-curricular discussions, even though they often made up the bulk of our meetings, as I found them disrespectful and distasteful. The nuisance this month was a management consultancy firm that we were using to design and deliver a series of new Senior Operational Manager (SOM) assessment centres. As I listened, the team seemed to be concerned about how the consultancy in question was getting the pick of the crop when it came to high-profile projects. They were accusing the Managing Director of the consultancy of using his connections with the Service to cut us, as advisors, out of the loop. This meant that we ended up with all the unchallenging pieces of work. Sue tried to explain that the governors were more likely to take development advice and submit to coaching from an external consultant than from an advisor who was below them in grade and pay. With a piranha-like frenzy, they devoured Sue's contribution to the discussion.

'What's the point in us being here then if no one is going to take any notice of us because of our grade?' said Karen Smith.

'We should be given the chance to show them what we can do. It shouldn't automatically be decided that we can't coach at that level. We're already doing MBTI across the organisation, why should it be any different in an assessment centre?' asked Karen Rushton.

'Sue, are you correcting governors when you hear them talking like that? You should be standing up for us,' challenged Pauline Duff. I watched the back and forth of the argument without comment, along with Di Watkins and Rachel White, the new starters. The team moved on to discuss, in light of their desire to raise their profile among the governors, whether or not we should deliver the MBTI component of the SOM programme instead of the consultancy. After some more heated discussion about how *we* should be dictating the kind of work we do as opposed to picking up what was left, the team decided that, as advisors, we would deliver the psychometric feedback during the SOM assessment centres, instead of the consultancy. I was especially pleased about this result because this decision meant I would definitely have to have the training I was promised, as now it was not just about me receiving the training for the East Midlands, this was a national project that would need all of us to deliver it, if it was to be successful. I sat in the meeting doubly confident that Sue would now arrange for my skills to be upgraded to enable me to contribute at the same level as everyone else.

Later on in the meeting, discussions turned to the development of a positive action scheme. Sue informed the team that Beverley Thompson, the Head of the Race and Equality Action Group (REAG) was looking for input from us regarding a programme set up for black and minority ethnic (BME) managers. Pauline asked if we were allowed to put a programme on for *just* BME staff and questioned if it wasn't a breach of the Equal Opportunities policy. Others in the group were nodding conveying that they shared the same concerns. Sue said the details were on the intranet and she would find out how we were expected to help.

I thought, 'How bizarre!' Although the nature of the programme wasn't made at all clear by Sue, I felt Pauline's reaction was quite naïve and almost offensive. It was common knowledge that BME staff were at a disadvantage when it came to promotional prospects in the Service, and retention of BME staff was also poor. It was visibly apparent that, the higher you looked in the organisation, the fewer BME people you saw. The bulk of BME staff resided in the lower prison officer and prison officer support grades. It was my assumption that this programme was probably a result of the need to address the lack of balance. Yet the team that was possibly going to design the programme was entertaining a discussion about whether or not positive action was in itself a breach of equal opportunity.

Over the next couple of days, I attended the non-operational manager's programme in Coventry. Sue thought it would be good for me to see what was on offer to managers who didn't work in the uniformed grades, since I was also responsible for their development across the region.

The programme ran well and the delegates seemed to enjoy it. There was a bonus for me in that each delegate was able to do a MBTI profile, so I got first-hand delegate experience of the tool I was waiting to be trained in. After the profiles were marked, the tutors announced our MBTI types in the plenary-group setting. They asked us to read thumbnail descriptions of our 'type' or personality preference, then did a series of activities with the group according to 'type' dynamics. The whole exercise made for very lively discussions both in and out of session.

According to the tool, out of sixteen possible profiles, I'm an ENTJ which stands for Extraverted iNtuitive Thinking Judging. The profile breakdown said ENTJs are natural born leaders. They live in a world of possibilities where they see all sorts of challenges to be surmounted, and they want to be the ones responsible for resolving them. They have a drive for leadership, which is well served by their quickness to grasp complexities, their ability to absorb a large amount of impersonal information, and their quick and decisive judgments. They are *'take charge'* people.

Well, after recent events, I didn't feel that way at all! Having said that, the profile was definitely the person I was used to being before I joined the college. It was quite fascinating to see so much of myself, on a good day, in print. My leadership skills, critical nature and inability to suffer fools gladly spoke volumes. Apparently, there is not much room for error in the world of the ENTJ. They dislike seeing mistakes repeated and have no patience with inefficiency. They may even become quite harsh when their patience is tried in these respects. No surprises there, I thought!

In terms of relationships, I found out that ENTJs expect to have their needs met while maintaining their independence, and when ENTJs are scorned by others, they may feel a passionate devastation and a strong sense of loss that is seldom shared with others. However, this sense of loss and gloom generally lasts only a short period before they are ready to move on.

Remarkable! This is me, I thought. I wasn't losing my mind– devastated one moment and dusting myself off the next, with a hap-hap-happy smile! That was normal behaviour–at least for an ENTJ! This piece of information was particularly illuminating. The emotions I had been feeling when dealing with Sue were off the charts and this profile facilitated the *'eureka'* moment I needed. Whether this was hogwash or empirical science was of no consequence to me in that instance; what I was learning offered some explanation and insight and I was grateful for that. My extreme emotion was making me vulnerable and this profile caused me to think about that. My emotions were giving Sue power over me, because they left me indecisive and floundering–which simply wasn't like me. Sue didn't like me, that was a given. She had difficulty treating me with respect, also a given. However the way she was treating me was wrong and I needed to handle the fear my inflamed emotions were generating, thus preventing me from dealing with the situation effectively. Only then would I be able to be objective and determine my best options. 'Ha! I am back!' I exclaimed in my head, for I was still on the training course.

For the afternoon of the final day, the tutors announced that they would give one-to-one feedback on the respective types in 20-minute slots, if we were interested. Not many of the group took them up on the offer, probably because it was a chance to get home early. I made an appointment for the feedback since I wanted to get as much exposure to the tool as possible. I spent my 20 minutes asking questions about the versatility of the tool, all the different ways it could be used and how I could get my hands on more materials. I left the session with a clear self-management strategy. I also gained a good understanding about how I could use the tool in my region and why it was so popular in the Service.

A few days later I had a meeting with Sue and Helen, the Admin Manager. They took approximately twenty minutes to explain how to interpret the 360-degree feedbacks I had inherited at the end of June. Surprisingly, Helen did most of the talking, as she shared her own delegate experience of what it was like to receive the feedback. Sue then spent a few minutes explaining that she normally started at the back of the profile booklet, summarised the findings for the client and moved on to the front. It was quite rushed and 'matter of fact'–I felt as if I was impinging on their time. I left the meeting thinking that if I had any hope of understanding the profile documents, I would need to take myself through them, much as I had done with the J-SAC DVDs, and develop my own system to build my confidence.

In the afternoon, I swung by the IT block to pick up my long-awaited laptop and RSA token. Then I travelled to Leicester and met Governor Edwards of HMP Glen Parva and Fran, the Head of Personnel. It was a meeting designed to introduce myself and the services available at the college. The meeting was going well until Fran asked about MBTI.

'Do you know how to do MBTI profiling?' she queried. 'I'm qualified in Levels A and B, so Brian and I have had discussions previously about doing some sort of personal development or coaching with a few individuals using tools that help to identify personality traits. And we think that this would be a good place to start.'

My heart froze. They had asked for MBTI profiling—what was I supposed to do? I was too embarrassed to say that I didn't have a licence to practise, especially considering this was my first opportunity to build credibility at this prison. Operational staff judged new staff very quickly. This is probably due to how often they have been in life-threatening situations and the need to depend on others for crucial support. In a prison, you need to know that you can rely on a fellow officer in a crisis. This capacity to weigh someone up, however, often spilled over into assessing almost everyone on sight. Hence, it was important to strike the right chords with the governor because, if he was not suitably impressed with my credentials or demeanour, he wouldn't work with me.

Governor Edwards picked up where Fran had left off. 'Several of my managers are working at a grade higher than their actual post dictates. I've got principal officers working at Manager F levels and Manager Fs working to a Manager E level. For some, this is working very well and they are thriving on the challenges set. For a few, it's not working as well as I'd hoped.'

He continued to elaborate. 'Now we're not just asking you to work with those whom we think are struggling—we have a mixture of individuals for you. Some need help to cope with the daily demands that are being made on them having to work up one level, and some will just need coaching in terms of their next career move and making sure they're getting developmental support. It's about me making the investment,' he said. 'Whether my managers could do better or are already doing really well, it's my view that I am still responsible for providing appropriate levels of support and investment.'

I was very impressed by his approach. I replied. 'As a response to development needs, this is a very positive approach and I think it's particularly insightful that the people you'd like me to work with are a combination of people who are doing well in their roles and others who aren't doing as well. I think this will eliminate any stigma that might be attached to the project. If, for example, I was only to work with individuals identified as struggling in their role, this could negatively affect the participants. However if there is a mix in terms of performance then hopefully all those involved will be happier to participate.'

I further explained, 'As a Leadership team', with the emphasis on *team*, 'we have a range of skills between us and as such we should be more than able to accommodate your identified needs.' Phew! Okay, so I was *winging it* a little bit. I was thinking that, having already asked for the MBTI training more than once, surely my training was being arranged now, especially after the last team meeting. I began looking ahead and determined that it would probably only take me five to ten days to qualify and get a licence to practise the tests. This meant I could quite reasonably begin working on the requests for HMP Glen Parva right away and probably wouldn't have to tell them I currently didn't have a licence to do what they were asking. God willing, my training would be arranged for me just in time.

The Governor continued. 'I'd like you to use the outputs from the psychometric tests as a platform for the one-to-one discussions we'd like you to do. There are a couple of individuals in the group who are not fully aware of how their behaviour affects others. So it would be difficult for you to coach them when their view of themselves is vastly different from the view others hold of them. We think the personality profiles will make for good discussion points that you could use to build a personal development plan that will challenge behaviour.'

I agreed with their proposals, except for where they talked about the managers who were not self-aware in relation to how they affected others in their team. For those individuals, I additionally recommended the 360-degree tool (as this tool would deliberately capture the perceptions of the team mates who worked with these managers in question). Understanding how other people see you alongside how you see yourself, is a powerful thing. Between them, Governor Edwards and Fran gave me a brief description of each candidate: their behaviours, any particular issues and overviews of performance, along with the kinds of outcomes they expected per individual. They were very thorough.

I emailed Sue a few days later, asking when my training was going to be because I had just had my third request for MBTI profiling. I was especially careful to explain that Governor Edwards and Fran were very specific and clear about what they wanted and why they wanted this particular approach to developing some of the senior management team. I further explained I was beginning to feel vulnerable about not having this skill.

I continued to convince myself I would secure the necessary training. With this request, along with the agreement at the last team meeting for the advisors to deliver MBTI during the SOM assessment centres, it was bound to happen. I couldn't have been more wrong.

Sue responded within a couple of days saying:

> Hi Olivea,
>
> Thank you for your e-mail.
>
> We are at this time planning further development for 'new' Advisors, we are constrained to a degree by our budget for this development and have to prioritise in line with department needs. The main priority coming up is 360 degree feedbacks and in order to do this everyone needs to be TLQ qualified…

In the face of another request from my area and in spite of the discussion at the last meeting, Sue had denied my request again. The denial frustrated me for a number of reasons. Firstly, TLQ (Transformation Leadership Questionnaire) training was not going to help me with the very specific backlog of MBTI requests that I now had. And training to understand yet still another brand of 360-degree profiles would not give me a licence to practise occupational psychometric tests. What equally concerned me was her reference to 'new' advisors. All of a sudden, my development needs were no longer important because new people had arrived. I had been at the college for nearly five months and on induction for four of those months; Chris had told me that this training would be arranged, yet my development needs were still outstanding and now the focus had shifted to the development of newly arrived advisors.

As I continued to read her email, I became more incredulous:

> ...*I disagree that you will lose credibility as Advisors work together on these projects. MBTI could possibly be used as one tool to support* [Personal Development Planning]...*at Glen Parva, but there are a raft of other tools that would be more relevant for this type of work namely the development grids. I understand that Brian has concerns about operational performance of these individuals and therefore the need would be to concentrate on core management skills development and less on the MBTI.*
>
> *I am a little concerned that as you haven't done the MBTI training that you are talking at length and agreeing to work that includes MBTI without having a very clear understanding of how MBTI impacts on both the individual and teams. Advisors role is to influence Governors/individuals on the best way forward following a clear needs analysis. You probably need to start by meeting the individuals concerned and talk through with them and their line managers (if not Brian) the issues they face. You probably also need to talk to the Head of HR in more detail before commencing the project.*

From the very first time I met Governor Edwards, I could see that he was not the kind of man who needed much guidance; he knew what he wanted and if you couldn't deliver it, he would find someone who could. I was eager to show I could deliver. This was my opportunity to work with a highly efficient team and with a prison that was doing well in the league tables. Yet, as I read her response, I noted Sue wanted me to go back to Governor Edwards and Fran, even after they had been so explicit with regard to what they wanted and why, and offer them the development grids. These grids were designed by the Service and listed all the operational skills that a manager should have at certain management grades like doing an investigation or managing a budget. The manager would assess him/herself against the grid and where they found they did not have enough exposure in certain operational skill areas, they would ask for training or development in those areas. This was not what Governor Edwards had asked for as he was already building operational skill in his team by having them work a level above their designated management grades. Instead, he outlined key personality traits and behavioural preferences that he thought needed challenging amongst certain managers and asked for MBTI as a widely used personality tool. I knew I couldn't go back and ask him to use the grids in place of occupational psychometric tests.

Then there was what Sue described as me discussing MBTI 'at length' even though I had not yet had the training and was without a clear understanding of MBTI. This was exactly what I had stopped myself from doing for precisely that reason. I knew I was not a practitioner; however I had seen the tool in action and been on the receiving end of feedback, so the governor's requests sat reasonably well in my, albeit limited, understanding of the scope and use of the tool. The governor had made a request that I felt duty bound to accommodate and I had entertained it under the guise of advisor team support along with the hope that I would soon receive the training.

I looked again at the bit of her email where she suggested that my role was to 'influence governors'. I thought, 'that's rich!' A governor had spoken to me with total clarity about what he wanted, he hadn't asked for the moon; he had asked for something that was readily available in other regions across the country; the tool he selected was a good fit to the needs expressed, yet I needed to 'influence him' to use tools that could not possibly do the same job!

As I revisited the email sentence by sentence, my irritation turned to anger at her capacity to dismiss my request and redirect me to activities that would only lead to embarrassment if I followed her advice. By this time, I was talking and gesticulating at the computer screen.

'Does she think I'm stupid?' I asked my desktop. 'What more does she want me to talk with them about? The conversation I had with them lasted some forty minutes, and was the tail end of discussions two competent people had *already* had about the issues they faced. They don't need me to give them options: they need me to facilitate their decisions. They're not feeling around in the dark: they know exactly what they want!'

I could feel myself losing patience, and talking to the computer was not helping! My frustration had nowhere to go. I decided to give myself a couple of days before I responded. I needed to make sure that when I did, I was only communicating my needs and not my frustrations.

On 28th September, I emailed Sue regarding her decision and reiterated that Governor Edwards and Fran, the Personnel Manager, were very clear about what they wanted. I also stated I didn't think that I should be at a development disadvantage to other advisors because of budgetary constraints. I concluded by asking for more help and for her to direct me to the *'...raft of other tools that would be more relevant for this type of work'* that she had referred to in her email. Sue never responded.

Throughout the month of September I delivered feedbacks, worked with the advisors in my team to deliver programmes, designed and delivered bespoke programmes and made consultancy appointments. The client feedback for my first month off induction was very good and I was feeling positive about working in the field or my region the East Midlands. I found it much less oppressive, as people seemed kinder and they were very receptive to me as a professional. I felt that, as my clients continued to appreciate my help and give good feedback about my performance, Sue would soon have to accept I knew what I was doing. I reaffirmed to myself that I was doing a good job and that eventually she would have to give me the same support she was without doubt giving others.

On 6th October, I received an email from Sue informing me she had deducted over £200 from my expense claims because I was not allowed to claim from home to base journeys. I was really upset, because I had been waiting for this to be sorted out since June. I hadn't even claimed for all the journeys I had made to Newbold, just the ones where there were LMD team meetings and appointments, which meant that I had claimed for the same journeys as everyone else. Neither had I claimed daily or overnight subsistence to which I was entitled. I had held on to my expenses for as long as I could in the hope that Sue was remedying this by taking note of the suggestions made by Zoë, the Head of Finance, in July. However when the admin staff started chasing me for the outstanding months, I reluctantly submitted the forms. I was wounded because Sue didn't even have the decency to tell me that she had finally made a decision concerning my base. Instead, she chose to deduct over £200 and then send me an email outlining what she had done.

And there it was again—the confusion about what was expected of me, what was available to me. And this was making me so unhappy. No one else seemed to be in any great difficulty in the team. The advisors were an especially vocal group. If they were unhappy about something whether on an individual or collective basis, they were sure to mention it during our team meetings or by global email. They never held back. Yet I hadn't heard of any difficulties with Sue from anyone, not even the new recruits. It was just me. Nonetheless, I decided that perhaps it was time to let the issue of expenses go. I chose not to respond.

On 7th October, Helen, the Admin Manager copied me in to a couple of emails she had sent to Nigel, a senior officer (SO) and trainer at Newbold, asking him if he needed any help from LMD regarding his development. I had not seen individual offers of help like this before coming direct from the admin team instead of an advisor, so I read the exchanges with interest. Nigel, having already contacted me in September, when he explained that he needed help to '*make* [himself] *more attractive to* [prisons] *to persuade them to promote an SO up to Manager F*', replied that he had recently been in touch with me and we were yet to meet. Helen responded to say that she would '*get* [me] *to contact* [him]' and then proceeded to apologise to him for having to wait so long for me to arrange a meeting with him. When I read this, I was annoyed that instead of checking with me, it looked as if Helen had assumed I hadn't been in touch with Nigel at all. When I had originally received Nigel's email in September, I recognised that his career plans were ambitious in that he wanted to skip past the principal officer grade and go straight to a Manager F level, in other words from a uniform on the wing to a suit in an office. On receipt, I had immediately forwarded his email to Sue asking her for guidance and as usual she didn't respond. In the interim, I had contacted Nigel and we made an appointment, which he cancelled a couple of hours before we were due to meet. We were yet to reschedule when Helen had made this unusual and unsolicited offer of help from LMD. I didn't think it was right that Helen should apologise in my stead and certainly not without finding out what the situation was. Furthermore, I felt she had not considered the type of message she was conveying about me to my client by suggesting that I needed to be chased up. The lack of respect and poor regard seemed to be spreading.

Chapter Four

An Impasse

On 12th October, I was ten minutes late for my one-to-one meeting with Sue. She had set the meeting for 8.30am, which meant that I had to leave the house by 7.00am to get to Newbold with time to spare. Leaving the house at this time was not normally a problem because, even though Rudy and I were primary carers for Mum, who had been chronically ill for many years with heart, lung, and blood disorders, we alternated the care between us. Six years ago, Mum's health started to deteriorate and she became depressed about living alone. I could not bare the sadness each time we had to say goodbye after a visit or the worry of living fifteen miles away in Northampton. Rudy and I bought a house in Wellingborough and Mum moved in with us. We were so grateful to God because the house we bought was perfect; it had plenty of room so that Mum could live an independent life with her own bedroom, bathroom, kitchen and lounge on the ground floor, whilst we lived in the rest of the house. Every morning we made sure Mum was awake and coherent before her personal carer arrived, to help her shower and dress whilst we went to work. Being on hand so readily was a comfort to me and to Mum, and Rudy reckoned she was a great mother-in-law.

Our usual routine was a little different this morning because Rudy had to leave especially early and Mum had had a bad night. When I popped into her room at 6.35am to check on her, I found her in pain and unable to get out of bed without assistance. I helped her to the loo and got her back into bed. We prayed for God's healing and then I made her a drink of mint tea. As she sipped the tea I could see her strength return. Her breathing was less laboured, and the dullness in her eyes was being replaced by an alertness and better awareness of her surroundings. I checked my watch. It was 7.05am and I needed to leave. Mum sensing this said, 'You can go now. I'm fine.'

'It's okay Ma, I want to wait for the carer to arrive before I leave. I'll let work know I'm coming in later today. It's a little early to ring in so I'll ring Sue in about half an hour.'

'Livie' she said firmly and lovingly, 'you need to get to work. I'm feeling much better now. When you get in call me and you'll see that I'm fine. Now go!'

It was difficult to argue with Mum. Once she had spoken, you obeyed. I checked that she had all her medications to hand and fluffed her pillows and asked if she needed another drink. When she gave me the look that said 'if you don't leave right now I will put you out myself,' I gave her a big kiss and headed for her bedroom door.

'I'll call you later and you'd better sound great when I phone!' I cheekily said. She smiled.

I got in the car and it was 7.15am. I could still make it at a push, I thought. One hour and fifteen minutes would have me arriving pretty much on the nose. Mum's fine–you can make it; let's go, go, go, I cheered myself on.

I prayed all the way to Rugby whilst counting down the minutes, and mapping where I was and recalculating the time for each miniscule part of the journey. The A45 was surprisingly clear; it was normally the first traffic bottleneck I would encounter on the way out of Wellingborough. The days of simple country drives across the county had long been replaced by tailbacks, congestion and gridlocks, yet not today; today I was sailing towards the M1. As I travelled up the M1 then on to the M45, I still thought that I could make it until things slowed through the quirky village of Brinklow. When I got through, I was four minutes away from the college yet my meeting with Sue was in two minutes. I was late! There was no point in ringing since I was virtually on the premises. I would have to apologise when I got in. I drove into the car park attached to the LMD building to find that it was full and people had already parked precariously on the approach road. I had to reverse out (which I hate) and drive back to the main car park and then walk back to our building. I got in at 8.40am! I was quite flustered. I hated being late and I just knew Sue would be irritated by my late arrival. As I came along the corridor I looked through the glass panel of her office door and saw her sitting at her desk waiting for me.

I knocked on the door and opened it, and stuck my head into her office whilst the rest of my body remained in the corridor. 'I'm sorry I'm late. Can I have a few minutes to pick up some paperwork for the meeting?'

She looked up from her computer screen over to me standing in the doorway and then looked back at the screen without saying a word. Okay, I thought, this is awkward.

I quickly shut her door, ran to my office, unlocked the door, stood and logged on to my computer and sent some documents to print. Then I ran upstairs, said a hurried 'Good morning' to anyone I passed en route, rushed to the printer, grabbed the documents I had printed, ran back downstairs whilst putting the documents in order, whizzed by Katrina from the admin office who was coming back into the building, having just had a cigarette, said a hasty 'hello' to her and ran back down the corridor to Sue's office. By the time I returned, Sue was sitting at the round meeting table in her office. I came in and sat down opposite her.

I was now twenty minutes late.

'I'm really sorry I'm late…' I began to apologise again. I was about to explain about Mum and why I didn't get to Newbold for 8.30am when Sue abruptly said, 'Do you know what this meeting's about?'

'It's our usual progress meeting,' I said immediately on my guard.

'No, it's a performance review,' she announced.

As I looked at her, I thought to myself, wow, I have spent four months on induction without positive feedback. I have barely completed my first month on my own and I'm achieving good results, yet now I'm subject to a performance review! Although stunned I remained calm. I had many years of dealing with difficult situations. Keeping my composure during such times was something I prided myself on, despite the fact that I was often running around and screaming like a mad woman inside my head– you would never know that you had rattled me even when provoked.

'Well,' she huffily began, 'you've been late to two team meetings without apology and *this*' she emphasised, 'is unacceptable!'

How ironic I thought, of all the days to be late, I had to choose today!

She continued, 'I mean it's not fair on the rest of the team. Some of them have to travel much further than you and they get here on time. You're only an hour away. Walking in late without apologising is bad for team morale.'

I had been late a couple of times, though not without apology, and it was true that out of all the advisors I lived the closest to Newbold. However in terms of context, it was also true that many of the advisors travelled up to Newbold the day before and stayed overnight so that they did not have to travel on the day of the meetings. My focus though was on her insistence that I did not apologise. I remembered both times vividly, and in each case I had called ahead and explained about being delayed in slow-moving traffic and asked for both my apologies and whereabouts to be conveyed. I couldn't understand why she kept talking about my not apologising because, in my experience, if ever anyone walked into a meeting late especially when the meeting room was small their entrance was often less than discreet. As such, there was always a compulsion to either apologise there and then, because they had almost certainly already disrupted the meeting, or at the very least they motioned to be excused for their tardiness with a raised hand and a mouthed 'sorry'. That was the situation I had found myself in both times: I had raised my hand, mouthed a 'sorry' and quickly found my seat. Then during the break, I had found Sue and asked if she had got my messages, apologised and explained in person. Both times, she had said that she had got the messages and told me that I was not to worry. Furthermore, on one of those occasions someone arrived after me.

'But Sue,' I objected, 'on those occasions I rang ahead to let you know that I was going to be late. I spoke to Louise and then in the meeting I apologised to you personally and explained again.'

'But you were late this morning and you didn't ring ahead.'

'No. I didn't because I thought I could make it, and very nearly did—though I did apologise as soon as I came in. I'm kicking myself right now for not calling and saying that I may or may not be late and when I arrived this morning there was no parking…and…' I stopped myself because I was making excuses. Had I left on time or at least the minute Mum told me she felt better I would have made it.

'—the fact remains that I *was* late and I *have* apologised *twice* already. If you'd just let me explain…'

Remarkably, Sue cut right across me and moved on to the next item on her list of offences.

'Where is Steve's laptop?' she asked in a most accusatory tone as if I had hocked it illegally on the black market for little profit, my gain being the thrill of illicit trading. I couldn't believe how random she was being. We hadn't brought the issue of lateness without apology to a close, yet she had moved on. Steve was the governor at my last prison when I was the Head of Learning and Skills.

I answered the question. 'I returned the laptop two weeks ago.'

She continued, 'Well, it's still unacceptable that you've held on to it for so long. And the fact that the governor had to ask *me* for it reflects badly on the team.'

Somewhat bewildered I tried to explain. 'The laptop was issued to *me* as the Head of Learning and Skills. Steve said that I could hold on to it until I got another one for my new role here. Also the laptop in question isn't even funded by the Service, it's funded by the Offender Learning and Skills Unit, so technically it's *their* property and they had no objections to me holding onto it for a while either. Frankly, it wasn't even that useful because I couldn't network it and I only kept it for so long because I wasn't scheduled to visit Leicester on the induction you put together for me. I didn't feel I could justify a drive to Leicester just to drop off a laptop. In the end I dropped it off at HMP Wellingborough because his wife works there.'

Like a rapid-fire automatic machine gun, Sue moved on to the next criticism. 'I understand that Helen had to apologise on your behalf to Nigel. He's been waiting for you to contact him about some development issues. When people come to you for help I expect you to respond quickly. It is unacceptable for you to keep them waiting.'

Wow! Helen had reported me to Sue! 'I *have* been in touch with Nigel. In fact we set up a meeting that *he* cancelled,' I retaliated.

Sue leapfrogged over to the next complaint.

'I think you're working too much in isolation and the admin team never know when you're in the building.'

Steadily trying to keep up with the erratic discourse I said, 'I always make my presence known when I come into Newbold. Don't forget that, because the printer, photocopier, stationery and my mail are upstairs, by default I always have to go upstairs for something. Whenever I do, I normally pop into each office and say good morning or afternoon as appropriate.'

It was incredible to me to hear that she was suggesting that I waltzed in and out of other people's offices without a word to anyone. I wondered what kind of person she thought I was and, having been here since May, how long she was suggesting I had been behaving like this?

Sue replied with, 'Yes, that may well be, but you're not actually *sitting* with the admin team to find out what they do from day to day.'

I don't know what I was thinking by this stage. I should have kept my mouth shut. I had been here before. Yet my mouth was open and the words were tumbling out. 'I don't understand where this is going,' I said. 'Isn't the admin team a support function? Wouldn't it make more sense for them to sit with me, to find out what *I* do?'

'I have an obligation,' she postured with her voice raised, 'under the rules of health and safety. People need to know when you're in the building.'

I struggled to grasp if we were even having the same conversation. I thought we were talking about her suggestion that I should be sitting with the admin team to familiarise myself with the work they did; however, now we were talking about health and safety risks. Okay I thought, let's deal with *this* issue.

'I always let people know that I'm in the office. And with regards to health and safety, I'm often left in the building alone. The admin staff regularly lock-up and leave without letting me know that I'm the only one left in the building. I generally tend to find out when I go upstairs to collect my printing, and all the lights are off and the office doors are locked.'

Again Sue moved on without resolving anything or accepting anything. Sue produced a printout of my diary and claimed that the way I populated it was sparse and meaningless, and gave no indication as to what I was really doing with my time. Whilst pointing at the printout to reinforce her concerns she asked aggressively, 'I mean, what does this mean: *"Awayday at HMP Whatton?"'*

Having inherited the East Midlands from Sue and having had very little by way of a handover or protocols, I was actually populating my diary in the same way she did. I had copied her example.

'This,' she said still pointing, 'is unacceptable. Your diary entries should include the names of the people you are going to see and not just the name of the prison. I have asked you to do this before,' she chided. Sue had sent an email to the team asking us to be more specific about our whereabouts a few weeks ago. I had started to record more details with the new entries I made but I had not amended entries made before her email.

'Yes, yes, you have and I'm sorry. This is something that I can remedy very quickly.'

'When was the last time you spoke to any of the advisors?' We had moved on again.

'I spoke to Ruth yesterday.'

'And before that?'

'I haven't spoken to any other advisors for maybe two or three weeks.'

'This is unacceptable. It's important that as a new team member you keep in regular contact with the other advisors. You must check what they are doing in their areas and discuss what work they're involved in.'

'As a new member of an established team shouldn't the building of relationships be a two-way thing?' I reasoned. 'We see each other once a month, if that, and I call when I have something constructive to say. No one initiates calls to me and if I speak to anyone like I did with Ruth yesterday, it's normally because they're returning *my* call. I have been here for five months and no one has ever called just to say hello or to ask how I'm getting on. I am very aware that I am dealing with long-standing relationships that might not ever include me on a deeper level; that's not an issue, that's life! It's not a problem for me; I get the help when I need it, they get support from me when they need it; the relationships are productive. What I don't understand is how it is that you expect me to chase after them to ingratiate myself and for what reasons exactly? If you want more exchanges between us, have you spoken to any of them about maintaining contact?' I barely drew breath.

I felt as if I was having some sort of out-of-body experience. Everything was incredibly surreal. Was this really happening to me? Were there hidden cameras in the room? I started to smile and shake my head in disbelief, to which Sue victoriously responded as if she had got me just where she wanted me, 'You may well laugh, Olivea, but this is exactly what I'm talking about—your attitude!'

The situation was irredeemable. I knew this and yet I was compelled to defend myself. Although Sue was extremely agitated by this point, I couldn't allow the meeting to end with a stream of unfounded criticisms. This was a performance review and I was beginning to feel that my job was in jeopardy. Sue had not outlined any good performance. If this was a performance review and she didn't have one good thing to say, then didn't this make it a *poor* performance review? I couldn't afford to have any of this nonsense recorded on my personal file. I needed to refute the allegations, otherwise I could blame no one but myself if I ended up with a poor performance review, ultimately leading to the termination of my contract.

I said quite calmly and resolutely, 'I don't believe my attitude to be in question.' Sue was blinking rapidly, her face and neck were blotchy rouge, and her lips pursed. She didn't respond. This break in her attack gave me a well-needed respite.

After only a few seconds of silence, I said, 'I have listened to everything you have had to say. The diary thing I can remedy immediately on leaving this meeting. I'll just go back in and put the details you want to see on there. But just for my own peace of mind, do you have any actual evidence of poor work performance that we can address in this meeting?'

In an attempt to answer my question, Sue went on to disclose that HMP North Sea Camp, had been identified as a priority in my area and I had not yet made an appointment to go and assess their needs.

Actually, I had. I reminded Sue I had only been managing my region for one month. I then informed her that I *had* made an appointment to meet with Governor Warwick and the appointment was in keeping with his request to see me later on in the year. He had made this request when I met him in August at the area governors' meeting. I went on to offer to forward an email that would confirm this.

Sue ignored the fact that the appointment she just accused me of not making, had indeed been made. She moved on to argue that I still had not done the outstanding 360-degree feedbacks.

Wearily, I explained that, since the 20-minute overview given by her and Helen approximately three weeks ago, I had taken myself through the profiles to build my confidence and I *was* now making the appointments in question. Again, I offered to forward proof that I had made some appointments as evidenced in my electronic diary. She said that if I had populated my diary properly she would be able to see *who* I had made appointments with as opposed to only being able to see *where* I was going.

Finally, I'd had enough. I couldn't imagine Sue harassing any other member of the LMD team like this. The advisors were so forthright and opinionated and I had never witnessed Sue trying to cut her new teeth on them or put her foot down. Not one of them would have sat for as long as I had and taken this abuse. They were a law unto themselves and would have told her in no uncertain terms that she was out of order! Perhaps this was why she had chosen to tussle with me. Maybe she felt that, because I didn't brawl like most of them, I was an easy target and weak. Our relationship was awful. I had tried to be diplomatic and tried to take ownership of the quality of our relationship in the past and perhaps I now needed to be more explicit so that she could become more self-aware and equitable in her treatment of me. It wasn't my fault that she was intimidated by the people she used to work alongside and now had to manage, and she shouldn't be directing all the frustration generated by her inability to control them at me.

'I don't understand why you're treating me differently from the rest of the team,' I ventured. 'I have been denied training that I was promised, yet everyone else who joined before me has had the training. I asked you to be flexible about my base, which again is no different from the flexibility available to other members of the team, and instead I waited for months without an answer and then, without warning, you deducted more than £200 from my expense claims. You know I don't claim for everything I'm entitled to claim for–I just want my petrol money back. I can't imagine you treating any other member of the team like this.'

Then it happened–something so off-the-wall that when I heard it I sat wide-eyed, stunned and silent.

'Are you accusing me of racism?' she blundered.

Her response completely knocked me for six! I had no idea why she was talking about racism. At this point, I made a conscious effort to not behave in a way that suggested any form of agitation on my part, as I needed to see where she was coming from and didn't want to redirect the conversation with a poor response. I cautiously replied. 'People treat people differently for different reasons. Why do *you* think that racism is in the equation?'

'Well, you've alluded to it,' she announced.

'*I* have given you ample examples of differential treatment by way of expenses and outstanding training. I should be able to point out such treatment without fear of being accused of playing the *race* card. It is evident to me that I don't have access to the same level of flexibility that is available to other members of the team and I'm merely trying to find out why that is.'

'—and furthermore,' I couldn't let her get away with using my race as a shield to deflect her inconsistent treatment of me, 'I find that your comments are both inappropriate and unprofessional.'

I looked at her and she looked at me. Nothing more was said.

Then Sue just got up abruptly and left me sitting at the meeting table alone. She went back to her desk and started shuffling paper. I remained seated. I waited a few moments for her to come back to the meeting table. This didn't happen. Sue stayed behind her desk and continued to shuffle paper without indicating if the meeting was over. I thought, 'How absurd!'

After at least a minute or maybe even two, I decided to break the silence. 'Has the meeting finished,' I asked cautiously.

'Well I haven't got anything else to say,' she busily replied.

She was visibly flustered as her face and neck were quite red, and shuffling the paperwork seemed to serve no purpose other than to occupy her hands. I slowly got up from the meeting table, I turned and said 'Thank you' and left her office. My words seemed out of place and somehow inadequate, but I couldn't think of anything appropriate to say.

The walk back to my office, although very short, seemed longer. I sat at my desk shell-shocked and tried to make sense of what had just happened. I revisited the criticisms, which had come hard and fast. I asked myself if she was justified, had I given her cause?

I was in my fifth month. I had had a meeting with Sue every month since my arrival. In that time, although I recognised our relationship was in trouble, my performance was never an issue, at least as far as I could tell. Even when I had passed on good feedback emailed from my clients, she never responded. I thought more about her wanting to know if I was accusing her of racism and felt her comments to be discriminatory. I considered that, if I was white, she wouldn't have been able to say anything about race, yet because I was black she decided to put racism on the table. I needed more time to think about this point in particular. I wondered if Sue's reference to racism was actually a disclosure of her underlying motivations. Maybe this was the way she *really* felt and, because she was under pressure in the meeting, she accidentally exposed her prejudices. Although a moot point, I found this particularly scary.

It didn't matter which way I looked at it, what had happened was unprovoked and undeserved. I phoned the personnel department to make an appointment to meet with someone to tell them what happened and how unhappy I was about it.

I met with Susanne, Head of Personnel for the college, at approximately 11.30am. I told her about the meeting with Sue and the things that led to my discomfort at the college. I made particular mention of Sue's reference to racism, and how demeaning her comment was to me. I conveyed that I felt it was discriminatory for her to make such a reference. It was at this point that I began to cry with humiliation and was immediately upset with myself for doing so. I didn't want to be written-off as some hysterical or temperamental woman. As much as I wanted Susanne to see that anyone would have been degraded by what was going on, I didn't want to cry.

I composed myself and continued as calmly as I could. Susanne asked if I wanted to make a formal complaint. Straightaway I said it wasn't my preferred choice, since I just wanted my relationship with Sue to change and become more positive. I felt a complaint was unlikely to achieve that.

Susanne then asked, 'Would you consider mediation?'

The thought of having a third party present for the next time I had a meeting with Sue was very appealing. I didn't want to have another encounter with her without witnesses. With a mediator present, we might be better able to uncover the issues and reach agreement, instead of Sue abandoning me and losing all sight of professional conduct. It was on this premise I agreed to mediation.

At 1.00pm, I went to the LMD team meeting. During the break, I briefly spoke to Helen, the Admin Manager about Nigel, the senior officer who needed help to get a Manager F posting. I wanted to make sure she didn't have cause to think that I was 'alluding' to anything, so I chose my words very carefully and delivered them in a measured tone—whilst remembering to smile. It was ridiculous that I had to work so hard to make sure I didn't cause offence or create more difficulties for myself, yet I felt constrained to take these measures in order to avoid any repeat of the morning's events.

I made Helen aware that I had actually been in contact with Nigel before her email and that *he* had needed to cancel our first appointment.

'Oh I didn't know that,' she said quite dismissively.

Stifling my annoyance at her tone, I explained that her email read as if she knew for a fact I hadn't spoken to Nigel, and that was not the case. I made her aware that I felt it was a little premature for her to apologise in my stead before finding out the full story.

She was a little red-faced and said 'Oh okay.'

I smiled and walked away. I was still reeling from the meeting with Sue and was beginning to feel that Helen was also scrutinising my work on Sue's behalf. I wasn't normally prone to bouts of paranoia, though Sue and Helen were quite close. They socialised both during and after work and they swapped stories about the horses they owned and the equestrian competitions they entered.

After the break, the team meeting continued as normal until around 4.30pm when it ended, with a view to picking up the outstanding agenda items in the morning.

The next day, the team meeting continued as planned. In predictable form the team started by complaining, this time about Richard and Tom from the Fast Track team. Fast Track is a two-year intensive graduates' development programme. It is also open to internal staff, who compete for a place in the same way as the graduates. Once selected, each candidate is exposed to various elements of running a prison, from searching a prisoner to sorting out prisoner complaints. During the two-year period, the candidates sit exams and are coached and mentored for management roles. Richard and Tom were helping us out by delivering some of the operational manager programmes. Apparently, neither Richard nor Tom had made a secret of changing the programme that had been recently redesigned by the LMD team and using some of their own Fast Track materials in place of the activities they had deleted. It seemed that they had decided the original programme didn't need much changing and preferred most of the old modules within it. The team asked me how I had got on working with Richard.

I explained, 'Sue asked me to partner-up with Richard because he was very nervous and *"out of sorts"*–her words not mine, with the new-look programme. She asked me to let Richard take the lead and I was to support him in whatever way I could. When I met with him, he said that he wasn't happy with some of the new material and preferred to use what he felt were tried and tested approaches and tools. So I followed his lead as instructed and put in a couple of new activities of my own. The programme received very good reviews, with an overall performance rating of 97%.' Uncharacteristically there were no interruptions.

I felt a little panicked. Maybe I shouldn't have told them I had added my own materials to the programme, as that clearly didn't go down well. However, in habitual fashion, my lips were still moving.

'I also worked in this way because I was supposed to observe the programme in two weeks before I had to deliver it. However, because of Sue's request,' I motioned to where she was sitting, 'I got a single day's notice to deliver a programme I had never seen. Once Richard showed me what he wanted to use and explained how he wanted the session to run, I actually felt more comfortable working with his material.'

O God, had I just made this worse? The internal question brought with it a sense of impending disquiet. I had done nothing wrong, yet the look on their faces suggested otherwise. They were cross. It was difficult to tell if it was because we had made some changes to the programme or if it was because the Fast Track team didn't like the programme. I knew I wouldn't have to wait long to find out which.

The team picked up where they had left off before my explanation and started to complain anew about how hard they had worked to re-write the programme from last year, and that changing the programme per facilitator meant that we could not ensure consistency of delivery. They went on to complain that the Fast Track team had no right to change *their* programme. They were only there to help LMD out; they were not there to take over!

Sue listened to their points. She didn't defend my approach, nor did she confirm that I was only doing what she had asked. Instead, she made a statement that she initially directed towards me. 'We won't always have the luxury of being able to see a programme before we have to deliver it Olivea, and…' she was addressing the rest of the team by this point, 'we should all work with the new-look programme without changing it, to make sure things are consistent from now on.'

Sue was right about the consistency issue; however, that was not the message she had given me when she asked me to help Richard. She knew Richard was uncomfortable with the new programme and didn't tell me why he was 'out of sorts'. She had instructed me to let Richard take the lead and, as the lead facilitator, he wanted to make changes. I felt as if she confirmed I was indeed the saboteur to the team's efforts. I had been hung out to dry.

As the discussion concluded, I was told the next time I delivered the programme it would be with Janet from Fast Track. And to make sure that we all stuck to the agreed design, Janet would be briefed by Sue personally on the operational manager programme as re-designed by the advisors.

On 17th October I went to the HMP Gartree's learning centre for an area strategy meeting in Market Harborough in the morning, then on to Leicester area office to do a 360-feedback in the afternoon. I met Eiwen for the first time; this was pretty much the norm as I developed into my role. When I started going through her 360 profile, she said how keen she was to get her results, especially since Sue had rung to find out if I had delivered them yet. I smiled and just made some comment about inheriting backlog. I apologised for the delay, though inside I was really troubled.

These feedbacks were outstanding when I joined the college, not having been done by Sue in the first instance, and now she was ringing my clients to check if *I* had done them yet. This was probably why she was so adamant during that awful performance review meeting–she clearly felt she had evidence she could use against me. Thank God, I had made the appointment with Eiwen before the meeting. I stifled my embarrassment, which seemed to be with me more often than not and I delivered the session professionally.

The following day I was at Newbold and I decided I needed to make an official response to Sue in relation to the encounter I had had with her previously. I spent time drafting my response to make sure that it was succinct and that I adequately conveyed the distress she had caused me. It was only half a page to register that I was unhappy and to make sure Sue's reference to racism was on record. When I finished, I sent it by email and simultaneously received an email from Sue. When I opened it I found that it was Sue's five-page rambling account of what had happened, and it read like a completely different set of events and there was no mention of her bringing up my race. In fact, there were places where she blatantly lied–I found that particularly distressing. Her version ended with an action plan that looked like the platform for a poor-performance hearing in anticipation of when I failed to meet her unilaterally drafted targets. No concluding actions were discussed in the meeting, because Sue was too busy riffling through her pieces of paper, trying to justify a performance review with incomplete and, at times, erroneous information. And because she made the mistake of raising the question of race, the meeting didn't even come to a close. She totally and unprofessionally abandoned me at the table. Ultimately, this action plan was presented as part of her summary of events, as if it was how the meeting had ended. I felt it was a devious attempt at manipulating anyone who was to read her account into thinking that she had been perfectly reasonable and I had been the opposite.

It seemed that, for whatever reason, Sue was unable to bring her original plan to fruition in that meeting–perhaps because she didn't anticipate I would defend myself so well, with facts, logical argument and memory recall. As I read her summary, it was as if, in the privacy of her office without the irritation of someone protesting in the background, she felt better able to recreate a version of events and subsequent actions much better preferred by her. In her new version, she was in charge, I had no defence, I was a poor performer, and she had followed protocol. And from that fantastical place she felt justified and emboldened to bark orders at me through the pages of her letter and expect compliance without question or resistance.

In the action plan she wrote:

> *...When you are spending only part of your day at* [a prison] *in the vicinity of Newbold Revel, I expect you come into Newbold Revel for the rest of the working day and notify Ros or Helen of your time of arrival and leaving.*
>
> *...At all meetings arranged you will be expected to arrive on time and contribute to discussions.*
>
> *...As part of your team role I will expect you to make regular contact with all Leadership colleagues to gain in-depth knowledge of how they contribute to the work of the department...*
>
> *...You are required to make yourself familiar with the initiatives that the other Area Advisors are working on and consider how you may take these forward in your Area in line with your Area Manager's expectations.*
>
> *...All outstanding feedbacks you have been given are to be undertaken as a matter of urgency and in any event, by the 7th November 2005...*

And so she went on.

It was beyond me how she couldn't see that some of these actions were unfair and demeaning. How she could not see that reporting my arrival and departure times to her secretary or Helen from admin was insulting, lodged outside of my comprehension.

Not only was I senior to both of them, in my mind her orders implied that I was abusing the flexibility of my role. I smarted at the image of my going cap in hand, to say that I had arrived or that I was ready to leave Newbold, like some Dickensian street urchin.

Sue's reiteration, that I was to be either at a prison or at Newbold, compromised me financially and she knew this. Each time my travel was interrupted by a trip to Newbold, I couldn't claim the expenses for that part of the journey, not to mention the fact that triangulating each journey to include Newbold significantly increased my mileage and time on the road.

What she detailed was a format for controlling my whereabouts and nothing more. Under the guise of an action plan, she was trying to bully me to work in a way that she couldn't justify, yet she was content to make me comply with anyway. I felt strongly that this unilateral and uncompromising approach was antagonistic and rife with unequal treatment. I felt unwaveringly that her approach was underhand and intolerable, so much so that I emailed Susanne in personnel to say Sue's actions had now made mediation impractical.

The next day came with more woes and burden. I arrived at HMP Woodhill learning centre to deliver the new-look operational manager programme that had caused so much contention in the last team meeting. In the spirit of doing as I was told, I didn't bring any additional materials with me, only the prescribed materials as discussed. These materials required a role-play from the two facilitators delivering the programme within 30 minutes of starting the programme. I hadn't seen the role play 'acted out' though the instructions looked fairly straightforward. The programme was due to start at 9.30am, so when Janet from Fast Track hadn't arrived by around 9.15am I rang the admin office a little concerned. I was assured that Janet knew she was co-delivering with me and was probably minutes away.

At 9.30am, I made a start. I had to face 15 operational managers, all white, all male, most of them older than me–on my own. I was anxious because I was uncomfortable with the programme and, as I was alone, the elements that needed two facilitators were now posing a real problem. Having worked with operational managers in my previous role as the Head of Learning and Skills, I knew that generally speaking managers at this grade could be quite resistant if they didn't trust you, thought you were too young lacking experience or too 'girlie'. There were gender issues in the Service. Some of the managers were what Sue termed as 'serial fails', meaning it didn't matter what you taught them as they would, in her opinion, fail again. These individuals could be very distrusting and bitter about the selection and evaluation of competencies and considered that the system was flawed. As a woman, to stand in front of a group of men who were cynical, long in the tooth and resistant to 'sucking eggs', whilst being nervous about delivering a quality programme, had all the makings of a challenging day.

During the introductions, some individuals expressed the opinion that the system was 'fixed' and that they didn't learn anything from the workshop they attended last year and that is why they failed. I was really under pressure; however, I focused on what they identified as their development needs. I promised I would deal with those needs individually if need be, during and after the session. The individuals in question seemed to appreciate the offer of one-to-one support.

I gave the group some exercises at approximately 9.55am. I dreaded what I was to do with them afterwards since the facilitator role-plays were next. I didn't have a partner or an alternative exercise. I just started praying in my heart for God to help me and then, miraculously, Janet showed up. I was both relieved and overjoyed.

Janet apologised for being late. She said that she didn't know I was working on my own. She said Sue had told her Rachel White would be working with me and she had been asked simply to look in on us because we were both new. She said Sue had told her she didn't need to show up until around 12.00pm. I couldn't believe it! Rachel was on holiday abroad and couldn't have gone without Sue's sign-off. I asked Janet twice if she was sure about what Sue said. She was adamant this is what Sue told her.

Janet kept asking 'Why would Sue tell me that I didn't need to show up until around 12?'

'Beats me! I'm just grateful to God that you decided to pop in earlier than you were told.'

Janet was brilliant. She didn't like the new revised programme either and had brought her own tools and activities just in case I proved to be flexible about the content. Despite what I had been told by Sue, I was so relieved that Janet had turned up and I was willing to do anything. Janet had been through the exams herself and had first-hand knowledge of the J-SAC. She fielded some of the more difficult questions from the resistant and sceptical members of the group. The course went really well.

On the way home, I phoned Val Woodcock and left a message saying that I felt I had been set up and that I was not at all happy about it. I called her because I had already spoken to her about the quality of my relationship with Sue. I felt that she would give me good advice about what I should do next. Val returned the call a few days later to say that she was sure nothing sinister had gone on and that there must be a logical explanation. I didn't share her confidence, especially not after my last conversation with Sue. By this time I was feeling completely alienated and targeted by Sue.

After nearly two weeks of deliberation pondering the possible repercussions of making a formal complaint, I decided to raise a grievance against Sue. I would file this complaint to Stacey, the Head of the college. I felt my life couldn't get much worse and something should be on record if it did. I wasn't especially confident that Stacey would do anything, not because I had any personal experience of her, though she did sanction Chris's march off the premises.

I wrote to Stacey outlining the main areas of concern to include queries as they related to my official base at Newbold, expenses claims, the MBTI training and Sue's proposed action plan. I also mentioned the embarrassment of Sue checking on me via my clients and undermining my credibility in the field, and her reference to racism. I didn't know how to complain other than simply writing it all down, because I found the policy on raising a grievance confusing. The forms were not standard and the grounds under which you could complain were vague. I wanted to complain about unfair treatment, but I wasn't sure if I should explicitly state if the grounds for complaining were race, bullying, harassment or a lack of care. It was confusing. I wasn't sure what I should ask for or how I should ask for it. In the end, I wrote a letter to complain under *PSO 8010 Equal Opportunities* with particular reference to the discrimination, harassment and bullying sections.

I also responded to Sue's version of events of the review meeting. I had been working on it over a number of days because she had put so much information in her response that had not been discussed in that meeting. I was careful to refute each inaccuracy and attached evidence of emails supporting my rebuttals. Simply writing back to disagree was pointless. Proof was important.

Whilst waiting for a response to my grievance, I continued to get on with my work. On 3rd November, I sent an email to the LMD team asking for help to deliver MBTI training at HMP Nottingham and HMP Glen Parva. By this time, requests from my clients for MBTI had been outstanding for at least a couple of months and I couldn't afford to keep my clients waiting whilst I tried to resolve outstanding disputes about my development. Rachel White, one of the new arrivals, was the first to respond to say she was unable to help because she was as yet unlicensed.

Later that day, Sue responded to my version of events regarding the horrendous meeting on that morning of 12th October. I was nervous about the contents. When I opened it, it said:

Olivea

I acknowledge your summary of our discussions regarding your performance dated 1st November 2005. However, I disagree with its content and therefore the original email outlining the issues discussed 12th October still stands.

And that was it. Nothing more. I was enormously insulted by how curt and dismissive the email was. She hadn't conveyed any consideration of my comments or the evidence I had attached. For example, in response to her allegation that I was late without apology or explanation, I attached emails confirming I had spoken to Louise when I was running late to meetings and Louise confirmed she had conveyed my messages to Sue. There was also an email confirming that various appointments had been made when Sue thought they hadn't been. I had proved that she didn't have all the facts when she was criticising me in our last meeting. I had proved she had been unfair, and she ignored the facts just as she had ignored them in the meeting. It was as if I had no voice and trying to be heard was making me hoarse.

The day wasn't all bad though as there was some good news. Di Watkins, the other new advisor, responded to my request for help to deliver MBTI training. She said that she was unable to help me with HMP Nottingham for the end of November–however, she was willing to talk about December dates for HMP Glen Parva.

On 10th November I was looking forward to working with Janet from Fast Track again at HMP Ranby in Retford. It was approximately a two-and-a-half-hour drive so I set out early enough to be there before 9.00am and set up. Janet was already there because she had arrived overnight; however, I had the programme materials with me. When I was about 20 minutes away from HMP Ranby, I received a call from Helen in admin saying that Ruth couldn't deliver the operational manager programme that was to be simultaneously delivered in HMP Blakenhurst (West Midlands) due to a family emergency. Karen Rushdon, who was supposed to co-deliver with her, had opted out previously because she decided that it was too far for her to travel outside of her region. This left the delegates, who had started to arrive, with no facilitator on site to deliver the programme. Helen asked me to go to HMP Blakenhurst instead, which meant I still had to get to Ranby, drop off the materials, re-plan my journey, and make my way to Redditch. Effectively this meant I had to drive for another three and a half hours.

When I got to the HMP Blakenhurst learning centre, the delegates were furious because they had been kept waiting all morning. As much as they appreciated that it was not my fault, they felt that the programme should have been cancelled and they should have been sent home. They wouldn't let me deliver the programme because they felt that they were being short-changed as it was now after 12.00pm. In a bid to appease them, I offered to stay until 6.00pm so that they could have a full day. They refused my attempts to placate them. One or two said that if they failed their J-SAC they would appeal on the grounds that they were not treated fairly by not getting the same training as their peers. They said that they were going home as soon as I agreed to another date to deliver a full day's programme. I had to liaise with Newbold to provisionally agree to another day to deliver the programme in full to these delegates before they calmed down.

After a date that was convenient to all of them was set, I offered to work individually with anyone who wanted to stay. As it turned out, once they calmed down, had a little lunch and realised that if they stayed it wouldn't jeopardise them receiving another full-day's programme, only one person decided to leave. I used my bespoke training materials and spent the rest of the day thinking on my feet to deliver a programme that wouldn't be repeated when they had their rescheduled full-day's training. The feedback was very good.

It took me a couple of hours to get home by which time my back was very painful, though I was extremely glad that I was able to deliver and hadn't let the situation beat me.

When I got into to Newbold the next day people already knew what had happened: Sarah, the Learning Centre Manager from HMP Blakenhurst had rung ahead to tell them how well I had done. She said I had successfully turned the situation around. Something remarkable happened next. I got an email from Sue, via her secretary, thanking me for the extra effort I put in. It was the first positive gesture from Sue since my joining the team in May. I was very much hoping my hard work had paid off and whatever problems Sue had with me would subside, that she could see I was a team player and that I could be relied upon in a crisis.

Later that morning, I also got called into a meeting with Sue, Helen and a company that was pitching for the contract to design training for the heads of learning and skills (HoLS). It was clear to me that the meeting had ground to a halt because Sue was unable to comment as to the specific problems faced by HoLS, which was why I had been called in mid-flow, as a former HoLS. I didn't mind being an afterthought; I took it as another positive step in our relationship that she felt she could call on me. Overnight, things had changed for the better and I was delighted.

Sue introduced me to Ian from Campaign for Leadership. I did my best to explain the difficulties faced by HoLS, starting with how we were recruited, the support we were promised and didn't get and so on. Then another amazing thing happened: Sue announced I would be 'the lead' on the project.

After the meeting concluded, Ian asked me if I had any more information on HoLS development. I said I would send him an overview I had done on a previous project to develop the HoLS. Sue then told me that another meeting was planned with another company vying for the HoLS training contract on Monday. She invited me to attend. I was absolutely thrilled. She told me to get the details from Helen. I did this and I also asked Helen to forward me all the information on the project to date, so I could bring myself up to speed. I was determined to excel and continue building bridges. Additionally, I contacted the HoLS in my region. Although I didn't have much information about the kind of training that might soon be available for them, I asked them to tell me what they needed and what had been made available to them so far. I felt that if even a couple of them responded quickly enough, I would have more to say in relation to their current needs by the coming Monday meeting. Although my grievance was outstanding, I felt that maybe by the time I got to meet with Stacey my relationship with Sue might have improved to the extent that the grievance would be quickly remedied.

Monday 14th November found me very positive about the HoLS development meeting. I listened along with Sue and Helen to proposals made by the competing company. I felt the meeting went well and I was looking forward to receiving all the proposals from the interested parties and contributing to any decisions made as 'the lead' for the project.

The team meeting on 16th November found me excited about finally being accepted by the group and Sue, as well as being involved in the HoLS project. I put together an outline of what I had covered at HMP Blakenhurst, so that whoever ended up delivering the full-day programme to that group in particular would have a good understanding of what I did and how the exercises went. During the meeting, I eagerly waited for Sue to say something about the event. She often made mention of individual LMD advisor achievements worthy of note and, hopefully, it was my turn. I was also waiting to see if she would deal with the way Karen had re-worked the schedule in her favour without regard for the rationale behind having two facilitators to a programme. The meeting started around 1.00pm. We had a short break, but by 4.30, I needed to use the bathroom. I checked where we were on the agenda and felt that if I was quick I wouldn't miss anything. Also the loo was in the next room.

When I walked back into the team meeting, the room fell silent. Val quickly spoke up to break the silence. She explained that Sue was just saying what a good job I had done at HMP Blakenhurst. I looked over to Sue, who remained silent, steadfastly looking ahead of her. I sat down.

After Val finished, Sue addressed the group and said simply, 'I think we should just make sure that you always work in pairs–because of what happened.' Then she moved on to the next agenda item.

I was devastated. I couldn't understand how we had been in the same room for hours and nothing was said by Sue about HMP Blakenhurst, even when I circulated my outline, when it was my turn to talk about what was happening in my area for the month. Sue could have said something then: it was the perfect opportunity to say that I had done well, yet she said nothing. Instead, she waited until I went to the toilet to revisit the event and talk about me. I have no real idea as to what was said because she didn't confirm what Val was saying about her. In any case, I couldn't understand if Sue was actually talking, why Val had to tell me what Sue said when Sue was right there. It didn't make any sense. The email that Sue sent via her secretary meant nothing to me now because I realised she had only sent it because people were speaking well of me and openly congratulating me–therefore her not acknowledging me might have looked petty or suspicious. I'm not sure what else happened in the meeting after that: I was overcome with a sadness I couldn't shake. I was in the meeting in body only. My mind and my heart were breaking.

On 22nd November, I met with Stacey Tasker, the Head of the college, about my grievance. When the time came to see her I made my way over to the Mansion. I was apprehensive because it was to be the first time we would meet and this was hardly the best of circumstances. As I walked up the wide, spiral staircase, which spoke of grander times, I wondered what kind of person she was.

Neither the advisors nor Sue had been particularly complimentary about Stacey as the Head of the college. They often referred to her lack of experience and understanding of training issues, as an ex-governor without a 'learning' background, and the irony of her heading up a learning function. My preoccupation was less about her understanding of learning management as I wondered instead if she was a fair woman. I wondered if she could sense my pain and distress from the letter that I had written her. I hoped that she would instantly see that I was genuinely worried about my future and that I was looking for help and not trouble. When I got to the door with her name on it, I knocked gently and waited to be called in. Gill, Stacey's personal secretary, opened the door.

'Olivea?' she said as she pulled the door open fully.

'Yes,' I said. 'I have an appointment with Stacey.'

Gill told me that Stacey was waiting for Susanne from personnel and asked if I wanted anything to drink whilst I waited. I said no. She left me to go and fill a jug with water for the meeting. As I walked over to one of the almost full-length windows, I took my glasses off to give them a clean. It had been raining all day and, despite walking over with an umbrella, I still managed to get rainwater on my lenses. When I put my glasses back on I noticed the view overlooked a large green with several football posts dotted about. I was sure I could hear geese, although I couldn't see any. When Gill returned I walked across the floor to the 1950s Art Deco-style, bright-blue easy chairs, set against tastefully painted powder-blue walls, and sat down. To my right, there was a grey marble fireplace with an emerald-green tile surround and a black cast iron inset. I noticed two old-fashioned oil-filled radiators, which added to the charm of the room. Susanne came in and said hello and then headed straight for Stacey's office. She went in and closed the door. A few minutes later Stacey opened her office door and greeted me. I stood up and walked across the room on the lightly patterned blue carpet that flowed into her office along with the same powder-blue walls. I smiled and shook her hand. Stacey was of medium height and thin. Her hair was brown, shoulder length and, apart from a fringe, was un-styled. She was casually dressed in a twin-set cardigan and a pair of black trousers. It was not uncommon for women to de-feminise in the organisation:

simple blouses with subdued colours, black, navy, or grey skirts or trousers; simple jewellery, if any and no makeup. I rarely saw vibrant hair colours or chic cuts, high heels or tailored well-fitting suits. Stacey had been in the Service for many years. Her dress sense, like that of the majority of women I had met since joining, was unvarying, plain and simple. I, on the other hand, had consistently resisted the compulsion to grey down. There was already too much grey in the world. I wore a military styled, multicoloured striped designer jacket with muted gold buttons down the front and on the cuffs. Rudy had bought me the jacket for my 40th birthday when he took me to France as a surprise. I loved the jacket because it fitted well and the different coloured stripes meant I could wear it with a variety of coloured bottoms. I chose to wear a deep green (nearly black), straight and full-length skirt, offset with shoes Rudy had bought me in Italy. It was important to me to look polished and to wear things that triggered happy special memories for me. If I got stressed in the meeting, wherever I looked I would see a good memory and remember how much I was loved. Also, with it being the first time I was meeting Stacey, I wanted her to see me as well put-together, and professional. As she welcomed me in to her office, she seemed businesslike and courteous. Stacey led me to a large rectangular meeting table with rounded edges and eight chairs covered in tawny, tweed-like fabric and finished with a dark varnished wood surround. Susanne was already seated, so I walked behind her and past a mottled-effect brown leather chesterfield settee and sat opposite her, leaving the head of the table and the two carver chairs, positioned at each end, for Stacey. We were almost ready to start, except that my representative had not yet arrived. Susanne said she would check to see what the hold-up was. Stacey popped out to the outer secretarial office and I continued to sit and look around her office. There were photos of cherished ones and special memories on the walls and around the room: a young girl on a black horse, someone skiing and a stunning shot of what looked like the city of Manhattan. There was a framed certificate award for long service on the wall above Stacey's desk, 25 years I think, and on the bookcase behind me, there was a photo of her receiving an OBE from the Queen. Everywhere I looked, I saw privilege and acceptance. But I also saw hard work and perseverance and was encouraged by it. Maybe she would have some understanding of disadvantage, as it can't have been easy to get where she was. Even the smallest amount of empathy would provide a platform for us to build on.

Stacey's office overlooked the front of the Mansion, which faced the private car parks, then spilled over to views of green land interrupted only by an intermediate and irregular tree line. Then there was more open space, framed by another tree line, that met the sky. Just outside one of the four large windows in the room, fitted with simple white roller blinds, the British flag fluttered brightly and energetically on a white flagpole, in contrast to an otherwise dull and lacklustre day. Even though the day was abysmally dreary, somehow on the top floor of the Mansion whilst looking over the expanse of land, the day seemed brighter. Maybe it was because the top floor lifted you above the other buildings and the open space allowed what light there was to dance with the wind and the rain across the sky. Whatever it was, I watched the rain falling, as it had done all day, yet I was sure I could see streaks of light teasing us mortals with a hint of warmth and mildness that we knew we would not taste during the approaching winter.

Stacey re-entered the room followed by Susanne. Apparently, there had been some mix-up with the representative from the Staff Care Welfare Team who had got the dates wrong, which left me unrepresented. Stacey gave me the option to postpone the meeting; however, I really wanted to move things forward so I agreed to continue without representation. Having prayed before the meeting, although a little tense, I felt confident that I was doing the right thing by going ahead. I was offered the obligatory glass of water, which I accepted. Then we set about addressing my issues.

Stacey began. 'I've looked at your complaint. I don't think that there's any merit in going through each item.'

I was taken aback. Although fairly detailed, my written complaint didn't cover everything I was concerned about. It simply outlined some of the more measurable and (I was hoping) less contestable aspects of my experience at the college. If Stacey wasn't going to allow me to fully articulate what I considered to be the difficulties, then how was she going to gain a proper perspective of my problems?

Whilst I deliberated, Stacey briefly summarised my complaints. 'Your main issues seem to concentrate around your relationship with Sue and her style of management. For example, there's the issue of how you manage your diary. I've seen your diary and by comparison, my diary is relatively full with entries on an almost hourly basis. But your diary sometimes only has a single entry for the day.'

I was confused. Was this a meeting to hear what my concerns were? Or was this meeting designed to tell me my complaint had been investigated and these were the findings?

In any case, I responded. 'Well, I should imagine that, as the Head of the college, a lot of people come to see you. However my role is mobile and I go to visit clients all over the East Midlands and sometimes further.'

'Yes, but…' she interrupted, 'I often have to go to Head Quarters and then I still have more than a single appointment.'

'I don't doubt that, but a lot of key people work at HQ which would make it easy to make multiple appointments for one day,' I countered. 'But when I have to go to HMP Ranby, for example, it'll be to see one manager. That's a five-hour round trip, assuming there are no difficulties on the road. Then with a two-hour consultation or meeting and, whether or not I take lunch, that's eight hours and a single entry in my diary.'

Unconvinced, she said, 'Sue has a responsibility to manage you in the way that she sees fit. I've known Sue for many years, she's a *nice person*. I'm sure if you do the simple things that she's asking, your relationship will improve.'

Sue has a responsibility to manage me *fairly* I thought, not as she sees fit! And why was there suddenly a focus on Sue being a nice person? Nice people do bad things and bad people do nice things. They were not mutually exclusive states. We went back and forth over the diary issue for a while as I tried to show her that my diary was properly populated. However, she continued to reiterate that if Sue felt that there was a problem then, based on her knowledge of Sue–there was a problem!

'Sue managed this region before you. She *knows* how long it takes to get to a particular site.'

'Sue', I responded, 'lives near here. Sue can get to work in 15 minutes. I can only do that with one prison–HMP Wellingborough. Every other site that I have to travel to is close to one and three hours away from my home.'

Stacey moved on to the matter concerning my timekeeping. A horrid sense of déjà vu started to creep in. She said, 'Sue has some genuine concerns about your timekeeping.'

After what looked like some thought of what to say next, Stacey said, 'Have you ever considered apologising when you walk in late to a meeting?'

I couldn't hold myself back. 'Whenever I'm late, I always apologise. It's simply rude not to.' I motioned to the complaint documents she was holding and said, 'I attached evidence that I had given appropriate notification I was going to be late, have you seen it? Louise is my admin contact and, if I have any difficulties, I always contact her when appropriate. There's an email in there from her confirming that she passed the messages on to Sue. I don't know why you would think that I wouldn't apologise when late.'

I was getting upset. I felt Stacey had already made up her mind. And with this being the first time we met, my opportunity to make a good first impression had evidently been taken away by Sue's version of events.

The conversation continued. Stacey told me things like: the reason I was not put forward for MBTI training was because LMD had enough advisors able to use the tool. This meant that I should use the other advisors to deliver the tool in my area. She also said they were looking at introducing new tools.

Then Stacey told me something quite incredible. She said unequivocally, without any doubt or question in her delivery, 'The reason Sue is monitoring you so closely is because her suspicions have been aroused by *other* advisors who have asked you for help. But you declined to help them because you were too busy. Then when Sue checked your diary to see why you couldn't help them, she couldn't see what was taking up all of your time to the extent that you couldn't help anyone else.'

What was she talking about? I hadn't refused to help anyone with a project. On the contrary, I was the one asking for help and being turned down. Desperate for some clarity I asked, 'Can you be a bit more specific, and tell me which tasks or projects I have declined to help with?'

'Oh well, I can't remember the specific details right now,' Stacey said dismissively.

I couldn't afford to let this drop. 'I'm sorry, Stacey, but if specific details have informed the approach adopted by Sue, then I should know what those details are. Otherwise I'm unable to defend myself or accept what you are saying.'

I was at odds with the way I was being treated by Sue, but if it transpired I was actually to blame for the level of scrutiny I was currently under, it was important for me to understand that in order to resolve it. I asked again, 'What have I refused to work on, or who have I refused to work with?'

'I don't remember the details of that right now,' she replied. 'But what's important is that you recognise Sue isn't doing anything wrong by asking you to properly evidence your work and checking that you've done so.'

I had to let it go. I didn't think that she was deliberately being evasive, it was visibly apparent to me she really didn't have the details I was requesting because it wasn't divulged in her meeting with Sue, no doubt because such evidence wasn't necessary. Stacey automatically believed that what Sue was saying was true; accordingly, she didn't then need specifics like which projects I had refused to work on, or which emails supported my alleged excuses of being too busy, nor did she need excerpts from my diary to determine my workload at the alleged times of unavailability. Sue's word was enough.

As Stacey looked over some notes to inform her next point, I listened to the wall-mounted grandfather clock by the door. The hypnotic pendulum swing echoed the endless back and forth of the meeting: issues revisited again and again to get me to accept the failings Sue had identified; issues pushed back by me in the fight of my life to prove that the faults were not all mine. Tick: lateness, tock: I apologised. Tick: diary, tock: it's accurate. Tick: no training, tock: you promised. Tick: Sue's nice, tock: so am I.

After some more talk about the need to move on from the way Chris managed things and the difficult job that Sue had inherited and what *I* could do to help *her*, Stacey suggested mediation as she believed it would work in our situation. Although I had considered it previously, by this time I didn't see the value in it. I declined the offer, but then accepted, since I didn't want to appear inflexible. The meeting lasted for approximately two hours. Unfortunately, I spent most of that time unpicking the lies that Sue had already told Stacey. Stacey showed me out of her office whilst Susanne, who had said nothing throughout, remained seated. Stacey reiterated that she thought mediation would work because the situation between Sue and me was not hopeless. She told me that she liked my jacket, asked me where I got it and confirmed that Susanne would be in touch as soon as the dates for mediation were set up. It had been just over a month since that awful meeting with Sue and I now felt as if I had almost had the same meeting again. The only thing I had to look forward to was mediation, the Service's panacea for all internal staff conflicts. Overall, I felt that the meeting hadn't achieved anything. I wanted to create a good first impression. I waived my right to be accompanied to demonstrate that I was flexible and sincere about moving the issues forward. I did not feel that I received the same level of accommodation. Susanne took notes and didn't say anything in the meeting. Stacey supported Sue to the hilt. And I left with a compliment about my jacket!

A few days later I received an email from Fran, the Head of Personnel at HMP Glen Parva saying that she was confused about the MBTI and 360-degree materials I sent her by post, in relation to the work I had planned to do for them. Having a client become confused as a direct result of my involvement with them was upsetting to me. With most training sessions, it was customary for the consultant to arrive with the materials and not have to involve the client in the storage or distribution of the materials. However, because the MBTI sessions were going to be handled by Di and now Alison, Di suggested that the materials be sent, for the delegates to complete the self-assessments before their sessions in December, in order to save time. I had therefore arranged for the materials to be sent to Fran along with some simple instructions. Evidently, this approach was causing confusion, whilst I was becoming more resentful that I couldn't facilitate this development need for my client myself. The whole exercise was incredibly convoluted. What distressed me most was that it was completely avoidable. I could have been trained by this point; I would have made appointments with each candidate and I would have carried the materials myself. Instead, I now had to forge a response for my client whilst trying not to look as if I was completely inept.

I tried calling Fran over the days that followed, since I felt more emails would only exacerbate matters. Unfortunately, I wasn't able to get through. I was between a rock and a hard place. I could have left some messages; however, I didn't want to do that because long-winded messages with instructions as to what needed to be done with the materials, was likely to cause even more complications. I didn't think to leave a simpler message so that she at least knew I was trying to contact her. I remained hopeful I would be able to speak to Fran and fully explain what she needed to do.

On 29th November, Sue stopped me in the corridor upstairs in the LMD building and said that we needed to catch up. She behaved as if there wasn't a grievance against her, as if she had forgotten how badly she had treated me in the last meeting. I was quite nervous, I felt awkward and my heart was pounding. I just stood in front of her like a rabbit caught in headlights; people were passing in between us and I didn't know what to say. She motioned for us to step into Chris's old office at the end of the corridor and shut the door behind me.

'I think we need to catch up, Olivea, because I'm aware that you're not getting the support you need.'

I said, 'I'm not sure what I should do under the circumstances.'

Abruptly she replied, 'We're not going to talk about the grievance and either you take my offer up or not. It's up to you. I'm aware that you're not getting the same level of support as everyone else,' she repeated herself, 'and I feel the need to do something about it.'

'Oh,' I said, 'I think it's a little late for that.'

She shrugged her shoulders and waited for my response to her invitation.

'Okay,' I said, 'Did you want to meet today?'

'Let's say in an hour's time,' she said assertively.

Then she opened the office door and left. I rushed downstairs and immediately contacted Susanne in personnel by an email marked 'URGENT.' I wrote that I was uncomfortable about meeting Sue alone and didn't want a repeat performance of the last time.

Whilst waiting for Susanne to come back to me, I busied myself with compiling my area report for Sue to read. When Susanne responded I was disappointed. She didn't offer to accompany me or send someone to support me. Instead, she suggested that I should ask Sue what the meeting was going to be about and then if I deemed it was *'something trivial'* I could proceed with the meeting.

I thought, 'She's got to be kidding.' How was that going to look? I imagined myself saying, 'Excuse me, Sue can you tell me what the meeting is going to be about before I commit myself. Only I need to determine if it's trivial or not!'

What was Susanne thinking? Was she totally oblivious as to how tense my relationship with Sue was? Did she really think I was in a position to vet Sue? I responded to Susanne stating that I felt she had not quite grasped the gravity of the situation, that it was inappropriate under the circumstances for me to ask questions like that, without sounding antagonistic. I reminded Susanne that the last time I met with Sue she accused me of implying that she was racist.

It was at this point, I realised that I was completely on my own. Susanne came back with a response to say that, due to other commitments, she was unable to attend the meeting with me and that she was the only person in personnel who did case management. Everyone else worked in an administrative role. Susanne asked if I wanted her to communicate her unavailability to mediate, to Sue. I was happier with that. I would meet with Sue, just not alone.

Within minutes, Sue's secretary Ros came downstairs to tell me Sue had sent an urgent email I needed to read immediately. After communicating with Susanne, I continued to update my area report just in case Sue still wanted to read it, so I hadn't noticed that Sue had sent me an email. Obviously, as I hadn't opened it and triggered a 'read receipt', Sue rightly deduced I had not read her email yet, so she sent her secretary downstairs with a hard copy.

Ros said, 'You need to read this' and handed it to me sheepishly.

I wondered what was so important that it couldn't wait until I checked my email again. The sheet handed to me was folded in half: I unfolded it and read it as Ros left my office. In the email, Sue said:

> *...Following our brief conversation. I think in view of e-mails just brought to my attention I feel it inappropriate to carry on with the brief meeting this morning.*
>
> *In light of my concerns that I feel that you are adequately supported and line managed within your job role, I am going to suggest to Val* [Woodcock]... *that she take on day to day contact and progress with you. This does not however mean that I will not be your line manager and therefore any sickness leave etc will need to remain reported directly through me.*
>
> *I will let you know today if Val agrees to this arrangement.*
>
> *Regards*
> *Sue*

She had changed my reporting line without any consultation. It was protocol for any changes in reporting lines, management structure or workload for there to be formal notice, consultation and recording of mutual agreements in the SPDR appraisal form. But Sue had not done this. On the one hand, she was talking about concern for me and making sure that I was getting the right levels of support, and on the other hand she was happy to ignore policy and the simplest of courtesies and alienate me further. I was now a problem to be handed over to someone else who was, ironically, being given options. Sue was so regularly off-hand with me by this point that I felt she probably couldn't even see how badly she was treating me any more: it had become second nature. I didn't have any objection to Val Woodcock who, since the last time we spoke, had been promoted as deputy to Sue. I objected to being off-loaded. I objected to not being allowed to have a voice. If this was really about my needs, why was I then not consulted?

Having spent a little time putting my area report together for the now cancelled meeting, I thought it best still to give my updates to Sue. Laughable really, I thought, that I could be treated so badly yet my thoughts ran to giving Sue the information she needed in order to get up to speed on what was happening in my region. Despite her email, I still felt obliged to respond to her original request. Forever bound by sense and duty, I girded up my loins with delusion and went upstairs to the admin office. Like a battered wife returning to an abusive husband, I told myself that Sue didn't mean to hurt me; I told myself that from now on she would treat me right. Sue was in there with Helen. When I arrived, she seemed annoyed. A roll of her eyes left a quizzical look on her face as if to say, 'Didn't you get the email?' She was staring at me without a word.

I quickly said in response to the unspoken question, 'I have read the email, but I wondered…um…do you still want to see the summary report of my monthly activities or…or do you want me to…er…give them to Val…instead?' Her stare destabilised me. I was tripping over my words.

She was as abrupt as she had been earlier that morning and said, 'Well there's no point now.'

She continued to look at me with her ears and forehead peeled back like a cat. With her eyes widened, her lips were pursed and angled upwards as if to say, 'Are you still here?'

I was so tired of being spoken to without any common regard. Yet I knew that if I at all challenged her about it I would be labelled as aggressive. Clutching my report, I turned on my heels and left the admin office.

As I walked down the corridor and made my way back down the stairs, I wondered what was wrong with me. Where was my strength to resist being treated so poorly? Even though I knew I would not be treated with respect, I had gone upstairs to approach Sue. Why was I working so hard to show respect to a manager who refused to afford me a modicum of reciprocal regard. Was I a hypocrite by not lashing out or was I a saint?

I needed some air. I grabbed my coat and went for a walk across the grounds to the library. It was well stocked with leading authors in learning management and I would find materials to help me design some of the programmes I was working on. But, as I searched the shelves, my mind ran to the unanswered questions about the mistreatment I felt duty bound to tolerate. Absorbing abuse and tolerating torment was a deep-seated and ingrained response to those who had power over me. I had been taught along with my siblings and my friends to behave like this from childhood. 'Respect your elders. It does not matter if they are right, they are older. Respect those in authority over you. It does not matter if they are right, they are in charge.' These mantras were the milk with which we were nurtured.

A leadership and management activity toolkit caught my eye. I grabbed it off the shelf and sat at a desk for a closer look. As I flicked through the pages, I thought more about how we were brought up. I remembered one particular occasion and the days leading up to it that perfectly answered my predisposition to show respect at all costs. My family lived in Wellingborough, a picturesque rural market town in Northamptonshire. Every so often, my sister and I would be excited to leave our sleepy hollow and travel to choir practice in Bedford in preparation for a regional event. When Mum could afford it, we would take a taxi to the train station, or at other times we would take a leisurely 30-minute walk there, even though Dad had a car. We tended to walk, because asking Dad was exasperating and belittling. On one such occasion, the youth in our church were going to London, picking up some friends at the next stop in Bedford, after which we would all make our way to the rehearsals for the Annual Church Convention. At these events, we got to touch base with friends from all over the country, wear our best clothes and check out all the cute boys! These occasions were important for us because it was before the days of the internet, IMs, mobile phones and text messages, before Facebook and Twitter. Meetings like these were where we swapped stories and mixed-tapes. It was where we felt like grown-ups. We asserted ourselves and demonstrated our skills in music, drama, poetry and prose—we made our mark and got noticed. And when we got home after each event, we savoured the happenings and stories and the people we met for months and sometimes years. In our uncomplicated and for the most part uneventful lives, going to these meetings was everything.

My sister and I (Suzie is three years older than me), had been talking about going to London all week. It would be the first time I was to be a part of the National Youth Choir, requiring a number of journeys to London and the use the London Underground! Try as I might, I couldn't get a sense of what it was like to travel beneath the streets of London. What time did the Underground close? Could we get trapped down there if rehearsals overran? Did Mole People, tunnel dwellers who, having shunned the 'above world' to live in their own ordered society, really exist? We would travel as a group of around 20 young people from Wellingborough and Bedford because only very strict Sister Agnes, the Choir Mistress, had made the journey before and knew how to negotiate the underground labyrinth of the capital. I was excited to bursting point!

Suzie and I knew what we were each going to wear to the last detail: appropriate attire befitting young ladies going to church being bra and proper knickers, our best but not matching underwear. Matching underwear, especially red or black, suggested that you dressed for seduction, harlotry, immoral intent and that wasn't the behaviour of the godly and the chaste. We wore chocolate-brown 20-denier sheer tights, which were held up by another pair of proper knickers, because the tights were one-size and not made for 13 to16-year-olds. To us there was nothing more unsightly than tights forming decrepit folds like jowls around ankles! Sometimes we wore girdles over the tights, even though they made me chafe and cut into me really badly. The girdles were not made for my very ancestral African bottom and thighs. Girdles were a real inconvenience each time we needed to use the loo; taking them off was like peeling rhino skin, but we were prepared to make the necessary sacrifices for beauty!

The next layer of suitable clothing would be brushed-cotton white vests and nylon petticoats trimmed with lace. For our underarms, we would use *MUM* roll-on deodorant. Then there would be A-lined homemade crimplene dresses and polyester cardigans regardless of what was happening in the fashion world. We never wore trousers because trousers on women were a sin.

We knew how we would style our hair. Mum had promised us a taxi to the train station so we didn't have to worry about getting too sweaty before we got to London. That was really important, because our hair was not chemically straightened; so to look good meant an uncomfortable sleep in our curlers. Once the curlers were out and the hair styled we had to avoid sweat and humidity at all costs, otherwise our hair would revert to an uncontrollable frizz and lose all sense of feminine proportions, ruining any chance of being chatted up! The look would be finished with a beret cocked to the side or a crocheted tam worn the same way. We would oil our skin so much we glistened in the sun (and indoors) but we never wore make-up because only Jezebel did that. We never wore jewellery because our preacher said we no longer slaves. Earrings, necklaces or bracelets were all indicative of us being owned whether by Egyptians, Babylonians or Colonials. We were free and were to resist being cleverly drawn into bondage again even if the chains were made of gold. Wearing jewellery also suggested we were burdening ourselves with the cares of a wanton world and lusting after the flesh, as opposed to yearning after spiritual things. There were so many rules. Many of them were unbiblical and misguided; some of them were plainly ridiculous—like not being allowed to cross your legs in church or whistle. I was terrified when I saw a bishop do both—I thought the sky was going to fall in! Yet we obeyed these rules and more without question. It was what we did.

The final layer of acceptability was perfume and for that we had *Avon*. We wore 'Occur', 'Moonwind' or 'Charisma' with accompanying creams for that total-body Queen Esther smell.

On the morning, everything was going to plan until we went to get the taxi money from Mum. We stood in her room as she rifled through her purse and then her handbag as she lay ill in bed. She was very sick and had been for many years. She had suffered two heart attacks and lived with complications involving high blood pressure. As children, we took turns in looking after her. She spent most of her time in bed weeping, praying and sleeping. But she was always everything a mother should be: loving and very much in charge.

Mum stopped searching for the money. She took her hands out of her handbag and folded them over it in defeat. Then she looked up and gently said with some sadness, 'Ask your Dad to take you.'

'Ooh Mummm...' I protested through gritted teeth in a typically whiney childlike manner. It was the only way you could respectfully object to anything in our household. Any other type of protest would suggest you were asserting yourself as 'the man' or 'the woman' of the house and there was already one each of those and only *room* for one each of those. Hence, no matter how old you were, if there were any complaints to be made, you made them as a child in subjection. So I whined and huffed, though as I looked at how tired and unable she was, I stopped pressing for a change in her instruction.

My sister dug me in my ribs. That meant it was my turn to ask him. I reluctantly went downstairs to the back room, as no one was allowed in the front room—except to clean it. Everything we did as a family was in the back room. The TV when it was working was there. The drop-leaf folding dining table was there. We ate and played our games there. The front room was sacrosanct and only for special visitors.

Dad was watching TV. It was Saturday, and apart from *Saturday Cinema* on BBC2 at 3.00pm (where we would watch the likes of Elvis, Gene Kelly or Doris Day in a musical or John Wayne and others in the obligatory Western) there was little else to watch but sports, and Dad liked to gamble. Dad liked to gamble a lot. He is a tall, broad Barbadian. He is a gruff man. The only times we heard him laugh out loud with unbridled haw-haws was at the antics of *Tom and Jerry* and *Foghorn Leghorn*. There was always time and relationship for those cartoon characters whilst his encounters with us were mostly joyless.

In quick succession, I noisily walked through the two sets of beaded curtains. One hung between the hallway and the kitchen and the other immediately adjacent divided the kitchen from the back room. Dad did not acknowledge my arrival and continued to watch the TV, seemingly oblivious to the clattering beads and my standing right by him, pointedly waiting to speak. I did not want to force my presence on him yet his refusal to recognise that I was in the room left me without a choice. I carefully and respectfully started to speak.

'Dad, we've got rehearsals today. Could you give us a lift to the station please?'

He didn't speak. Dad continued to watch the TV as if I wasn't there. I hadn't done anything to upset him. This was just what he did. Every encounter with Dad was always about him remaining in control and having the upper hand. He loved to hold us to ransom. I stood there like a spare part waiting for a response; still nothing. I looked around the tiny room with darkest brown (to hide the dirt) corduroy fold-out foam bed settees and bare off-white matt walls. There was no wallpaper, no pictures, and no photos. That was because Dad said that the council house was newly built so we weren't allowed to put paper up or anything for twelve months or more. The house needed to 'settle'. Of course, we knew that wasn't true. Dad just wanted to spend his money on other things. Why waste money on paper to cover walls or carpet for the floor when you could bet on a horse and win hundreds of pounds to bet again and win more? After what seemed like an age, I left the room and ran back upstairs to the bedroom I shared with my sister.

I went in and flopped down disappointedly on the bed. Suzie, whose real name is Paulette–I don't think I will ever understand why West Indian parents named us one thing and called us another–said 'Well, what did he say?'

'The usual,' I said, 'nothing. He's watching telly. Should we just go?' I asked. 'We've still got time, we can walk.'

'Well we've asked him *now*. If we walk out before he's said yes or no we might get into trouble. Let's wait for a bit.'

So we waited. After a short time, I went back to Mum.

'Mum I've asked Dad like you said but he didn't answer me. Can we just go?'

'Ask your Dad again,' she said in a measured tone, 'if he still doesn't answer you *then* you can go.'

As I went back down the stairs, I felt I knew what Mum was doing. Dad would always pick fights with her no matter what she did. Had she found the taxi fare he would have quarrelled about her wasting money when *he* had a car. If we had chosen to walk without asking him to take us to the station, then he would have accused her of training us to disrespect him. Once he felt he had sufficient evidence of our impertinence, he would punish us by taking the plug off the TV and hiding it, or turning off the central heating in the winter, whilst forbidding us to turn it back on. Then he would go upstairs and tell Mum what he had done, looking for an argument. All this we had experienced before, sitting at the bottom of the stairs listening to him rant whilst she lay ill in bed. We only ever heard his voice; Mum was often too sick to respond and if she did she was so weak her voice never carried, even when their bedroom door was open. Afterwards he would go to work for the night and we would sit in the cold without at TV. Central heating was new to us. The boiler with the 'on/off' switch was in the backroom. The thermostat controlling the temperature was in the front room, but we never knew it was there. Dad would switch off the heating in the backroom, then slip into the front room and turn the thermostat to zero, so no matter how we flicked the forbidden switch after he left for the night, the heating remained off, and Mum never knew how to work it. As the night progressed, the cold would seep into our bones and the tension Dad left, fuelled resentment in our hearts that no child should have to deal with.

I took a deep breath, parted the beads and stood beside him. 'Dad, could we get a lift to the station please?'

Again, he said nothing! He just continued to stare at the telly. 'No matter,' I thought, 'we were free to go now anyway.' I bolted back upstairs, told Suzie we could go, grabbed my bag, kissed my Mum who told me to behave whilst I was out–as if misbehaving was even an option–and made my way back downstairs, where Suzie joined me. Coats on and bags in hand we went to say goodbye to Dad.

'Bye Dad,' we said in unison.

'Sit down,' he said slowly and sternly as if about to rebuke us. 'I will take you,' he said without removing his stare from the TV.

If only we had taken our chances and escaped through the front door without saying goodbye, but that would have provided him with ammunition to attack Mum with. Now we were certain to miss our train, for telling him the train time would give him the power to keep us waiting in the house until we had all but missed the train before we saw any movement from him. Yet not telling him meant he did not know what time to leave. Either way we were snookered, for he would resist any prompting or urgency on our part–we always had to dance to the tune that he was playing. He didn't ask what time our train was and we didn't dare tell him. We grudgingly sat down. Coats on and bags in hand. With our big conditioned-to-respect brown eyes, we silently watched the clock as it became too late to walk to the station. We watched the clock as it become too late to run to the station. We watched the clock until we had 15 minutes to buy our tickets and board the train.

Then Dad stood up. So we stood up. He stretched and made his way to the downstairs loo. He came back, then patted his trouser legs for his car keys. Where were his keys? He never knew where they were. We scurried around helping him to look. I ran back up stairs and Suzie looked in the hallway on the telephone table.

'All right,' he said, 'I've got them.'

Nine minutes to go. Our gamble had paid off. We could still make it. We shouted more goodbyes to Mum, left the house and got in the car—we were pulling off. 'Yes!' I encouraged myself by envisioning the journey in my head: a quick left, then a right turn on to the main road and we will be there in five minutes, maybe six, tops. But Dad took a right and another right! 'Where is he going,' I thought? Incredibly, even though we had no time to lose, Dad had decided to take the back streets to the station. There was no need to take the scenic route as thirty-odd years ago there was no such thing as rush hour traffic in Wellingborough. There was traffic, however not nearly enough to ever discourage anyone from travelling along the main roads. Our hearts were in our mouths in sheer frustration because, as if taking the scenic route wasn't bad enough, Dad who was normally a speed freak was only driving at an excruciating 20 mph!

I wanted to scream and ask him why he took such pleasure in tormenting us in this way, but of course I didn't and neither did my sister. It simply was not done. In our households, respect was not earned—it was an automatic right due to all adults. You would never see a scene from *Eastenders* played out in a West Indian home in the 1970s. You would never see a teenager shout at an adult and say things like 'I hate you!' or 'You're supposed to knock before coming into *my* room, get out, I don't want to talk to you!' *If* you lived long enough to gather up your things—and by *your* things I mean anything that you actually managed to purchase with your *own* money, because if it was something that your parents had bought you, including the 'grip' (suitcase), you would have to leave it behind—you would be out on the street *minus* a few teeth! So we said nothing; in any case we were always mindful about how Dad could use our behaviour to start an argument with Mum—we needed to protect her.

We were tense and visibly impatient, looking out of the windows, leaning backwards and forwards as if our doing so would increase the velocity of the vehicle. If we could have done the *Flintstones* thing and pushed our feet through the floor and started running, we would have done.

After an agonising meander through the back streets, we could see the station but the train was pulling in! We were sure we were never going to make it! Dad drove into the station. I lifted up the door lock and grabbed the lever in the side panel to open the door but, unbelievably, the car was still moving. Why had he not stopped yet, I thought? Ah, he was *manoeuvring*! But of course. 'Oh my God,' I screamed in my head. Then I prayed in my heart, 'Father please help me not to explode. God please make him stop and let us out, we need to catch this train!'

The car stopped. We leapt out and threw the doors closed behind us.

We shouted 'Bye Dad,' as we ran.

'We're not going to make it,' Suzie said as we ran up the steps without buying our tickets—we would have to buy them on the train. Whilst running across the bridge, I heard a clang. The guard was closing the carriage doors; then another clang and another. We had begun our descent down the other side; *clang* followed *clang*. There were far too many clangs for the number of people who would normally board the train at sleepy Wellingborough. I wondered how many doors this guard was closing. As it turned out, he was closing virtually all of them! Our friends had seen us arrive and proceeded to open almost every carriage door in an attempt to slow the departure down before they boarded the train! This was not the first time they had had to rescue us in this way. They were frantically waving from their carriage and we breathlessly thundered down the platform towards them as they opened their door. We jumped on. Two more clangs and the whistle blew—we were on our way and, remarkably, with not a hair out of place!

And now some 30 years later, even though I know that whenever I am being treated shabbily I should be screaming or offering some sort of resistance, I freeze and take the abuse, just like I did with Dad. I don't say 'Hang on a minute Sue, you can't change my reporting line without so much as a word of conversation' or 'Who are you looking at like that?' Instead, I wait for the juggernaut to hit me with blinding speed and careless force leaving nothing recognisable, only the horror. It is afterwards, when I reassemble in a different place (like the library) and a different time (like now) that my brain allows me to mull over some kind of recourse and, even then, my response is seasoned with measured and pre-emptive considerations. When my emotions are set to blow like Mount Vesuvius, there is always a part of me that thinks, 'Yeah, a volcanic eruption would be great about now but think of the mess you'll make! And then you'll probably be the one who has to clear it up. Do yourself a favour and calm down.' And these considerations often have me choking on my own smoke.

Yet the truth is that, even if my upbringing or personality had not precluded resistance to mistreatment in the Prison Service, the historical odds were still stacked against me. My struggle for respect and acceptance up until joining the Service has been a longstanding, faceless one. And whether or not I have consistently engaged in the warfare, I have always been aware, if only on a subconscious level, that certain bastions of British societal inequality remain unconquered and have thereby affected my entire life and livelihood. In themselves, they are de-motivating and as much of a deterrent to thinking straight and speaking up as any threat to existence. Differential treatment is not a new phenomenon and its corrosive effects often bring about reluctance to challenge inequality. This knowledge, coupled with my experiences of growing up, had made for much introspection and some floundering in terms of doing the right thing or even knowing what the right thing was.

At around lunchtime I was back at my desk with the leadership toolkit in tow when I received an email from Susanne informing me that mediation would be arranged. I was still sceptical of mediation because I felt that my case was too complex for this particular mode of resolution. I was nonetheless eager to put an end to this nightmare, so I didn't resist her attempts to set the meetings up.

Throughout December, I continued to work and enjoy my time in the field. What I did not enjoy, however, was trying to finalise arrangements for MBTI delivery at HMP Glen Parva. I received an email from Di on 30th November stating that both she and Alison potentially had problems with the 12th December date selected to deliver MBTI at the prison. She said that they had problems with partners, parents and children. And then, in justification for postponing the event, Di said that I hadn't confirmed the date was firm anyway. I responded to both of them to say that *'as agreed'* I had been confirming timeslots with the candidates for the 12th; however, I would now need their new dates of availability.

I was really at a loss as to what to do. Trying to organise this development for the staff at HMP Glen Parva had become so difficult. At the last LMD team meeting I reiterated my need for help with this project. During the break, Di and Alison approached me and said they could help. They suggested working on the same day, if possible splitting the delegates between them. They agreed 12th December was the best date for them. I said I would need a little time to contact the delegates and set up timeslots with them for that day. I agreed to forward the confirmed timeslots in due course. We all agreed that 12th December would be the date that I would work towards, especially since no one else from the team had come forward with other dates and we would soon fall into the Christmas season. Now it was looking as if neither of them could make it and I would have to cancel the appointments I had made. I knew this would reflect badly on me and I was not looking forward to cancelling the timeslots already booked.

On 5th December, I received an email via Sue's secretary to inform me that Val Woodcock had agreed to line manage me in relation to my area activities: Sue would remain my line manager in all other respects. It was like a scene out of Shakespeare's King Lear, *'Only we still retain the name, and all th' additions to a king. The sway, revenue, execution of the rest, Beloved sons, be yours.'*

I was confused. Technically Sue was saying that I, like chattel, would be divided between two managers, and I had no real idea how this was supposed to work. It certainly didn't work for King Lear! On the one hand, I was supposed to liaise with Val for day-to-day issues, yet for any real management decisions I was supposed to speak to Sue. This meant that, even though our relationship was very poor, she had complicated matters by introducing an additional reporting level but I still had to go to her for any significant decisions—she still retained the name and power of a King. I felt quite defeated, as it was plain to see that my opinions and desires counted for nothing and it was okay to just move me from pillar to post without consultation or regard for my needs.

Over a week had passed and I still had not resolved the issue of contacting Fran at HMP Glen Parva to explain what she needed to do with the information I had sent her. I had made further attempts to call and still couldn't get through, so I reluctantly left messages with the personnel department and on Fran's phone. Even though I didn't leave lengthy and detailed messages, it was important that she knew I was trying to contact her and resolve the confusion around the MBTI and 360-degree packs. And now, even worse, the cancellations. As I did this, I knew that I had made a mistake by not leaving messages before. When I didn't get a response by the end of the day, I resorted to sending her an email to explain and, to cover my back, I also sent an email to Val, to make her aware of the difficulties I was having organising this bout of MBTI training. On the back of that email, I additionally explained why there were gaps in my diary. I particularly wanted to do this because I knew that Sue, and now Val, would be watching me and I needed to account for my time. Despite the fact that, as advisors, we all knew that tying clients down to specific dates was often fraught with difficulty, I didn't believe that I would be afforded any leniency because of this.

For example, since July I had scheduled training for aspiring managers and middle managers to commence in September at HMP Sudbury with the Training Manager, Peter. I had managed to deliver two workshops out of the series; however, Peter had either cancelled or not confirmed the other dates and, as a result, we had rescheduled several times. Each time he did this, I would have to provisionally block book dates in my calendar in order to ensure that I could consecutively roll-out the programme on finalising the plans. By December, he hadn't confirmed the December dates, which meant I had to take them out of my diary, creating the gaps I had tried so hard to avoid.

It was an impossible situation and one that I was sure Sue and Val were aware of. Clients cancelled all the time. As much as appointments were made with plenty of notice, my clients worked in highly reactive environments. Prisoners tried to kill themselves and some succeeded. They tried to escape and some succeeded. They would hold dirty protests where they would smear excrement on the floor and walls. At other times fights would break out. Managers and officers alike needed to deal with these incidents on a daily basis and they would naturally cancel appointments whenever their priorities changed. Yet here I was, panicked by a few gaps in my diary that I could no more control than birds in the air and worms in the soil. I was desperate to pre-empt any further criticisms relating to diary management.

It wasn't long before another team meeting was due. With everything that was going on I was a little detached, though something happened part way through this meeting that immediately got my attention. The team were doing their usual random complaining except that, this time, they were berating a senior black manager who worked in the personnel management group (PMG) at Head Quarters. Her name was Althea. It was so bad, I felt uncomfortable and personally affected. There were suspicions around the way the PMG were going about their business, as word had got out about possible organisational restructure and streamlining. I had not heard anything about it before this meeting but it seemed as if the team felt that something underhand had gone on and that our roles might be affected. Apparently, the Service was looking at creating a number of new roles, one of which had clear overlaps with our role. Sue, adding fuel to the fire said, 'Robin Wilkinson and Cathy James are clearly stipulating that the Area Business Partners role overlaps with the LMD role without any concern for us!'

I didn't really know who the people they referred to were, except that they were senior personnel people. Sue then waved a questionnaire in the air entitled *Change Management Approach/Change Readiness*. Then she passed it around for us to look at. Believing Althea to be responsible for the document, she said, 'Look at it, it's a load of dross. I don't want to be a part of it. As a Senior Manager B, Althea has no clear vision of what she's doing!' As we looked at the document in turn, Sue continued, 'Althea has commissioned consultants to scope out this work without going through me. I have been waiting for a week for her to call me and update me on the meeting she had with them and she has not returned my calls. We need to distance ourselves from Althea because she cannot be trusted.'

The team, suitably riled by this point, started to respond. Rachel Boyling said she thought Althea was on our side and understood the work we did. And now it seemed that she was stabbing us in the back! Alison Richardson commented it was her view that Althea had never been on-side with us. Pauline Duff suggested the HQ personnel group always had their own agendas that didn't include our welfare.

As always, I was horrified that they could talk so openly and negatively about anybody, but I was especially stunned that Sue, having already made one faux pas in her dealings with a black person (namely me), was content to continue in this vein without any fear as to how this could be construed! I made notes about the comments and who said what during the meeting. I wasn't quite sure what I was going to do with them.

The discussion ended with an agreement that, for the time being, the team needed to be 'seen' as being compliant and working with Althea. Then they simply moved on to the next agenda item as if there hadn't been a disgraceful display of unprofessional conduct.

The meeting continued with Helen giving a number of updates to include the positive action request from Beverley Thompson that was briefly shared in the September team meeting. Helen outlined that there were now twenty-two Black and Minority Ethnic candidates who put their names forward for the programme and that Beverley was looking to us for the content. She then proceeded to tell us the project had been handed over to the external consultants who were the designers of the Senior Operational Manager (SOM) development programme.

I was very disappointed that I had not been involved in the project even though I knew that I didn't necessarily need to be involved in every project given to the Leadership team. It seemed that it didn't matter that I had relevant skills and experience in the voluntary sector, teaching and training black managers; nor did it matter that as a black manager on a team employed to design bespoke programmes for governors and managers, meant I had first hand insight into what it felt like to be a black manager in the Service. Then as if to add insult to injury, Helen announced the HoLS programme might not go ahead because of some budgeting issues and the project had been passed to procurement. Apparently, the people they had ultimately chosen to design the programme were not on the approved providers list.

Hang on a minute! In November, Sue said that I would be the lead on the project and I had asked Helen to keep me up to date. Although there had been a few email exchanges, as the lead for the project I had not been involved in any more discussions or decision making, despite my enquiries. Yet there had obviously been deliberations about the project without my involvement; a decision had been made about the choice of consultant for the project and now the provider of choice was tied up in Prison Service bureaucracy. I was embarrassed and upset that between them they couldn't even show some common civility, they simply cut me out of the loop and discarded me. I couldn't find a way of asking how all of this had transpired without it looking antagonistic or pedantic, so I said nothing. I was already in trouble having raised my grievance, Stacey had already made it clear to me that she was supporting Sue and I didn't want to look like I was reacting to every little thing as discriminatory practice.

After the team meeting Val asked if she could have a word. We went into my office. This was to be our first meeting since Sue had changed my reporting line. I thought perhaps that Val wanted to outline how we should work together because it was not at all clear to me how she was going to manage me day-to-day whilst Sue managed me at the same time.

As we sat, without any pleasantries to ease us into the new dynamics of our relationship Val said, 'LMD has received a complaint from the head of personnel at HMP Glen Parva. I just wanted to understand the nature of the problem.'

I knew this was going to happen. There had been far too much 'faffing' about over this MBTI training and with the scrutiny that I was under, it would only look like incompetence on my part.

I began to explain. 'This has been a nightmare from the beginning.' I told Val about the initial consultation meeting with Governor Edwards and Fran, the head of personnel. I even provided her with Fran's original notes in her own handwriting clearly citing MBTI as her preferred choice. I told Val that because I didn't have a licence to deliver MBTI, I took Sue's advice and asked other LMD advisors for help. Di and Alison agreed and then both dropped out at the same time, forcing me to cancel the individual MBTI sessions. I commented on how convoluted and drawn out the whole project had become because I had to involve too many people to do something I should have been trained to do by now.

Val left saying she would sort it out. I immediately set about forwarding the emails related to the difficulties I had encountered to Val. I wanted her to see how hard I tried to meet my client's requests and how long the whole thing was taking. I'm not sure what I was expecting Val to do—explain to Sue that I had done my best under the circumstances or perhaps even organise my MBTI training at the eleventh hour? What actually happened next however was quite unexpected. Later that day I read an apology from Sue to Fran explaining how it was *my* assumptions that contributed to the confusion. Then she personally put herself forward to do the MBTI feedbacks and proffered a couple of appointment dates for the New Year.

As I read between the lines I could hear Sue saying replete with regal airs, 'even though I've been promoted and don't do this level of work anymore and should really be devolving this to one of my direct reports, I will personally do this for you because you are such a valued client and because Olivea's messed this all up.' All that was missing was the cape, tights and supersonic speed.

I wished there was another word for embarrassment, as I seemed to be using it on a regular basis. I felt completely inept. Had

HMP Glen Parva asked any other advisor bar one new starter, the project would have been well underway. Yet because they had asked me and I had to rely on the good graces of others, this meant they had been waiting since mid-September for something as simple as 'meet my people and use this tool as a platform for discussions.' Now they had to wait until the 20th and 27th of January 2006! I had never in all my years of consultancy, let my clients down like this. I was ashamed.

Feeling the need to do something to help my cause I wrote again to Stacey Tasker asking if she would deal with my expenses and outstanding training needs. With the mediation still some way off, I needed to know I was not coming back in the New Year with nothing resolved. I felt I could probably face the New Year more positively if something was in place. I was looking for anything as the smallest gesture of good will that would give me hope for the year to come.

The following day I was due back into Newbold. Rudy left before me at around 7.00am and was travelling to Northampton to work. At approximately 7.30am he rang to say there was no point in my trying to get to the M1 because the A45 was gridlocked. He said if I didn't need to leave the house yet it would be best to leave later. He suggested I check the news to find out what was going on.

I checked teletext, and listened for the news and found there had been a fatal accident on the M1 early that morning. The northbound and southbound lanes were closed from junction 15. I had a middle managers meeting at Newbold in my diary for 2.00pm so I decided to work from home for a couple of hours hoping that the motorway would be reopened by then. I checked teletext and the news every 30 minutes until 12pm like a madwoman. At this point, the M1 was still closed however I thought I would try to get to Rugby via Weedon Road in Northampton to Kislingbury, Daventry, then Rugby.

I set off and got into Northampton with a deceptive amount of ease. But as soon as I turned off the A45 I got caught in traffic on route to the Daventry turn off. After about an hour of not moving, I decided to ring Newbold and explain that I was not going to make the meeting. It was about 1.15pm. I had been listening to the radio and people were ringing in with their stories about trying alternative routes and being stuck in traffic since the morning. I really wanted to get into Newbold because I knew that missing the meeting would be another mark against my name yet in an hour I hadn't moved more than thirty feet.

I speed dialled Newbold reception on my hands-free and asked for anyone in LMD admin. Once I was transferred, no one picked up the phone so I dialled '0' and asked for anyone in the Fast Track team. I got through to Tom and I explained that I called LMD and no one picked up their phone and that it was important that they knew I had rung in. I told him I was expected at a meeting for 2.00pm however couldn't get out of Northampton. He said he'd pass my message on.

A few minutes later Helen rang me. 'Hello Olivea', she said tersely, 'I've just had a message from Tom, but I can't understand why you didn't ring me or any of the others.'

I was somewhat puzzled by both her tone and her query. I replied, 'I rang the switchboard as normal on speed dial and asked for anyone in the LMD team. With it being lunchtime I wasn't sure who would be at their desk. Whoever the switchboard put me through to, didn't pick up the phone.'

Did it matter who I spoke to, I thought? Wasn't it more important that I had rung in and managed to get a message across? I mean, they were in the office next door to Tom's. I couldn't see why this would be a problem.

'Well I've been by my phone for the last hour, *if* you had rung in,' she emphasised, 'I would have answered. And there are other people here too.'

'I don't know what happened,' I reasoned. 'Maybe I was put through to the wrong extension, but it rang and there was no answer.'

'Well, I was *definitely* here. I've been here all afternoon. If you had called you would have got someone…' she continued.

Alright already! I thought, surely she didn't ring me back to have an argument about why I spoke to Tom instead of her. I exhaled. Then I changed the subject and explained I wouldn't be able to make it to Newbold for the 2.00pm meeting because of the accident and resultant motorway closures; and as soon as I could, I would turn around, return home and work from there.

Helen snottily responded with, 'The Middle Managers meeting was actually at 10.30 this morning. I don't know why you would think it was at 2.00pm.'

I couldn't believe it. She was starting with me again.

'Oh,' I said temperately, 'I must have written it down incorrectly. It's in my diary for 2.00pm.'

Again, not wishing to get into an argument, I reiterated that all the traffic was headed the same way and that there was a roundabout up ahead. It made sense for me to turn around as soon as I could, as the opposite carriageway was virtually empty.

I ended the call. 'Was it me?' I wondered. Was I reading too much into this or did Helen seem bent on arguing and showing how irritated she was with me? What had I done to upset her? Why did she feel she could talk to me in that way? Maybe she couldn't see it. May be I saw too much. It was becoming more and more difficult to make sense of everything. I felt I was losing my grasp of reality. Was I seeing antagonism where there was none? I couldn't tell anymore. From the moment Sue asked me if I was accusing her of racism, everything changed for me. I couldn't trust her or anyone she had influence over.

I finally got home around 4.10pm. Normally a round trip to Northampton would take twenty-five minutes and this had taken four hours, though it was worth it because I knew that if I hadn't even tried to get into Newbold, Sue would have disciplined me for working from home unnecessarily.

A few days later, I took Mum to the Warfarin clinic at Isebrook hospital. Afterwards, whilst on my way in to Newbold, I received a call from Katrina in the admin department. She called to check where I was. According to my calendar, I was due in at Newbold and I hadn't arrived yet. I explained I had taken my mother to the clinic and was on my way in.

I was annoyed by the call. I especially resisted outlining what I was doing in any more detail than what was on my electronic calendar to the admin team; I was senior to them in rank and at no time since joining the college had I been told I had to account for my whereabouts to them. I felt horribly demeaned by the call. I felt sure this was something Sue asked them to do. I couldn't imagine the admin team ringing each advisor every time they were due into their base office, to check if they were there yet.

I had worked over the weekend on a Performance and Competency Assessment project for HQ and didn't feel it inappropriate to start later in the day, as long as I did my hours. I certainly didn't expect that I would have to outline every waking moment to the admin team. I could almost tangibly feel Sue watching my every move through them. They had become her extended eyes and ears. She could reach me anywhere. They were empowered to challenge me and ask me where I was and what I was doing. When was this going to end? Since raising my grievance in November, things were noticeably worse for me. Yet this boldness to check on my whereabouts by the admin team was a new development and particularly worrying. Interestingly enough, no one ever checked how long I worked at home in the evenings or at the weekends.

I arrived in the office by 10.30am. When I got in, there was a letter on my desk from Stacey. I was stressed and a little apprehensive. I needed some good news, please. I pleaded in my heart. I began to read. Stacey had quashed the need to move my base. In response to my request for training, Stacey reiterated that there were enough trained advisors and there was no more money for further MBTI training. And even if there was, it would be spent on extending the LMD portfolio with other tools. In short—it was another rejection. These rejections now seemed routine. I felt powerless to change anything. Nothing I had done to date had posed any challenge to Sue or Stacey. They were the ones with the power and they had no issue showing me who was in charge.

On 21st December, I sent an email to Helen with an attachment that detailed the responses from the Heads of Learning and Skills (HoLS). The HoLS had confirmed the development already received and outlined their outstanding training needs. I put a report together and forwarded that to Helen. Although I knew I was no longer involved in the project, I had committed to do the work, so I continued collating the responses from the HoLS and any other useful information for the contractor to use. Helen responded by email and said the contract had been awarded and the consultants were about to start work on the programme. It was very difficult for me to think I wasn't being toyed with because of the grievance I raised.

I worked towards the end of the month very much looking forward to having a good Christmas holiday. The break would give me time to think. I was increasingly uncertain about whether I should continue working for the Service. Since I wasn't sure if I had the strength to return after the Christmas break, I took all of my personal belongings home. My rationale was that if I decided not to come back, I didn't want the added embarrassment of having to call in to collect my things. The office hadn't felt like 'my office' for a long time anyway and often when I came in, things like my stapler or pens were missing. On a few occasions people actually helped themselves to the snacks I left in the drawers and this was even though the office was locked after each use. Even more bizarrely, there was a turquoise two-seater settee in the office when I arrived in May and then one day, it just vanished without a word from anyone. I did not feel valued. I saw little point in staying in an organisation that didn't want what I had to offer. I deserved better. To leave would mean I didn't achieve the goals I set when I joined the Service. They still mattered but I was tired of feeling like I didn't belong. I was outgunned. I had been in the Service for just over two years trying to inject my enthusiasm, culture, experience and intelligence into an ailing system. But this organisation didn't want to get better. It was rejecting me like a transplanted organ.

I had an assignment due for the Masters degree that I was doing in Training and Performance Management that I would have to work on over Christmas. I took annual leave instead of study leave to work on it. Even though I was entitled to study leave, I didn't have the confidence or courage to ask Sue for it. I couldn't bear the thought of her having any more power over me. It had become too much for me and it was clear I wasn't going to get equal and fair treatment. This was truly breaking me.

I became ill over Christmas. I spent most of the time in bed because my back gave way to painful spasms and I could hardly move because of the pain. Rudy and I discussed the financial impact of my leaving the Service. He said that we would find a way to manage and that he would support me whatever I decided. I knew he would. I thought long and hard about going back to work and prayed. During one of my quiet times God spoke to me. I heard his words as clear as if it were Rudy in the room with me, 'This is bigger than you.' And with those five words I knew I had to go back. I knew that God wanted me to stop thinking about myself and what I thought I deserved. With those words, I knew the Service had done this before and gotten away with it. They had picked at, niggled and worn down individuals before me. And if someone didn't make a stand–they would do it to someone else. I would have to go back and wait for the right moment to act. Everything in me wanted to run in the opposite direction. But I believed God had spoken to my spirit.

There were financial implications to leaving the Service. Things would have become very difficult especially as I had my mother to look after. We would have managed though, if God had said to leave the Service. But he didn't. I knew I had to stay. I knew I had to wait and when the moment came to act–I would know.

Chapter Five

New Year–Old Fear

Despite being in a lot of pain, I completed the assignment due for my Masters Degree to time and I was very pleased. Although doing my Masters was very taxing, it challenged me in a deeply positive way. I was learning a tremendous amount. I was excited and nervous about my grades all at the same time and I was being critiqued in a constructive way on each assignment. It was healthy and it reminded me unequivocally that I was capable, and that was not a message I was hearing back at work. In fact, when I looked back over my educational journey, it was not a message I had heard often. I never realised until much later in life that I had been abused by the school system, and neither did my Mum. She expected the school to educate me and never had any reason to think that they wouldn't. What she didn't know was that assumptions were made about my abilities and I was treated in line with those assumptions to my detriment. I was considered slow and lazy when in fact I was smart and bored. And due to my upbringing, I neither challenged nor complained about it because I had been taught that such behaviour was wrong and brought with it dire consequences. One never corrected an adult or directed them in any way. At home, we were taught to obey even when we didn't agree or thought something was unfair. We were taught to keep quiet. Consequently, when I was nine years old at junior school, it was assumed that I was a slow learner needing remedial English lessons. I said nothing to the teachers who explained this to me, and Mum was never informed by the school. Every Thursday afternoon, I would be asked to join the remedial learners in the main hall, while the rest of my classmates would enjoy musical education and a sing-a-long on the radio. I remember hearing my class singing in the distance. The melody and lyrics for *Yellow Bird* sung one line at a time as they followed the voice on the radio, still brings back a sense of being abandoned and excluded. With it comes the memory of how I sat, for what felt like hours, reading books about *Miffy* and *Harry the*

Dirty Dog. I of course read them within minutes of taking my seat because they were so easy and spent the rest of the afternoon daydreaming. I was eventually saved by a substitute teacher who actually asked me to read *to* her. When I did this with the usual books I was given each week and then did the same with the hardest books that she had in her selection, I was *formally* assessed. I remember being told at nine years old that I had a reading age of around twelve to thirteen years old, by which time I had wasted a full term as my teachers thought I was too slow to bother with.

Secondary school was not much better, as I was left to vegetate at the bottom of the top stream for all five years of my secondary education. And poor me–I didn't realise that I was doing myself a disservice by not actually wanting to do any real work. I enjoyed coasting along without a care in the world. At the start I was 11 years old; no one had ever sat me down and said you can be anything you want if you work hard enough for it. And I had never seen a black professional. I lived in my daydreams and never thought about what life was about and the things I might need to commit myself to in order to get what I wanted. Apart from my drama tutor and, latterly, my dance tutor who didn't arrive in my life until I was fourteen, no one took any interest in me. I was allowed to fail at everything remotely cerebral or deductive. My teachers happily mistook creative thinking and a deeply reflective nature for disinterest. It was more convenient to dismiss me as unwilling or unable. It was less work. No one thought to review my file either to suggest that, if I was consistently at the bottom of the A1 stream (which I was), perhaps I might achieve more at the top of the next stream down, the A2 or B1 stream. Or, dare I say it, maybe I should stay in the A1 stream with more investment. As the years rolled on, I stayed at the bottom of the A1 stream without intervention. I was happy not to be pressured at school because there was enough pressure at home. Besides, I was a great pupil–I never caused a fuss. In six years, I never got a detention. I loved drama and dance and, as I got older, I became more and more involved in school productions. I loved acting and I was good at it. My drama teacher said that I had the ability to tap into difficult emotions at the drop of a hat. In an instant, I was where others would need further explanation and encouragement to go. She described me as a little 'off-centre, with a capacity to see patterns, make connections, and draw obscurities and the unexpected together'. I was a rare talent. Of course, I didn't truly understand what she meant (until now). But I never forgot her words, for she spoke well of me. What mattered was that she was sowing positive seeds into fertile ground that would one day spring up into trees of confidence and self-efficacy. For each play or dance performance, I would secure letters of excusal from the classes I should have been attending. I would be excused from maths class, history, geography, French, biology and science. I would always be released without hesitation. Not once did any of the teachers refuse to excuse me, because I had fallen behind in my studies. Between the critical ages of 13 to 15 years old I didn't do any quality work, unless it was on the stage. No one managed my education and I was far too busy having fun and taking it easy to notice that I was falling into the under-achievement trap. I was not meant to achieve and that's why my education was so bad. I went to a school where nothing great was expected of me. Once exam time came around I was hugely unprepared, to the extent that the English teacher (who was a very tall, broad, stern and completely bald, Mr Rowley) told me that I wouldn't pass my CSE-level English exams, even if the answers were written on the back of a cornflakes box on exam day! Well, I did pass it and now I was doing my Masters, albeit in my forties and under tremendous pressure.

My life has always seemed to be blighted somehow in the work of progression. I have invariably ended up where I intended to be, yet it is as if everyone else was taking the elevator whilst I was taking the stairs. I arrive at my desired floor hot, sweaty and oxygen-starved, to find the cool, calm and collected takers of the elevator way ahead of me. I often wonder where I would be in life had I had the investment I was due–not special treatment or classes, just notice, involvement and recognition of potential. What would life be like for me now had my aptitude for languages, maths and music been properly encouraged?

As the New Year rang in, I remained apprehensive about my future in the Service. Nothing had been resolved since I had raised my grievance in November. It was a terrible burden weighing down on me yet I could see no other choice than to persevere. Having spent much time in prayer, I decided to wait on God for more answers. He would direct me and, until that time, I was not going to take any more action. I was not going to rock the boat or make waves; I was just going to work hard and wait.

I was due back to Newbold on 12th January, but as I hadn't been able to drive since Christmas, I decided to ask Val if I could work from home for the next couple of days. Although I felt much better, I thought some more time away from the car would do me good. When I called, I explained this and outlined which projects I planned to work on whilst catching up with email and so on. Having been out of circulation since December, I felt sure there would be plenty to keep me occupied. She agreed.

Although I had a full-day's leave left, I decided to try and make some headway with the backlog of emails. I logged on to my laptop and opened an email from Helen in admin advising us of the new tools that would be used in the assessment centres that were being set up for the senior operational managers (SOMs). She detailed that the Hogan Development Survey was the tool that the design team and the external consultants had decided to use. She also outlined arrangements for us to receive training on the new tool so we could support the consultants during delivery in the SOM development centres. Yea! I thought, I'm going to get some new training. That was good news. I read on.

Helen went on to convey that any advisor who was not already psychometric Level A and B qualified *could not* do the training or even facilitate at the assessment centres. 'Unbelievable!' I said aloud. I had battled with Sue to get some psychometric training under my belt for months and now, because I didn't have a licence to practise MBTI or any other occupational psychometric tool, I would be excluded from the most recent national initiative. I wondered how this could be justified. I understood Stacey's point about wanting to invest in new tools for LMD, yet how could she deny me training that was the lynchpin to the new tools they wanted to invest in? At this rate, I considered that I would never be brought up to the same standard as my peers. I started to imagine the future possibility of LMD investing in another tool further down the line and offering development that was again contingent on having pre-existing skills or licences I didn't have. I could see myself falling farther and farther behind in terms of my development, whilst constantly being criticised for not delivering service to the required standards. It was hopeless. I had come back to work in the New Year, having drawn a line in the sand, and decided to just do my job to the best of my ability. Within hours of resuming my work, I was being excluded again.

On the first official day back at work, Val rang back to say that Sue recommended that I consider taking the time off 'sick', as I had been ill over most of Christmas. I declined, saying that, even though I was ill over Christmas, I accomplished the work I took annual leave to do, and was officially back at work. My real fear, however, was that Sue would use my taking time off sick as evidence of poor performance or letting the team down or something; she was working so hard to discredit me and devalue my efforts and I couldn't afford to give her anything she could use against me. It was then I decided to keep timesheets just in case I needed to prove I was doing my hours. I felt I needed the extra security.

The following day, I opened an email calling for an emergency team meeting in London on 17th January. It sounded serious. Val called later to make sure I had read the email. When I asked her what the urgency was, she said they were in the throws of making some decisions about our roles, but somehow word had got out and people were talking without full knowledge of what was really happening. She explained the meeting was being called to quell the 'rumourville'.

On 17th January, I was the first to arrive at Abell House in London. I made my way to the meeting room, which was quite small. I wondered how all of us would fit in and noted there were not enough chairs. The building was unfamiliar to me, so I didn't try to find additional furniture. In any case, I had no way of knowing how many members of the team would attend the meeting at such short notice. Maybe there were enough chairs.

As I sat and waited, I pondered on how it would be the first time anyone had seen me since before Christmas. At almost a month, it was the longest period I had been away from the team and all the madness.

Sue arrived next. The door was open so she came in the room. Remembering my commitment to do well in the face of discomfort, I said a hearty, 'Good morning, Sue.' She mumbled something under her breath whilst looking around and, without acknowledging me in any way, walked out of the room and stood outside the open door. She stayed there until a few other team members arrived and then she said something about needing more chairs. The voices disappeared for a few moments and then re-emerged as members of the team came in with extra chairs and plenty of conversation. I felt incredibly small and really hurt. It was as if Sue couldn't even bear to look at me, let alone speak. I could have gotten the chairs with her, if she had told me where to go. I couldn't understand why she despised me so much. Everyone who came in acknowledged me and asked how my Christmas was. I smiled and responded appropriately, even though inside I was dying. I wondered how much they knew about my situation and if Sue had told any more lies in my absence.

During the meeting, we were told that our jobs were about to be absorbed into the organisational restructure, but there were no definitive answers as yet. There was going to be a conference on 2nd February to explain everything in more detail. After the meeting, Val asked to speak to me in the corridor. I instantly knew what she wanted to talk about. The conference in question was on the same day as the mediation meeting with Sue. Val suggested she go to the conference in my place. However, I responded that I felt a proper, first-hand explanation as to what was going to happen to my role was more important. I said I had little faith in mediation in such a complex case and perhaps it was better to cancel it all together. Then, still hurt from the morning, I started to ramble and told her that I hadn't seen Sue for weeks and that she couldn't even bring herself to say 'Good morning' to me in response to my greeting, much less allow mediation to resolve anything. I maintained I was a member of the team and not a stranger in the street and if Sue couldn't manage a simple 'Good morning' when I was taking the lead to re-open dialogue, then what was the point of mediation?

Val didn't comment on Sue's behaviour. Instead, she agreed for me to go to the conference and recommended that I rescheduled the mediation.

The week played out as normal. I had to keep reminding myself that, even though nothing had changed, *I* had changed: I was going to walk the extra mile. It was Thursday 20th January, nearly the end of the week. I could make it to Friday without incident, I told myself. All I had to do was take it one day at a time. And this particular day I was to work with Sue, who was going to be giving the MBTI feedback at HMP Glen Parva. We hadn't worked together since my induction and we hadn't had any real interaction since the performance review in October. Though apprehensive, I was convinced I could do this. All I had to do was observe Sue in action and take notes on which to build delegate performance discussions. I could do that, I convinced myself; I could be *invisible*.

As I drove to Leicester, I considered that the scheduled feedback was to be the first MBTI session delivered since I had been requested to do this last September. It had all taken such a long time to organise and had caused me considerable embarrassment, yet now at least the sessions were underway. Having already gained permission from the delegates, I thought it would be good to record some of the observations given by Sue and use them as a platform for further discussions in the follow-up sessions, as originally suggested by Governor Edwards. I figured that most of the delegates wouldn't remember many of the observations made during their feedback, so if I recorded them it would be a firmer starting point to discussions about behaviours and preferences. In addition, I couldn't be sure what printed information would be given to the delegates to remind them of their 'type'.

When I attended the MBTI session last September for the non-operational managers, we were given our MBTI types as a group. This led to various group discussions and exercises, all of which helped consolidate our understanding. We were also given an MBTI booklet with all the types explained in relation to strengths and areas for growth. This was done over a period of two days; however, Sue's individual sessions with delegates were only going to last for an hour. The chances that the delegates would remember enough to form the basis for further discussion were slim, in relation to how people learn. It is accepted among training professionals that we only remember 10% of what we hear, and 10% of an hour's discussion is a capacity to recall six minutes of content. My plan was to record the delegates' reactions to the disclosure of their 'MBTI type': to record if they accepted or disagreed with some of the outcomes, if they had already seen certain things about themselves or if the information was deeply revealing, and so on. I was excited about using the outputs from the sessions, along with the assessments of each individual as provided by Governor Edwards and Fran, the Head of Personnel, to form both challenging and enlightening one-to-ones.

I arrived before Sue and met Mark, the delegate, for the first time. He was a little confused as to who would be doing the feedback and felt the organising of the project was mystifying. Of course, he was right. I attempted to explain without sounding as if I was making excuses that I wasn't a licensed practitioner for MBTI. This meant I had to rely on the availability of others. I assured him the confusion was over and we were well on our way to rolling-out the agreed personal development programme. I checked with him again if it was all right for me to sit in the session and observe the feedback. I reminded him I would use the outputs from the session with Sue to form the basis of the one-to-one sessions I would later have with him. I asked if we could firm up the first follow-up session after the feedback with Sue; he agreed and then showed me into the meeting room we would use.

He left the office for a short while because he needed to see someone quickly. Within minutes of him leaving, Sue arrived. I said, 'Good morning', to which there was no reply—she just looked round the office and asked, 'Is Mark about?'

'He said he needed to nip out for a moment,' I explained. 'He knows the session starts at 9. I'm sure he'll be back on time.'

I pointed to the room we were going to use. 'He said we could use this room. There's a rack to put your coat on.' I led the way.

We went into the room. She did a quick scan of the layout and said with a superior air, 'I don't understand, Olivea. What are *you* doing here?'

I was a little taken aback and not only by her tone; I knew she knew I was coming because I had copied her and her secretary into the emails I sent confirming that I would be observing the sessions. In fact, that's why Mark was confused as to who was actually going to do the feedback, me or Sue. I had been clear about my intention to observe the session from the outset.

'Um,' I said. For a moment, I couldn't think of the right words to say. In my head I heard, 'Just tell her what you said in the emails.'

I tried again. 'I was hoping to observe you delivering the feedback. I figured my clients were likely to forget most of the content of the discussions by our next appointment and that would be counterproductive, since I'm supposed to use the feedback as a basis for further meetings.'

Sue was staring at me.

I continued to justify my presence. 'I find…that normally clients either don't take enough notes or they don't make any notes at all during one-to-one sessions.'

'Well that's not going to work, because you being in the room is a breach of the psychometric confidentiality protocols,' she announced.

That can't be right, I thought. Last September I got my MBTI type in a room with 14 other people in it and 'types' were shared and discussed openly. Although confused, I continued to make my case. 'I was planning to use the outputs from your feedback anyway as a basis for the follow-up discussions with the clients. This is what Governor Edwards wanted. I think this is a good way of ensuring I make the best use of the feedback you give, first-hand. Also I've already gained the permission of the clients and we've individually agreed how the information will be used. This was something Val recommended. She even gave me a template letter to follow to secure client agreement.'

Sue simply repeated herself, 'I don't understand Olivea, you're *not* supposed to be here.' Her words were laboured and deliberate.

My head was buzzing with questions like, if she knew that I shouldn't be here then why had she not responded to the emails that I sent confirming I intended to attend? I had sent the last one a couple of days before. She could have mentioned it at the emergency team meeting earlier in the week. We were going around in circles and someone needed to back down. I knew, once again, that that person would have to be me.

'Okay, what would you like me to do?' I asked politely.

'Well, you can't listen in,' she said coldly and sternly.

Sue stubbornly stood in front of me and continued to stare right at me. I stared back! I rapidly went through a montage of mental states steeped in emotion: confusion, intimidation, flashes of anger, calm, reason, rage. As my eyes fixed upon her intransigent smugness, I wanted to fold my fist like the character Sofie from *The Color Purple* and beat her down! Who does she think she's talking to! Oh it's *on* now–she's going to know that she's messing with the wrong person! In a microsecond, I was 10 years old again. Mum would send me to the corner shop and, as soon as I left the house, a little white boy who lived down the road (between our house and the corner shop) would be at his door chanting at me on the way to the shop and on the way home, 'Nigger, nigger, blackie, paki; nigger, nigger, blackie, paki.' It didn't matter which route I took, down the back ally to the shop and then up the street to the house, he would wait at his front gate and then at his back gate until he saw me emerge, then on and on he would chant. If I turned round as if to make after him, he would run inside his house. But one day, one day he was brave enough to taunt me a few steps too far from his house and didn't get back to his back gate quickly enough. I showed him! I fought like a street kid; I fought like a boy. He never called me names again. He would still watch me–from *inside* his house from his window, behind closed gates and locked doors–but never another word. I can see to it that Sue never shows such disrespect to me to my face again! I revelled in the prospect.

Olivea Ebanks! I rebuked myself. What are you doing? What are you thinking? Is this really the way to go? She's goading you, can't you see that? Is this God's love? Is this his wisdom or his way? The realisation that I was neither loving nor wise brought with it shame, that covered every conflicting emotion; then remorse, for failing and pity that I ever thought myself good or kind. What's happening to me?

As the shame overwhelmed me, I lowered my eyes in defeat and asked again, with all the respect and politeness I could muster, 'What would you like me to do?'

'Well, you'll have to go back to Newbold. You can't stay here, Olivea.' My name seemed to curdle in her mouth.

'Sure–no problem,' I said, smiling and nodding.

And, like a plate of hot food knocked to the floor no good to anyone, I gathered what little dirty dignity I had left along with my bags and my coat and made a dead-man-walking exit out of the still-open door. By this time, Mark had arrived back in the main office. He looked at me with my coat and bags in my hand.

'I'm sorry,' I said whilst making my way to leave the building, 'Sue's in the meeting room, but I've got to shoot off to Newbold straightaway. I'm… I'm sorry.'

He looked a little puzzled and said 'Oh…okay.'

I rushed out of the main office door. I didn't want to give him enough time to formulate any questions. I needed to avoid any further humiliation.

It was still rush hour so it took me about an hour to get to Rugby. All I could see for the whole journey was the way Sue looked at me; like she was in a room with an overrunning, smelly, dirty toilet! She spoke to me with such disdain and, apart from a flicker of retaliation, I smiled and nodded like an imbecile. Sue was goading me to respond in a way that she could later say was aggressive or unreasonable, and I very nearly did. The tears ran down my face and I didn't have any tissues. I could barely see the road and I didn't care. I was upset because I didn't like being hated.

All the confusion and embarrassment surrounding this project could have been so easily avoided had I been trained in MBTI. I was now faced with the problem of building five or six personal development sessions per client on the back of feedback meetings that I was not privy to. I would have to rely totally on each client to remember their MBTI type, respective traits and responses to the information. Organising these personal development sessions had caused me so many problems: arranging and rearranging appointments, apologies for causing inconvenience or not responding to clients in the way they expected. I had never been so ill-equipped to do my job and it was all because Sue had issues with me.

On 23rd January, I forwarded details and the client profiles I had put together for the staff at HMP Glen Parva to Di. She had given me another date to deliver the MBTI feedback alongside Sue. I expressed my gratitude for her help in the covering email. I didn't bother with a request to sit in on her sessions after my encounter with Sue. I'm not sure whether or not she would have said the same thing in relation to the protocols; however, I felt sure that making the request would get back to Sue. So I had to find another way to build on the individual feedback given to the clients.

My 'one day at a time sweet Jesus' strategy didn't seem to be working very well. I had only been back for a couple of weeks and there was a negative encounter each week. My motivation was already waning and I couldn't think what to do to spur myself on.

We had our LMD team meeting on 26th January and, true to form, it was another whinging session. This time, most of the complaints were in relation to the lack of clarity surrounding our roles. I suppose, under normal circumstances, I might have had the same concerns, except that for me the changes represented an opportunity to get away from Sue and the college.

During the break, Val Woodcock approached me saying that she needed to 'have a word'. She proposed we met during the lunch break. Even without any further information, I knew deep down that I was about to get a telling-off for something. At lunch, after we had all had some sandwiches, I went over to her to ask if it was a good time to have this talk. She said she had decided what she needed to discuss with me, would take more time than the 45-minute lunch break would allow, so we would have to meet after the team meeting. This naturally made me even more stressed. And she again gave no indication as to what the meeting was going to be about, which meant I couldn't even mentally prepare for it.

We met up in my office around 4.30pm. It had been a long day and having to wait for this meeting left me anxious. As we sat, there was no conversation. This just made me more uncomfortable. My eyes darted around the room as I waited for Val to arrange some papers. She produced a printout of my electronic calendar from December to end of February. She angled it on the desk so that I could read it. As I looked at the printout, Val proceeded to tell me that there were too many entries for Newbold, including entries from last year. And February (this year) was looking a little light in terms of appointments. I was terribly uneasy.

'If you recall,' I was treading very carefully, 'in December I explained what was happening with regards to the gaps that were in my diary in an email I sent you as part of my monthly report. I was very careful to point out that Peter, the training manager at HMP Sudbury, who had asked me block book dates to train his middle managers, had formed the gaps, when he failed to confirm the dates. I had to take them out of the calendar. That's what created the gaps.'

I continued to elucidate. 'Also, I have been off for nearly a month, and although I returned back to work on the 12th you know that I've been in the field, so it's difficult to both make and firm-up appointments. When did you print off this copy of my diary?'

I reached out and looked at the date on the bottom right hand corner of the printout. It was one-and-a-half weeks old. Val had printed my diary before I had even spent a single day in the office! I turned to face my computer, and opened up my electronic diary and showed it to her.

'If you had checked my diary today, you would have seen that it is better populated since receiving confirmation from my clients.'

She peered over my shoulder as I tabbed across the diary screen to show her January, February and March appointments.

'Yes, I can see that now,' she said, as it barely registered that she was wrong to be challenging me over out-of-date information.

I went on to explain that I tended to populate the calendar with confirmed dates, except for block bookings, which is why, when she printed off my calendar from the previous week and a half ago, there were some gaps.

'Well I can see that the current updated calendar is less of a cause for concern, but there does seem to be an unusually high number of days spent here at Newbold.'

'I've got a couple of complex programmes to design as part of a series for HMP Morton Hall, I've got some feedbacks to do that I need to familiarise myself with and J-SAC DVDs to review.'

I started to pull up my electronic task list that I used whenever I was at Newbold. I was instantly grateful that I was disciplined enough to make regular entries. I asked her if she wanted to see it.

'No, that won't be necessary,' she replied.

Why didn't she want to see it? I thought. It was beginning to seem like a pattern was emerging in that, each time Sue and now Val made an accusation, I would provide evidence to substantiate myself, and they would either ignore it or refuse to look at it. I started to wonder what was really happening here. Were they expecting that maybe, just once, I might not be able to provide evidence for my work or was this all in my head? Had I completely succumbed to paranoia?

'I understand that you've got things to work on,' she continued, 'but your role is a consultative one. You should be in the field more. You should be working towards a rule of one day at Newbold and four days in the field.'

'No one has ever told me this before,' I objected. 'Plus, I don't see this rule reflected on the movement sheets of the other advisors. And how am I supposed to have dedicated facility time to design programmes if I can only come into Newbold one day per week, bearing in mind that I'm not allowed to work remotely from home?'

I found her suggestion to remedy my plight quite asinine. 'Perhaps you don't need to do quite so much bespoke design and could recycle more.'

'You mean I shouldn't be giving an individual design response to the individual prisons?' I needed to get this right in my head.

'You don't have to design a completely new package every time you have to deliver a programme on, say, team building,' she offered.

'I think it's worth considering,' I countered, 'that it is because I spend quality time designing to meet the individually expressed needs, that I am getting such good results from my client base.'

'Yes,' she said, 'but there has to be a balance with the consultancy aspects of your role.'

'But isn't the purpose of consultancy to generate the design work I'm doing now? What's the point of consultancy, if it isn't to inform design and delivery? And isn't the level of design work and booked training a testament to the levels of consultancy that I've been doing. I mean, doesn't it confirm that I'm already doing the right level of consultancy because I've got all of this design work to do? And, as you've already seen, I've got dates booked up to March for consultancy and the delivery dates for the courses I'm now designing will take me up to August for fieldwork.'

'Yes, I understand that. But you still need to be in the field more.'

I have no idea why I was trying to get a rational response. She was clearly following orders.

'Fine,' I said, 'it's important to me that the quality I offer my clients doesn't diminish so I'll follow your quota of one day in and four days out and find my own way around the problem.'

It seemed pointless to have a debate about finding the best way to deliver quality work as that evidently was not the issue. The issue was for me to do as I was told. As I sat there, I was disappointed with Val. My early encounters with her had showed her to be a rational and independent thinker. Yet, since taking over line management of me, she had dealt with me in a way that suggested she had lost the capacity to think freely and to reason objectively. I felt that her dealings with me were careless. She had become cold and accusing without once explaining how we would work together. We had met twice, and both times she had immediately launched straight into whatever problems she felt I was causing. Val concluded that part of the discussion by telling me that this was the last time I would get an informal warning about my calendar. I sat defeated and speechless.

As if I had not been rebuked or belittled enough, Val then asked me if I was still letting the admin team know when I was on site at Newbold.

'Yes,' I answered politely while my insides tied itself in knots. I very much resented the question, as it made me feel like someone who couldn't be trusted and it reiterated how one-sided everything was. Whenever I was in Newbold, I spent most of my time alone downstairs. Although Sue's office was also on the ground floor, she was rarely in it and seemed to spend most of her time with Helen and the admin team. None of them seemed to notice that, after making my presence known, having a quick chat about the weekend or some other incidental, I would go back downstairs to work alone, as if banished. None of them came to see me, ask if I wanted a coffee or invited me to lunch and it had been like that since my arrival. Yet here I was again with the suggestion that I was the unsociable one, the distant one. I wasn't sure how much more of this I could take. I had been back at work for approximately ten days and in that time my resolve to keep my head down and work without getting into trouble had been ground to dust.

Val summarised our meeting in an email at the end of the day. When I read it, I noted that she stated I agreed that my diary was light in terms of outputs for November to January. It was my recollection that I agreed that, in December, I didn't have as many appointments as normal due to a number of factors and I had been at Newbold and could provide evidence of my work. I thought about responding to correct her, then, I remembered my commitment to just get on with my job and to not make waves.

On 7th February, I was at Newbold doing my admin. I sent an email to thank Di for her support in helping to deliver the MBTI feedbacks in response to an email she had sent on 25th January. She said that she had enjoyed herself and that the feedback was received well. I hadn't had much opportunity to respond earlier due to a combination of concentrating on programme design, annual leave and being in the field. It was something I had meant to do for days. Although sure she wasn't waiting for formal thanks, I was grateful that the project was now under way and I wanted her to know that.

The next day I was out in the field for the entire day and therefore had to deal with emails in the evening. When I logged on, I opened an email saying that the mediation between Sue and me would now take place on 16th and 17th March. I told myself, 'Not long now, hold on, it will all be over soon.' It was only February and I was already fatigued. I had immediately started working to the new rule of one day in and four days out, which meant I was working at home in the evenings and some weekends in order to design. Though the end was in sight, we had a date for the mediation, and maybe I'd be able to talk freely about what I felt was unfair treatment.

The following week brought with it more paranoia and uneasiness. During our LMD team meeting on 14th February, we were taking turns to outline our commitments for the next month. When it was my turn, I firstly made sure I publicly thanked Sue and Di for doing the MBTI feedbacks in my area. Even though they had not completely finished, it made sense to use the meeting as a platform to register my gratitude. Then I went on to talk about what I had planned for my area.

When it was Di's turn to outline her plans for the month, she said, 'As you all know, next month I'll be in Barbados with Sue.'

Everyone responded with knowing smiles, nods, and chorused, 'Yes we know you're going to Barbados.' I, on the other hand, couldn't understand how everyone knew except me. As usual, questions were racing through my mind like: how is it that this is the first time the trip was being discussed openly? I wondered who had applied to go and who did the selection. It was becoming increasingly difficult to ignore the fact that I was being systematically excluded from anything that would develop me. I didn't know what to do. Once again, I decided to leave it alone. I reminded myself that the mediation was just around the corner.

I had my one-to-one with Val the following day and I was grateful she couldn't fault my work, because I used the opportunity to forward the client feedback that I was getting so that she could read them before our meeting. I wanted to make sure she had much more than Sue's opinions about my capabilities. The feedbacks varied from simple gratitude for a job well done to high and detailed praise about the impact on the learners. During the meeting, Val commented on how positive the client feedback was. I felt good that, for the first time since she took over management of me, a meeting had started on a constructive note. Yet what I considered a positive start deteriorated into familiar signs of harassment in mere moments. As Val put the feedbacks on the table and pushed them to one side, she said, 'Are you still going upstairs when you arrive to say good morning?'

I was incredulous as to the speed with which we moved from praise to what I anticipated was about to become criticism.

I said 'Yes,' tentatively.

She continued. 'Some of the staff are hurt that you don't spend time with them.'

I felt as if I was on an emotional rollercoaster, as I went from praised to despondent. I took a deep breath and said very carefully, '*Hurt?* I find it difficult to believe they would be conveying such strong emotions as hurt over my popping upstairs to say good morning and spending time with them. I have to be honest with you Val, I don't understand why this is such a big issue to the extent that we have to keep revisiting it. I have said repeatedly I *do* go upstairs and I *do* say good morning.'

As I waited for her to respond, I tried to make sense of everything in my head, my safe place. It's not as if I ignored the admin staff when they spoke to me, I reasoned. If I did then that would make more sense. I'm not rude to anybody. They sit upstairs in an open-planned office and have each other for company. And I have to sit downstairs on my own. Yet I'm expected to go upstairs on arrival, engage everyone and then come back downstairs to work alone and, even though I do this, everybody's still upset with me?

Val offered an explanation. 'Maybe this will help,' she began. 'When I was a manager working for a different company, I used to just come in and get on with my work and that practice generated some very revealing feedback about my management style. Sometimes staff just need you to engage with them about weekends and soap operas.'

'I understand about manager and subordinate dynamics, but I am not the manager for the admin team. I don't give them instructions per se, I don't do their appraisals, and therefore, I shouldn't need to build a relationship with them that is more complex than the one I already have. I already make small talk and I already engage with them.'

Unconvinced she continued to educate me. 'The team perceive you to be...' she said, searching for the appropriate words, 'detached and distant; you're a bit of an enigma. Perhaps you just need to work on your water-cooler skills.'

I sat deadly still as the helplessness deepened. Not once, since raising my grievance, had there been a consideration from her, as my manager that *I* might be the one who needed some TLC (Tender Love and Care), that *I* might be the one who was hurt. There had only ever been the impact I was having on others, the things I was not doing well enough and the problems I was causing. It was clear that she wasn't going to let this go, so I said I would take her words under consideration so that we could move on. I wanted so badly for the meeting to end, but it wasn't over yet.

'How well do you feel you get on with the LMD team as a whole?' she asked.

'Why do you ask?' I replied wearily.

'Well, Di has complained that you haven't said thank you for the MBTI work she has done in your area.'

Whilst I sat completely shell-shocked, Val continued by extolling the virtues of teamwork and patronised me by saying that both Di and Sue had taken valuable time out of their busy schedules to help me. 'I mean, it's not easy to leave Yorkshire and Humberside to come over to *your* area to do a piece of work for you. Di had to leave her own area commitments to help you,' she laboured.

I felt like throwing my hands up in the air and screaming, '*What do you want from me!*' Of course that's not what I did because she wouldn't have understood my response. Val was oblivious to the offence she was causing; she was ignorant of the smooth transition she had made in taking over from Sue to bully me. Sue passed the baton and Val was racing towards the finish line. She would have considered any exclamation uncalled for, unnecessary and maybe even aggressive—such was her focus to secure a win for her team.

Instead of screaming, I reminded Val that I had thanked both Di and Sue for their help only yesterday in the team meeting in front of everyone, including her. I also told her I had thanked Di by email at the beginning of the month.

'Yes I know you did, but Di is upset that it took you two weeks to respond to *her* email.' I was back in my safe place and this time I was shouting. Incredible! I say 'thank you' by email when I get a chance; I say 'thank you' again publicly as soon as I see her and she's upset enough to complain to my manager. *And* my manager, in turn, thinks that there is enough merit in the complaint to bring it to my attention. What about the five months it's taken to deliver the MBTI profiles—a single day's work? Five months! And in that time I've been conveyed as assumptive and incompetent, sufficient for Sue not only to apologise in my stead, but actually to step in and do the work *for* me. I've been embarrassed and belittled, and now I'm being told off for being ungrateful for all the hard work and sacrifice of others. Nothing I did was good enough. How could I get everything so completely wrong all of the time? Maybe I was inept. How had I managed to win both national and various company in-house awards for competence? How had I managed to progress in my career to date, if I was consistently making the most fundamental mistakes? Never before had I managed to alienate groups of people and bring such displeasure of my managers on my head.

As I sat saying nothing, Val continued to look through my diary commitments and noticed that I had a meeting booked with REAG (Race and Equality Action Group). She asked me what it was about. I told her I had done some work and made a few proposals last year with regard to supporting BME staff in the organisation and REAG wanted to discuss them with me. Her response was, 'I didn't think that you'd be interested in that kind of thing.'

I was faced with a choice. I could either ask her what she meant by 'that sort of thing' or I could leave it alone. I left it alone, because I couldn't see anything good coming out of pursuing that particular line of questioning. I felt sure it was destined not to end well and any further engaging with her would mean that I would have to stay in the meeting that I was, by this time, climbing the walls to get out of.

Val, however, seemed fairly content with continuing down this route. 'LMD was invited to a Black and Minority Ethnic (BME) forum to outline what we as advisors could do for the group. We didn't include you, Olivea, because with you being the only black manager on the team it would be somewhat tokenistic.'

'Now I've heard it all!' I thought. I didn't respond, I couldn't respond because I was numb. Val continued, totally unaware that her comments were inappropriate, and explained that the forum was set up to discuss the concerns of BME staff in relation to lack of development and progression within the Service, with the intention of feeding outcomes into any evolving LMD training packages. She went on to say that the meeting turned out to be quite difficult, as there were questions she was not best placed to answer. Apparently, one individual stated that she was held back by a triple-glazed glass ceiling, in that she was black, female and assertive. She asked directly what the college was going to do to help people like her progress. Val said that not being able to provide solutions or answers was an uncomfortable experience and that she could perhaps had done with me being there.

When Sue mentioned this project last year, I thought as a black manager I would have useful insight to add or could simply benefit from being in a room with other black managers in the Service to bolster my own confidence. It seemed though that, having considered my involvement, Sue and Val thought otherwise and did not even ask me for my input.

As Val drew the meeting to a close, she said, 'Is there anything you want to talk about or anything you need help with…except of course anything to do with your grievance and your relationship with Sue. Sue and I agree that it's best that I don't get involved with any of that.'

Great, I thought. The one thing that is actually ruining my life I'm not allowed to talk to my manager about it.

I politely said, 'No, I have nothing further. Thank you.'

She stood up and said that she would send me a summary of the meeting. Then she left. As I sat in the seclusion of my office, I felt empty. 'Oh God,' I prayed, 'how long will you have me endure this? Can you not see my heart is breaking? I cannot endure this. They are killing me. Please Father–release me. I need to leave this place.' I reached for my Bible and in the privacy of my office read Isaiah 51 aloud:

> … *Listen to Me, you who know rightness and justice and right standing with God, the people in whose heart is My law and My instruction: fear not the reproach of men, neither be afraid nor dismayed at their revilings…*
>
> *I, even I, am He who comforts you. Who are you, that you should be afraid of man, who shall die, and of a son of man, who shall be made [as destructible] as grass, that you should forget the Lord your Maker, who stretched forth the heavens and laid the foundations of the earth, and fear continually every day because of the fury of the oppressor?…The captive exile and he who is bent down by chains shall speedily be released; and he shall not die and go down to the pit of destruction, nor shall his food fail.*
>
> *For I am the Lord your God, Who stirs up the sea so that its waves roar and who by rebuke restrains it… And I have put My words in your mouth and have covered you with the shadow of My hand…*

I meditated upon his words and through the course of the day, I felt hope and peace return to my mind and heart.

On 20th February, I travelled to London to meet with Richie at REAG. I was excited about being invited to discuss the proposals I had made in December regarding improved race relations in the Service. As I walked along the third floor of this maze-like eight-floored building, I was immediately struck by the high levels of ethnic diversity as I passed each office. I saw a balance of black, white and Asian. I even saw a man in traditional Muslim dress, with a small white hat and beard. This was something I hadn't seen since joining the Service. I walked along the corridors, awestruck. When I finally got to the REAG office, I stood at the door and asked for Richie. He stood up to greet me.

'Olivea?' he said, 'I'm Richie, come in. Can I take your coat?' Richie looked like a dark Asian or a Caribbean Indian, but I couldn't be sure of his ethnicity. I found out months later he had a mixed heritage. His father was an African American in the Air Force who he has never met and his mother was white English. Richie was about 5' 8" tall. His build was stocky and his hair although very short was sort of wavy black with flecks of grey—definitely not afro hair. Richie wore a salt and pepper beard. It suited him—yet beards were uncommon in the Service. Most men chose a clean-shaven look accompanied by a regimented short-back-and-sides. Richie's face, though kind, was heavily lined and maybe even a little weatherworn, but his smile was wide and warm. He was casually dressed in a polo shirt and trousers.

The atmosphere in the office seemed totally different from what I was used to. People were smiling as they looked up to acknowledge me, everything seemed lighter somehow. No doubt, it was all in my imagination, yet it felt good to imagine; it felt good to feel as if I wasn't being judged the minute I walked through the door.

We made our way to the meeting table in the open-planned office and Richie went through my document. In it I had posed questions and strategies about the complaints procedure and protection for victims, and developing staff to manage diversity and career development for Black and Minority Ethnic staff.

The meeting went well and Richie answered a lot of my questions about the complaints procedure and management of the complainant. Then he caught me off guard with his next question. 'What was the inspiration behind these proposals?'

I didn't quite know what to say. I had prepared for the meeting, and I came armed with suggestions for improvements and such. However, I hadn't for a moment contemplated an answer to this question. I didn't know this man. I couldn't just tell him my plight, yet there was no other possible answer to the question. The inspiration behind the proposal was purely due to the problems I was facing at the college. It was because I suspected that the treatment I had endured was racist and I needed to be sure that there were adequate systems in place to support me should things get worse after mediation.

Pensively I said, 'I didn't expect to be asked this question, the answer is…I wrote this proposal because I have serious doubts about how I am being treated at the college. It looks and feels like racism but I am loath to confirm it as such. It feels more blatant than anything I have experienced in my entire professional career and when I tried to look for help and resources, I kept running into dead ends. So I decided to highlight the areas that I felt needed attention and made proposals in a bid to help others like me in the future.'

'Right,' he said gently and then continued to listen for more.

Feeling somewhat encouraged, I said, 'I wanted to see if there was some work being done so that whilst people like me were experiencing discrimination, that somewhere in the Service positive changes were being made—changes sufficient to help those of us who were struggling. I was trying to find out how many people had made complaints about racism and if they had been handled fairly and sensitively. In other words, is it worth making a specific complaint or would I be signing my own death warrant? I needed assurance, I suppose…that after the hurt and the pain there is going to be a place for me in the Service and there's going to be…capacity for us all to learn and grow through the discomfort of a complaint being made and prejudice being exposed. Because if there isn't, then there is no point to enduring the difficulties.'

Richie was listening intently.

'When I put this proposal together in December it was because I didn't feel at that time that Newbold was taking my concerns seriously so I needed to see some indication that the Service as a whole would take me seriously if I pushed a little harder. Whilst searching I had hoped to find evidence that complaints were centrally recorded. I was looking for intelligent analysis of complaint types and levels of resolution and satisfaction actively used to inform policy and practice. On finding this, I would have been assured of the Service's commitment to eradicate racism. But I couldn't find this information, which brings me back to why I'm here.'

I knew I was rambling a little, but I hadn't prepared for this. In hindsight, I don't know why I didn't prepare for a question like that. In reality, how often does someone produce a detailed piece of unsolicited work, which challenges the way an institution is set up, with the expectation to simply deliver it and walk away without so much as a 'what prompted you to do this?' inquiry. Actually, all things considered, Richie's question made perfect sense and I should have been expecting it.

He was still listening. I was still talking.

Finally he spoke. 'Are you a member of the Black Manager's Forum?'

'I don't really know anything about it apart from its existence,' I replied.

He looked surprised. 'I'll be honest with you Olivea,' he said, 'but I hadn't thought about your ethnicity when I read the proposal. I noted your name and the fact that you worked for LMD. But when you walked through the door and I saw that you were black and a manager for LMD, I thought immediately: why weren't you at the most recent meeting that LMD were invited to?'

So I told him. I told him that I wasn't there because Val Woodcock had expressed the opinion that my presence might seem tokenistic.

Richie looked at me in sheer disbelief and said, 'Really?'

Having gained more confidence and trust since the conversation had changed direction, I proceeded to relay my one-to-one meeting with Val, which had taken place the previous week, in its entirety. Oh, it felt so good to talk to someone in the Service, someone who could give me some objectivity and context, someone who could say: 'Olivea, you're overreacting, you're paranoid, you're crazy!'

Thankfully, Richie said none of these things; he was genuinely surprised by my comments. Although he offered no judgement or assessment of my situation, I could see he was concerned. It was something I hadn't seen from anyone in the Service in relation to this situation– not that I had discussed it with many people. In the early days, I had shared it a little with Val when she was still an advisor and she was convinced it was all a misunderstanding. We never talked about it again. By year-end I had mentioned to Rachel White, one of the newcomers, that I was having a few problems with Sue and she lost all power of speech and if the earth had opened up and swallowed her it wouldn't have been a minute too soon. Of course, in the processing of my complaint I had spoken to Susanne and Stacey. Thus far, genuine concern for me, or a realisation that there was a serious problem that wasn't all emanating from me, was something I had not seen before.

As the meeting got back on track there were some questions Richie didn't think he was the best person to answer, so he provisionally invited me to another REAG meeting that was due to take place in a couple of days on Wednesday, 22nd February. He suggested that I could meet the individuals who would be better able to help me at the meeting. He promised that he would confirm as soon as he could. I was hugely grateful and optimistic about the offer of attending the meeting, not least because I had a gap in my diary for the Wednesday.

I had previously hoped to be at HMP Lincoln on the Wednesday. It was to be the culmination of several attempts to get an appointment. I had finally received a personal invitation from Jane, the personnel manager, once she had heard about the good work that I had been doing at another prison. In response, I had offered 22nd, 27th or 28th February for her to choose from. Because I was under so much pressure to fill my calendar because Sue and Val were randomly printing off my calendar, I had resorted to inputting unconfirmed appointments with a *'(tbc)'* proviso. At the beginning of the month, in anticipation that Jane would choose one of the three dates offered, I had gone ahead and randomly selected 22nd February, with a view to moving it if Jane chose one of the other dates. However, when Jane eventually responded to say that the people I needed to see, including her, were unavailable for all of the proposed dates, due to holidays and a combination of other events, my plan had spectacularly backfired.

Undeterred at that time, I decided not to remove the entry until I had made another appointment at a different prison to replace it. Unfortunately, over the week and a half that followed, other clients were also unavailable on that day. Hence, I had begun this week in torment because the gap in my calendar meant that I would have to fill it with a Newbold visit. I had reached the point where I didn't even want to be there for the permitted one day a week, preferring instead to completely book myself field appointments and catch up with admin at home in the evenings. Val had been quite clear at the end of January that, if I had any more gaps or was spending too much time at Newbold, then I had had my last informal warning. I was living in constant fear of breaking the rules, both spoken and unspoken. I was compulsively double-checking and triple-checking my own work. I felt as if I was being physically beaten in places no one would look for bruises. Yet help was on the way, at least for this week. Unknowingly, Richie had offered me a lifeline for 22nd February and, by God's grace, Richie would confirm it and I wouldn't have to go into Newbold at all.

When the meeting finished, Richie directed me to Deborah in the same office and said that she would put me on the files for any other meetings for the Black Managers' Forum. He also asked her to give me the minutes of previous meetings so that I could catch up with the issues. Then he left the office.

Deborah, having overheard the part of the conversation I had with Richie about the tokenism comment made by Val, said that she couldn't believe that I had to work under such conditions. She continued to speak without inhibition.

'You should have been at the Black Managers' Forum meeting because Val did a crap job and it was really embarrassing for her because she couldn't answer any of the questions the managers asked. It would have been better if you had been there because you might have been able to give assurance to fellow colleagues that LMD were serious about helping black staff get past institutional barriers. Instead it was just embarrassing and it was clear that the college has no idea how to help us.'

The following day I was at HMP Wellingborough. When I left after my appointment, I checked my messages to find a voicemail from Richie, formally inviting me to the meeting the next day on Wednesday 22nd February. 'Hallelujah!' I said aloud in the car park whilst raising my hand to the skies. I didn't care who was listening because I was relieved and thankful. I jumped into my car and before I turned the key to start my engine I called Ceri in admin and asked for an electronic train ticket, as there wasn't enough time to wait for one in the post.

When I got home, I tried to update my electronic calendar with the new details; however, the network repeatedly sent pop-up messages about not being able to synchronise files. The network crashed each time I attempted to remove the HMP Lincoln details in order to replace them with the REAG meeting information. This was a common problem with working remotely in the Service; no one was ever sure whether the problem was due to security protocols or outmoded technology but everyone knew how slow and cumbersome it was. As I couldn't tell if I had updated the files successfully or not, I logged out with a view to update the calendar retrospectively from the desktop, the next time I was at Newbold.

I got on with some design work. At around 5.15pm, I realised no one had called back with my ticket reference. As it was after 5.00pm and unlikely that any of the admin team would still be in the office, I decided to log back on to my computer and check my emails to see if they had sent it that way. I didn't find the ticket reference. Instead, I was mortified to find an email written by Helen on behalf of Val saying:

Hi Olivea

Val has asked me to contact you regarding this. Ceri has asked me to sign off a form to authorise your travel again to London tomorrow. From your calendar it appears that you were going to HMP Lincoln tomorrow, which was a priority you and Val had highlighted and discussed as important to your current work, and that you were already in London on Monday to see Richie… from REAG. You are going to London again on Thursday for a project board meeting with Stephen Seddon. In light of last week's meeting when we discussed getting prior approval to travel and to bear in mind budgetary costs, particularly at this time of year, we are wondering why is there a second meeting in the same week with Richie...which appears to be outside your area work remit?

At this moment we are not able to approve this travel. Please call Val/Sue to discuss asap as a matter of urgency.
   Thanks
   Helen

I was livid. My ticket would cost approximately £29.99 and they wanted to talk to me about budgetary constraints when they weren't even reimbursing me for all of my expenses! As I hotly read the email again, I couldn't understand what she meant about this meeting being outside my 'area work remit'.

I forwarded the email to Richie because, if it turned out I couldn't make the meeting, I was too ashamed to say I wasn't *allowed* to go or that they wouldn't pay for my ticket even though I was a Manager E responsible for the development of governors across 15 prisons. I decided he could judge for himself from a simple email what I had to put up with almost every day.

I called Val as instructed and got her voicemail. I left a message and set about responding by email. I banged out a response, giving little thought for the choice of words. I was so angry. I told Val that on both counts I had been *invited* to REAG, that HMP Lincoln had cancelled and that I couldn't understand how this was outside my remit with me not only being a black manager but a black learning and development specialist. I pressed *send* without even checking my spelling.

Had I taken a moment to compose myself I might have told her that HMP Lincoln had refused the dates I had offered and that I was too panicked by the prospect of having gaps in my calendar to take out the provisional date that I had offered, until I had something else to replace it with. However, on further consideration, I might have thought better about conveying so much vulnerability–but in any case, it was too late now, the email had gone. I don't know how long I then sat at my laptop stewing in my own juice. I of course knew that HMP Lincoln was a priority prison. I had been trying to get an appointment with the governor since September the previous year without success. I had even tried making appointments with the Head of Operations whom I had previously worked with at HMP Leicester, in the hope that it would informally lead me to meet with Governor Taylor and her team. Then one of my informal routes had paid off. Sandra, the personnel manager at HMP Morton Hall was very good friends with Jane, the personnel manager at HMP Lincoln. When I had mentioned that I was having difficulty meeting the governor, Sandra said that she would recommend me to Jane because she was so pleased with the work that I was doing for them—and that's when I got the invitation from Jane to meet with her and the governor. Whilst thinking through how to sort this mess out, I opened an email cancelling the Performance and Competence Assessment Project Board meeting, which was scheduled for Thursday 23rd February. My house of cards couldn't take another hit: this email demolished it, because it meant I would now have to go into Newbold after all. The email sent me into more of a panic as I realised that if Val refused to let me go to the REAG meeting in the morning, I would be in Newbold for Wednesday *and* Thursday. And if that happened I had nothing to look forward to except a formal warning.

When Rudy came home, I filled him in and he was furious. It takes a lot to rile Rudy.

'You don't need to take this, Liv,' he said. 'You're a manager and they're treating you like a *child*. Aren't they paying you to make these kinds of decisions and to manage your time? You're supposed to be training governors and they don't trust you enough to make your own judgement calls about travel and which meetings to attend? That's pathetic. I mean, you're going to see people who work in the Service. If you were going for a jolly to see someone who didn't have anything to do with the organisation, fair enough. If there wasn't a connection, fair enough. But, *Liv*, you're going to your head office. You're doing Prison Service business with Prison Service people. This is ridiculous. This is messed up!'

When the house phone rang around 7.15pm, I sensed it was Val. Although a good hour had passed since I told Rudy what had happened, he was still angry. He sat across from me as I picked up the phone. It was Val.

She began by saying that she had read my email, yet she still asked for an explanation as to why I needed to see Richie again. I felt it best simply to reiterate what I had said in the email. It didn't make sense to say anything else. She tried to justify her approach as necessary because I hadn't given enough notice to travel and my journey was incurring additional expense for the department that they could ill afford. As she talked I marvelled, because it was as if we were talking about the way I had flouted the expenses rules to organise an unauthorised trip to Dubai to have a meeting to be followed by an extravagant lunch and dancing, when in reality I was asking for an off-peak standard ticket to London!

When she had finished talking about how, as the budget holder for the department, she was accountable for all the expenditure and so on and so forth, it was my turn to get some answers. I needed to know what she meant by the comment about me concerning myself with things outside my 'area work remit'. I was curious. At my last one-to-one meeting when I told her that I had been invited to REAG, she had sown a seed of disregard with the remark, 'I didn't think you'd be interested in that sort of thing', and I hadn't pushed for clarity then. However, her reaction to my involvement with REAG was much stronger this time. I wanted her to tell me plainly that she didn't want me to work on a project to do with black people in the Service and if that was the case she needed to explain herself. As it turned out, Val couldn't answer the question!

'I just needed to know what you were working on, Olivea.'

'Val, you knew what I was working on and yet you refused to authorise my travel. That has never happened to me before in any place I have ever worked as a manager. I would like to know what it was about this project that made you think that it was outside my work area remit.'

Val avoided the question by suggesting that perhaps she hadn't chosen the best wording to query my reasons for travel, and then she dispassionately said that it was too late anyway to arrange a ticket. I said that I would pay for it myself. There was no challenge to this.

'Right then, have a good evening, Val.'

'You too, Olivea.'

When I put down the phone, I was very hurt. I couldn't understand why I was being picked up on every little thing. As Rudy had quite rightly said, this was a legitimate meeting at head office; it was a project to which I could add value and one which would have a positive impact on my area the East Midlands. Yet I was being treated as if I was doing something underhand or illegal. I didn't feel as if I was being treated like an experienced manager capable of making effective and informed decisions, though I did feel that I was being treated like a child who couldn't be trusted to be responsible and who needed to be kept on a tight leash because she was badly behaved.

In the morning, I bought my ticket, got to London and went to Cleland House. On the way to the meeting, I was joined in the corridor by Beverley Thompson the Head of REAG—we had met briefly at the HMP Whatton's Diversity 'awayday' in October. I was impressed that she remembered me.

As we walked she said, 'I understand you had some difficulty getting here today.'

I replied that it was standard treatment for me at the college. She asked if my travel had been paid for. I told her I had paid for my own ticket. Beverley suggested I fill in an expenses form and pass it to her and that she would authorise it. Although grateful for the care and the concern, I said I would send my expenses in as normal and, if the fare was deducted by Sue, I would then pass it to her.

When we arrived at the meeting room, I found a seat and introduced myself to the people who had arrived before me. Beverley quickly called the meeting to order and explained that during the meeting we would review Race and Equality training materials and set new protocols. I did my best to contribute by giving learning specialist direction. We were all asked to review in full the materials that had been compiled so far and make observations and recommendations where appropriate. At the end of the meeting, Beverley asked if I would help with the training strategy she was working on as it was evident from my contributions in the meeting that I would be able to provide useful insight. I happily agreed to review the REAG training materials as requested along with everyone else. However, I respectfully declined the invitation to work on the strategy and said that I was happy to talk with her about my reasons in private.

I followed Beverley back to her office. Once there, I explained that I was under a lot of pressure because of unfair treatment at the college. I told her that Sue was contacting my clients in an attempt to check up on me and that I was under constant scrutiny. If I took on a large piece of work that wasn't commissioned by the college, I believed Sue would say I was failing to meet my core responsibilities. I explained I was already working at home in the evenings and at weekends to make sure the college couldn't fault my work and that the REAG training strategy development roll-out was a substantial undertaking I couldn't commit to, for those reasons. Then she asked me a question that was like an oasis in the desert.

'Would you be prepared to work on the training strategy on a full-time secondment for a few months?'

A way out! An actual way out of the college, I thought! Even if it was for a few months, it would be enough. Either I would get one of the new roles in the restructure or maybe the secondment might last longer than a few months.

I said 'Yes'.

Beverley said she was due to see Stacey that day in a meeting and would approach her about the prospect of my being on secondment to REAG. She gave me what she had done so far on the REAG training strategy and asked if I could look at it and comment in the interim.

I floated all the way to the tube station and praised God as I made my way home, all the while hoping this was my chance to get away from Sue's prejudice and jealousy. I was incredibly motivated again by the prospect of making my mark, progressing and adding value.

When I got home, I logged on to find a response from Val to the email I had sent her the previous night. She had come up with a flimsy explanation as to what she meant by the phrase 'outside your area work remit'. Apparently, she now needed to know about the days I was spending outside my area, the East Midlands *before* they happened rather than afterwards, as agreed at the last team meeting. It seemed that she had forgotten that the second REAG meeting was confirmed to me the day before I intended to travel. What is more, everywhere I intended to go was normally plotted ahead in my electronic calendar to which Val, Sue and admin had electronic access. Since joining the college I had delivered workshops, attended meetings and assisted colleagues in London, West Midlands, Birmingham, Hemel Hempstead, Huntingdon, Milton Keynes, Coventry and Doncaster–all of which were outside the East Midlands. Except for plotting these events in my calendar like everyone else, I never had to *ask* for permission to travel outside the East Midlands. In a recent team meeting, there had been some discussion about providing notice about travel so far outside your area you needed overnight stays in hotels. But that wasn't the case with my day trips. Additionally, in the same meeting, Sue had said that at the last senior management team (SMT) meeting, a request was made for everyone to fill in forms requesting travel, but that she had, quite proudly, in our defence said that that would be impractical for the advisors. Rather, she had stated that the electronic calendar was the 'advisor way' of gaining permission to travel, and should remain so. Sue went on to confirm that this had been accepted by the SMT.

Currently, I was working on a project team looking at simplifying and redrafting the Staff Performance Development Record (SPDR) appraisal forms and the meetings were all in London. I was due to deliver feedback at HMP Long Lartin in Worcestershire as a favour to Ruth, the advisor for the West Midlands. Again, although it was in my calendar and available to view by Val, I was not challenged over these or others being outside my area. However, the REAG meeting was a problem and so much so that, henceforward, I was required to gain permission from Val for *all* travel outside the East Midlands. I had been with the college for nine months; the rules kept changing and I kept finding myself on the wrong side of the tracks. I was sure no one else in the team was being micro-managed like this, because if they were, based on the extrovert personalities in the team and the high levels of autonomy inherent in the roles, there would have been an uproar. Yet for me, even though there was no evidence to suggest I was abusing the flexibility of my role and, in the face of excellent feedback, it was still acceptable to treat me like an incompetent employee who was not able to make the most rudimentary decisions in her own area, let alone outside the East Midlands boundary.

In line with my new instructions, I went through my calendar and highlighted the appointments that were outside the East Midlands. I formally reported them to Val, stating that I had already agreed to support the events in London, Worcestershire, Birmingham and wherever else I was going, long before she had told me about this new rule. I sought permission to travel and felt horribly demeaned by having to do so—not because letting my manager know what I was doing was a problem, it was because I felt that there was prejudice and contempt behind the instruction.

On 1st March, I was working at Newbold, having had to reschedule a feedback session with Davis who was based at Cleland House, London. His was an additional feedback I had agreed to do because the team had been asked to cover feedbacks for HQ because the newly arrived advisor for HQ was on induction. Davis had contacted me on the afternoon of 23rd February to reschedule. I agreed and we rescheduled to 23rd March. I updated my calendar immediately; however, because of the problems I was having, I didn't delete the entry on 1st March. Instead, I put an additional note in the time-slot field that the meeting had been rescheduled *to* 23rd March. Then to cover myself further in the 23rd March 'field' I put the new entry in with a note saying it was rescheduled *from* 1st March. It all felt quite preposterous and smacked of overkill; however, my experiences to date had taught me that no amount of caution was too much.

Unfortunately, the rescheduled appointment caused me to be at Newbold, as I was unable to get another appointment for 1st March. I did, however make sure that I was scheduled to be in the field for the rest of the week. As I came to terms with having to be at Newbold, I got a call from Val on my mobile. She was on her way to Coventry to the SOM assessment centre to facilitate using the new tools that I wasn't eligible to be trained in because I didn't have Level A and B psychometrics. She asked if I was at Cleland House. Instantly, I was on my guard. The rearranged appointment had been in my calendar for a week now, along with the supporting explanation for the change, yet Val was asking me where I was. Warily, I explained that I was at Newbold because the appointment had been rescheduled at Davis's request. She then went on to ask what I was doing instead of being at Cleland House and requested a blow-by-blow account of what I had planned for the week, despite the fact that my whereabouts and plans were well documented. As always, I complied.

After the call, I was quite disturbed. I felt I was being systematically harassed and made to feel small. It seemed that I couldn't get the balance right and no matter how much detail I recorded about my whereabouts or what I was doing with my time, it wasn't enough.

I was still waiting for the mediation with Sue, having been offered it in November the previous year. Over Christmas, I had decided to return to work with an attitude of obeying God and single-mindedly working towards doing my job well. It had only been about eight weeks and, since then, I felt that I had been warding off daily assaults on my integrity, intelligence and professionalism. I wasn't sure how much more I could take or even if I could make it to mediation, without registering the discomfort and disappointment I was regularly feeling.

On 7th March, I was back at Newbold. Of late, I had felt an increasing sense of oppression and isolation. Being based on the ground floor in itself was not a problem: it was the aloneness that came with the negligence and harassment that I couldn't cope with. Sue's office was there along with a couple of classrooms and a hot-desk office for the other advisors if they came in. Despite the layout, however, I tended to be on my own and quite cut off: Sue tended to sit upstairs with the admin team and the other advisors were rarely at Newbold using the hot desks. Although I went upstairs to greet the admin and Fast Track teams, it was rare for people to come downstairs to talk to me. Whenever I worked late at Newbold, the staff would turn off the lights and leave me as the only person in the building, without letting me know that they had gone home.

After arriving, I went upstairs to greet the team and collect my mail; however, this morning I noticed that Sue's name was on Chris's old office door. Instantly, I realised Sue had arranged a move upstairs: I was officially the only member of staff based on the ground floor. The impact of this deepened as I walked along the corridor and into the open-planned offices. I suddenly became painfully aware that everyone upstairs was white and I was black and downstairs—on my own. I was completely alone! I had never seen my predicament so plainly until that moment. The employees in this building were now separated by race. 'How callous and short-sighted,' I thought. It was bad enough that Sue could barely speak to me or look at me—now she had put a whole floor between us. It was as if she had become so powerful that she didn't even need to shield her prejudice anymore.

Chapter Six

No Retreat

The date for mediation finally came around on 16th March, months after my complaint. After all the treatment I had endured since making the commitment to last, I commended myself because I was here now. I had made it.

Before the meeting, I was organising my files, opening and reading emails as normal. During these times, I especially took note of the movement sheets to see if the other advisors were adhering to the same rules that Val had given me. I regularly found that, not only were there days with no activity recorded, all other advisors regularly recorded themselves as working remotely from home or being at base for more than one day in a week. Rachel White, the advisor for the Eastern Region popped her head round the door to say 'Hello', which was nice. I commented on the fact that I had seen another two advisors on site and that it was unusual for so many of us to be at Newbold, unless there was a team meeting.

I jokingly asked, 'Am I missing something?'

She said, 'No. I'm here because of the Bermuda project.'

'What Bermuda project?' I asked.

'I'll be going to Bermuda in June to deliver training,' she replied rather matter-of-factly. I felt my eyebrows rise and my eyes open widely. I couldn't hide my surprise.

'I don't know anything about a trip to Bermuda. How did you get to know about it?'

The blood drained from her face and she took a step back nearer the still open office door. 'Um, I think maybe it was discussed in one of the team meetings or something…'

When she registered the continued look of shock on my face, she sheepishly left my office without another word. Still staring at the now closed office door, I thought, how could this happen? I couldn't understand how two trips to train abroad hadn't been openly discussed or how I had managed to fall out of the loop somehow. Was it possible that I had been excluded again?

Yet now wasn't the time to deal with this. I had to shake myself out of this: the mediation was approaching and I still had work to do. I continued with my admin and had a quick look at the movement sheet week commencing 6th March. Something was troubling me about it, yet I couldn't quite put my finger on it. I stared at each entry per advisor, and when I got to Rachel's whereabouts at the bottom of the sheet, her entries suddenly leapt out at me. It simply said, *'SHL Level B, Surrey'*. I knew that SHL was a people performance consultancy and they provided occupational psychometrics development for Human Resources and Training professionals. The next step was to look them up on the internet to see if they had a training centre in Surrey. As I scrolled down their list of contacts and venues, I found it. The address grew large as I stared at it.

I called the number. I needed to get to the bottom of this.

'Good afternoon, SHL. How can I help you?'

'Yes, hello. I'm calling from the Prison Service. Could you check if one of my colleagues has attended the Level B training this month?'

The receptionist asked for the date and the name, then told me that Rachel had attended their management centre from 8th to 10th March. The receptionist also volunteered that Rachel had attended Level A, the precursor to MBTI training, for three days from 14th February.

I was incredulous. I had been asking for this development for at least eight of the ten months I had been at the college. First of all, Sue told me that I had to wait until the new advisors arrived so we could train together. Then she told me that Di arrived with the MBTI licence and the focus was on new advisor development and new tools. Then Stacey told me in December that she, quoting Sue, didn't believe further MBTI-qualified advisors would provide value for money. Yet here we were with an advisor who had secured the MBTI training within four months of arrival, having arrived after me.

I didn't know how I was supposed to feel about this. What possible justification could they give for this blatant preferential treatment? I started talking to myself in my office.

'They've given her the training! The training they didn't have any more money for. The training we didn't need any more of. They have given *that* training to someone who has just arrived. Why can't they train me? I have tried. I have really tried to see this from every angle except race. I have put this to bed a hundred times. I have endured one dehumanising experience after another and each time I've walked away trying to make some *other* sense of it. But what do I make of this? Come on, Olivea, you dozy bat! These people are taking you for the biggest mug there is!'

My face burned hot, my mouth was dry, and my hands were shaking. I couldn't think. I was pacing. Up, down, up again.

'Father, please help me! Please, please, give me your peace. Give me your grace.'

If I wasn't sure before, I was sure now that I was on the receiving end of racism. There were no burning crosses on my lawn or hooded lynch mobs baying for my blood. No one was telling me to my face that they were superior to me, but the ambiguous prejudice and camouflaged bias was palpable. As the realisation hit me, I could barely breathe and my chest started to tighten. I told myself that I needed to calm down. I took a number of deep breaths, then I sat down and I printed off the SHL programme for reference. I went to the mediation knowing that their remit would not allow them to investigate these events properly. Nevertheless, I sat for two hours in a small room with two mediators and explained everything I could recall, from Sue's treatment of me to Rachel's training. At the end of my disclosure, the mediators agreed the scope of mediation could not adequately support my needs.

Five months had passed since Sue and I had sat in that horrendous meeting in October, and now I was no further forward. In fact, I was further behind in terms of better treatment and remedy. I went home knowing that the college was walking all over me and I needed to raise grievances for racial discrimination. It felt as if they were taking pleasure in degrading and humiliating me, excluding me from their professional and social circles and creating a hostile environment for me to work in. And, worst of all, they had the gall to tell me that it was all my fault. I was the enigma. Therefore, it was acceptable to use me as the catalyst and the originator of the troubles, because it was *I* who was not like *them*, and if I were more like them, then everything would have been fine. All I had to do was a little code-switching, and play the game a little. If I drank more than I ate; if I smoked and had fag breaks with them; if I had no life outside work; if I 'slagged off' management; if I gossiped about who was sleeping with whom; if I joined the lottery pool or discussed who I fancied along with my husband or *instead* of him; if my blackness had not been the vehicle for social apartness and distinctiveness—I would have been fine!

I knew there would be no turning back after this and I would probably lose my job. Yet I couldn't, in all conscience, allow myself to be treated so poorly and do nothing. Maybe this was what God wanted me to wait for—something tangible, more than a feeling of exclusion. Actual proof.

The following day, it took me a while to discover the appropriate way of filing a complaint about racism at the college—the information available was non-standardised and inconsistent. It was evident the forms had been customised from the ones used in the prisons for prisoners, but they made no allowances for recording a series of incidents that culminated into a total racist experience. They were designed in a way that presupposed that a solitary thing had happened: where you could detail names, times and numbers of persons present, with a box for a brief explanation. Then as if the process wasn't difficult enough, there was the additional confusion that Susanne was both the Equal Opportunities officer who was to receive the forms and the Head of Personnel who was to receive copies of the forms!

I raised four Race Incident Reporting Forms (RIRFs pronounced rifs). I decided it was logical to look back on all the incidents and detail the ones that I felt were harming my career and demeaning me most as a person. After Sue had raised my race as an issue the previous year, it made sense to me that, in every subsequent encounter with her, my race was a factor in her mind and, as the main decision maker and the person Stacey relied upon for the truth, it was possible that everything Sue did concerning me was stained with racism.

In the first grievance, I complained about being refused MBTI training and explained how not having it curtailed future opportunities for development. I went on to explain how I believed that I would suffer even more detriment when the time came for us to apply for the new roles in the new structure. In the formal application pack we had been given to aid preparation for interview, the skills required were recorded as the applicant needing to have *'an understanding of learning evaluation tools'* and being *'able to use and deploy development assessment centres and methodologies (e.g. 360 and Psychometrics) as part of a wider development programme'*.

My second RIRF outlined Val's comments about 'tokenism' on 15th February and my exclusion from the BME staff development project. My third complaint queried how the Barbados and Bermuda trips had come about and that I was not included in any of the arrangements, discussions and design work. And the final complaint was about how I had been left on the ground floor as the only member of staff and the only black member of staff.

It was really alien to me to be writing about my race so deliberately and without concession: to be talking about black and white, the haves and the have-nots. I sat and asked myself if we were really in the 21st century and if this was really a national institution with a national heritage and international pride and presence. I wondered how we had got here: was it me? Could I have been more tolerant, less sensitive? As is my way, question followed question. My internal dialogue was in conflict. 'Okay,' I said, 'so you've written it all down–don't you feel better already? You don't need to actually send it. If you do, your career will be over. Your life will be over. You'll face financial ruin, and you can't afford to give up work. What did God say? What about Rudy? You don't want to become a burden to him do you? What about Mum? Who's going to care for her when you both lose everything because you couldn't tough it out?' On and on, the questions came hard and fast all with possible consequences that I could ill afford to ignore. Yet, in a moment, everything was quelled within me with the answer to the next question. 'Aren't you worth more than this?' I pressed the *Send* button.

I continued to work as normal, whatever that was–normal being doing as best a job as I could do, whilst people treated me like dirt. Doing a great job whilst being disrespected, dismissed and denied; doing my job, knee deep in the nonsense of still arranging for Sue to do MBTI feedback at HMP Glen Parva on my behalf. Yep, I thought...pretty normal!

20th March found me at HMP Onley. I had a meeting there with Kate and Laura who were heading up the personnel and training function there. They had invited me to discuss their staff development needs. When I got into reception, there was a small queue of four women. They were all white and middle-aged. They looked like 1970s volunteers from the Women's Institute trapped in time in floral dresses but minus the straw hats. They came across as quintessentially the product of privilege and English country life. They were busy chatting about how they had each got lost on the way, who had taken which turn, who was still to come and what sort of identification they had each brought with them. One of them had brought her passport whilst another queried if her utility bill would suffice. They were excited and chatty, which wasn't a sight you often saw on the way into a prison.

As I waited to sign in, I watched the officer check and record the visitors' particulars and I listened to him ask the first woman, 'Do you have a mobile phone on you?'

He processed each woman in the same way, each time ending with the same question, 'Do you have a mobile phone on you?' This was standard practice as many people tended to miss the numerous signs clearly stating that mobile phones were not allowed in the prison.

The last lady then said, 'There are a couple more of us to come– should we wait here until we're all together before someone comes to get us?'

The officer agreed that was a good idea.

Finally, it was my turn. 'It was a good job I had arrived with time to spare,' I thought. I pushed my prison service photo identification pass through the hatch and under the security glass that separated us. I stated that I had an appointment to see Kate in personnel. The officer logged my details and then rang Kate. He told her I was in reception. He ended the call and pushed my photo pass back under the security glass.

'Do you have any contraband on you?' he asked.

'I'm...I'm sorry, what did you say?' He hasn't just asked me for 'contraband', I thought. I started to smile in disbelief and gave him a wry look with my smile. I was thinking, maybe he thinks I'm someone else, someone he thinks he knows; maybe this is his idea of a joke.

He repeated himself. 'Miss, do you have any contraband…anything you shouldn't bring into a prison, like alcohol or drugs?'

He was deadly serious. As the smile vanished off my face, I simply said 'No.'

'Someone will be down to get you in a minute.'

I walked over to a free seat and sat in a daze.

After a couple of minutes, two more ladies in floral frocks came in and instantly recognised the others waiting and the energy level was up a notch again. The two new arrivals went to the counter, handed over their identification, waited until their details were recorded and then answered this simple question, 'Do you have a mobile phone on you?'

I sat incredulous thinking that you couldn't make this stuff up. No one would believe you, I told myself as I mused on the fact that truth really was stranger than fiction. I was confident that the officer if questioned wouldn't even recognise his change of tack. Was racism that endemic in the organisation, I questioned–so much so that officers blatantly treat black people differently without even noticing? My being sensitive to matters of race considering everything I was going through was one thing, but this–this was undeniable and inexcusable racial prejudice and differential treatment.

I contemplated what I was to do; take down his epaulette number? Challenge him? Make a complaint? Make a scene? So far, my complaints were contained in that they only involved Newbold and the people there. I was still relatively safe and respected in the field. If I was to complain, I considered, even about a single prison, then news of the difficulties I posed would spread like wild fire. I'd have nowhere to feel safe to just do my job without fear of reprisals. One battle at a time, Olivea, I counselled myself. I let it alone.

March now seemed to be the longest month ever. On 24th, I had a meeting at the area office in Leicester. Afterwards I stayed there and worked from a spare desk, because I couldn't face going into Newbold. It was Friday and I was glad it was the end of the week: all I wanted was to stay out of Sue's reach so that I could get some peace. I wanted to finish the day well without any contention. Around 2.30pm, I received an email from Sue. My initial response was 'What now!'–though afterwards I told myself to stop being so reactive and to open the mail.

I took my own advice and opened it. It read:

Olivea

I was very disappointed to see that you weren't in attendance with the rest of the team at the above [TDG] *conference* [yesterday].

At the January Advisors meeting the conference was discussed and the team were asked to give the conference high priority for attendance supporting [the college]. *I understand you had subsequently arranged a J-SAC feedback. The J-SAC feedback would not have been considered high priority over the…Conference, could you have rescheduled the feedback?*

I look forward to hearing from you.
Sue

Clearly, I wasn't far enough out of reach, I thought. I took a deep breath, replied with an apology, and explained that I had already rescheduled Davis's appointment in London from 1st March to 23rd March and the decision was driven by his availability. I thought it pertinent to give her a little background to help her understand my reasons and explained that Davis had been seconded to work up north on a project, which meant that he was no longer conveniently located in the south, so he had postponed the original appointment for his return. However because he was very keen to have his feedback as soon as possible, I had agreed the first alternative date he could do.

I then tentatively brought to her attention that I wasn't the only member of the team who had made other appointments for that day and hadn't gone to Newbold for the conference. Naturally, I stopped short of asking her if she had conveyed her disappointment to them. Such a momentary lapse in judgement would have no doubt brought with it grave consequences. I heroically concluded by saying that the feedback in question was an additional feedback that I had agreed to do, to alleviate team workload pressures for the Head Quarters area, and to support Steve, the newest member of the team. I continued by explaining that I, therefore, considered it to be high priority because: 1) it had already been postponed and 2) I didn't want it to drag on to the extent that Steve would inherit outstanding feedback. I ended with another apology.

I felt good because I had responded without taking the bait. I apologised, I explained, I contextualised. It was over and I could go home soon in peace. I don't know why I thought it would be the end of the matter, because it wasn't. I was really surprised to receive another email from her. This one said:

> *Olivea*
>
> *Thank you for your email, and I note your comments re above.*
>
> *Whilst I'm grateful for your apology I'm extremely disappointed that once again you have failed to consult with your line manager before departing from your agreed programme of work.*
>
> *The request for attendance at the conference to support…colleagues was as a direct request to all* [college] *staff from the Head of Group. This was discussed at the January Advisors meeting.*
>
> *Yes, you were quite correct in that you weren't the only member of the team not to attend the conference, however all other team members discussed priorities and sought approval from their line manager prior to making alternative arrangements.*
>
> *As you have already been asked on several occasions it is again expected and appreciated in future, if you would*

> *make a point to discuss changes to your calendar with your line manager.*
> *Sue*

Wow, I thought, I had really rattled her. Maybe it was the comment about not being the only one not to attend the conference. It was difficult to know how not to upset Sue and I was so wearied by trying and failing miserably. Even though I couldn't understand why I was being reprimanded by her and not spoken to by Val, as my line manager, I decided to apologise again followed by another explanation. This time I made it clear I had indeed confirmed changes with Val my line manager on 1st March when she had rung to check my whereabouts and had asked me to outline my plans. Although I had been annoyed at Val's call that day, I was now glad that she had called because I was able to recall everything with accuracy.

But it was now very difficult to mask my frustration with Sue. I found myself asking her why she felt the need to keep conveying this extreme disappointment she felt concerning me. The gloves were off and my teeth were showing! I told her that she made me feel as if I had committed a crime when in actual fact all I had done was to make a judgement call and to choose to accommodate a client. I chose practitioner activity over a conference. I suggested I shouldn't be in hot water for making that decision and that it didn't seem fair. Then I ended with *another* apology. I didn't hear from her again on the matter.

I brooded over the exchange. What was that all about? It wasn't as if I was needed at the conference: outside of attendance I had no other role to play. I hadn't boycotted the event or refused to go. I hadn't deliberately found something else to do on that day. I had accommodated a client, purely and simply. I had also made my manager aware of my movements and change of plans and it still wasn't good enough. There were others who didn't make the event—however, their decisions were applauded because they had apparently, *'discussed priorities and sought approval from their line manager prior to making alternative arrangements'*. Nonsense! I thought. It would be nigh impossible and totally impractical for everyone to check with Sue or Val every time a client moved or cancelled an appointment. They only expected that of me. Besides wasn't I supposed to be spending more time in the field and less time at Newbold, I belligerently queried?

It was 4.25pm and I couldn't do any more work. I needed to get out. I switched off the computer and got myself together. I was just about to leave the office and my phone rang. 'Please God let it not be her,' I prayed. I rummaged in my bag and grabbed my phone, but when I looked at the display, I didn't recognise the number.

'Olivea Ebanks, good afternoon.'

'Hi Olivea, this is Dave Clifford.'

'Hello Dave' I said, grateful that it wasn't Sue.

'Yeah, I'm getting back to you because you sent me an email about sitting in on the *Listen to Improve* focus groups.'

'Oh thank you so much for getting back to me. I understand that nationally we are running these focus groups to hear what staff have to say about the Service and how they feel about working here and so on. And I was told that you were running the sessions in the East Midlands.'

'Yes that's right. You said in your email that you wanted to tag along for when it was HMP Lincoln's turn?'

'If I could, that would be great. I've been trying without success to get in to see the governor. I figured that if I could hear from the staff directly what their concerns were and what they wanted by way of development, then that first-hand information would put me in a stronger negotiating position with the governor.'

'No worries. I'll be at Lincoln on 6th and 7th of April. Can you make it for those dates?'

'I'm sure I can.'

He wrapped up the conversation with a 'That's smashing–see you then; looking forward to meeting you.'

Finally, I was going to get to spend some quality time at HMP Lincoln. I determined that on Monday I would send an email to Jane, the Personnel Manager, to let her know my plans and to ask again if she could slot me in to see them at any time over the two days the focus groups were due to run.

As I drove home, although pleased that things looked as if they were heading in the right direction with regards to HMP Lincoln, my mood soon darkened when my mind returned to the previous email exchange with Sue. By the time I got home, I was numb and defeated. I broke down in tears to Rudy. I said I'd had enough and that I was tired of being criticised for every move I made. If I did extra work, I was criticised. If I worked on my own initiative, I was criticised. If I worked from home, I was criticised. If I went into Newbold, I was criticised. I was in hell–and instead of red devils with tails and pitchforks, they were white professionals in business suits. Their pitchforks were conveniently relabelled policies and one-to-one meetings where they repeatedly tortured me by conveying disappointment in my work and patronised me with advice to help me to fit in.

On 28th March, we had our LMD team meeting. When I picked up the agenda from a pile on the table as we entered the Revel room in the Mansion, I noticed that Barbados and Bermuda were items for discussion, almost as if it had always been that way. I took my seat wondering if Sue and Val knew that I had raised grievances about racial discrimination. A week had passed and I had not received any acknowledgement from the personnel department that they were dealing with my case. Was I supposed to interact as normal? What if Sue or Val wanted to talk to me about the grievances– what was I supposed to do? What was the protocol? Had they told anyone in the team? I was on edge. As the all-white team made their way into the meeting room, I was acutely conscious of my blackness and difference. Today Derek, the Fast Track manager, and a couple of people from the admin team additionally joined us.

Outside the cleverly crafted agenda, there were no other surprises as the meeting played out as normal until around 4.30pm, when Di and Sue gave an update on their trip to Barbados. Sue suggested that Di began with her experience of the trip. Di started with comments about how lovely the people were and how remarkable it was that they had managed to achieve so much with so little by way of resources since their prison had burnt down. Then she went into the detail of the programme content, making particular reference to MBTI. 'More salt for my wounds,' I thought.

'I *really* enjoyed doing the MBTI,' she said with great embellishment. It sounded as though she was gloating–yet how could she be, I thought; she didn't know my circumstances. I was struggling to keep the paranoia in check.

'MBTI was so well received,' she continued gleefully. 'And the delegates were really impressed by the accuracy of the tool—*it was as if white woman bring medicine!*'

I felt as if someone had burst into the room, slapped my face and run off, leaving me to wonder what had just happened. What did she say? And, as if she had heard the conversation I was having with myself—she said it again.

'Yes,' she said excitedly, 'it was as if white woman bring medicine!'

I did a quick scan of the room. Some of the advisors looked a little uncomfortable and I was sure I heard a nervous titter, yet no one said anything by way of registering a protest.

Before I could collect my thoughts to consider an appropriate reaction, Di continued to elaborate by praising the intrinsic worth of the tool and the subsequent reactions it generated from the delegates.

'—and when we gave them their Myers Briggs type they asked, "How did you do this?" It was as if we had done magic!'

All that was missing was for her to tell us how she then offered the natives mirrors in exchange for gold and precious stones. Again, I waited for one of my managers to stop her in her flow, to address this travesty, yet uncharacteristically, they all sat and said nothing.

By this point, having received no indication from anyone that she was on a slippery slope, Di remained unguarded about her comments and further disgraced herself. She continued divulging the particulars of the programme content, the delegate reactions, and the culture of a Barbadian prison. She concluded her outline of the training by conveying what she and Sue did in their spare time. I can't imagine why she felt the next statement she made would have been okay to say, even in jest.

'—and the evening activities were interesting once you cut through the clouds of marijuana!'

Before anyone could gather some semblance of what was happening, Sue endorsed Di's commentary by smiling and saying 'Yes, the evening events were *very* interesting.' Then they exchanged knowing smiles between each other.

I was at a loss as to what to do. If I said something, I was sure I'd be judged as pre-empting a response from either Sue or Val. Even worse, any response could be construed as insensitive of Di's feelings, knowing an immediate addressing of the issue would have embarrassed her. I figured if I did anything other than what I was doing–which was nothing–it would backfire and the focus would shift from Di to me. So, I spared her feelings, even though it seemed no one was considering what it must have been like for me to have had to sit through this blatant disregard for my race. They knew I was part Barbadian; it was one of the first things they found out about me. I cannot say if this happens to black people the world over, but in Britain, white people will ask black people where they hail from within minutes of meeting for the first time. And no matter how I say plainly that I was born here, the very next question is, 'Where do your parents come from?' It is almost as if they cannot begin to engage with you until they are satisfied that you are not originally from Britain, confirming that Britain is still theirs. In any case, even if I didn't have a Barbadian heritage–Di was talking about black people in a derogatory way. I was sure she didn't consider Barbadians different from Jamaicans, or Jamaicans different from Africans. She was talking about educated and professional black people in a way that demeaned them and *that* by extension demeaned me. She had spoken about them as if their limited resources and a need of help made it okay to ridicule them. She had leapt to their rescue and they were eternally and unashamedly grateful. I didn't doubt that the managers and officers from Barbados were respectful and appreciative, but this image of simpletons speaking broken English and fawning over her was most offensive and suspect.

Then I felt a sickening feeling in the pit of my stomach; maybe this was the kind of response Di had wanted from me last month. She had complained that I had not said thank you *quickly* enough. She wanted me to applaud her skill so that she could tell others how grateful I was for her rescue of me! But I had not given her that fix. I had expressed simple gratitude without the superlatives. It was not a deliberate move on my part not to praise her skill per se. I was grateful that she had done the work and conveyed as much. At that time, I hadn't yet met with the delegates for the follow-up discussions and no one had sent an email detailing how well Di had done. Had anyone done this, I would have passed their comments on. I thought I was doing the right thing by saying thank you for the work she did for me–I could see now that anything less than kowtowing wouldn't have been enough. I didn't know it at the time that she needed more. And that's why afterwards I had to listen to Val lecture me about the sacrifice Di had made to leave her area for the day.

The meeting continued for another 30 minutes or so, and then ended. As much as I felt like bolting from the room, because by this time I felt nauseous, I sat and waited. I'm not sure what I was waiting for. Maybe either Sue or Val were going to address the team, having given everyone a chance to reflect or maybe they were going to ask to speak to me after the meeting to check that I was okay. Maybe I was going to witness them ask Di if they could have a word with her. As I sat in my quiet storm, I looked for anything that communicated to me that they had recognised that something was horribly wrong.

After the customary checks between advisors as to what time they should meet up for drinks and a meal, people started to leave the room seemingly unaffected by what had taken place. This can't be happening, I thought. They can't possibly be letting people leave the meeting thinking that what had happened was fine. This was totally unacceptable. My eyes were flashing from side to side as I scanned the length and breadth of the room to see activity confirming that my managers were about to take action. There was no such evidence. Even Di was leaving now. There seemed to be no point in waiting any longer, as it was clear that nothing was going to be done. I gathered my things and, along with the stragglers, made my way out. As I walked slowly down the stairs, I observed team members ahead talking and laughing. A couple squeezed by me whilst talking; all this talking, I thought, yet no one was talking to me.

I went back to my office and emailed Di immediately to explain that her comments were racist and why I considered them to be so. I asked that we could meet so that I could help her to understand. I knew that it would be an awkward meeting, yet I felt if we had any chance to get past this we needed a full and frank conversation. She also needed to say sorry and I needed to hear her say it, because she had hurt me.

I then filled in a fifth Race Incident Reporting Form (RIRF) because it was unacceptable that neither Sue nor Val challenged what had happened in the meeting. They should have responded to the fact that the statements were made without any regard for my ethnicity and were highly offensive. The comments implied that not only do Barbadians not speak English properly, her choice of words suggested that Di went to Barbados with superior knowledge as a white person. I was fully confident that she could have communicated the delegates' enthusiasm without implying that they had a poor command of the English language or that her colour was the vehicle for specialist knowledge and delivery. I kept asking why no one had said anything. Why was it always up to me to object? Was something only offensive if I considered it to be? And if I thought it was okay, then did it cease to be offensive or racist? I strongly believed that with Derek, the Fast Track manager, Sue as the Head of Leadership and Val as her Deputy in the room, that I shouldn't have had to say anything. I wondered if they realised that they were now complicit in Di's behaviour because they had done nothing to stop it. And when I considered how quick and ready both Sue and Val were to constantly reprimand me about alleged gaps in my diary or the level at which I engaged with the admin team, or some other criticism—yet they had sat and let something this monumentally immoral happen and done nothing—I got angry. 'This is the sort of thing they should be concerning themselves with,' I grumbled. 'This is where they should be stepping in.' Even as I filled in the complaint form, I was still in disbelief that they had done nothing in the meeting. I was repulsed by their inaction and devastated by their cowardice.

When I got home, I told Rudy, I told my Mum and I phoned my sister and told her. I phoned the Elders in our church and told them. No matter how many times I spoke about it to free myself of the anger that had welled up inside my chest, the impact was not lessened. And each person I told was equally shocked and angry. The first reaction was always something like: 'She said what?' quickly followed by, 'What did your managers do' or 'Did anyone say anything?' And every time I answered 'No, no one said anything; no one did anything', there was outrage. I didn't get to bed until the early hours of the morning, as I dreaded what the next day would bring. I was to be at Newbold for the second part of our team meeting. All I could think about was how awful the atmosphere was going to be.

The next morning, when I got in, I found out as I made my way back to the Revel room in the Mansion that we were to spend the morning looking over the applicant profiles for the new jobs we were all eligible to apply for and that the session was optional. 'Oh, thank you, God', I breathed. I chose not to attend. As I turned to make my way back to my office, I saw Di coming up the winding stairwell. I continued down to meet her and, when we were in speaking distance, I motioned for her to stop. I smiled and said 'Good morning' and told her I had sent her an email and would welcome a chat after the meeting, once she had read it. As I said this, I felt she would instantly know what I was talking about, so I was very careful to be calm and non-threatening, as I didn't want to give her an excuse not to come. I wanted her to see that I wasn't looking for a showdown of any kind. I just wanted us to talk. She looked at me quizzically and then said she would have a read and pop in afterwards. I continued down the stairs as my heart pounded and my knees shook with a combination of sheer terror and relief. I had taken the first nerve-racking step towards turning this mad state of affairs around. I went back to my office and waited.

Di never came. Instead, she chose to drop me a quick emailed apology in the afternoon. It said:

>Olivea
>
>*I apologise unreservedly if my comments offended you in any way whatsoever. I accept my choice of words was inappropriate.*
>
>Regards
>
>Di

If the comments offended me? *If,* I read? Hadn't I made it perfectly clear that her comments were racist? This meant even if no one was offended, what she did was *wrong*. Yet here she was apologising *if* she caused offence, whilst noting her choice of words were inappropriate. How gracious, I thought! How is it, that she couldn't see that her comments went beyond being inappropriate and that they were racist? She hadn't simply offended me, she had breached the Prison Service code of conduct. I stewed for the rest of the day.

On 30th March, I met with Stacey Tasker, the Head of the college and Susanne, the Head of Personnel to discuss the Race Incident Reporting Forms (RIRFs) I had submitted. I opened by saying that I was quite distressed that I had now raised five RIRFs and, if we included the complaint from November, the grand total was now six outstanding complaints without resolution.

Stacey responded almost in a panic 'We are taking the complaints seriously but we don't have this problem here! These are the first complaints we've *ever* had about race, we simply don't have this kind of problem here!'

As if it were possible to be any more upset than I already was, Stacey managed to upset and insult me that very instance. What was she suggesting? I wondered. That this problem only existed because of me? *That I was the problem?* What did she mean? Was she really intimating that everything was fine until I came along?

This organisation was inexcusably heaping layer upon layer of racism and insult on my head. How typical a response from an institutionally racist organisation, I thought. She might have well have said, 'There must be some mistake, Olivea—we don't have this problem here. It can't be racism because it didn't exist until you arrived', because what she was actually saying didn't sound much different to me. It was such an historical and archetypal reaction. And in that moment I could hear the sentiments of every bigot I had ever heard in my life speak. This was only happening because people were able to take one look at me and decide that I didn't belong and that my very presence would bring hitherto unwarranted problems. The realisation that Stacey genuinely believed everything was fine until I arrived hit me hard and then the cynicism hotly followed. Britain wasn't racist until the immigrants arrived! It wasn't the superior attitudes, the prejudice or meanness of spirit that caused racism…it was the immigrants!

I couldn't understand this reticence to accept that racism was woven into the very fabric of the Prison Service and then it dawned on me. If there was any acceptance that unwitting racism existed in the organisation, it was only that it existed at officer level, like officers were a lower order of being. And even then, one had to accept that there were no out-and-out racists at that grade apart from the odd bad apple. Instead, what we had were officers doing a challenging job in a challenging environment, because it is difficult trying to align concepts of punishment with fairness or align equality with criminality. Somewhere down the line there is bound to be some jarring. A distinction had been made between the clumsy oafishness of the officer, and the intelligent finesse of the manager, so much so that if you even suggested that there was racism within the management grades it was met with incredulity and an inability to comprehend. In the management grades, racism didn't exist even in its most basic, unwitting form.

And here I was, not only accusing the organisation of racism within the management grades, I had given names and those names had faces. Indeed there was no way that Stacey could accept what I was saying because I was talking about people she knew, people she liked. To her, racism was about systemic failures within an organisation. No one owned the problem, no one person was responsible and certainly no one person treated another person poorly because of their race. If anything, it was an institutional collective failure; it was systems failing, like a whirring antiquated computer in the basement churning out policies that Asimov's robotic emissaries executed indiscriminately. Yet I was not sitting in front of a system or robots. You can't have a collective failure without a collective of individual people failing. I was sitting in front of people who had failed me. I knew who they were and I wanted something done about them. As far as I was concerned there needed to be acceptance that racism was endemic throughout the organisation and was being perpetrated by several individuals within it. I felt strongly that the Service shouldn't get away with relegating racism to the lower ranks, as if officers struggled with matters of higher intelligence. This divide needed to be challenged: there were racist officers *and* there were racist managers.

Stacey, oblivious to the offence, moved on from her incredulous stance that this was even happening at the college because they had such an unblemished record until now. She told me that my claims were about to be formally investigated. My sense of insult remained, though her comments that a fresh pair of eyes would be looking at my problems and not just Sue's myopic counterparts, brought some relief.

After she had finished outlining the role she was going to play as the commissioning officer, I pushed two envelopes across the table. The first contained another letter of complaint about Susanne being both the Head of Personnel and the Equal Opportunities Officer. I summarised the contents for expedience.

'Since having raised the five RIRFs,' I said, looking squarely at Susanne, my hand still on the envelope, 'you have not acknowledged receipt of them or responded to me beyond confirming that the meeting we are now having had been arranged. You didn't offer me any counsel or support in your role as the Equal Opportunities Officer nor did you give me any direction as the Head of Personnel as to what to expect from this meeting. I feel strongly that your dual role has compromised the options available to me, as the complainant, to get independent advice.'

She took the letter and said nothing. Then I briefly said that the RR65 questionnaire was contained in the second envelope. The RR65 is a questionnaire that employees can serve on their employers if they believe they are being discriminated against on racial grounds. It helps in preparation for Tribunal cases, should an employee decide to go that far, as the answers given by the employer can be used as evidence. If the employers deliberately give vague or ambiguous answers, the Race Relations Act 1976 allows Tribunals to draw inference that discrimination has occurred, solely from the answers given in the questionnaire. The form is downloadable from the internet and the Race Equality Council in Wellingborough had advised me to serve the Prison Service with one. There were standard questions on the form and some flexibility for me to ask my own questions. I additionally asked questions about the ethnic breakdown of the college, who had had training, how special projects (like Barbados and Bermuda) were advertised, what the level of grievances were at the college, and so on.

Stacey then moved on to some of the specifics of my case. She mentioned that Di had been 'dealt with', inasmuch as Sue apparently spoke to her immediately after the team meeting. My instantaneous reaction was to state that I had remained in the team meeting room after the meeting concluded and I didn't see any such thing. I explained I wasn't the first person to leave the meeting and, when I did leave, it was with the last members of the team. Stacey continued to assure me Sue had tackled the issue straightaway, as if Stacey had been there to oversee it personally! She went on to say that Sue didn't address Di during the meeting because she didn't want to embarrass her.

'How is it that my feelings were not spared,' I asked pointedly, 'was it right for me to leave the meeting belittled and embarrassed?'

No one answered this question. I was not satisfied. I protested further.

'Do you realise that two days have now passed and not one of my managers has come to me to say that what happened was wrong. Nobody has had the decency or courage to speak to me about this. No one has even bothered to find out if I'm okay. And I can tell you now—I am not okay!'

What Stacey might have intended as diplomacy, I interpreted as rudeness as she moved the conversation on and enquired if I still wanted the complaint about 'the comments' to be a part of the investigation, seeing as Di had had a 'note' placed on her file. Why wasn't anyone listening to me, even now, I thought? Even after such a blatant show of poor judgement and poor management, and racism, no one was listening to me.

Wearily, I said that I wasn't prepared to make any decisions on the spot. Then Stacey suggested that, in view of the circumstances, I needed a new line manager. She offered me a full-time REAG secondment, as if it had been her idea all along. I had been waiting to hear something about this role for six weeks! But now that I had raised five racial complaints, it was suddenly okay for me to go. I was in a predicament because, as much as I wanted the secondment, I realised that I needed to be able to see what was happening to our jobs in the restructure. What is more, I felt that it sent completely the wrong message to the perpetrators just to have me vanish in a puff of secondment smoke to London. Because I didn't want to miss out on the opportunity entirely, I proposed a mix of both roles and said I would get back to Stacey after having thought about it in more detail. She agreed to let me think about it and said the decision regarding the role would be all mine.

Stacey summarised the meeting in writing later on that day. She reiterated that the decision regarding the secondment to REAG would rest solely with me and that she would be happy with whatever I decided. I encouraged myself that at least her promise of flexibility was in writing and there would be no argument or confusion regarding the REAG role. It was everything else that would take time to work through.

Susanne also responded on the same day, stating she would no longer be the Equal Opportunities Officer. And, just like that, I had even fewer options. Since there was no one to replace her, the position would be advertised and filled through normal recruitment and selection routes. She did not propose any alternative support mechanisms to help me in the interim.

Over the next few days, I crafted my response to Stacey with regards to the proposals made in our last meeting. I specifically asked her not to change my reporting line. I already felt like a parcel that nobody wanted. I was being passed from hand to hand. I was painfully aware that complaining about my managers didn't make for the best working relationship—but then, neither did bullying me! And I had managed. All I expected was for Sue and Val to treat me fairly and with respect. Stacey seemed more concerned about their comfort levels and the difficulties they faced having to work with someone who had complained about them. I was not asking for anything less than professionalism. When they brought up issues relating to my performance, I did not ask to be moved. I was still expected to do my job to the best of my ability. I was still expected to carry myself professionally. Why was it different for them? How was it that they were afforded the luxury of having the 'discomfort' being moved on? If they had accused me of inappropriate language or behaviour, changing my reporting lines would not even be a consideration. What they failed to understand about me was that respect is something I was taught to do. It didn't matter if it was earned or not. I would never roll my eyes, snap my fingers or refuse to do a piece of work. I would never go out of my way to make life difficult for them—I would do my job. It wasn't necessary to move me again and it was important that Stacey understood this.

Furthermore, moving me again would mean starting a new line management relationship with baggage. I was not convinced that whoever Stacey had in mind would not be primed that I was a problem and to watch his or her back. What good could come from starting a relationship like that? Then of course, there was the fact that whomever Stacey had in mind would be outside of LMD. This person wouldn't understand my workload or pressures. They would be torn between taking my word about what the role required or Sue's and Val's. Whatever angle I looked at it from, the outworking was negative and I would suffer detriment.

Regarding the full-time secondment offer, I stated that I would be happy to work on the training strategy on a part-time basis as suggested during our last discussion. In essence, I would be a shared resource between REAG and LMD. I gave her the example of honouring the commitments I currently had in the East Midlands for two days a week, whilst not making any new ones for the next eight weeks or so. I could then work on the REAG training strategy for three days a week, citing that this was similar to the arrangement Val had as Deputy to Sue. I was careful to point out this pre-existing arrangement, as I didn't want Stacey to think she was setting precedence for me. I offered to confirm dates that I was already committed to and draw up a draft schedule, which would enable Stacey to see how my suggestion could work. I told her that I considered the REAG training strategy to be quite a sizable piece of work and, as such, difficult to manage without some adjustment to my normal core duties. I made sure I was clear to ask for the opportunity to work on it. In Stacey's summary of our most recent meeting in March she had said, '*We discussed the possibility of a mixture of the two* [roles] *but I made it clear I was happy with whatever you felt most comfortable with and the decision would be yours.*' The words seemed emphatic enough; however, I didn't trust her, though I didn't necessarily need to trust her, she just needed to keep her word. My confidence was not so much in what she said, it was in the fact that this promise was in writing. She couldn't go back on it. Although I was used to being denied anything I specifically asked for at the college, in this case, being proved wrong would be to my advantage.

Chapter Seven

Beasts of Burden

On 6th April, I was at HMP Lincoln to meet Dave Clifford as arranged. He had agreed to let me observe the *Listen to Improve* focus groups set up to understand staff issues directly from the staff in a reprisal risk-free environment. I had struggled for months to get a prison-wide sense of the development needs of the managers and officers–this was another way in. I planned to sit in all the sessions across both days, record the outputs and ultimately report my findings back to Governor Lynne Taylor as soon as my report was ready. I had hoped to see Governor Taylor and Jane, the Head of Personnel as well, at some point across the two days; however, Jane had once again responded to say that neither she nor the governor were available at any time on either day.

   I arrived early enough to go across the road from the prison to the Lincoln Hospital to get a drink in the café. I had just started writing in my diary when Dave turned up and introduced himself. He was of average build with short, dark hair. He was smartly dressed in a well-cut, dark suit. As he stood holding my hand, he smiled widely. I could see a glint in his eye denoting charm and cheekiness. Straightaway I thought, 'This is going to be fun.' The rapport between us was instant. Without any bashfulness, he immediately asked what I was doing. With a mischievous smile, I said it was private.

   He said cryptically, 'Well, between the phone calls and the diary writing I'm drawing my own conclusions.' And off he went to get himself a drink.

   I put my diary in my bag. I could hardly wait for him to come back to ask him what he meant. He returned, sat down, and proceeded to unwrap a pastry and sip his coffee. Then he smiled, as if to say 'Your move'. This was excruciating. I took the bait.

   'What did you mean by that comment about the phone calls?'

   'Oh that,' he said. 'Sue sent me an email asking me to contact her.'

He was still baiting me. I responded, trying not to sound too eager. 'What did she say when you got in touch?'

'Oh she talked around the houses a little' he said nonchalantly. 'And then she asked me if *I* had arranged this meeting with you or if you did. She asked about the nature of the meeting and how the meeting came about.'

Unbelievable! Why was she still checking on me? Even though I had pointedly complained about this behaviour as undermining my credibility in the field, she was still allowed to do this. In matter of fact, why was she asking Dave? She must have seen the *Listen to Improve* events in my electronic diary along with Dave's details. Everyone knew that these events were a national initiative to improve the well-being and motivation of the staff. Everyone knew the events were a part of the people strategy that was being rolled-out from Head Quarters, as it had been widely publicised. If she was unclear as to what I was doing, why didn't she simply ask me? Better still, why didn't she ask my manager? Hadn't she identified HMP Lincoln as a priority? What better way to understand the prison than to listen to a cross-section of the staff who have been given carte blanche to say whatever they wanted? I tried to laugh it off, even though I was deeply embarrassed. We went back over the road to the prison and ran the sessions.

The following day I was back at HMP Lincoln. In between the focus group sessions, Dave was still probing. He directly asked why Sue was checking up on me. 'I used to be an investigator y'know—I know when something's up! C'mon, you can talk to me,' he encouraged.

I didn't want to tell him, but by this point I was so desperate for approval and acceptance. Although I had only just met him and he could have been anybody, I was awash with the compulsion to prove I wasn't a problem and didn't deserve this kind of treatment. So I told him. I told him that I was having real problems and I gave him a few instances. He was truly shocked and sympathetic, whilst I was further saddened by being reduced to telling total strangers my business.

I had raised six grievances by this point exposing Sue's mismanagement of me, and a formal investigation was underway.

Yet I couldn't shake Sue's overbearing presence in my day-to-day life. I wondered what it was going to take.

Day followed day and week followed week; for the most part, I was increasingly consumed with what Sue would do next and what I would then need to do about it. By this stage, it was nigh impossible to not read something sinister into everything she said or did. This wasn't at all like me, though it was what I had become in just under a year. I knew that my race was at the forefront of Sue's mind—she had told me as much—and that wasn't something I could afford to ignore. Months had passed and her comment about racism hadn't been acknowledged or addressed by anyone despite my efforts. It was almost as if she had never said it. Yet I couldn't forget that she *had* said it. It was the elephant in the room and I couldn't get past it.

It was Monday, 24th April and I was working in Liz's office (she was the personnel manager at HMP Foston Hall). I was doing J-SAC feedbacks and in between appointments, I was catching up on other pieces of work and checking email. I was looking for an email from Sue.

At the beginning of the month, I had had an accident in my car just outside HMP Nottingham and was waiting for my insurers to sort out repairs when I found out that I wasn't entitled to a courtesy car. I asked Helen if she would do me a favour and arrange a hire car for me. I was due to keep it from Wednesday 19th April to Monday 24th April; however, when the garage phoned to say that they would need to work on my car for longer, I extended the hire until Wednesday 26th.

Now there was an email, that Katrina from admin had phoned and left a voicemail to alert me to. She had called confirming that, after I had spoken to her in the morning, explaining that I needed the hire car for longer, she had amended the hire details on the Newbold system. Then she ominously directed me to read an email from Sue that had been sent the previous Friday regarding hire cars. As I scrolled through, the first thing I found was an email from Katrina entitled 'Car Hire' with the day's date, reiterating her voicemail message. It said:

> *Olivea, Please be aware of Sue's email sent on Friday 21 April to all advisors who do not have a lease car regarding hire cars.*

I continued to scroll down looking for it whilst thinking how strange it was that Katrina didn't simply tell me what Sue's email was about, yet I had been directed by voicemail and now email to read it. I decided that it wouldn't contain anything good and was probably another rebuke or that Sue had found some other way to make an example of me. She wasn't there when I had originally asked for the hire car because she was on holiday and perhaps, if she had been there, she would have denied my request. I thought perhaps she wanted to watch me cancel appointments for a whole week because I didn't have a car. That would have enabled her to give me a warning for letting my clients down. My mind was racing and going through scenario after scenario. None of them were good. I hadn't made the request because I felt I was entitled to a hire car, I had made it because I was in an awkward position and, as advisors, we couldn't do our jobs without a car. I was without the funds to sort the problems myself; otherwise, no one would have known that I was in difficulty. So I had asked for help and Helen and Katrina had helped me. Yet now it very much seemed that trouble was brewing. A horrible sense of foreboding overshadowed me and I had to tell myself that whatever was contained in the email, I would get through it. For months now my anxiety levels were so high that whenever I checked my emails and saw that Sue was the sender it filled me with absolute dread. Even though I knew that that wasn't a rational response to something as commonplace as an email, my heart was still pounding at speed and my breathing was shallow.

So there I was looking at the screen. In the short time it took to scroll down, read Katrina's email and then scroll down to Sue's email, I was too upset to read it. I was over-anxious and angry because someone had reduced me to this quivering wreck. I felt I was losing the battle to stay sane.

I calmed myself. Eventually I opened the email and it said:

> *Dear All,*
> *As you have elected not to take the lease car option, from immediate effect, L&MD will no longer provide hire*

> *cars. You will need to ensure that you have sufficient insurance cover that provides for a courtesy car during periods such as repair/maintenance etc., or alternatively you would be required to take annual leave.*

So I was right. I couldn't help but conclude that Sue was still trying to get at me because the wording of the email mirrored my situation exactly: I was the only member of the team who had a hire car due to not being able to secure a courtesy car whilst mine was being repaired. I was just grateful I had re-hired the car the previous Friday some four hours before Sue got the notion to make things impossible for me. I had made the call to the hire company before calling Newbold, because I wanted to query if I could keep the same model that I was driving and, after they confirmed that I could, they automatically extended the hire arrangement. If Sue was unhappy about this, she would have had to contact the hire company directly to cancel the extension, knowing it would have left me without a car. So she probably signed it off begrudgingly and then crafted this email to prevent further re-hiring. Although emotionally upset, I felt largely unaffected by the immediacy of the email: I had a car to do my job and that was what mattered most. I was due to get my car back on Wednesday (26th) anyway, and my situation hadn't forced me to cancel any appointments. I was grateful for that.

The following day the garage phoned to say they had underestimated the timescales and would need to keep my car until Friday 28th April. My heart fell to the floor and panic set in. I didn't know what to do. I couldn't ask Sue for an extension because I believed her email, and the immediacy of it, was engineered to prevent further extensions to my current arrangement. Furthermore, I was feeling incredibly humiliated and demeaned by her, and having to ask for an extension would have felt more like having to beg, which was degrading. Additionally, I was fairly sure she would simply re-route me back to the email. She had used the same tactic when it came to dealing with my expenses, where I was to be based and gaining financial support to do my Masters. Each time she had let me explain my dilemma, let me make the request and then humiliated me by saying 'no' whilst simultaneously directing me to my contract or a policy of some kind. She revelled in her power. I rarely got any kind of flexibility or accommodation from Sue. I didn't feel strong enough to go through that cycle again. I was so wearied by what was happening to me. I had started to experience dizzy spells whilst driving over the last few days and they were scaring me. I was either close to tears or crying. I was constantly watching my back and going over my own work two and three times to make sure I hadn't done something Sue or Val could pick me up on. And now I was expected to beg. I just couldn't do it! The next day the hire company came to collect their car and I was left without a vehicle to do my job.

I spoke to Rudy about it and we agreed we didn't have the funds to re-hire the car ourselves. Although payday was looming, it simply wasn't close enough. He proposed that he drive me to HMP Glen Parva in the morning and then go on to his workplace. However, we ruled that out because he had such an early start, so putting the hour he would need to get me to Leicester and then another hour for him to get back on track on his journey would have made it impractical for both of us. I decided to take the train.

The next day, when I arrived at Leicester station there were only black cabs available. I couldn't afford the fare, yet I remained upbeat because I was only a 10-minute drive away, traffic permitting. I would take the bus. I had plenty of time as it was just before 8.00am and my appointment was not until 9.30am. I had no idea just how the best-laid plans of mice and men could go so awry.

The bus that was due in five minutes didn't show up. The next bus scheduled to arrive half an hour later, was nearly half an hour late. I started to panic because, by this time, I only had approximately 20 minutes to get to my appointment and the bus had already started to go along unfamiliar routes. Whilst I was on the bus my mobile rang. I could see that it was my client. I was too embarrassed to answer my phone and tell him I was on the bus. And I didn't know where I was or how long it would take to get to him. I didn't answer the call. I kept thinking how even the prisoners got taxis ordered for them and there I was on the bus. The bus went all over Leicester and because I wasn't familiar enough with the geography of the city, I dared not get off just in case I was miles away from the prison. I kept looking for landmarks that I knew so I could leap off the bus and run to the prison gate. By the time I got to the stop nearest the prison, I was an emotional wreck. I needed the 10-minute walk to the gate to compose myself and carry myself in a professional manner.

I arrived at approximately 10.00am. My client took around 15 minutes to collect me. When he arrived, I apologised for being so late. He was fine and he went on about how bad the traffic was in Leicester. He'd assumed that I had driven. I let him ramble while I agreed with his observations about rush hour traffic.

When we finished his one-to-one, I walked back to the bus stop, waited for half an hour in the rain for the next bus, then got the next train back to Wellingborough. By the time I walked home I felt as if I had been in the ring with Mike Tyson—I felt battered, disoriented and exhausted. I was unbearably miserable. I couldn't understand how things had come to this. However, it wasn't over as, when I got home, there were a number of letters from Stacey.

When I opened the first one, I found that she had changed my reporting line again—despite my objections. She also refused my proposals to work on the REAG training strategy on a shared-resource basis. The other letters related to each grievance I had raised. As I read them, it seemed to me that Stacey was proposing a few quick fixes in an attempt to avoid doing a full investigation into all of my claims. With each grievance I raised I was actually hoping that Stacey would see that something was fundamentally wrong at the college; instead, I felt as if she was making me look as though I was over-sensitive and finding problems that didn't exist.

For example, she offered to move me from the ground floor to the 1st floor as if I hadn't been affected by this oversight, forgetting that, even if I moved, that that wouldn't necessarily stop the room from falling silent when I walked in or persuade Sue to treat me like a human being. Concerning the trips to Barbados and Bermuda, Stacey had sent an attachment copy of an email addressed to the LMD advisors including me, detailing both trips abroad dated 25th November 2005. I wondered how had I not seen this email before. Even more curious—as I turned the page there was also a 'read receipt' attached; this suggested that I had read it back then. Instantly, I thought that this was damning evidence and that I needed to remove the Barbados and Bermuda trips from the investigation request. I had made a mistake. But then as I thought, I remembered that a 'read receipt' wasn't categorical evidence that an email had been read because, when in 'preview' mode in *Outlook*, the highlight bar activates the tracker mechanism whether you have opened the email or not. It was good to see proof that an email had indeed been sent even though I couldn't account for how I managed to miss it in November. Maybe I deleted it without reading it as some days there were over a hundred emails to read. So the fault *was* mine. Yet my concerns around exclusion went beyond my being copied in on a single email, inasmuch as there was no active communication about the project, even though we had met as a team on four other occasions from that date. The first time it had been mentioned, and then only in passing, was 14th February– some three months later, by which time teams had been selected per project. Up until that point, it hadn't been an agenda item or discussed under AOB. There were no follow-up emails or reports on progress; there was nothing–radio silence. I felt that there could have been any number of reasons why I hadn't read the email and I had no choice whilst holding the evidence in my hands but to accept the responsibility for missing it. What I couldn't understand was how missing that single email all those months ago resulted in my having no knowledge of these opportunities until it was too late to either apply or contribute. The silence about the projects abroad was an uncharacteristic departure from normal practice within the group. In our team meetings, it was customary to give an update or outline of the respective stages of a project. Yet in this case, there had been no announcements of how many people had shown an interest. There had been no announcements about who had been successful in securing the appointments. There had been no announcements as to the type of content that might be covered and no requests for volunteers to support. Had there been any such broadcast before 14th February, it would have given me equal opportunity to get involved on many levels.

    As I confirmed to myself that I still needed to include this complaint in the investigation, despite the November dated email, I noted in the 'tracking' record that, unlike me, Rachel had not activated a 'read receipt' yet she was still going to Bermuda. I wondered, if she hadn't read the email then how did she get to know about the project sufficient to secure selection. What's more, closer scrutiny revealed that Pauline wasn't even on the original circulation list of the email, yet she was also going to Bermuda. After all this deliberation, I was satisfied that sending a solitary email didn't secure or promote active involvement. It was clear that other mechanisms had been employed to include others, yet not me. I was confident that the question of my involvement in the projects, or lack thereof remained a key issue worthy of investigation.

The next morning, I got to HMP Wellingborough by taxi, as Mum paid my fare. She was appalled I was going to walk to my appointment. I told her it was only about one and a half miles; however, she maintained it wasn't about the mileage, it was about the principle. She was upset that things had been allowed to get this far. I took her kind offer. I was due to receive feedback from all the tests I had sat in relation to the new roles we were going for. Because the new role was considered a managed promotion, all advisors who expressed an interest in it had to do a ninety-minute case study, a 360-degree assessment and psychometric tests. Then the results were to be triangulated, and fed back through a coached assessment interview by an external agency. A development plan would then be drafted and forwarded to the area manager, who would use the outputs when the advisor went for the internal board interview. All of this extra effort was necessary in order to justify a managed promotion to Manager D level. Personnel were clear that, just because the restructure process created the new roles, an advisor couldn't apply unless he/she went through this compulsory process which was specifically designed to allow candidates to clearly demonstrate that they had the aptitude, competencies and skills to work at a higher level.

The new role for the region was 'ring-fenced' for me and the area personnel manager, Val Perry, who had interviewed me right at the beginning of this journey. The role was ring-fenced insomuch as no one else was eligible to apply for the role unless either Val or I proved to be unsuitable. This was part of the fair competition protocols that were worked into the recruitment and selection strategy, in recognition that the job was made up of elements of both our current roles. Rumour had it, however, that Val Perry wasn't going to compete for the job because she was going to retire within the next 18 months with Bob, her husband and area manager for the East Midlands. In any case, as long as my results were adequate, I would be eligible to compete for the role. I prayed that my results were good enough, as I didn't think I could take another blow that week.

My feedback was excellent. I had so few development needs in relation to the new role, the consultant said I should be proud of myself. And I was. I went home on a high. This was good news. It meant there was nothing in terms of skill deficits or operational and Human Resource knowledge, standing in the way of a promotion. Indeed all I had to do was get through the interview, which would be by the end of May. And, if successful, I would be promoted to Manager D. I would be able to leave the college and work from area office, reporting into the area manager.

It was all finally coming together. I had a few years in the Service under my belt, which goes a long way in a place where people are 'civilian phobic'. I had good rapport with many of the governors and their staff in the East Midlands. I was about to finish my Masters degree. And this new job meant a long-awaited promotion and the facility to start earning what I used to earn before I joined the Service. I could finally see the light at the end of the tunnel. I knew I wasn't there yet but, for the first time in a while, I could see a future. I could see myself being strategically positioned to effect change in the Service and progressing. And, better still, these assessment results and, hopefully, a successful interview would speak louder than the criticisms I had endured to date.

Rudy came home early so I could pick my car up. I decided to raise another grievance about the whole car-hire saga. I think the buzz from the good feedback and the hope that I could move on gave me the impetus I needed to continue to address the inequalities at the college—at least for as long as I was there. I was not going to forget that Sue put racism on the table, not until I had an explanation as to why it was there, along with remedy for the humiliation she caused me.

I was finding it virtually impossible to distinguish between Sue genuinely doing her job and getting at me. It was evident to me that she didn't like or respect me, yet I couldn't tell when she was simply doing what she would normally do with anyone else, and when her prejudice was influencing her decisions. As such, I couldn't afford to let any incident pass just in case she was discriminating against me unlawfully. I decided it was better to raise the issues and be told later that there was nothing in it, than to suffer endless torment wondering 'what if'.

Whilst in consideration mode, I prayed a prayer of forgiveness for Sue, Stacey and the Service. It was important that I approached this situation without bitterness in my heart, since bitterness clouds judgement. I was already unwell and had much to deal with. I didn't want to start behaving as they were.

I met with William from the PCS trade union on 2nd May to go over the proposals made by Stacey in her response to the grievances. PCS are the trade union for the civil service and government agencies. I had contacted them in March and William was assigned as my representative. We had met briefly at the end of March but this was to be the first time we were to actively work on my case.

William was very tall and pale. Both his jacket and his trousers were too small and his shirt was un-ironed. He perfectly exemplified Ichabod Crane, the fictional character from *The Legend of Sleepy Hollow,* the short story by Washington Irving. He more closely matched the Disney animated version where Bing Crosby was the narrator. William was pleasant, quietly spoken and well mannered.

As I couldn't face going into Newbold, William met me at the Wellingborough local college. We used one of the business suites on the premises. We spent three or four hours discussing Stacey's responses and our best and most constructive approach to them. William was so patient with me. I think he realised that when I spoke to him it was the only time I had been able to talk at length to someone in the Service about what I was experiencing. Even though I was fairly random and repeated myself several times, he just let me vent. I'm not sure how productive it was for the matters at hand but it was certainly cathartic for me.

As we responded to Stacey, William outlined that another change to my reporting line was expressly what I had asked her not to do. I had already endured a line management change, and when Stacey had made me aware that she was considering another change in the meeting we had in March, I was adamant that I didn't want this. Yet here I was responding to her decision to change my line management again.

William and I also responded to Stacey's refusal to formally investigate everyone who was present at the meeting when Di made the racist comments. I had previously responded to Stacey about this on 6th April saying that I was *'appalled that* [the college], *a centre for learning excellence with* [LMD] *charged with the responsibility of shaping and encouraging core behaviours…amongst our up and coming governors and leaders, listened to these comments with indifference'*. Although I was sure she was aware, I also reflected on how I had frequently watched team members advise managers in training to stop any form of racist behaviour immediately, quoting appropriate breaches in policy under threat of failing exams if they didn't challenge inappropriate behaviour in this way. I reminded her that these advisors were embarking on the delivery of J-SAC feedback to countless managers who had failed when they were measured against Prison Service principles. Yet, bizarrely, this same group of trained professionals and managers sat through a meeting where racist comments were made implying 'white superiority', and did not flinch at references to marijuana reinforcing negative stereotypes about black people. I outlined that, in view of the sombre responsibility for addressing inappropriate behaviours sitting squarely on the shoulders of *these* advisors in particular and managers who were present in the room when the racist comments were made, they should absolutely be included as part of the investigation. They had failed to act in a way that they regularly stipulated others must and she should want to know why that was.

Yet now William and I were responding to her view that… *'I consider the other individuals present at the meeting not to be directly relevant to this and that this is a management issue for me to take forward as I feel most appropriate.'*

The final considerations for the day were with regard to the flexible working option I proposed in relation to the REAG secondment Stacey had offered me. Stacey had ultimately decided that, *'it would be best for business continuity that* [I] *continue*[d] *with* [my] *work in the East Midlands'.*

I conveyed my upset to William that she had broken her word; however, after a little more discussion we decided that we would leave that battle and concentrate on the war.

Chapter Eight

Reverberations

On 3rd May, I was planning to go to HMP Morton Hall in Lincoln to deliver a workshop. Mum had been quite ill for the previous few days and at around 6.30am she was so ill I had to call the NHS emergency number. The nurse listened to me outlining her symptoms; however, when she heard how Mum was breathing in the background she told me to call an ambulance immediately. It was all very frightening: Mum was shaking violently; she was incoherent, having difficulty breathing and crying out in pain. I tried to remain calm, but I was absolutely terrified. I called the ambulance and texted my family and the Elders of the church, asking them to pray.

When the paramedics arrived, they spent around thirty minutes with Mum trying to get her breathing and temperature under control, after which they decided to take her to A&E in Kettering. The paramedics asked me if I wanted to ride in the back of the ambulance with Mum; however, I was paralysed by the dilemma and couldn't decide. If I went in the ambulance and on arrival at the hospital she started to recover, I wouldn't be able to get back in time to pick up my car, drive to Lincoln and get there before the start of the programme. There was no way I could cancel. Sue would find out and crucify me. For what felt like an eternity, I was crippled with indecision fearing the repercussions of not going to Lincoln. In desperation, I asked Rudy to follow the ambulance without any regard for what he had planned for the day. I would take my car and do the same after sending an email to the client to let them know that I would like to start the session later, at around 9.30am or 10.00am, and the reasons why.

The ambulance left with Mum with Rudy following behind.

I tried three times to log on remotely and was thrown out by the system. At 7.45am, it was still too early to ring HMP Morton Hall; I knew the training manager wouldn't yet be on site. In the end, I tried to guess the email addresses and sent a mail from my home computer. I locked up the house and went to get into my car, which wouldn't open with the key pad. After a couple of attempts, I assumed the keypad was dead and went back into the house to get the spare key, but I got the same result. I hadn't driven the car since I had picked it up from the garage on Friday 28th April, so I rang them to find out if this had something to do with their workmanship. I finally got a response at 8.15am: the receptionist said no one was available until 8.30am. I went back inside the house to wait. At about 8.45am I received a call from Emma, the Training Manager at HMP Morton Hall and I explained everything. I must have sounded like a complete head-case as I rattled off my dilemma. She very kindly acknowledged that my first priority was Mum's wellbeing and suggested that we merge Wednesday's and Thursday's delegates together because both groups were below the optimum numbers anyway. I was so grateful and relieved and thanked her. I finally got through to the garage who claimed that if there was a problem that it was not likely to be down to their workmanship. I called the RAC. When the mechanic arrived, he found that the boot had not been closed properly and the little light had been on draining the battery probably from the time I dropped the car off at the repairers. He charged the battery and I had to leave it running for about an hour. After this, I went to see my Mum.

On the way to the hospital, I was racked with guilt because I sent her in the ambulance alone. What was I thinking? I chastised myself. The picture of her with an oxygen mask and an ECG attached to her chest flashed before my eyes and the guilt deepened. How could I have watched her suffer so? Instead of being concerned about her welfare, I was consumed with worry about being told off by Sue. How pathetic had I become? Even Emma, the Training Manager for HMP Morton Hall, a person I barely knew, had instantly recognised what the priorities were, yet I had become incapable of putting my family first. Irrational fear had devoured all sense of reason.

When I arrived, I found Mum resting comfortably. The worst seemed to be over but the doctors wanted to keep her in hospital for observation over the next few days.

The following day, after returning from a long day at Lincoln, I picked up a letter from Stacey. She had responded to my grievance about the car hire saga. She decided that, had I asked Sue for an extension, I would have got one. I was disappointed she had again formed a judgement about a situation I had asked her to enquire into, without speaking to me. I couldn't understand why it was so difficult for her to hear my side of the story. Why was no one listening to me?

I had a quick shower and changed into a pair of jeans and a tee-shirt. Then Rudy and I went to visit Mum at the hospital. As we drove, I fought back tears that seemed to spring from an underground well. I turned my head as if to stare out of the passenger window and bobbed my head to the music playing on the radio so that Rudy couldn't see just how out of control I was. But, as the despair swelled in my fragile heart, the tears surged pushing themselves through my tightly closed eyelids. Stop crying Olivea– you'll get caught. Come o-o-o-on, pull yourself together, woman! I was losing myself: falling deeper and deeper into a hole that had no sides and no bottom. All I could see was the rapidly diminishing exit above me. Then when Rudy asked if we should get a Chinese takeaway meal or a pizza after visiting with Mum, the jig was up! My face was completely wet. I tried to wipe the tears but it was too late: Rudy could see.

'Oh sweetheart,' he said, his voice full of equal emotion. He reached over to touch my hand. It was all I needed.

Mum came home a few days later. She was quite delicate, yet she was home. The infection was under control and she had some new medication to take. She is such a soldier. She has battled many illnesses for most of her life, yet you couldn't keep her down for long. I was glad she was home.

As May continued, I became more withdrawn both at work and at home. I felt completely beaten by the systematic bullying and harassment. I was filled with anxiety every time I had to go in to Newbold: it was a hostile and intimidating environment. I was having dizzy spells more often and becoming more anxious about them. There seemed to be no way to end the vicious cycle. I didn't want to go to the doctor for fear that I would be signed off sick. I felt that was just what Sue wanted: something tangible to say I was unreliable, unable to perform. So I carried on.

Yet blow followed blow like day followed night. During our team meeting on 10th May Sue announced that Di had secured the position of National Fast Track Manager D. I could not believe it. Last month Sue had secured promotion from Acting Head of LMD to Head of LMD, even though there were six active grievances of racial discrimination, unfair treatment and harassment against her with formal investigation outcomes pending. Although there were very serious and unanswered questions about her management capabilities, her style and some of the decisions she made, she was nevertheless promoted. And now, the person who had made racially offensive comments in a public setting had secured promotion too. We were in the middle of the investigation and people were getting on with their lives as if nothing was happening. Of course, I had seen the job advertised and I was more than qualified to do it; however, with my application needing to be signed off by Sue and the likelihood of her being on the selection board *and* interview panel, I felt my chances were, at best, nil. In fact, I had seen a number of jobs at the college that had been created as part of the restructure but thought that, if I could barely persuade Sue to say 'Good morning', in response to a simple greeting, that I had no hope of getting a job where she was involved on so many levels.

As the announcements continued, to make matters worse, Sue explained that Di would be working on a shared-resource basis: two days managing her core duties and three days in her temporary promoted role. What I was feeling at that point was so complex that words like *disappointed* or *let down* seemed puerile and inadequate. As the news settled that the very arrangement I had asked for was denied me, yet was readily available to someone who had made racist comments not two months ago and who had not spoken to me since, I despaired. I couldn't think what to do. I didn't see the point of raising another grievance because things were just getting worse for me. If I did complain again, it would be the eighth official grievance. I thought, how ridiculous that anyone could raise two or even three complaints in such a short space of time, but eight…eight was ludicrous. If I did this, I would be seen in one of two ways: either I was crazy and complained about absolutely everything or I was sane and there was something seriously wrong at the college. My confidence levels were such that I thought the former view was gaining in momentum. I wanted to be taken seriously, though I was becoming confused about the best way to do that.

I met my new interim manager, Steve, on 12th May. He explained that the meeting would be relatively informal; it was just so we could introduce ourselves. He talked at length about his career in the Service and asked me to talk about my employment history. Afterwards he explained that he wasn't involved with the ongoing grievances and I was to let him know if I needed help in any other area. I took a chance and asked for special leave in June after I explained I had already booked annual leave for 12th to 16th June but due to stress had fallen behind with my studies. I felt I needed more time to complete my Masters assignment and dissertation. He agreed to an additional six days from 19th to 26th June and asked me to send the request in writing. I did so when I returned to my office. I was fairly guarded in the meeting, not only because I didn't want yet another line manager, but also because I couldn't be sure what he had been told about me. I felt judged nearly all the time. Having a new manager who already had some insight into my situation (though not from me) served only to increase my anxiety.

I was fortunate to attend my first meeting of the Black Manager's Forum on 23rd May in North Kilworth, Leicestershire. It was such a complete departure from everything I had experienced at the college or, indeed, the Service. To be surrounded by so many black professionals was an extremely positive experience. The consultant hired for the day, also black, took us through a very simple exercise. We were asked to plot on a grid what we felt our relationship and expectations of the Service were, from when we started to the present day. We used a scale from the number 1 (being 'very poor') to 10 (being 'excellent') on the vertical measure. The horizontal measure was the number of years worked in the Service from five to 25 plus years. I was shocked to see the level of consistency when the delegates shared their graphs. Many of them, including myself, had high expectations within the first year of employment–mostly between 7 and 10. Afterwards, however, most graphs showed a rapid decline over the years. A few individuals showed the 'relationship with the organisation' line plummeting below zero and plateauing there for several years. I measured myself as starting at 8 and spiralling down to 0.5.

This was quite sad. It gave rise to several managers sharing their experiences of the Service, the lack of support and blatant racism they had encountered. One Asian woman had just come back to work after six months sick leave due to the stress caused by the racism she had faced. She related how she was treated with indifference on her first day back. She didn't get a 'return to work' interview; no one assessed her fitness to return; no one updated her on what had been happening in the prison or the organisation during her absence. It was as if she had never been away and having returned she was invisible. She was hurt by it. On the verge of tears, she expressed that she was unable to say how much longer she could stand being ignored. Everyone was refreshingly candid about their experiences and their expectations of the Service; it was just sad that not one person expressed any kind of hope for a brighter future. We were like rats trapped in a cruel experiment. The stories shared included being passed over for promotion, being challenged about the need to have a Black Manager's Forum in the first place, facing discrimination for needing the time off to attend the Forum meetings, being scrutinised unnecessarily and having to do more than their white counterparts, whilst remaining unrecognised and unrewarded. There was anger in the room about Phil Wheatley, the Director General, needing yet still more statistical evidence of racism in the Service before he was prepared to commit to an effective programme to combat it. It was almost as if he was unconvinced that racism existed in the organisation. The managers were tired of having to answer more questions and take part in more surveys, as it was clear that nothing was going to be done. All they wanted was an honest response to the racism they were experiencing. Instead, they got an inability even to accept that there was a problem and a lack of will to comprehend the devastating effects of racism on the human spirit. There was an indisputable sense of powerlessness and weariness amongst the managers, many of whom had been facing racism for their entire stay in the Service. I shared their despair.

When I got home, I checked my email to find that William, from PCS, had sent me the responses to the RR65 questionnaire I had served the college with in March. I wondered if they had answered all the questions properly and transparently. I was intrigued and hopeful that there were things in their responses I could use as evidence later down the line. As I opened the document, the first thing that struck me was the answers to my questions about the ethnic make-up of the college. Out of 296 people employed to work at Newbold, 288 people were white and only eight people were from a BME background. It was no wonder Stacey believed that they didn't have a problem. How could they have a problem with integration and acceptance when there was barely anyone to mix with! And, who would want to make a complaint in an environment like that? I had only done it because my back was against the wall. Had God not spoken to me, I was getting ready to run as fast as my little legs would carry me! I wondered how many black and Asian people had chosen to leave over the years, rather than take the college on, knowing that they were grossly outnumbered. In response to my questions about diversity training for all the staff, none had been done since 2004. I also asked about training that went beyond the cursory awareness training, because I knew the current package was out of date and lacking in depth and challenge. Their response was that the senior management team had undertaken group training in 2003. When I asked how many staff had been trained in investigation techniques and their ethnic make-up, the response was 24 staff, none of whom were from a BME background. I was trying to get a picture of how confident black people would be to raise a concern. Certainly, if at any time you felt racially compromised and you could only talk to someone who represented those who compromised you—there was little incentive even to broach the subject of unfair treatment.

The training records were very illuminating. The college had attempted to make the entries anonymous (Person 1 to Person 15), but it was easy, from start dates and anecdotal information I knew about the individuals in the group, to work out whose details I was reading. In appreciation that people had joined the team with previous skills and training, I had asked the college to specifically outline the training that *they* had paid for, for members of my team.

The training account in this report spanned three pages, with numerous entries for all the advisors—except me. I had three entries against my profile and they were: induction, familiarisation visits (which of course was induction by another name) and a two-day 360-degree training entry. I did a calculation of induction days for the team to find that each member had received between 0-10 days' induction. This included the people who had joined the college after me, with no prison service experience. I, on the other hand, had had just over 70 days' induction across four months. Even civilians joining to become prison officers at six weeks were on a shorter induction than I was.

When I looked at the level of investment of the various accredited programmes, qualifications and workshops for all the staff, it made me feel worthless. Furthermore, I had thought that only Rachel had secured MBTI training, as Di had joined the team with the Level A and B licence. Yet, according to these records, Di had additionally received more MBTI training and another psychometric tool. This meant that they both now had the suite of skills that were necessary for the new roles in the restructure, whilst I was without them. In that moment I empathised all the more with the managers I had met at the Black Manager's Forum earlier on in the day. It is the most demoralising of feelings to suspect that people don't care about you or consider that you are not worth much. Yet there is always something at the back of your mind, hoping that your suspicions are not proven. But when they are, even when you were the one who pushed for the disclosure, you want to return immediately to moments before, when there was an element of doubt. That doubt provided an unlikely comfort. It always whispered, 'You might be wrong about this—of course they like you; of course they value you.' But once you know that they don't, once you know that they don't consider you worth the investment—the finality of the discovery hits you hard and replaces the unlikely comfort with deadness.

As I read through the 25-page document, I saw that the college had given national responses to many of my questions, quoting national Prison Service statistics and attainment. This made it difficult to get a localised picture of what was specifically happening at the college. An overall pattern was beginning to form. At the college, there was little to no experience of or appreciation of the fact that people of different colours and cultures worked there. No one had been trained recently, even to basic awareness levels. They had not looked at their ethnic make-up to put positive action in place or, at the very least, made sure the few ethnic staff they had were comfortable and happy about treatment. How hard would it have been to ask eight people if they felt they were being treated fairly? We were so disposable, so incidental that we were not even on the radar of equal and fair treatment. Indeed, it seemed that there were so few people of difference in the college, it was no wonder people like Stacey, Sue and Val struggled to understand different ways of working or different needs. They only understood themselves and people like themselves. Virtually everyone at the college was white and I was in no doubt that it had been that way for a very long time.

Chapter Nine

The Investigation

On 26th May, I planned to be at Newbold for half a day to meet the investigation officers for introductions and I had an appointment at HMP Nottingham in the afternoon. I had been compiling an evidence file so the officers could see what I was specifically upset about. It mostly contained email exchanges and printouts of my diary, so that they could see that criticisms of how I managed my time were unfounded.

True to form, after printing some documents, I went upstairs to say 'Good morning' to my co-workers. I found Sue and Helen in the admin office. Helen had her back to me and opposite her was Sue, who was facing me as I came through the door. I smiled at Sue and said a hearty 'Good morning', even though inside I felt as if I was dying. I kept telling myself, 'Don't let them see you break.' Helen turned round and said 'Good morning' in response; Sue continued to read a document aloud to Helen, without breaking to acknowledge me. She completely ignored me. I felt as if my legs were made of lead. My brain was processing the fact that I had been blatantly ignored and slighted yet again. Then I realised that I was just standing in the doorway and not moving. I came to my senses, walked across the room, picked up my printing and left the office.

On the way back down the stairs I reflected on how energised I had been when I joined the Service and how I now felt as if I had been ground to dust. I came on board with real passion and drive and high expectations but found only indifference, ridicule, and prejudice.

It was going to be some three hours before I met the investigators, so I settled into getting on with my work whilst waiting for William from PCS, who had agreed to accompany me. I wondered how the investigators would see me. Of course, I knew that they would be objective, though they had already interviewed a number of staff. I wondered if there were any early indicators to support my allegations or if evidence to the contrary had been provided.

William arrived approximately thirty minutes before the meeting started. He asked how I was and I told him I was incredibly wearied by the whole thing, yet grateful I was meeting the investigators to arrange the interview. I had no idea what to expect, never having been on the receiving end of a complex investigation before. He assured me the investigators would tell me what to expect and I could ask as many questions as I wanted to.

When the time came, we made our way to the meeting room and when we got to the building, we knocked on the door and were called in. As we entered the room, I was totally caught off-guard to find a microphone and tape recording equipment already set up. Panic set in before I had even taken my seat. Apparently, there had been some sort of mix-up and neither William nor I had realised that I was actually going to be interviewed there and then. All the anxiety that I had tried to keep in check burst its banks.

Rob, the lead investigator, could see my confusion and discomfort as I spluttered that I wasn't expecting to be interviewed.

'If you're not prepared to have the interview we could reschedule to another time?'

Richie, whom I'd met earlier in the year from REAG, was the supporting officer and concurred with Rob. Their recognition of my plight and the will to accommodate me brought instant perspective. I needed to get this out of the way.

I took a deep breath and said it made sense to have the interview. They were running a little behind schedule and asked us to come back in an hour. William and I went back to my office to wait and I cancelled my afternoon appointment in Nottingham.

Although mentally unprepared for the interview, I was glad that I had been working on an evidence file. It wasn't complete, but I felt it would be useful and I brought it with me when we returned to the interview room.

Rob started the interview with introductions. He was tall and dark-haired. He looked very sure of himself and this put me a little more at ease. He looked as if he meant business, and that was what I needed. After stating his name for the purposes of the tape, Rob went straight in to asking me to explain my role and history at the college. Then he got into the real business of the interview.

'In our interview with Sue, she describes your and her relationship up until a meeting in October as pretty okay, pretty straightforward, no particular issues. Is that how you would describe it?'

Wow! What an opener, I thought. Everything was fine until the meeting when Olivea lost all sense of proportion and reality? How could she say that everything was okay up until that point? By that time, I had already complained about expenses payments, my induction, home working, her management style–yet she says there were no issues? I was astounded.

Rob was waiting for an answer. It wasn't the right time for me to try and make sense out of what Sue had said: I needed to answer the question posed.

'No,' I said.

'How would you describe it prior to October 2005?'

I started to explain the difficulties with my induction, how I had questioned the quality of our relationship and so on, when he began to query the timelines and I started to get a little confused. The evidence file that I had brought with me was not only incomplete, it wasn't well organised yet. It was divided into themed sections like the car hire, MBTI training and so forth; however, I hadn't got round to putting things in chronological order. As I tried to be more specific about dates and some of the things that had actually been said, I could feel my anxiety levels climbing again. I was flicking through the pages in clear hole-punched pockets, hoping to stumble across vital information, and I could hear myself stating that an event had taken place on a certain date and, before I finished the sentence, I had changed my mind as to what had happened and when. Oh no, I thought to myself, I must sound as if I don't know what I'm talking about! Within minutes of this muddle, I asked if we could stop the interview so I could get my personal diary from my office. I just had visions of undermining my evidence by messing up my dates and confusing incidents.

When the interview resumed, the investigators decided to focus on the 12th October meeting. They wanted my take on how it had gone, since Sue had described me as aggressive. They also mentioned that Sue didn't consider that there was anything wrong with the quality of my work, it was the quantity she questioned: I wasn't doing enough of it.

How disappointing to find out that she saw me as black, aggressive and lazy–hardly original, I thought and yet highly offensive. I wondered why there was this reliance on stereotypes, why white people so readily adopted this default position, whenever their treatment of black people came into question. It wasn't until I received a copy of the transcripts from all the interviews the following month that I realised just how determined Sue was to ascribe the same instability of character typified by pro-slavery arguments. When asked about the events of 12th October Sue had actually said:

SB: *Olivea did get very aggressive.*

RD: *Oh right. Why do you use the term aggressive?*

SB: *Because* [of] *her body language and the way she was speaking. She was speaking in a very aggressive sort of manner. She came over as what I see as aggressive, with her body language and her eye contact. It's what I would define as aggressive.*

RD: *What would prevent it being–that same demeanour, being defined as assertive?*

SB: *Assertive is standing your own ground and making somebody see something from your point of view. Olivea was quite, well she was very accusing and the way she was speaking, I mean it's a fine line but to me I would describe it as aggressive not assertive.*

RD: *She was very accusing?*

SB: *Yes.*

RD: *Can you example that…?*

SB: *She was saying 'you have no evidence'…and 'you can't do this and you can't do that' was the terminology she was using and I think it says in there* [referring to the complaints] *she kept saying to me 'you're treating me differently and I don't understand why,' and she said that about six or seven times!…*

> (p.674 of Investigation Transcript ISS 54/2006 Sue Brookes Interview)

Sue never departed from her reliance on black stereotypes. In her witness statement, she recorded my behaviour as demonstrating increasing levels of anger and aggression:

> *Para 34: The conversation* [on 12th October] *had deteriorated by this point and the Claimant* [Olivea] *seemed to get angrier as the meeting went on. As I raised issues she got more and more angry…(para 37) and she also seemed very angry with me for bringing up these issues in the first place…(para 40) Towards the end of the meeting, the Claimant got very angry indeed (para 41). I said that I would confirm the outcome of the meeting in writing. She was very aggressive at this point.*

My interview lasted around three hours and when I came out I felt numb. Everything made perfect sense now: Sue's inability to trust me when I worked from home, her resistance to allowing me to manage my own timetable, her need to scrutinise me constantly. I hadn't given her cause to think about me in this way. Her suspicions about my work practices were without merit and had surfaced within weeks of my arrival in May, yet she didn't tackle my alleged poor performance until October, despite having had one-to-ones with me each month. Even then, she wasn't really faulting my work per se, she was just finding fault in general and making specious observations. And, of course, there was her indefensible mention of race.

William said I had done well, though I didn't feel the same. I felt there were too many gaps in my information. I thanked him for his support, said goodbye, and made my way back to my office. I sat at my desk for a long while as I considered how painfully difficult it was to be fully assured of something yet lack unequivocal evidence to prove what you knew to be true. I tried to work out how exactly someone ought to go about proving that someone else or an organisation was racist today when no one is calling you a nigger to your face anymore. I considered that even the British National Party (BNP) doesn't admit to being racist and fiercely rejects the inference. Rather they portray themselves as existing purely to protect the future for the indigenous people who first migrated to this country. I smiled at the concept of indigenous migrants. If ever there was an oxymoron—that was it!

After revisiting all the questions and my answers for what felt like an obsessive-compulsive one hundred times, I simply hoped I had done enough at least to convey there were very real problems at the college. I was not over-sensitive or paranoid. I also hoped the investigators would be able to uncover the information and records that I didn't have access to. For example, I had good reason to believe that certain team members had the flexibility of where they could be based worked into their contract, not least because they admitted as much; however, the personnel department would hold those files as confidential. Maybe that information, among other things, might show that Sue had racially discriminated against me and that, in a bid to cover her tracks, she had compounded matters by victimising me.

By the time I eventually left the office and made my way home, I was mentally and physically exhausted. I told Rudy what had happened and went through everything again. All we could do now was wait.

I was at Newbold on 30th May and did my duty by popping upstairs to greet the team. I was feeling increasingly alone on the ground floor each time I came into Newbold. Although I often enjoyed the variety of working with teams and alone, knowing I was down there because Sue couldn't even bear to look at me or hear my voice was hurtful. My illness was escalating: I was having panic attacks at home now and more dizzy spells. I was having difficulty sleeping. Every time a client cancelled an appointment, it sent me spiralling into crisis until I found someone else who could fill the space in my diary.

Once my head had cleared about the interview, and after much deliberation, I decided to raise another grievance about Stacey's rejection of my proposal to work on the REAG training strategy on a shared-resource basis. It just made sense to raise it whilst the investigation was under way so they could look at it as part of their enquiries. I thought a lot about how I was being perceived. However, I concluded that, as these things had happened to me, they needed to be formally recorded, no matter what perception people held about me. As bad as things were, if I didn't speak up, then I would be doing myself a disservice. I further thought that, in some strange way, any refusal to speak would have made me complicit in the abuse.

It was now June, yet I had no sense of summer. I hadn't noticed the days getting longer, lighter or warmer. I wasn't looking forward to a holiday or fun in the sun. It was just another month filled with days that I would have to go into Newbold, hours where I would be on my own, minutes where I would be despised.

On 2nd June, Stacey notified William that, due to recent developments, she was about to be questioned as part of the investigation and this meant that she could no longer be the commissioning officer. She informed him that she would be passing the latest grievance, about my not being allowed to work with REAG, to my interim manager, Steve. I didn't know whether to be happy or sad. I couldn't see how my interim manager (who was subordinate to Stacey) was going to get to the bottom of *her* decision. How was Steve supposed to investigate his manager? It wasn't so much that he couldn't investigate someone who was a higher grade, but to investigate his boss whilst still reporting to her for his day-to-day work, I thought was totally preposterous! Exactly how objective could he be? The whole thing was farcical. I wondered if Stacey really thought I hadn't realised that, had she followed protocol, my complaint would go to her superior, the Director of Personnel for the Prison Service, Gareth Hadley. The complaint would no longer be 'contained' at the college. People in high places would have to get involved. However she wasn't about to let that happen, so she devolved the complaint to her subordinate and breached policy. Yet what could I do, I thought– complain again? I decided to take comfort in the fact that the complaint would at least be added to the grievances that were a part of the ongoing investigation. This would ensure it was looked at properly. June already felt incredibly old and tiresome and I was only two days into it.

I was delivering feedback at HMP Wellingborough a few days later. Afterwards, on my way out, I bumped into Dave who had facilitated the *Listen to Improve* focus groups at HMP Lincoln in

April. He ominously said we needed to talk. Instantly worried, I asked him to pass by my house once he finished with his appointments. He arrived for around 3.00pm and, after a cup of tea and some catching up about some of the prisons in the East Midlands, he said that he had been contacted via email by one of Sue's 'people' from the Newbold admin office. They wanted to know if I had turned up to the meeting at HMP Lincoln in April and whether or not the meeting was productive.

I was stunned and couldn't believe my ears. I slumped back into my settee, took a deep breath and expelled the air from my lungs, puffing my cheeks out as if to exorcise Sue from my body. It seemed nothing could stop her from slighting my character and undermining my professionalism.

'I'm sorry I'm bringing you bad news, but I couldn't believe it when I got the email. They're really out to get you aren't they? Why are they trying so hard?'

'I wish I knew. What did you tell them?' The defeat resonated in my tone.

'I told them that you attended both meetings and that I was glad that you were there because you brought an extra dimension to the discussions. And I told them that you helped me with documenting the points that were raised in the meeting and that you were very thorough. I also told them that it was a pleasure to work with you.'

'You know, I sent them copies of the observations I had made during the meetings within a couple of weeks of having written up my notes,' I said. 'That was over a month ago. Do they think that I pretended to go and then made up fictitious notes to cover up my absence?'

'Well I can't believe how blatant they're being. They're not even trying to cover up.'

'Look, I really appreciate you telling me. And thank you for being so positive about me in your reply.'

'No need to thank me, it was the truth.'

'I know, but you could have responded in a way that fuelled whatever it is they're looking for and you didn't. Listen, I need to ask you a favour and if you can't do this I won't think less of you because you've been such a blessing to me already. Could you forward the email exchange to me?'

'Oh I'm not sure if I kept it–I didn't think that far.' He started to look disappointed with himself.

'No that's fine. If you can't find it, then can you send me an email detailing *this* conversation?'

'I tell you what, I'll have a look, and if I can't find it, then I'll do what you said. Do you think I'll be called as a witness? 'cos I'll do it, y'know; I'll give evidence.'

'Let's hope it won't go that far.'

We talked some more about the investigation and my health and he left my house going up to 5.00pm, after wishing me luck and promising to stay in touch. As I waved him off on his motorcycle, I wondered what I had done to deserve such thought and consideration from a virtual stranger. I had only met him on the two-day project in Lincoln and since then he had supported me without faltering and without any thought for his own reputation in the Service. My own colleagues, whom I had known for a little over a year, had not behaved so gallantly.

By 7th June, Dave responded to say that he couldn't find the original email from Newbold; however, he was kind enough to summarise what had happened in his response to me so I could use it as evidence. And I did exactly that. I forwarded it to the investigation officers as further evidence of unreasonable treatment.

I avoided going into Newbold whenever possible, as the thought of running into Sue or any of her accomplices filled me with anxiety. I had suspected some time ago that the admin team were spying on me and now, because of the information provided by Dave, I had confirmation. It seemed as if there were increasingly great forces against me: Sue, Val, Stacey and now the admin team. The institution was ganging up on me. They had committed resources and co-ordinated effort. They were sneaking around just to try to catch me out.

The dizzy spells were getting worse, yet I was due a break of sorts soon, to work on my last assignment before completing my dissertation. I wanted to hold out until then.

On 8th June, I received an email cancelling an appointment I had made to meet Governor Taylor and her team at HMP Lincoln. This was not good news. Both Sue and Val had been making a fuss about this particular prison since February and stressing how important it was for me to do some work there. I still hadn't managed to get in to see the governor. I didn't disagree with them about making HMP Lincoln a priority. I had been offering dates for months since September 2005. And each time, either the dates were not suitable or people became unavailable. I knew that, despite my efforts, Sue and Val would make out that I wasn't doing enough. They had this unwavering negative view of me that I couldn't shake, no matter what I did. On the one hand they acknowledged my work as good, yet there was this prevailing attitude that I could do better, I wasn't as committed as everyone else or I just didn't work as hard as everyone else.

Even though I regularly managed to get into HMP Lincoln to do personal development work with individuals, I knew that it was not the same as running a governor-led, establishment-wide development programme—and this could only be facilitated by meeting Governor Taylor and her team. Neither Sue nor Val had acknowledged the work that I had done with the individuals at HMP Lincoln. Their focus was solely on the one thing that remained just outside my reach.

The following day I received a call from William, my union rep. We were dangerously close to the deadline for logging my claim with the Employment Tribunal (ET). The Employment Tribunals are independent judicial bodies who determine disputes between employers and employees over employment rights. They give you three months less one day from the event that you consider to be racist, to log your complaint with them on an application form (ET1). If you miss this deadline, your application is rejected. This deadline is emblazoned across all ET documentation. I had asked William, weeks earlier, to get confirmation from the union (PCS) that they were going to support my application and help me fill in the necessary details. But now, he was calling to let me know that PCS believed I was entitled to an automatic extension to the deadline because the internal grievance procedure was still ongoing. I therefore did not need to make an application to the ET for another three months. I couldn't understand what he was saying because I hadn't found any such information. I reminded William that I couldn't risk missing the application deadline, especially as he was unable to explain where the union was getting their information from. He said he would call back.

By 12th June I was on annual and study leave. I spent the first day sending emails and checking my work commitments. I couldn't relax until I knew there was nothing that Sue could dig up in the two weeks I was going to be off. William called back as promised to say that the union were adamant I didn't need to complete an ET1 form–the form used to register an application with the Employment Tribunal. Instead, PCS were finally ready to meet with me to discuss the merits of my case, two days before the deadline! PCS also sent me an email strongly advising me not to take any action until they had met with me. I was very confused. I rang the ACAS helpline (the Advisory, Conciliation and Arbitration Service. This is an organisation that provides independent employment relations advice). And I rang the ET helpline and told them about the conflicting information I was being given. Neither could confirm the option for extension to deadlines and both advised me to meet the deadlines as originally intended. I thought, great! I am supposed to be doing my assignment but instead I have to fill in an ET1 form. I didn't even know where to start. What if I left vital information out? What if I didn't properly convey the gravity of my situation? Having read the guidelines to filling in the application, I could see that applications were not automatically accepted. Suppose I messed this up, I fretted. I spent virtually the whole day filling the form in. I had aimed to make the post that evening; however, by the time I had looked through my complaints, recorded the dates and tried to decide which parts of the story I would tell, it was after 5.00pm.

The next morning I worked on the form a little more. Then I rushed to the post office. I arranged a next-day, recorded delivery. I was so nervous about being out of time. I never wanted to raise an ET1 in the first place; however, I felt I needed the extra security if the Prison Service investigation proved unhelpful. As I had no idea when the investigation would be complete and when the report would be ready, waiting was not really an option. I sent the ET1 form off, went straight home and started on my assignment. I was fairly distracted and didn't achieve very much. That night I had difficulty sleeping and, when I did drift off, I had nightmares about filling in the form incorrectly. Then I would wake up to tell myself that it was gone now and there was nothing I could do about it; it didn't help.

When I woke up in the morning, I considered the level of support I had received from PCS to date, the conflicting information I received from them and how dangerously close I came to missing the deadline for my ET1 application. I decided to terminate my membership. As much as I appreciated William's support, I thought that if they could leave me unsupported at such a critical point in my case, that they were not going to be much good to me and my membership money would be better spent elsewhere.

It took most of the week for me to really get into my studies. I refused to log on or open any mail from Newbold, because I knew they would say something to derail me and I had to get my assignment done. It was hard enough trying to focus, do the necessary reading, and complete the assignment without feeling compelled to respond to communiqués designed to unsettle me.

By the weekend, I was relieved to receive notice from the Tribunal that my claim had been accepted. I thanked God.

On 26th June, I managed to complete my assignment by the end of the day. I was very pleased and exhausted. The 'high' however didn't last long as I thought about returning to Newbold.

In the evening, Rudy and I made a point of watching the BBC documentary, *The Boys who killed Stephen Lawrence*. We were mostly silent. We couldn't believe that the police let so much slip. It was surreal watching these racists talk so openly about the terrible things they wanted to do to black people. It made us wonder how these demented, barely literate fools could think they were better than anyone. In the documentary, there were references to police corruption, which made perfect sense to us. How else could the Acourt and Norris family have evaded questioning when the public were volunteering these boys' details the day after the murder? Someone had to have turned a blind eye, and that's not done unless it's made worth their while. Witnesses were mishandled–in essence, the police actually got *in* the way of finding Stephen's murderers. We were stunned. And then we were angry. The injustice of the system and the brazenness of the racists was repugnant. Afterwards, we talked about how commonplace it is for institutions to protect their own no matter the cost to quality of life or the life itself of the victim. It's as if we are of no consequence and our lives are cheap. Rudy especially commented about how shocked and horrified he was to think that, behind closed doors, this sort of thing is actually happening around us. He said he was reminded of a quote from Jane Elliott's *The Eye of the Storm*, where she remarked how disgracefully people behaved when their inhibitions were removed. He wondered how many colleagues he had worked with over the years would have responded poorly, if their inhibitions had been removed. If no one was to face any recrimination or reprimand for how they felt or for what they wanted to say, how would we really be treated in this country? I considered that the lies and deception, the refusal to explicitly make race a core component of the police investigation, was sadly familiar to me.

When I returned to work the following day, I had 197 emails. Whilst going through them, I opened one from my interim manager, Steve. I was immediately panicked by his request for 'an appraisal/grievance meeting' to discuss my complaint about the REAG placement for the very next day. I spent the next couple of hours trying to find someone to accompany me before I remembered it was counterproductive to have an appraisal and grievance meeting at the same time. I emailed him and told him I couldn't find anyone to accompany me at such short notice; however, I agreed to attend for the appraisal part of the meeting.

The following day, Steve set new targets for the coming year. He explained he couldn't review my performance because I had raised grievances. He said my performance would be reviewed after the outcome of the investigation and that he had sent me a letter confirming what he was now telling me. I told him that, in order to concentrate fully on my assignment, I hadn't read any of the letters sent to me at home and had not yet seen it. I commented that I didn't see how he could do my SPDR properly without a review of the previous year's performance, yet he continued to set new targets.

Afterwards, I asked why the last grievance, relating to the REAG placement, was being dealt with by him, outside of the current investigation. I explained it was a victimisation claim and, by its very nature, was connected to the other grievances. He said I would need to take it up with Susanne, in personnel.

Steve then questioned the way I had gone about securing annual leave. He said no one in admin knew I was taking the week commencing 12th June. He stated that the only thing he could account for was the following week he had signed off as study leave for me.

'You do realise,' he admonished, 'that if you didn't secure annual leave in the proper way, it could be construed as an unauthorised absence which would carry disciplinary action.'

Patiently, I explained I had asked for annual leave in the way I was instructed on joining the college, which was now over a year ago: to send an email to admin and they would present it to Sue. I confirmed that I had had the dates marked as annual leave in my electronic diary since April (since I knew my assignment deadlines a year in advance). I conveyed how I had sent an email requesting leave as normal and that several people, including him, the admin department, Sue and Val had access to my calendar entries so that anyone who needed to know what I was doing could see at a glance. He asked me to send him a copy of my original request, if I still had it.

Steve concluded the meeting with what he called 'a few reminders'. He said I needed to keep my calendar up to date and reminded me that I needed to communicate actively with other members of the LMD team. He also reminded me that Newbold was my normal place of work and working remotely from home was not to be the norm.

I was so offended. Since I had been reporting to Steve, we had never had any discussions or issues about any of these things. And now he was *reminding* me about them as if, since reporting to him, I had failed in these areas. I couldn't understand why he felt the need to remind me to talk to my team members or why he felt that I wasn't contributing to team activities, as he had never been to one of our meetings. I didn't say much at this point, I did what was all too familiar, I sat in disbelief. To me it was evident that he had been told he had inherited certain problems when he became my manager. It would seem these particular issues were the problem areas he needed to keep an eye on. What was especially upsetting to me was that, rather than ask me about the issues or waiting to see if they manifested themselves during his watch, he chose to talk to me as if I had already let him down. No one had any faith in me.

When I got back to my office, I found the original request for annual leave, dated 20th April, where I asked for time off from June 12th to 16th inclusive. I forwarded it to Steve.

Disappointment weighed heavily on me. I had been back for two days and already I was being spoken to about disciplinary action! I was dazed and confused. I very much felt I hadn't covered my back well enough to avoid being picked up on something. I thanked God I had kept the email requesting annual leave. Steve responded an hour after I had forwarded it with a 'thank you'.

I ploughed on through the unread emails, since I had not previously made much of a dent in them. As with most days, I worked through lunchtime before I realised what time it was. I was feeling stressed and unhappy and thought perhaps a sandwich, some sun and fresh air might pick me up. I made a mad dash to the canteen to see if they had anything left: an egg mayonnaise sandwich, a packet of bacon-flavoured crisps and a fruit juice. I walked across the grounds to the lake to watch the ducks and have my lunch. The sun was lazy that day, hardly making an effort to reveal its glory. It was masked by heavy, opaque and laden clouds and refused to rescue me with its heat and brilliance. I always feel better when the sun shines. Its warmth can penetrate the deepest mood and make me glad. Long stays in the sun change my skin from caramel to Jamaican rum cake: dark, moist and intoxicating. Whenever I can, I lie in the sun until my sweat becomes as diamonds on African soil. My heart pumps faster, pushing more blood around my body in response to the extra solar energy, throbbing in my fingers and toes. My body breaks down into particles that float up into the stratosphere on escalator rays. No longer head or arms or legs, just essence being carried up to the heavens above the pain. Way up, up into the sun, with every weight and care formally taking residence in my very solid shoulders, neck and lower back as stress—but now un-massed, flowing and separated from me to be consumed by violent, unforgiving heat, leaving me pure again. Then I am gently laid down in green pastures to rest. But not this day. The clouds and the wind had made a pact with my oppressors to shield the sun. They were a strong coalition, grouping and regrouping, cutting off any chance of remedy and deliverance. As I sat in the gardens, expecting majesty, silently willing and commanding the sun to make an appearance and purge me, I felt an unwelcomed cool breeze on the exposed parts of my arms and legs, drawing up goose bumps. Then a few specks of cold rain confirmed that this English summer would not allow me to be cleansed any time soon.

When I got home, I decided to contact the new commissioning officer directly. His name was Paul Carroll. The investigation was due to end the following day, 29th June, and the investigating officers had been in receipt of my last grievance since the 30th May. They had had plenty of time to look into it and I felt it was important that I conveyed that keeping this complaint separate could limit the weight of my grievances overall. Maybe that was the plan: to split the grievances up and look at them independently of each other. I couldn't allow that to happen. I needed to let them know that if they were up to something, I had sussed them out. (All hail, the queen of paranoia!) I sent the letter to Paul Carroll and then, at around 8.40pm, opened the mail I had been sent over the fortnight I was on leave. The stress in my body was escalating. I was experiencing tightness in my chest, yet I told myself to hang on because the investigation would be over soon. The investigators would only need another week at most to include my last grievance; all I had to do was hold on. The dizziness was still a worry. I wasn't sleeping and I was starting to forget things. I was doing things like booking the same people in twice for the same feedback or not booking them in at all. I was taking 400mg Ibuprofen for my neck and back, Kalms (herbal tablets) by day and Natursleep (more herbal tablets) by night to manage my anxiety and help me to sleep. I started taking vitamins, doing breathing exercises and, basically, anything that reduced anxiety and pain.

On 29th June, the long awaited report into the death of Zahid Mubarek was published. I heard it on the news that evening. As I listened to them quote Martin Narey (he was the Director General at the time of the murder) describing it as 'a preventable death', I realised that no one at work had talked about it for the whole day. I was at HMP Glen Parva doing feedback, and Newbold and everyone had gone about their business as usual. I wondered why we had not been notified that the report was due and why we had not been told as an organisation to prepare. I decided to look the report up on the internet and read the findings for myself. The Investigation report found that:

> *38.1 Many of the things which led to Zahid's murder were down to the failings of individual officers at Feltham. No one on Lapwing told the Security Department about Stewart's racist letter which had been intercepted. No one in the Security Department checked Stewart's security file when he returned to Feltham for the last time. It never occurred to anyone on Swallow that Stewart might be racist and that Zahid might have been uncomfortable about sharing a cell with him. Zahid's personal officers took no particular interest in him. And his request to move cells and the way his cell was searched left much to be desired.*

(House of Commons, 2006)

As I read, I thought that it was not improbable that these officers were trained at Newbold. I wondered what they had learnt: if they had shown any inappropriate behaviour whilst in training, had they been challenged? Whilst looking after Zahid they had exhibited an intolerable lack of care and sensitivity. They had missed blatant warning signs. For instance, on 23rd February, a month before Zahid's death, Stewart wrote this letter (exerpt)…

> CANNOT SEE IT STICKIN IN ERE, IF I DON'T GET BAIL ON THE 7TH, I'LL TAKE XTREME MEASURES TO GET SHIPPED OUT, KILL ME FUCKIN PADMATE IF I HAVE TO, BLEACH ME SHEETS + PILLOWCASE WHITE + MAKE A KU KLUX KLAN OUTFIT + WALK OUT ME PAD WIV A FLAMING CRUCIFIX + CHANGE THE † ON ME ED TO ✝ THEN ⤴ WID A BIRO, (HA) NAR, I DON'T THINK I'TIL BE THAT HARD, THESE SCREWS DON'T KNOW ME LIKE THOSE AT HINDLEY, I SENT YOU A V.O LAST WEEK WITH THE VISITORS NAMES, ADOLF HITLER, CHARLES MANSON, HAROLD SHIPMAN, + CHILDREN UNDER 10 AS

Commission for Racial Equality (2003a) p.3

In 2003, Stewart, in an interview with the Commission for Race and Equality said,

> *Well, before they put me in a cell with him they had put this note in my file saying that a letter was sent out by this inmate with racially something material, so they shouldn't have put me there in the first place. If they had done the job properly, and put me on a remand wing, then it wouldn't have happened. If they'd read the letters when they were supposed to, they should have thought, get the guy out, and the previous files with all these fights and assaults and that in the past, somebody should have thought I was a time bomb ready to explode.*
> Commission for Racial Equality (2003b) p.12

I continued to look and found out that, four years on from Zahid's murder, a report was conducted by Hounslow Racial Equality Council as part of the Commission for Racial Equality's investigation into racism at Feltham. They found that *'ethnic minority inmates were being pushed by white prison officers to such an extent that they would find it difficult to cope and might attempt suicide'*. The study also revealed that white prison officers often launched a diatribe of vociferous racist abuse at ethnic minority prisoners, calling them 'monkeys', 'black bastards' and telling them to go back to their own countries!

I considered what the ramifications of Stacey's involvement, as the Head of the Prison Service College, in acts of racism were. And Sue, as the Head of Leadership and Management Development, responsible for shaping the minds of our governors and officers. The Service trained all its officers in the same way. It was hard, and I considered perhaps even irresponsible, *not* to see a causal link between the way these officers were trained and their negligence in this tragedy. Yet, some six years after Zahid's death, I was accusing senior managers, responsible for overseeing and owning training policy for the Service since this tragedy occurred, of being racist. And I had had first-hand experience of their insensitivity, arrogance and obstinacy. I believed that my situation could have been drawn to a close quickly; yet turning a blind eye until something hit the public eye seemed to be the norm for the Service. It was accepted practice.

I thought back to the innumerable times I had spent with officers and managers who, even after failing their J-SAC, had expressed that there was too much focus on diversity matters. The situation felt hopeless. During the exams, these officers and managers missed vital indicators of prejudice that had been deliberately sown into the fabric of the scenarios, which they were expected to unpick. The role player always delivered the cue for reaction to an inappropriate reference, two or three times, and many candidates still missed it. Having failed, these officers and managers went back on the wing to miss vital cues again. As I surfed the net, I remembered how one officer had complained to me that he was sure that there was a diversity element (race, disability, gender) to *all* of the scenarios that year, and that that wasn't mirroring real life on the wing. He felt that as officers they were being set up to fail because, as the driving test has quotas for how many passes are allowed, he rationalised the J-SAC was the same. Hence, it wasn't so much that *he* had failed to recognise the elements of discrimination on grounds of religion or sexual orientation as presented in the exam, he had simply been 'marked down' because the quotas were full! Another manager I had rung to arrange his feedback had shouted down the phone at me, 'Yes, I want my feedback because I need to know how the hell *I* failed on diversity!' Shouting at someone he had never met before was not going to help, but it certainly gave me insight into his capacity to deal with sensitive or emotive issues appropriately.

Remarkably, both men had been trained, had passed through the system to their current management grades, and had spent more than a decade in the Service. Yet they were shamefully void of understanding, embittered by having racial tolerance rammed down their throats and wearied by the playacting, which left them no further forward in their careers. I wondered what a single session with me, lasting maybe one or two hours, could realistically achieve against this backdrop of ignorance and lack of will to change. I was in no doubt that, in the main, my clients were grateful for the input and acuity, though I was dubious as to whether the feedback sessions I ran became life-defining moments for them. I considered that maybe a few might have gone back to work with many a good intention, only to be faced with the reality of 'how we do things around here!'

It is difficult to say what might have averted the heartbreak of the Mubarek murder and the many others that didn't make headline news. I wondered about the others who sadly chose to take their own lives instead of facing another day of abuse, neglect and mistreatment. What I was sure of was that our officers and managers could easily arrive at a training session with prejudices and leave with them intact, unearthed and unchallenged. Another certainty was that there was resistance to impose sanctions on managers who performed poorly, even when formal investigations had determined that discrimination had taken place. This was common knowledge in the Service. And finally, if the institution was racist and protected those who demonstrated racist behaviour, having wrapped the facts in the sacred shroud of poor management, then what possible deterrent was there for the racist officer? All he or she needed to do was bide their time, secure promotion and then as a manager they would be free to unleash their special brand of maintaining order and control—all this without fear of reprisal or exposure.

I figured that perhaps it wasn't that much of a stretch to recognise the interplay between the racist behaviour of staff on staff, and the racist behaviour of staff on prisoners. For if an officer could insult me and openly discriminate against me on sight, in my good suit and with my official Prison Service-issued photo ID pass, then what was to stop him or her from doing the same with a prisoner of colour? What was to stop them from prejudging such prisoners and subjecting them to unwarranted scrutiny and the all too often resultant overuse of force? Presumably, that's when the training should kick in. Yet not when the head of the college was unable to recognise her own behaviour as racist. It was my view that the Service would protect Stacey. She was, after all, an OBE, an Officer of the Order of the British Empire. Stacey had met the queen, had shaken her hand. It simply wouldn't do to accuse this long-standing member of the realm of something as unsavoury as racism. Stacey would in turn, shelter and protect her minions under her wings of privilege and her watchful eye, and every attempt to expose them as unsuitable to be in charge would be vehemently rebutted and thwarted with outraged, righteous indignation. I was jumping to conclusions, but I couldn't help myself. The constant pressure and mental anguish left me imagining the worst about everything and everyone.

The night was far spent, and Rudy was already asleep. I crawled into bed and lay awake for another three hours. After thinking long and hard about whether or not the Service had learned anything from Zahid Mubarek's murder, my thoughts ran to whether or not there had been any change for the prisoners on the receiving end of the abuse. When I considered my own treatment and the lack of support I had received as a manager, I reckoned that there was no chance for the prisoner who, because of the colour of his skin, was instantly marked as a troublemaker, someone who needed watching. After all, I had experienced this myself. It sent shudders down my spine and I shivered next to Rudy to think that there, but for the grace of God, I could have experienced all this as a prisoner! I could have experienced the frustrations of not being heard, the aloneness and alienation, the disrespect and dismissal as a prisoner! I thought 'Lord, if I'm hopeless and broken now, barely able to confront the full intensity of my pain—what would I have been like if I were a prisoner?' What would I be thinking tonight as a prisoner who was alone and complaining again and again of differential treatment? Or what if, as a prisoner, I chose to suffer the indignity of racial comments silently for fear of making things worse; mortified and humiliated as I realised that I was not worth speaking up for? All of this I had endured at different times as a qualified professional with the freedom to go home at the end of a working day to the embrace and acceptance of loved ones. Yet my anger, shame and wretchedness mingled together to mix a cocktail that I could hardly stomach. I daren't think how I might have survived this ordeal if I had been a prisoner! If the Prison Service staff didn't respect or care for the black and ethnic officers, who were supposed to be their comrades in arms, laying their lives on the line without question and on demand, then what chance did the black prisoner stand; what chance for civilians like me? And what of other black staff? What were they experiencing? Who was helping them? I lifted my head to see the digital clock; it was 4.45am—I would have to get up in an hour and I still wasn't asleep. Yet my mind was overactive and revisiting facts, considerations and scenarios. I wondered if, after all of this, the Service would learn that people die when racist attitudes and behaviours are given air time and remain unchallenged. There is a heavy human cost, when pervasive and insidious philosophies surface, and are then justified or minimised, and I couldn't decide which one the Service was going to do regarding my case. I'm not sure what time I finally fell asleep, and even then my dreams were weird and my body was restless as I dreamt about my teeth falling out.

July came with no promises that my ordeal was about to end. The temperamental weather matched my moods and the worry associated with how quickly my body was deteriorating, compounded things further. Every day was a burden as I struggled to keep from passing out or seizing up in pain. Like a junkie needing a fix, I had taken to slipping out of meetings or training sessions, right in the middle, to lock myself in a toilet cubicle so that I could say a quick prayer and have a quick cry to release the pain. This was the only way to get through the most oppressive days. I continued like this day after day painting a progressively wider smile on my face as a response to anyone politely asking 'How are you' or 'How was your weekend?' 'Fine,' I'd say whilst the words liar and fraud would rattle around in my head. I went about my duties like a normal person.

On 3rd July, I went to HMP Whatton to deliver J-SAC feedback to Schubert. Schubert looked like most officers. He had a lean build and short-cropped hair. He was clean-shaven and in uniform. Schubert failed in 2004 and I inherited his feedback late because Sue hadn't done it. Having watched his DVD several times the previous year, I was able to give him detailed feedback on his performance and spent quality time coaching him. I was so pleased that he had passed this year. When the results came through, originally sometime in April, Schubert had been recorded as failing the J-SAC again this year, but on Friday Katrina in admin had handed me his DVD with a sticky-note attached saying 'passed on appeal.'

When I met Schubert at the gate, he escorted me to an office that we could use. Naturally, I started the session by congratulating him. Surprisingly, he thought I was playing some kind of cruel joke. He had been told he had failed and hadn't heard anything to the contrary. Stifling my embarrassment, I told him I had got his DVD and marking papers with me and I showed him the note stuck to the DVD saying 'passed on appeal'.

'But I didn't appeal! There must be some mistake. I've been told that I failed and received a letter to confirm it. But no one's told me that I've moved from a fail to a pass because my appeal was successful. What's going on?'

I was mortified. Outside of the sticky-note, I didn't have any official notice of his passing the exam either. Schubert's life and career was about to change–or not–depending on whether he had passed. Everything was hanging in the balance, and I was on the verge of crushing his dreams or helping him to realise them. The pressure was immense.

I immediately put in a call to Adrian, the manager at the assessment centre; however, he didn't pick up the call and the voicemail message said he was on annual leave, though it did leave a number for emergencies and another staff member's name. I called every number, including going back to Newbold to query what had happened.

I spent the first half hour of Schubert's feedback time making calls and no one could confirm his exam status one way or the other. What a mess, I thought! I was conscious of the time and couldn't imagine how awful it was for Schubert waiting for the phone to ring, so I decided to give him his feedback—whether he had passed or failed, the moderator observations of his performance remained the same; whatever happened 'on appeal' would concern the points awarded per scenario. I was responsible for giving him feedback on his performance as it was detailed, and as seen on the DVD. I would be required to do that regardless of the outcome of the expected call. Schubert was naturally, and quite understandably, very distracted during the feedback. Yet even that was better than just sitting and waiting.

He kept saying things like, 'MSSU (the assessment centre) would know if I passed…maybe the governor already knows and wants me to be surprised…he did look at me a bit funny at morning meeting…I think it's because he knows…'

About half way through a scenario, Adrian called me back to say that Schubert had indeed passed. Adrian explained that someone had made a successful appeal and that, for each candidate the appeal decision affected, their scenarios were moderated and graded again. As a result, eight out of 21 candidates were moved from fail to pass. He then went on to explain his disappointment: he had made a special trip from London to Newbold the previous week on Wednesday to see Sue, specifically to update her on the situation fully so none of her advisors would be caught out. He apologised to me and said that he would update Katrina in admin himself and speak to Sue to find out what went wrong. Fortunately for me, Schubert was so ecstatic that he had passed he wasn't bothered about how poorly this had been handled.

Of course, I was again embarrassed. I felt quite humiliated about being put in such a vulnerable position, especially as it was completely avoidable. Yet I was grateful that, due to Schubert's euphoria, my discomfort was not apparent to him and I was able to give him his feedback professionally. I was still, however, troubled about why this had happened: there was clearly some information available about Schubert's transition from fail to pass, otherwise the sticky-note wouldn't have been there in the first place.

That evening, I decided to check my email to see if there was an official word to all advisors after what had happened to me. It was around 10.00pm and there was no communication on the matter. I wrote to Adrian to thank him and to ask if he could draft an official note from MSSU to save other advisors the embarrassment I had experienced. After all, I thought, there were another seven candidates who had made this transition and it was important that the situation should be handled well—not every client might be as accommodating as Schubert.

Adrian replied the next morning. He said that he was sorry I had found myself in an awkward situation with Schubert. He went on to say:

> ...*As stated on the telephone to you, I feared this situation might occur if the circumstances were not communicated effectively. Hence, my meeting with Sue last Wednesday. I will be speaking with Sue regarding this event and communication issues in general as I feel I did 'MSSU's bit' last week. I'm disappointed to hear that there's still no official word out. I spoke to Katrina yesterday who said she would communicate this to the advisors it affected. Perhaps she missed you out because you are already aware?*

I really wanted to believe there was nothing underhand about this situation. However, based on everything I had endured at the hands of Sue, there was no way I could think that. I genuinely believed she wanted me to fail horribly. This was not the first time I had gone into an account without vital information—information Sue had held on to in the hope that I would be humiliated and end up looking completely inept. Credibility is a fragile thing in the Service: once it's gone, it's gone forever. If your face doesn't fit, management can be extremely unforgiving about displays of incompetence or shortfalls in performance—they never let you forget it. Sue only needed me to make one big mistake or to lose the faith of my clients and my career in the Service would be over. I had been fighting against this since joining the college and wasn't sure at this juncture that I had anything left to fight with.

I attended the Fast Track conference on 5th July. I would have preferred to carry on working in the field; however, after the last conference I missed in March and the way Sue had registered her 'extreme' disappointment, I knew not attending was not an option.

When I arrived, Sue was talking to Althea in the doorway to the conference room. Althea was the senior manager the LMD team had talked about disrespectfully in December. I had to walk pass them to get in as they were partly blocking the entrance. I said 'Hello' whilst passing behind Althea, with Sue facing Althea and me. Althea turned round, responded to my greeting and asked how I was. I said I was fine and continued to pass by them, recognising that they were talking. Sue ignored me again. I was amazed at how duplicitous Sue was being. A few months ago, she didn't have a kind word to say about Althea, yet at the conference she didn't have any issues aligning herself with her.

Overall, the day was quite painful for me. Throughout the afternoon, Val was too busy even to catch my eye. I tried talking to the other advisors, yet it felt strained. Over the two days of the conference, the LMD team gave me a wide berth and I mostly spent my time with the newly arrived Fast Track students on my table.

By the end of the week, I received a copy of the Post-Interim Report Action Plan (one of the outputs from the investigation), which Stacey had compiled. It was in response to the observations by new Commissioning Officer–Paul Carroll–that it was unacceptable that those present at the LMD team meeting on 28th March had been allowed to leave, without it being made clear that Di's comments were unacceptable. Finally, I thought, someone could see that situation had been handled badly! I was pleased that a fresh pair of eyes could see my point concerning this. I began to have a smidgen of hope that, even if I hadn't compiled enough evidence, that the actions of both Stacey and Sue would be judged as inadequate, inappropriate and unfair.

On the same day, I also received Paul Carroll's response to my request to include my grievance about working for REAG (on a shared-resource basis) as part of the investigation. Unfortunately, he decided that to include the final grievance would delay the investigation results. I was back on the rollercoaster of emotion again: good news, whoa bad news, ooh good news, whoa bad news!

I couldn't see how this was going to help me finally to resolve matters. His decision meant that the investigation results would be published, and I would still have an un-investigated, outstanding grievance. This would only complicate matters and keep me in an awkward and vulnerable position. Furthermore, I was trying to demonstrate that the discrimination I was experiencing was ongoing: it wasn't so much about a single incident (although each incident was important in its own right) but it was also about overall treatment, overall impact and detriment suffered. Keeping a complaint separate from the investigation could result in the decision that there was not enough collective evidence of institutional prejudice. Yet, there was nothing else I could do. I had already tried and failed and it was pointless getting into an argument with the Commissioning Officer.

On 10th July, I responded to letters from the Employment Tribunal (ET). I was asked to respond to the request of the Respondent (that is, the Prison Service) for a stay of proceedings. Didn't anyone want this to be over, I agonised? I wrote back and explained how much time had already lapsed and that it was causing me stress. I explained that, since raising my complaints, I felt as if I had been in professional limbo, while the discrimination continued, yet my counterparts–Sue, Val and Di–had all secured promotions. I outlined how the Leadership and Management Development (LMD) group had been undergoing significant change and that my current role had been absorbed in the restructure. Although there were a number of new roles created to complement our new HR Strategic model, my capacity to advance was severely hampered by the fact that applications for most of the positions suited to my skill set and career plans were contingent on my line manager's approval: technically Sue– as Head of LMD, she led the interview panels. I expressed that, in view of the current situation, I had little confidence and even less courage to apply to Sue for a job and expect fair treatment. I used whatever argument I felt would help them to allow the application to proceed without undue delay, because if I didn't secure a new role as part of the new HR initiative, I would be placed on the Home Office surplus list—and that was not a prospect I relished. I had worked too hard and too long to end up that way. The surplus list is a redeployment pool. If, as part of a restructure, your role is made redundant or your skills are no longer a match for the new programme of work, you are placed in the surplus pool for redeployment. You remain employed for a period of time, with the expectation that you will find another job in the organisation. As a surplus employee, you are supposed to get first refusal of any job matching your skills, but it doesn't always work like that. It's a horrible position to be in, as the core work you were doing becomes less and less. You end up getting a bit of work here and a project there. You gradually become invisible and very soon actually feel surplus to requirements. The culture of the Service is such that anyone in the surplus pool is regarded as being there for good reason—i.e. they were not that good at their jobs. I have heard comments from governors like, 'I really need to advertise this job but I've got to go through the dregs in surplus first!'

On Saturday, 15th July, Rudy took me out for a meal to celebrate another 'Distinction' pass for my Masters assignment. All that was left to do was to wrap up my dissertation. We were also celebrating Pauline's recovery from cancer. She was a member of our church and a woman of great faith. She had just been given the all-clear and we were grateful to God for her. She was an increasing source of joy, with an infectious smile and raucous laughter. Her laugher always sounded as if it should be coming out of a much bigger and jollier person. There was something quite unexpected when she laughed and you turned round and saw this five-foot, petite woman who looked as timid as a deer, yet she would bellow and belly-laugh like an old sailor. She had been on the phone telling of the goodness of God and how she couldn't wait until Sunday so that she could share her testimony with everyone who had prayed for her.

'Don't worry Pastor—you'll get your victory soon and then it will be your turn to testify. And I can't wait for that one. It's gonna be awesome! God's gonna deliver you in such a way that will blow our minds. He's done it for me–he'll do it for you!'

It was 2.30am and I couldn't sleep. We had had a good day. We rejoiced about Pauline and thought positively about our future after the Masters and the court case. Rudy had kept me out most of the day to tire me out like a toddler, but it hadn't worked because he was snoring and I was awake. Sleep, the one gift I could rely on, had abandoned me many months ago. It's sweet, sinking solace had long been replaced by a haunting of obsessive thoughts twisted by the deprivation my duvet was designed to keep at bay but no longer had the power to do so. Agitation, restless legs and a knotted brick for my left shoulder was my portion now. Eyes wide open in comfortless dark, ears alert to every sound. Is that Mum? Is she okay? Better go and check. Is the front door locked? Better go and check. No rest until you do–no rest afterwards either. I hadn't tasted heaven for a very long time.

My latest obsession was over the new Commissioning Officer's refusal to integrate my last grievance into the investigation. I got up, went to the kitchen and made myself a hot drink. I decided to write how I was feeling in my diary and maybe afterwards I would be able to sleep. Before long, I was rhyming:

Tormented and hunted
Disadvantaged, abused
Broken and stunted
Advancement refused

Stifled and silenced
Battered and bruised
Taken by violence
Discretion unused

Voiceless complaining
Nameless petitions
Faceless bewailing
Accused of seditions

No end in sight

Frustrated and broken
Denied every right
In lies that are spoken

The time they have taken
For fair play to reign
To prove I'm mistaken
To prove me insane

The truth is they fear me
And what I'll become
They seek to destroy me
Before I am done.

Over the next few weeks in July, I continued to deliver J-SAC feedback to the candidates who had failed. In total, for my area, I had 39 (pass and fail) feedbacks to do along with all other design, delivery and consultancy responsibilities. I had also agreed to help other advisors who were struggling with workload. I put a schedule together and I was steadily working through it. Some of the feedbacks for my clients who had failed were more difficult because a number of them directly complained about the quality of the feedback they had received the previous year and six clients actually named Sue as failing to give them useful or constructive feedback. These clients in particular were somewhat resistant at the beginning of the sessions and resentful that they didn't previously get the help they felt they needed. Now that they had failed again, they were ready to apportion blame.

Ian from HMP Sudbury said, on 11th July when I went to see him, that feedback with Sue the previous year had been a complete waste of time and he had walked out after only ten minutes! He said Sue was unprepared and didn't come armed with any notes about his performance and that she simply wanted to offer her opinion of his performance, rather than give him quality feedback. Gary from the same prison, also having previously complained to his line manager, outlined that he was apprehensive about whether or not it was worth attending the feedback session with me. Thankfully, Liz, the Head of Personnel had convinced him that I would do a better job. (Liz was now also covering the personnel manager role for both HMP Foston Hall and HMP Sudbury.) In fact, after I had delivered the feedback to these two clients, Liz had quite helpfully sent an email to thank me. She said that each client had made a point of telling her how useful the feedback was. She skilfully made reference to their levels of apprehension prior to my session based on 'previous experiences'. She copied this email to her governor and to Sue.

On 13th July, both Barry and Robert from HMP Onley complained about the poor quality of Sue's feedback to them the previous year, similarly stating that they had barely got thirty minutes of her time and that they had not learned anything of substance that they could then apply to working practice. On 24th July, Debbie from HMP Morton Hall complained that she had driven to Newbold to see Sue for her feedback and it that it had been a waste of a four-hour journey. Debbie said that she left the session in tears of frustration because she genuinely didn't know what needed to be different about her performance—which meant she was destined to fail again. The fact that she had now done so, plainly aggravated and upset her further. Then on 28th July, Gordon from HMP Lincoln also complained. I made the original appointment to see him for 19th July; however, he took a half-day's leave on the day in question without telling me, even though he had previously confirmed he would be there. Fortunately for me, I also had an appointment to do a senior operational manager feedback with his manager, Karen. She said she would speak to him to find out what had happened. It was after this that he contacted me and rebooked me for the 28th. When I asked him why he hadn't shown up for the original appointment, he apologised. He said his scepticism with the J-SAC process had got the better of him, he was angry and he didn't see the value in attending another pointless feedback session. He said that the previous year, Sue had left him with a vague understanding of 'not digging deep enough to deal with issues' but that he didn't then know how to fix the problem. After I had commenced giving him feedback, he said I gave him more clarity in the first 15 minutes than he had had in two years of feedback.

Whenever anyone complained directly about Sue, I turned the conversation to their own performance. I didn't want to spend time talking about her; I had done enough of that. I was blessed in each case where there was a complaint about her or anyone that I was able to move the client on and was ultimately commended by them for the thoroughness of the feedback and the insight I brought to the session. It was so good to receive positive feedback, reminding me that I was good at what I did, no matter what the people at the college said.

Stacey and Sarah, the new Equal Opportunity Officer, joined us in our team meeting on 1st August to report on the interim action plans that were driven by the investigation. I thought this could go one of two ways: either Stacey would explain things fully and outline plans for improved professional working or she would deliver something so sanitised and bland that nothing would change.

Stacey began by reiterating the inappropriateness of the comments made in March–however she didn't say what was said in March or who said it. No names were mentioned–not even mine! As much as I understand the rationale behind not repeating offensive comments, I feel that part of the problem in the Service is that many people don't know what racist behaviour is or why something is racist. After all, knowing that something is wrong is only part of the equation; people need to understand *why* something is unacceptable so that they can fully apply their learning. Nothing is worse than people who become so acutely uncomfortable and socially impotent around diversity because they have no idea as to what they are allowed to say: they freeze in conversations or avoid diversity issues altogether, which in turn alienates anyone who is different.

As Stacey continued to outline findings and recommendations, I watched Di bury her head into her chest and remain like that for the whole debrief. The rest of the group sat in silence. When Stacey had finished no one asked any questions. I was disappointed: I had been publicly subjected to racist comments yet there was no public apology. I was appalled that, to date, no one in my team had said anything to me about the offence. No one had said, 'Sorry Olivea, that must have been awkward for you', no one said, 'How are you feeling Olivea, are you all right?' Not one team member or my managers had said that this was unfortunate, unpleasant, or that it shouldn't have happened. In fact no one even asked *if* I was offended. My managers had made no attempt to see if there was any bad feeling between Di and me since the incident. They didn't question if we had rebuilt our bridges–or if we needed help to do that. There was nothing. This had all happened nearly five months ago and I didn't have a single viewpoint or sentiment from my managers or any of my peers. In the meantime, my professional relationships were being eroded either by silent prejudice or sheer awkwardness. Proper communication between me and my team members had noticeably diminished, yet there was no attempt at restoring workable relationships and dealing with the mounting discomfort which, if not experienced by anyone else, then was at the very least experienced by me. I was simply expected to cope. I sat feeling quite sad and dissatisfied in Stacey's handling of the situation. I was further aggrieved by the inadequacy of the proposed remedy: in September, we would all have to sit through a three-hour session on diversity, run by actors depicting true-to-life scenarios! How was that going to uncover or tackle personal bias? How would it ease tensions?

During the break, I overheard Karen Smith ask what had happened in March. She was not at that meeting in question, so she couldn't make sense of what Stacey had just said. For me, that very much made my point about skirting around the edges: people were leaving the meeting without a full understanding. Furthermore, not everybody was at this current meeting (at least five people were missing), so they had missed Stacey's debrief, and I doubted very much that the summarised minutes of the meeting would be any more insightful. On the whole, I was miserable and unhappy that people were leaving *this* meeting not knowing I had been hurt and was still hurting.

We were still on a break and almost everyone had got up to have a cigarette or stretch their legs. I decided to get some water. Whilst I was walking down the corridor to the kitchen, Di was on her way back to the meeting room. The corridor was very narrow, making it difficult to walk past someone without some sort of acknowledgement, because you couldn't avoid walking into each other's personal space. I didn't have much to say to Di, yet I couldn't walk past without saying anything. So, as we drew closer, I started to smile, tried to make eye contact to engage her and opened my mouth to say hi, hoping other words would follow. However, Di's gaze was locked on the meeting door behind me and she maintained that gaze. She walked past me as if I was a ghost.

The following day we were all back for the second day of the team meeting. As a way of maximising the time in our meetings, we had recently been asked (about three months previously) to write a monthly report outlining our activities. Although there wasn't a template per se we were to briefly outline problems, areas where support was needed and so on, by way of a few bullet points and it was to be no longer than a single side of A4 paper. Then we were expected to circulate the reports before the meeting so everyone was updated before arrival. I documented my activities as I had done in preceding months; however, due to the complaints about the previous year's feedback sessions, I had spent much more time with my clients in July than the one-hour slot as prescribed by Sue. Even though I wasn't behind with my schedule, which was amazing with 39 feedbacks for my region alone, I couldn't afford to have Sue tackle me about how long my feedback sessions were. I felt sure she would find a way of suggesting I was taking too long to deliver feedback because I wasn't proficient or because I was not doing something or other properly. On average, I had taken two and a half hours: the shortest session being one hour and the longest being four! So far, nothing had stopped Sue from checking up on me or criticising me—not two reporting-line changes or even the investigation. I was clearly in breach of her directions by doing longer feedback sessions, so I felt I needed to cover myself.

In my report, I deliberately didn't mention the names of my clients or which prisons they worked at. I also didn't mention Sue's name regarding the client complaints, because not everyone had mentioned her by name, although six specific mentions was quite significant. I was mindful that, as we cover each other's areas from time to time, this meant it was possible that feedbacks in the East Midlands were done by someone other than Sue on occasion. My only concern was to convey adequately why my feedback sessions were taking longer than an hour, and why some days I only managed to do a single feedback. I believed that Sue was still checking my electronic calendar and would see days where there was only a single appointment. I didn't want to get a formal warning for poor management of my diary.

It took ages to think of a single bullet point that would convey what I did with my time, whilst simultaneously covering myself without causing trouble. I finally settled on saying: *'extra care taken as a number of complaints raised relating to the quality of feedbacks and short length of feedback last year'*. The rest of the report outlined the other activities I had had for July and the commitments for August.

Before we went into the normal business of the day, Karen Smith was given the floor by Sue with a cursory, 'Oh Karen, you had something that you wanted to say…?'

'Thanks Sue,' Karen began, almost like a newscaster taking over from the anchor newsperson.

'I must admit I don't usually get round to reading the monthly reports, but I managed to do it this month and I felt that your comments about J-SAC feedback, Olivea, were unprofessional and smacked of having a dig at a valued colleague's efforts.'

Did she just call my name? I was expecting some sort of update on a project or something, but Karen was talking about me! What did she say I did? Having a dig? Is this for real?

She then proceeded to labour the point that, if I had an issue, I should take it up with the individual concerned and not publicly and negatively broadcast other people's efforts in this manner. I fought every impulse to lash out and ask her how she was currently demonstrating her own recommendations about dealing with things privately. The room was silent and Sue said nothing. She simply let Karen deliver blow after blow. I let Karen talk, as I felt even the slightest interruption would have been viewed as unnecessarily defensive. So I sat in silence too. This was wretchedly reminiscent of when Di made the racist comments: there was no one willing or able to step in then either.

'People complain all the time, especially when they've failed,' she toiled on. 'That doesn't mean it's okay to have a pop at someone in the team. I mean, one of my fails told me that the woman who did his feedback last year was crap, without realising it was me because

I'd changed my hair. A complaint doesn't mean anything and you shouldn't use it to attack another member of the team. I think it's unprofessional as we're all doing our best and working very hard with little thanks!'

When Karen finally finished berating me, I simply said that there was no 'dig' intended. I calmly and resolutely explained that, against a backdrop of being instructed by Sue (like everyone else) to cluster appointments for the last feedback round and see as many people in one day as possible for approximately one hour, I was taking two and a half hours, on average, because people had complained. I'm not sure what she was expecting—maybe acceptance that I was out of order or an apology. She had spoken with such triumph and confidence about my alleged display of unprofessionalism as if it was her duty to correct me in front of everyone. Yet as I spoke, I saw the steadfast gaze that she had used to convey conviction give way to eyes that were darting across to Sue in uncertainty. I continued to explain that, for me, this meant that it was absolutely imperative that I gave the client the commodity they valued most–a timely feedback session. I was giving them time to reflect and accept observations about their performance, giving them time to challenge and ask questions because feedback wasn't about me simply passing on what I had seen thus discharging my responsibility to inform and instruct; feedback was about the client actively learning. I told her that in each case, without fail, I had been thanked for my attention to detail and commended on the investment that I had made in my clients' development. I further outlined that I wouldn't change my approach and thoroughly enjoyed delivering the J-SAC feedbacks to people who were so visibly appreciative of my skill, as it was extremely rewarding. I thanked Karen for her observations and rejected her point about un-professionalism.

'Oh…right,' she said, 'well, that makes sense. I didn't realise, I thought you were just having a dig.'

'Well, I wasn't,' I said.

That's when Sue got involved. 'I'm going to need the names of all of the people who have complained in order to address this,' she said coldly.

What exactly did she want to address, I thought? I didn't say anything because I most certainly wasn't going to agree to that, yet neither was I going to make myself any more of a target than I already was by further argument or disagreement. My heart was beating so loudly in my head that I felt sick. I could see Sue's lips moving but I could no longer hear what she was saying. All that external poise and composure I portrayed contradicted the chaos in my members. It was regularly taking all of my energy to remain calm throughout these exchanges and meetings, to avoid reacting in a way that could later be construed as somehow negative. For so long I had had to stifle normal and rightful reactions to the indignities I was suffering, for fear of further unjust reprisals. It had left me mentally and physically bereft of strength. My working environment was so hostile that now anybody could have a go at me without challenge. I had become fair game and it was hunting season.

As soon as I left the meeting, I emailed Sarah, the Equal Opportunities Officer, and asked to meet with her. As I thought about it, I determined there was no way I was going to breach confidentiality and give Sue the names of my clients. It's not as if they had asked me specifically to take their complaints forward, they were just frustrated and venting themselves. Had I not been in such an impossible predicament with the level of scrutiny I was under, I wouldn't even have mentioned it. But I felt it was the only way to pre-empt an attack from Sue or Val and protect myself.

Sarah was unable to meet me that day; however, she made an appointment for the following day. About an hour before I saw her, I got an email from Sue, which read:

> ...*Following the Advisors meeting yesterday where Karen raised concerns over comments you made in your monthly area report. As agreed, I would be very grateful if you would forward to me any information regarding particular candidates who raised concerns over the quality of feedback they had previously received. As part of the team's commitment to quality and continuous improvement I will, of course, follow up on all information received.*

I hadn't agreed to any such thing. This was madness. The feedbacks in question had taken place in 2005—it was now 2006.

And due to the restructure, the new role wouldn't even involve J-SAC feedback for 2007. It didn't make any logical sense to do a review for a function that was about to become obsolete for leadership advisors. Any kind of review would be a waste of resources. It was amazing to think that Sue was simply incensed by me and couldn't bear the thought that some clients preferred my approach to hers. It seemed that Sue was so desperate to prove that I wasn't good at my job she was prepared to commit significant resources to lift something—anything! Just one unhappy client, that's all she needed. She had scrutinised my work, undermined me with my clients and, after fifteen months of unrelenting harassment and discrimination, couldn't find any tangible evidence of poor performance, yet still she was driven by her obsession to discredit and humiliate me.

I often asked myself *what* I had done to provoke such unremitting attacks from her. I could never find an answer that would support her attitude or treatment of me. Even if I deserved micro-management or poor performance reviews surely they would need to have been borne out of evidenced ineptitude. I found Sue's behaviour inexcusable and Stacey's constant protection and endorsement of her sickening. It wasn't any wonder the Service was in such a mess: they protected and promoted those who feared change and hated anyone not like themselves.

When Sarah arrived, I gave her my single-page report to read and asked her if anything stood out in any way. As she read, she said that she couldn't see anything worth picking out. When she finished reading, I pointed to the statement in question and asked her for her first impression. Again she didn't see anything worthy of note. So I told her what had happened.

Her response was, 'You can't do right for doing wrong, can you?'

Sarah couldn't believe my report was the only one that had been scrutinised in the meeting; neither could she believe that I was scolded in front of the other advisors. I told her I didn't want to divulge my client's identities as they had spoken to me in confidence and I was sure that refusing the request would be construed as antagonistic by Sue. Even if I didn't give Sue the names of the clients and gave her the prisons they worked at instead, it would be easy to tell who they were from the list of pass and fail candidates that was issued by the assessment centre, which grouped everyone by region and then by prison. She asked me if I wanted her to speak to Sue on my behalf and, without hesitation, I said, 'Yes'. I also asked if she could speak to Stacey as well, because I was sure Sue would get to her as normal and make me out to be difficult and resistant.

After Sarah left, she sent an email to say that Sue and Val were now going to do a sample phone survey instead. How ridiculous, I thought! The whole department was in a state of flux, every member of the team needed to find a new job. Instead of our managers channelling resources to make sure there were no casualties in the restructure for 2007, they were going to do a phone survey across over 100 prisons to see who was unhappy about their feedback in 2005. I couldn't believe that the Heads of the Leadership and Management Development team had nothing better to do, and I told Sarah as much.

I didn't hear from Sarah again until the end of the working day. On the way home, I received a call from her apologising for taking so long to get back to me. She said that she had had to wait a while to see Stacey because 'Sue had got in there first'. Fortunately for everyone's sake, Stacey had had sufficient presence of mind to say there was no value in doing a phone survey.

On 7th August, I wrote to Trevor Phillips, Chair of the Commission for Race Equality (CRE). Things were getting to the point where I needed to arrange legal support. I didn't know what I needed to do first, but I expected CRE to be able both to support and represent me. Although I understood that the CRE didn't take every case, I was hoping that, because a formal agreement was already in existence between them and the Service to execute the Mubarek inquiry recommendations, that the CRE could use me as a test case and practical example of the outworking of the current partnership. I lifted elements of the five-year action plan that specifically reflected the situation I was in so that he could see that the Service was failing to discharge the actions it was committed to. I was hopeful they would get involved because, on the CRE website, Trevor Philips said:

We cannot afford to fail… In the end greater equality and increased professionalism is our joint goal… Achieving the targets set out in [the CRE and Prison Service] *Action Plan will be the sign that we are on our way to success.*

Chapter Ten

The Findings

The investigation report and findings finally arrived on 14th August. I was due to leave for Newbold when the postman arrived at my house. I picked up the A4-sized brown envelope with the college's postmark and stared at it for a while without opening it. I was so nervous. I walked into Mum's kitchen where she was making a cup of tea. She urged me to open it. I lifted up the sealed end and slid my finger across the top of the envelope. I put my fingers inside and slowly lifted the report out. I read the front page which said in bold underline,

> *'Investigation into allegations of racial discrimination, bullying and harassment by Olivea Ebanks against her line manager Susan Brookes, Head of Leadership and Management Development, Val Woodcock, National Manager, and Di Watkins, Leadership Advisor as set out in her complaints.'*

It went on to name Paul Carroll as the commissioning manager, the investigating and assisting officers as Rob Kellet and Richie Dell, followed by the words 'Final Report, 2006'.

I opened the document and immediately started to look for an executive summary. Mum was watching intently.

'Well, what does it say?'

With the biggest smile I had worn for many months I said, 'Listen to this.'

I read aloud.

> *Having considered the evidence available to us we have concluded that* [the College has] *failed to demonstrate that they have not discriminated against Olivea on the grounds of her race. That Olivea was treated in a manner that amounts to harassment and victimisation as defined in PSO 8010.*

I flicked through to find it identified significant management failings on the part of Sue as my manager. It further stated that the college had paid insufficient attention to race and diversity issues, their approach to management training had been poor and that there was scope for the college to be identified as 'Institutionally Racist'.

'Yes!' I shouted and hugged Mum.

At last Stacey would have to believe me: the report proved that I was telling the truth. I was so tired. I knew it wasn't quite over yet but at least we could begin talks from the perspective that I really was the victim and it was now time for remedies. As I read random excerpts, I was especially grateful for the comments in the report citing that I was effective and my work was of a high standard. Thank you, Jesus!

I made my way in to Newbold with a view to reading the report in detail. When I got in, I sat down and took a deep breath. I read the executive summary again. Then I went into the body of the report. As I did this, certain things jumped out more than others. I noted that, during her interview, Sue had accepted that the requirements she made of me in October in the action plan she had drafted could be seen as a punitive measure. Regarding expenses in relation to assurances about where I might be based, the report also noted that:

> *It would have been reasonable for* [Sue] *to have accepted that* [I] *had been given reassurance at the time of...signing* [my appointment] *letter...instead* [Sue] *gave the impression that she had a closed mind on the issue...*

I was particularly pleased to see there was more than one reference to the quality of my work being of a high standard, based on the views of those interviewed and the feedback I had provided. I was also glad the report highlighted that Sue had a tendency to move forward with decisions without involving me as the person most likely to be affected by her decisions. The report highlighted inconsistencies concerning Sue's and Val's management of me.

I was equally encouraged by references to 'Institutional Racism'. I hoped this would finally cause Stacey to realise that something was fundamentally wrong at the college and that her own behaviour had actually endorsed Sue's actions. I believed that, had she been prepared to consider that I was telling the truth from the outset, things might not have become so painful or prolonged.

As I read on, there were a few things that I found disappointing and a little perplexing about the report. The first issue was in relation to my access to occupational psychometric training. The report concluded that the reasons for not allowing me to undertake MBTI training were 'managerially sound', even though they noted conflicting evidence. They mentioned that the information I had given them relating to others being trained after me was correct, yet they didn't present evidence to explain why others were able to secure the coveted training. I couldn't understand how they were then able to come to the conclusion that the decision not to train me was still managerially sound. In May, I had reviewed the responses to the RR65 questionnaire, which detailed the training records of the LMD team. I found that, in the training year of 2005-2006, Person 14 and Person 15 had received psychometric training, listed as Fundamental Interpersonal Relations Orientation-Behaviour (Firo B) and MBTI conversion training. I deduced, from the start or appointment dates as recorded in the RR65 response, that Person 14 was Di Watkins. I also based this deduction on the requirement that one needs already to be a practitioner of psychometric tests in order to do the Firo B training. I then deduced that Person 15 had to be Rachel White, because of the start date to the college and because this person was recorded as having received Level A and B training in February and March 2006, which tied in with the LMD movement sheets. I had actually found evidence that both Di and Rachel had received occupational psychometric training, yet it wasn't clear to me if the investigators had considered this information when drawing a conclusion, because the RR65 wasn't recorded as 'documents consulted' in the document list appendix. Furthermore, the investigation report only focused on Rachel and didn't mention Di. I wasn't sure whether to press the matter or not. Additionally, I wasn't sure if the investigators realised just how important psychometric training, practice and policy were to an advisor in the daily execution of their duties. Psychometrics was regularly referred to in team meetings in one way or another, emphasising its importance and the many development programme boundaries it crossed. I wondered just how different the outcome might have been if I'd had all of this information to hand for the investigators for my interview. In any case, I was at least grateful that the evidence was now available for the Tribunal should I still need to attend.

I was annoyed at myself for not adequately conveying the issues surrounding the trips to Barbados and Bermuda, as well as the car hire saga. I felt that if I had, the outcomes again might have been different. I was disappointed that, even though Di had made racist comments, the investigators considered it had been adequately dealt with, along with the interim report recommendations. As far as I was concerned, her comments were symptomatic of prevailing attitudes and prejudice that manifested themselves in various ways in the team. I couldn't help feeling that Di had got away with racist behaviour that was blatant, whilst I was being repeatedly rebuked, reprimanded and picked on for the slightest thing. Sue and Val's treatment of me was mercilessly unforgiving: they constantly reminded me about what they considered to be shortfalls in my performance and demeanour, yet for Di, her shortfall, her mistake was forgiven and forgotten. A note on her file had absolved her of all sin. She was allowed to move on whilst I still had to face the fallout of the investigation. It just seemed that there were double standards—one rule for them and one rule for me.

As I continued to read, the recommendations left me quite concerned. For such an extensive report of over 20 pages there were only four very simple recommendations: firstly, that the college should address the outstanding diversity training issues for all their staff; secondly, that I should get an apology and, thirdly, that my line management arrangements should be reviewed to gain my confidence. The last recommendation concerned Sue. The report said she should receive support and guidance to make sure she learnt from her poor approach to managing me.

For at least three years, Sue, as a leadership advisor, had been responsible for designing and delivering training on group levels. She administered one-to-one executive coaching, core management skills, and encouraged attitudes and behaviours determined as essential by the Service. This was her job. Like me, she had been responsible for analysing personalities, behaviour and performance against agreed competencies and standards. Additionally, she had been responsible for spotting management potential in officers and identifying where individuals lacked sufficient capacity to meet the required competencies. Most recently, she had progressed to become the Head of Leadership and Management Development, where she governed eleven leadership advisors and teams of trainers responsible for delivering new governors through a fast-track scheme. She also supervised numerous support staff. How is it that, with all this skill and experience, she needed more support and guidance? If this level of ownership and responsibility couldn't inform her decisions, than what good would a little guidance do? Why wasn't anyone talking about sanctioning her? Sue knew what the policies were. She was not inexperienced. She had treated me this way because she didn't think I would fight back and if I did it would have been of little consequence. Sue's mishandling of me wasn't because she didn't know how to recognise unfair treatment. She could have stopped doing what she was doing from the minute I had said our relationship was poor. She could have stopped after my first complaint. But she didn't. It wasn't guidance that she needed. She needed to understand that there were consequences to her actions. And that was not a message that had been communicated up to this point. Sue *chose* to behave the way she did, and Stacey and all that is the Prison Service encouraged her to stand her ground. Guidance and support was not going to change anything, not when the college had already affirmed her behaviour with promotion–twice!

On balance, however, I was pleased the findings, and conclusions thoroughly highlighted examples and references of:

Unhelpful behaviour by management…ineffective practices by management…poor practice in relation to training at [the college]…*poor management generally…poor treatment and inconsistent management concerning* [me]…*significant management failings…*[And finally citing] *institutional racism.*

Looking at these factors made me feel that most of my claims were upheld, even where the outcome on a particular allegation was inconclusive. The way I was being treated in relation to those allegations was still highlighted as ineffective or inappropriate. Ultimately, this was what I wanted. I wanted Stacey, as the Head of the college not to count up how many of my claims had been upheld per se. I wanted her to see that a member of her staff was being bullied, harassed and victimised. I wanted her to see how precarious a situation the college was in, if discrimination on racial grounds couldn't be ruled out. This meant that, if this went to court, discrimination on racial grounds might be ruled in! I wanted her to see that the systems she had in place had failed and that some of her managers were ill equipped in terms of management style and were responding in unacceptable ways. I felt that, if she could grasp this, we could move forward. In any case, I was sure that the final reference to institutional racism would be enough to galvanise the college into effective and meaningful responses.

I was fairly confident the report had been circulated by now. William from PCS had rung me the week before I received a copy, to say he knew it was ready. I had also received a couple of calls from Stacey's staff officer, to check if I had received it yet in the post, and that was around 7th August. Now that the powers that be had the report, work was no doubt underway to make things right.

It wasn't long, though, before the relief I felt in reading the results gave way to apprehension. I wondered how I would be treated, in light of the report, by everyone concerned. I managed to convince myself things had to get better now that my performance and demeanour were no longer under the spotlight. It was now time for the college to turn the spotlight on itself and its managers.

The following day, I was at Newbold. After sending a couple of documents to print, I went upstairs to say hello to the admin team and retrieve my printing. Sue and Di were in the admin office with a visitor and the door was closed. I thought that, if the meeting was private, they would have been in Sue's office, which was a few yards down the corridor. The admin office was not a private office because several offices in the building needed to use the same printer and access the same resources. I figured the door was closed because they were having a good old gossip—it wouldn't be the first time. So I opened the door because I needed to get on with my work. As I stepped in, all heads deliberately turned towards me. The immediate silence prompted me to check if I had misjudged the situation and ask if the meeting was private after all. When I asked, no one responded. Instead, they looked at me as if I had just parachuted in.

After what felt like an age of uncomfortable silence, the visitor said, 'Oh it's just an informal meeting.'

'Oh okay, does anyone know where Katrina is?'

And again, except for my documents printing, there was silence. This time the visitor wasn't in a position to answer me, so I continued to wait. Then Sue responded in a tone conveying annoyance and, without even looking at me, said, 'She's on holiday.' I asked for another member of the team instead. Again, with the same tone as if it was a recording, without looking at me, Sue said, 'She's on holiday.'

By this time, my documents had finished printing. I crossed the room, picked up my printing and left.

After approximately 20 minutes, I went back to collect more printing. This time the admin door was open and Di sat in the office alone, typing. I went over to the printer and waited as it churned out copies. It was a large document and the printer was quite slow. I stood in silence for a good couple of minutes with my back to her as I collected each sheet. Then I thought, 'This is silly and uncomfortable.' I figured, having read the report, that maybe Di was embarrassed by the whole thing and didn't know how to begin rebuilding our professional relationship. I wasn't sure I knew what to do either, but someone had to try something. She had been on annual leave for about four weeks in Australia, so I thought that as a popular dream holiday destination for many people it would be a good topic to start a conversation with. In an attempt to reopen dialogue, I turned to face her and bravely asked how her holiday was.

'I heard you went to Australia,' I ventured. 'That must have been great. Did you have a good time?'

She looked up fleetingly and with robotic speed said, 'Yes, I had a lovely time, thank you.' There was no emotion and no smile. In the split second I caught her eyes, they were cold and unfriendly. Although unsettled, I pushed a little harder to engage her, thinking if we could get past the pain it would be worth it.

'So…who did you go with? Did you go with your partner? Did the kids tag along…? It must have been really great to have four weeks off; I've never taken a break like that.'

This time Di continued typing and looking at the screen, then said 'mm hmm.'

Her empty impersonal 'mm hmm' was followed by a continuous 'clickety-clack, tab, clickety-clack' on the computer keyboard. Even though I was standing right in front of her she ignored me completely. She typed and stared at the screen. She had poured contempt on my efforts. I should have taken the hint first time round when she had quickly rattled off that she'd had a lovely time. But I thought she was being dismissive because she was perhaps finding the whole thing too upsetting; she had no doubt been affected by the investigation too. It can't have been easy to see your name in print as the perpetrator of racist comments. Maybe she felt ashamed. But I could see now that this was not shame, this was anger. She wasn't talking because she was angry with me. As I watched her I could see it on her face. The investigation report had not engendered regret–it had hardened her heart. She was vexed that I had made trouble for her. I turned back to face the printer and continued to collect my document, sheet by agonising sheet in silence whilst the resentment in me burned. I thought to myself: these people have treated *me* badly, they were in the wrong as borne out by an official report, yet it means nothing since people are still allowed to be antisocial and refuse to engage with me. Di and I hadn't spoken since 29th March, when I stopped her on the stairwell in the Mansion to tell her that I had sent her an email. It was now August, five months down the line, and she was behaving as if, by being offended, I had offended *her*. It seemed it was still okay to look at me as if I was something nasty stuck to the bottom of their shoes, or look past me as if I was a ghost. I was so tired of being treated like a second-class citizen. I couldn't understand at which point in time I had become less than everyone else.

At lunchtime, I sent a thank you note to Sarah for sorting out the issues surrounding Sue's attempts at further harassment during and after the last team meeting. I conveyed my exasperation with the fact that there seemed to be no end to the differential treatment I was receiving and that the release of the investigation findings seemed to have made little difference. I was especially grateful for Sarah's diligence. There was genuineness about her that was refreshing and I felt I could trust her. She had fought harder for me in a few days of meeting me than any of my managers or colleagues. Sarah gave me the benefit of the doubt and demonstrated her willingness to help. She was proof that passion for fairness could be found in the Service and I was touched by the care she had shown.

On 18th August, I raised another victimisation grievance. The penny had finally dropped. Denying me a performance appraisal (SPDR) because I raised grievances was a breach of policy. I am not sure why it took so long to register that I was still being treated unfairly; however, the trigger was the investigation report. I remembered Steve telling me at my SPDR target-setting meeting in June and in writing that I wouldn't get a performance review until after the investigation because I had raised grievances. Now that this had come back to my remembrance, I sent an email to Susanne in personnel and asked her to explain the position better, as well as what was going to happen now that the investigation was over. She replied saying that the relevant policy did not specifically address the situation I found myself in. I thought *I* didn't find myself in this position—I was *put* in this position by managers treating me unfairly. I was so reactive.

Then Susanne went on to say that the policy did *'not refer to the situation where a member of staff has lodged grievances against their line manager, which until concluded means the report cannot be completed'*.

I had a look at the policy and it stated:

The Job Holder and their Manager **must** *meet at the end of the reporting period to discuss performance…The Job Holder* **must** *be offered an opportunity to comment on their performance…and the Manager* **must** *award a performance level.*

None of this had been done. This left the college in breach of Prison Service policy and procedures. I asked Stacey to investigate fully how this could have happened.

Chapter Eleven

Best Foot Forward

In August, I had my interview in London for the Regional Development Manager, senior Manager D role that I had fenced for the LMD Advisor and the Area Personnel Advisor. Val Perry, the Area Personnel Advisor for the East Midlands had opted out as expected, leaving me as the sole applicant. If I secured this role, it would mean promotion. This was very important to me and represented many things. Firstly, being promoted to a Manager D would increase my credibility no end as an organisational and learning and development specialist in the Service. Managers who have come up through the ranks (and uniformed staff) have been known to be extremely suspicious of civilian staff, who appear to arrive in senior roles without any Prison Service background. However, I was in a good position because I had joined to look after prisoner education, I had managed prison officers and managers; then I had moved on to developing governors and managers with an understanding of what they faced every day. Being promoted to Manager D from these vantage points would communicate to the people I had to work within the new structure that I was promoted because I fitted, because I understood the culture and because I had the relevant skills, knowledge and competencies. It would communicate that being promoted was in recognition of the value I had already brought and would continue to bring to the organisation and that I was not an unknown entity from the outside. I was one of them.

Secondly, I would get a well-earned pay rise. I had been at the top of the Manager E pay scale since I joined in 2003. As a direct result, I had been unable to influence my earning capacity even after exceptional work. Thirdly, this promotion would mean that I had successfully completed a rigorous and thorough assessment of my capabilities. This was important because, at this stage, I felt that in the absence of an appraisal, the only things on my file were unsubstantiated complaints about my performance by Sue and Val.

I imagined there being notes about how poorly I mixed team and reminders about updating my diary. I felt that, de hard work, there was nothing positive on my file since join college. It was easy to track how I arrived at my suspicic started when I met Stacey for the first time on 22nd November was further compounded by Val and Steve as my interim manag In each case, their approach was assumptive, and they spoke to about the things Sue had complained about as if they had witnesse the offending behaviour personally since taking over managemen of me. In each case, it was impossible for me to start with a clean slate because the starting point for each new relationship was whatever Sue had said and whatever she had recorded on my file. For each relationship, I was compelled to prove that I was observing protocol and I was being sociable etc. I was mentally and emotionally exhausted and it was very disappointing to see that not one manager could wait long enough to evaluate me on merit. Instead, they had each chosen to start with what they had been told, and made judgements and recommendations on that basis. My hope was that this promotion would cancel out all suspicions of poor performance, poor attitudes and unsuitable personality traits on my part. The tests I sat in the lead-up to the interview measured these areas and found me competent and suitable. Securing the new role would uphold and further endorse those findings.

    Finally, the non-operational staff were about to undergo organisational restructure and that is always a time of change, displacement and vulnerability. I had invaluable knowledge and experience of change management tools and best practice. In this newly promoted role, I would be able to draw from my extensive experience to set up and monitor change whilst taking care to support staff by building trust and confidence in the new structure.

    With all this in mind, I had a degree of confidence because the new role played to a lot of my strengths. I had completed the selection tests well and I was experienced at working at higher management levels in previous roles outside the Service. This meant that my legitimacy for applying for the role was academically sound and verified by knowledge and experience. I also had a good HR generalist background and I was the only person eligible to apply for the role at this stage. All I had to do was get through the

Chapter Eleven

Best Foot Forward

On 22nd August, I had my interview in London for the Organisational Development Manager, senior Manager D role that was ring-fenced for the LMD Advisor and the Area Personnel Advisor. Val Perry, the Area Personnel Advisor for the East Midlands had opted out as expected, leaving me as the sole applicant. If I secured this role, it would mean promotion. This was very important to me and represented many things. Firstly, being promoted to a Manager D would increase my credibility no end as an organisational and learning and development specialist in the Service. Managers who have come up through the ranks (and uniformed staff) have been known to be extremely suspicious of civilian staff, who appear to arrive in senior roles without any Prison Service background. However, I was in a good position because I had joined to look after prisoner education, I had managed prison officers and managers; then I had moved on to developing governors and managers with an understanding of what they faced every day. Being promoted to Manager D from these vantage points would communicate to the people I had to work within the new structure that I was promoted because I fitted, because I understood the culture and because I had the relevant skills, knowledge and competencies. It would communicate that being promoted was in recognition of the value I had already brought and would continue to bring to the organisation and that I was not an unknown entity from the outside. I was one of them.

Secondly, I would get a well-earned pay rise. I had been at the top of the Manager E pay scale since I joined in 2003. As a direct result, I had been unable to influence my earning capacity even after exceptional work. Thirdly, this promotion would mean that I had successfully completed a rigorous and thorough assessment of my capabilities. This was important because, at this stage, I felt that in the absence of an appraisal, the only things on my file were unsubstantiated complaints about my performance by Sue and Val.

I imagined there being notes about how poorly I mixed with the team and reminders about updating my diary. I felt that, despite my hard work, there was nothing positive on my file since joining the college. It was easy to track how I arrived at my suspicions. It started when I met Stacey for the first time on 22nd November and was further compounded by Val and Steve as my interim managers. In each case, their approach was assumptive, and they spoke to me about the things Sue had complained about as if they had witnessed the offending behaviour personally since taking over management of me. In each case, it was impossible for me to start with a clean slate because the starting point for each new relationship was whatever Sue had said and whatever she had recorded on my file. For each relationship, I was compelled to prove that I was observing protocol and I was being sociable etc. I was mentally and emotionally exhausted and it was very disappointing to see that not one manager could wait long enough to evaluate me on merit. Instead, they had each chosen to start with what they had been told, and made judgements and recommendations on that basis. My hope was that this promotion would cancel out all suspicions of poor performance, poor attitudes and unsuitable personality traits on my part. The tests I sat in the lead-up to the interview measured these areas and found me competent and suitable. Securing the new role would uphold and further endorse those findings.

Finally, the non-operational staff were about to undergo organisational restructure and that is always a time of change, displacement and vulnerability. I had invaluable knowledge and experience of change management tools and best practice. In this newly promoted role, I would be able to draw from my extensive experience to set up and monitor change whilst taking care to support staff by building trust and confidence in the new structure.

With all this in mind, I had a degree of confidence because the new role played to a lot of my strengths. I had completed the selection tests well and I was experienced at working at higher management levels in previous roles outside the Service. This meant that my legitimacy for applying for the role was academically sound and verified by knowledge and experience. I also had a good HR generalist background and I was the only person eligible to apply for the role at this stage. All I had to do was get through the interview. My development plan, which was drawn up from the outputs of my assessment, had already been sent to Bob, the Area Manager. I was glad the development plan was so positive and hoped Bob would use it appropriately whilst considering me for the role.

Having said all this, however, my confidence was still threatened by a number of other factors. To begin with, my interview was three months late–this created tension and a high level of paranoia for me. All interviews for this part of the restructure were to be completed by May. All other advisors who were interested in their respective areas had had their interviews to time. I wasn't sure if the interview was delayed for the same reasons that I was denied my appraisal. I thought that perhaps they were waiting for the investigation to prove that Sue's approach was justified because I was a poor performer. I thought that perhaps they were considering that, based on my test results, they couldn't risk me being successful at interview and securing a promotion before the investigation results proved I really was a poor performer with poor social skills. I was also nervous because I was being interviewed by the Area Manager, and I didn't know how much he knew about my predicament. At the conference in February, we were told that the Area Manager's decision was final and that there was no appeal. As the Area Manager for the East Midlands, I expected Bob to know everything, especially as my claims were the first officially recorded racial grievances in the history of the college. So I suspected he had already made a judgement as to whether or not he wanted a black senior manager on his team who was taking the Service to court for racism. I suspected he wouldn't want me. I considered that, even though my test results were very good, he would have already seen my file or have been briefed on what the performance issues were– and not forgetting the fact that I was making history on his patch just months before he retired. Even though the concerns on my file were unsubstantiated, I doubted very much that he would think the information recorded was untrue and in need of challenge. As a manager, one never assumes an employee's file has been maliciously compiled, the assumption is that the details are correct. Besides, I was still shaken by the way I was being treated: it was already beginning to feel that the investigation report would not ultimately change very much for me.

I was imagining so many things. I had finally been worn down. I had to dig deep to find a smile and the kind of energy you need at interview. I was suspicious and resentful. The investigation concluded that I had been systematically victimised and harassed, yet I was still expected to put my best foot forward and secure a promotion while people were still treating me like dirt. If I had been on the senior management team in receipt of the investigation report with such damning indicators of institutional racism, I would have consulted the victim. As much as I understood the principles of open and fair competition, this report had just confirmed that the applicant for the role was a victim of long-standing poor and detrimental treatment. The last thing she probably needed was to be treated as if she was on an equal footing with everyone else, when the report clearly showed she had been on the receiving end of unfair treatment. I would have been aware that this might have a baring on her performance. I would have considered that there were mitigating circumstances warranting a different approach. In light of the fact that she had worked at a high level in the past, and had produced good work for the area, and not forgetting that she was the only applicant, I would have at the very least, assessed the extent of her suffering and asked if she felt able to continue. I would have considered if there was room for some concession.

It had only been eight days since the issuing of the investigation report. It was too soon to put resolutions in place to deal with the negative and devastating effects of harassment, bullying and victimisation. And it was certainly too soon to judge which measures, if any, would have restored the confidence, motivation and trust of the victim. I would have consulted the victim for these reasons.

But that isn't what happened. I was not consulted about whether or not I felt able to do the interview or if I wanted the panel to take anything into account when assessing my performance. No one considered that I was under huge amounts of pressure due to the discrimination I suffered. No allowances had been made at all. I, therefore, had no choice but to compete, even though I had repeatedly told them with each complaint how ill I had become as a direct consequence of the discrimination. As usual it was all up to me!

I did not feel able to raise these issues for discussion, neither did I think it appropriate for me to raise them. Any such direction should have come from the organisation as a response to the pain they had caused me. Instead of complaining, I made peace with the fact that I was desperate to get out of the college. Hence, I needed to secure the promotion to make my life better. Even with the positives though, I still felt that the odds were most definitely against me. But I encouraged myself that, if I could perform to the same level I had done on the assessment tests, they wouldn't have any grounds for denying me a promotion.

I had been preparing for this for months. Although I felt I knew my area of speciality well, I revisited old learning and development models I had used in the past and refreshed my knowledge. I had been doing this periodically since March. I put a reference sheet together with many of the recognised models and practices. I created mnemonics and practiced referring to them without disrupting the flow of a conversation. In addition, Rudy (who is a training manager) put me through mock interviews using the 'Person Specifications Outline' for the organisational development manager role. He devised quizzes by using the reference sheet that I had put together. Rudy asked questions that were difficult and obscure, and gave me feedback on my answers and approach to the questions. From July, we were doing these exercises on a weekly basis. Angie, a friend who was the Head of Human Resources in her company, conversed with me regularly on HR organisational matters, both current and hypothetical. This helped me form fluid answers about strategic planning and execution.

I was interviewed by Bob, the Area Manager for the East Midlands, and Althea, as a member of the HR from Head Quarters. I was so nervous, I barely noticed the size or layout of the room. My focus was to give this my best shot. The meeting opened with an apology for the delay in arranging the interview. Bob explained that it was due to deliberation about whether or not he was the right person to lead on the interview since he was due to retire by the time the new role became active. I immediately thought I was at a disadvantage: I could have had the opportunity to be interviewed by the new Area Manager, who perhaps hadn't got much history on my situation. Of course, there was no guarantee he or she wouldn't have checked my file or spoken to Stacey or Sue, but this person would at least be making a judgment having met me for the first time. We would both be new and perhaps more understanding of the need to support each other.

However, I quickly put this out of my mind so that I could concentrate on the interview. The interview lasted approximately two hours, and was a little tough and obscure in places. I felt I answered questions well, even though some of them were quite vague. On occasion, it seemed as though the board was looking for something that I couldn't quite put my finger on. This was especially noticeable in the area of strategic planning. Bob asked for my opinion about the priorities in the East Midlands. I told him that I felt succession planning was particularly poor and that the development of individuals in line with succession planning was equally poor. Although I understood overarching responsibilities to hold prisoners securely, reduce the presence of drugs in prisons and so on, I explained that the Service was too target-driven. I ventured that there was more to organisational effectiveness than meeting audit requirements, like preventing escapes. My personal view was that proper investment in the development of staff would improve the treatment we gave to prisoners. I further challenged that it was possible to meet all the Key Performance Targets and never change as an organisation. I demonstrated that there was no strategy for consistent investment in staff development in the region and that an organisation was nothing without its staff. I gave him the example of LMD, and how it had taken three years to establish it as a support for localised management development, yet now the roles were obsolete with no one to continue the work. I gave further examples of how individuals had become accredited for a promoted role through J-SAC, even though there were no roles for them to migrate into, leading to criticisms of the system. I showed him how we could make sure that individuals, having secured successful exam results, got an opportunity to practise and develop new skills.

Bob didn't seem too impressed by my candour. He felt you couldn't develop individuals and succession-plan at the same time and my proposals were unrealistic. Although I felt this was a strange view, I determined that a miscommunication had occurred, probably because I had not explained myself well enough. So I gave him examples of how I had facilitated this in the private sector with sustained high performers and high potentials. I explained that I would like to pursue some of those initiatives in the East Midlands, if I was successful at interview. I put it to him that we could work with the governors in the region and devise a strategy to develop and place individuals–if successful, it could lead the way to better development of management potential for every region. I believed that, if we looked at these issues as well as pursuing targets like basic skills for prisoners or Control and Restraint training for uniformed staff, we would be well on our way to organisational effectiveness. This would also facilitate better provision for prisoners and a more justifiable use of the public purse. Bob remained sceptical, though I felt I had made a good case. I had demonstrated that I had made it work in the past and was able to work closely with him or the new Area Manager to devise a suitable strategy with clear measurable deliverables for the East Midlands. His scepticism did worry me, though, because my success was dependent on his decision alone. I was aware that I had disagreed with him. It was at this point that I particularly felt disadvantaged because the new Area Manager might have a different view about the priorities for the region. Althea made notes during the exchange between Bob and me. Then she asked a few generic questions and recorded my answers.

When I got home, I went through everything again with Rudy. I explained where I felt there was a sticking point; however, I was happy that I had tried my best to show initiative, confidence and new thinking. Having listened to the answers I said I had given to the questions, Rudy said it sounded as if I handled myself well. His assurance was very welcome.

The following day I got a call from Bob. He told me I hadn't got the job. Apparently, my grasp of the strategy for the East Midlands and the area plan was 'a bit weak'. I was devastated. I thought 'a bit weak'? It wasn't weak, it was different. I had worked in the area for nearly three years, including my term at my first prison. How was my knowledge weak, I wondered? I instantly speculated if this was just because I had disagreed on a few points. Surely not.

Yet hadn't Bob asked for *my* views on the main priorities to focus on in the area, and that's what I had given him—my views. So what, if they had differed from the area strategy in places? He had asked for my opinion, he disagreed with my stance and I justified my position. I was aware that internal politics dictated that I towed the party line and said what was expected. But this was a brand new role, calling for brand new thinking. The way that we approached organisational effectiveness was under review because Head Quarters had recognised that we could work more smartly. The inefficiencies I had outlined during the interview were not his to own. I had not highlighted any personal failings on his part—they were organisational shortfalls. I would have worked with whatever mandate the current or the new Area Manager had laid down, despite my personal assessment of priorities.

Although deeply disappointed, I was still realistic. I didn't think it was impossible to go for a promotion and not get it. Yet I couldn't help thinking there was more to this. I had accepted that, just because I was the only applicant, that didn't automatically make me the best person for the job. However, in April, I had been appraised against the role and the standards set. The external assessors reported that I demonstrated *'strong evidence of organisational analysis and planning: strong evidence of organisational development, change management and strategy, planning and metrics'*. I was also reported as showing *'strong evidence of corporate and prison awareness'* along with *'strong evidence in project management, consultancy skills and coaching'*. With regards to the Human Resource Management section, they identified *'strong evidence in performance management, legal and policy framework'*. I was not simply hoping that, because the role was ring-fenced for me, it was a guaranteed outcome. I had more than enough evidence to suggest that I was a strong candidate. I not only possessed the relevant and recently assessed skills necessary to do the job, I was also actively working in the East Midlands, and had a good relationship with the governors who would be most affected by the restructure. As much as I accepted that I had development needs, I had a lot going for me as well and could develop into the new role with appropriate levels of support. Despite my fears, I had been very hopeful about getting the promotion, based on my skills and experience—but it didn't happen.

The weight of not getting the promotion really hit me, when I considered I was going to have to face Sue and all the people who were talking about me and waiting for me to fail. How was I supposed to tell them that I didn't get a job for which I was the only applicant? What did that say about me? I could just see Sue rejoicing. For her, it was only a matter of time before I failed and proved her right—and it had finally happened. A kind of panic set in, that I didn't know how to manage. I cried and then cried some more. I didn't know what the future held for me. Not securing this promotion meant that I would soon become surplus Home Office staff. I would be expected to look for jobs and hope to find one before my role as Leadership Advisor became obsolete. Yet I was painfully aware that I would be facing the same prejudice with each application. As much as I would try to put my best foot forward and detail examples of competence in each application, selection managers would always have the option of speaking to my manager and/or checking my file. It was a much-complained-about practice, that governors and managers would simply make a call about an applicant that they didn't know, and if the applicant's manager felt that the individual was unsuitable or not quite ready, that this would curtail the applicant's chances of success. I had even heard governors say that they endorsed a member of staff's application not because they thought the individual would get the job but because the individual needed the interview board experience. And, more bizarrely, I had heard governors say that they had signed off applications for fear of a grievance being raised against them if they didn't. Then, once contacted by an interview panel member, these unwritten reasons would surface, putting a kybosh on the individual's application.

I felt I had no chance of getting another job, and the facility to hold on to the job I had was taken away by the restructure. I believed that, just like she had done during the investigation interviews, Sue would always take the opportunity to sow seeds of doubt about my performance, by saying things like, 'the quality of her work is good, I just have issues with the quantity of the work'. Little comments like that wouldn't inspire anyone to give me a job. Not securing this promotion meant I was still at the college ultimately reporting to Sue, however many times they changed my reporting line, and any attempt at moving onwards and upwards would be sabotaged by her. Sue would always have power over me.

The negativity swirled around in my head. Two days ago, I was cautiously hopeful–one incident later and I was on the floor. I was so unstable! I had fallen flat on my face. But then that's what falling does–it throws you violently from one level down to another. There's no gracefulness involved. No considered and deliberate descending. Falling is synonymous with the dramatic, with speed and disorientation. There is no control. If you catch yourself early enough, you may be able to lessen the impact, by reaching out to steady yourself. But I had unceremoniously flown through the air and landed with my skirt around my neck! I was wearing big, 'Bridget Jones' style pants and everyone was pointing and laughing. I was hurt, ashamed and exposed.

Not getting the promotion didn't make any sense to me, other than that there had been some sort of conspiracy. (Maybe I didn't fall unaided, maybe I was tripped!) I couldn't see how I could prove that the interview was unfair. There was no facility to appeal, as outlined at the meeting in February and by the Summary of the *Job Matching and Assessment Process Outline,* that had been sent to all parties affected by the restructure. There was something fundamentally wrong with a process this complex not having an appeals procedure. This left me very confused about the next steps. I believed that my grievances and outstanding claims against the Service had influenced the decision not to promote me, but in the absence of an appeals procedure, I was left with raising another grievance. I didn't know what to do, since neither grievances nor investigation outputs had made my life more bearable. At the very least, I felt, I should ask for feedback.

The following day, I sent an email to the clients (mainly a mixture of governors and personnel managers) who had expressed, over the last few months, a genuine interest in my getting the job. I didn't go into detail; I simply stated that I had been unsuccessful at interview and thanked them for their encouragement. I was overwhelmed with the responses. People were really surprised and sympathetic. They talked about me bringing 'star quality' to my work; they said that I deserved to get the role, and so on. There was even one from a governor who felt I should appeal, to make sure I had been turned down for valid reasons. I wondered how that governor would respond, if she knew just how many grievances or appeals against unfair decisions I already had in the system!

I found Beverley Thompson's response especially comforting and full of insight. In it, she said:

> Hi Olivea,
>
> I am really sorry to hear about the result of your interview. It must really have knocked your confidence. I am sure you are right that the effects of what you have been going through has affected you more than you had perhaps expected or recognised. You are only human after all and we can all sometimes be over confident that we are dealing with adversity better than is actually the case. We all have a tendency, particularly black people working in highly stressful situations, to parade a professional exterior even when we are dying inside.

How true, I thought. I knew many black people who spent a disproportionate amount of time covering the dents in their demeanour, their deportment stoic and noble, so much so that, when they finally announced any semblance of struggle, it was met with disbelief and resistance. And I was one of them.

On 1st September, I had palpitations on the M1, as I made my way in to Newbold. I had to pull over onto the hard shoulder, wind down the windows, and wait for the bad feeling to pass. I hadn't seen anyone since failing at interview and felt that everyone had to know by now. I was embarrassed and over-anxious. When I got in, I went straight to my office and logged onto my computer. My feedback from the interview had been sent. The interview pass mark was 60 points out of 100. I had achieved 55 points. Thus, for the sake of five points, the Service was now prepared to open my role to anyone who failed to secure the same role in their own area. And if the personnel department failed to find a suitable candidate from that pool of people, they would spend thousands of pounds to advertise nationally. This made no sense to me at all. I kept wondering how this new person was going to demonstrate *their* understanding of the East Midlands Area Strategy, having quite possibly never worked for the Service before. As far as I was concerned, the Service was making it clear it didn't want me. It was hard at this point to truly believe that I had simply failed to demonstrate competence at interview. I looked at all the indicators that built my case and at my suspicions again: the lateness of my interview, leaving me looking like the last person in the country to have my interview during phase one (phase two was already well under way); being interviewed by an area manager who was retiring and didn't need to open his mind to new ideas; that I had failed by a margin of five points, in an area where I had disagreed with old thinking for a new organisation structure and a new role. Was my performance really that bad? And didn't they also have my valid Prison Service experience, and my independently assessed 'strong' suitability for the role to draw from?

I read through the interview assessment marking sheet they sent me as feedback on my performance and saw that there was a maximum of 20 points for five areas of competence. For two areas, I had secured 15 points out of 20; for two areas I had attracted a score of 10 points; the final area on 'Strategic Planning' was where I scored five points. Aha, I thought. I had tried to demonstrate a new approach and the marking sheet recorded this as my having a 'good understanding of role opportunities and its strategic nature', yet not presenting 'operational reality'.

I couldn't understand what it was that the Service wanted from me. I saw myself as keen, intelligent and hard working. Of course, I didn't know everything, but for the Service not to want to invest in me sufficiently enough to upgrade my skills by such a small margin, was humiliating. As I considered that they would rather employ an external candidate instead of developing me, I became more and more despondent. They had just made me go through the motions so that it would seem fair and now for the sake of five points, I had no hope of promotion and I had no future. I was devastated and felt trapped at the college.

As the days rolled on, I thought more about the investigation report. I noticed it was actually ready by the deadline of 29th June, yet had not been circulated until August. I wondered what they had been doing since then. I continued to be obsessed about the recommendations—how light they were in terms of sanctions and how limited their scope to inform changed behaviour. The investigators proved that I had been discriminated against. They fell short of explicitly saying that it was on racial grounds. Despite their conclusion that I had been subjected to victimisation and harassment, they did not then determine this as a serious breach of Prison Service rules of conduct. Hence, no sanctions. I found this confusing. Regardless of what they thought the grounds or motives were, I had been victimised and harassed. We weren't talking about a single action or mistake. We were talking about systematic abuse for over a year. In my view, this pointed to strong cognitive preferences and entrenched thinking. Yet the Service felt that the remedy for consciously choosing to abuse and belittle others should be a one-off, theatre-based diversity-training half-day, along with undefined support and guidance for Sue. I could see that the recommendations seemed broad enough to include many initiatives, yet I believed that if Stacey's performance at our last team meeting was anything to go by, she would only put a few meagre initiatives in place, without ways of measuring effectiveness.

I knew there would be nothing to challenge behaviour or cause people to consider the gravity of their actions. There would be no consequences, except for perhaps a derisory 'note' on a personal file. I thought, 'Big deal!' There wouldn't be anything that would cause Sue, at least, to think twice about victimising someone else again. She would get away with it and the college would continue to make out that I was being petty and unreasonable.

I decided to write to the Tribunal. I wanted the Tribunal chairperson to see up front that, between now and the court case, the college would only pay lip service and give me the run-around. I wanted to declare in writing that I knew they were going to continue to drag their feet and play with my life, and that it wasn't so much paranoia on my part but it was the nature of the beast on theirs.

Chapter Twelve

Defence without Honour

After the release of the investigation report, I had received an apology from Gareth Hadley, the Director of Personnel, expressing sorrow for the way I had 'at times been treated'. He asked if we could meet to discuss the investigation report. I was pleased, as it would give me an opportunity to address the lightness of the recommendations and find out what he was really going to do about my situation. Stacey had also requested a meeting with me. She said that she wanted to resolve any outstanding difficulties and move forward. I initially responded to Stacey's request to say that I was happy to move forward but, after a couple of days, I felt there needed to be some clarity in relation to the content of the discussions she was proposing and the structure to the meetings. With this in mind, I wrote back and outlined that discussions about outstanding grievances and moving forward needed to remain separate.

Stacey responded on 31st August, saying that she wasn't anticipating a discussion about the level of investigation I required into my outstanding grievances and maintained she just wanted the opportunity to hear my views about the future. Stacey and Paul Carroll had created the situation I was in, because they had refused to include all of my grievances in the investigation. I was now in this position, where I was expected to move forward in relation to the things that were covered by the investigation report, yet remain in limbo over the things the report did not cover. I couldn't understand how Stacey expected me to attend a meeting about forgetting the past, whilst I was asking for another investigation into outstanding complaints. I felt it was ridiculous to expect that I could compartmentalise my situation like that. I responded the next day to say that, *'any attempt to push for resolution before careful consideration of* [all the] *facts, motivations or rationales* [would] *only lead to flawed and inadequate proposals* [for moving forward]'.

I maintained there needed to be proper inquiry into my outstanding grievances and reminded her that she was legally bound to answer them. She didn't respond until the day of the meeting, 4th September, only to apologise for not responding because she hadn't been able to get to a computer. Even then, she didn't tell me what she was going to do about the points I raised.

Jaswinder from RESPECT, a support group for BME staff in the Service, was supporting me and although we had spoken on the phone, I hadn't yet met him. I had been without PCS union representation since June and was tired of not having an independent and objective pair of eyes to look over things for me. Everything was reliant on whether or not I spotted something. If I didn't spot it, it wasn't dealt with, as in the case with my appraisal. This level of vigilance and the weight of the fear of missing something had left me worn out and constantly panicked about every occurrence. Even though I could often see rational arguments about a certain incident, they were being overruled by arguments like, 'What if it was racist, maybe you don't have all the facts' and 'You know it's racist because the other incident was racist, they don't just switch it on and off like a tap you know. It isn't a tool they're using for some jobs and not others, it's who they are!'

I tried so hard not to interpret everything against a backdrop of racism. It was becoming a daily battle.

Jaswinder arrived and introduced himself. He was a tall, heavily set Asian man. He came across as quite sociable. He later told me that he played rugby when he wasn't being hindered by his dodgy knee. One of the first things he said was that where my office was situated was unsuitable. He said that anyone could walk in, abuse me and leave without anyone knowing. It wasn't safe.

'Does anyone else work down here?'

'People hot-desk from time to time, but I'm mostly alone down here,' I said. I was amazed that his first thoughts were about my safety.

Jaswinder hadn't had time to read the investigation report fully; however, he decided that he at least had time to sit with me and look at the conclusions, before the meeting. I sat in silence wondering what he would make of it. Then it came like a bolt of lightning across the sky.

'If the college is institutionally racist...then it doesn't make sense for you to talk to the Head of the college, as she could be seen as one of the perpetrators.'

But of course, I thought. How is it that I didn't see that? Now this is exactly what I was talking about. Someone was picking up the stuff I had missed. Praise Jesus!

Jaswinder continued. 'You shouldn't be talking to Stacey. You should be talking to her line manager. The college has been implicated and with Stacey being the Head, then she's implicated too.'

It was almost as if, when he repeated himself, there was more clarity.

'You shouldn't go to this meeting,' he announced.

Shouldn't go? I mused. Maybe, I considered. Except that not going was not an option as far as I could tell. It wasn't his fault; after all, he had only just arrived. He couldn't possibly know that they would use that against me. I thought it best to explain.

'If I don't go to the meeting they could tell the court that I was being difficult and making myself unavailable. They are so transparent. I can see how Stacey is trying to play it, in that she has already implied in her emails that my unavailability, whilst you were on holiday and couldn't support me, was slowing up her desire to move forward.'

I told Jaswinder that lies and deception came so easily to the college and that I couldn't risk simply not going. Attempts to assassinate my character were many and I didn't want to add to the list the arrogance of failing to show up to a meeting apparently designed to help me.

Jaswinder said that the college would be obliged to fix what was wrong and demonstrate that they had fixed things, whether I showed up for the meeting or not. He still thought I shouldn't go; however, I think he could see how fearful and weary I was, so he conceded. He suggested I did a quick bullet point note for Stacey, reminding her of what was outstanding in terms of grievances and actions. He recommended I kept it simple as it wasn't to be a letter as such, rather a summary of points I could leave with Stacey, if I got too upset to speak.

I spent some time updating him on some of the occurrences of the previous month, especially the last team meeting. I told him how ill I was, that I was having dizzy spells whilst driving and that I was going to make an appointment to see my doctor after the meeting with Stacey.

About an hour later, we went to meet with Stacey and Susanne from personnel. During the meeting, I found Stacey particularly patronising. She was trying to engage in first-stage informal discussions about my outstanding grievances. When I asked her what she was doing, she used an analogy to explain.

'When anyone raises a grievance it is best practise to try and resolve it at the lowest level and try to avoid escalation. For example, if there were disagreements between us as to what colour to paint my office—let's say I wanted it pink and you wanted it to remain blue—we would have to engage in discussions at the lowest level to choose the right colour. We would meet and if we couldn't choose a colour, we would have to meet again and maybe agree to a compromise—say light purple.'

Was I losing it, I thought, losing my grip on reality? What had just happened here? Was I talking to the Head of the college or Lawrence Llewellyn-Bowen, interior designer? Jaswinder's comments came back to haunt me. He was right: Stacey is not the person I should be talking to. Yet I was here now, I couldn't get up and walk out.

I decided to remind her I had a solid HR generalist background and fully understood the nature of and rationale behind an informal discussion. I also reminded her that she had not dealt with each grievance in that way, that the equal opportunity policy stipulated that informal discussions might not always be appropriate and that I had wanted my claims to be formally investigated. 'How many times do I need to say this?' I thought.

Jaswinder, no doubt sensing my disbelief and irritation, moved the conversation on. He suggested that, once Stacey had received the report, she should have immediately arranged a special leave of absence for me. 'You should have realised that Olivea was under tremendous stress. The report proved that she was telling the truth all along and she shouldn't still have to come into work every day until you fix the problems. Olivea needs to get away from the college. This is a stressful environment for her and since the report, she isn't even safe from further abuse.'

'What do you mean by further abuse?' Stacey asked.

'Olivea told me about the last team meeting. That's harassment!'

Stacey's response was immediately on the defensive. *'That* incident,' she said firmly, 'occurred not because Sue was harassing Olivea, but because *Olivea* had put something inappropriate in her monthly report!'

It felt like déjà vu. Again, Stacey was able to form an opinion and a judgement about an incident involving me without actually talking to me about it. Again, Sue was not at fault, it was me. After everything that had happened, everything that had been proven—the fault still rested with me! How was this even possible!

I didn't have anything left in me. I just wanted to leave the room. Was it really so hard for someone on my team to defend me, for someone to say that Olivea deserved better or that she deserved some consideration? The war of questions raged on in my mind. I could feel my head starting to cloud over and grow dark, as if I was going to pass out. I started to breathe deeply and tell myself I couldn't pass out, and that it wasn't long to go now, and that I just needed to hold on. I wished that something would bite me so that I would know that I was dreaming. Any minute now, I thought, I will stump my toe or fall out of bed and, like Bobby Ewing's death in Southfork, Dallas, Texas, this was all a bad dream—every dreadful, unbelievable moment of it. When I came back to myself, Stacey was asking me how much special leave I needed and was one week enough. I couldn't speak. I felt as if I was having one of those horrible, debilitating nightmares where you are being held down on the bed against your will and you can't move or scream as danger approaches. I was powerless to respond.

I desperately looked at Jaswinder and he stepped in. He said we should agree on one week and then if I didn't feel fit I should call in and ask for more time. Stacey was not happy and expressed disappointment that we couldn't discuss the grievances any more. I still sat in silence. Jaswinder continued to keep the meeting moving. He said he would confirm another date for discussions after he had properly read the investigation report. He thanked her for her time and stood up. I watched him make his way to the door before I realised I was still sitting at the table with Stacey and Susanne. Although dazed, I pushed the reminder note over to Stacey without a word and left the room with Jaswinder.

When we got back to my office, we couldn't get in. I had left my handbag in Stacey's office and my office keys were in it. I felt so pathetic. I went upstairs to the admin department and asked to borrow a key. I came back downstairs, let Jaswinder in, made him a drink and went back upstairs to return the key. Then I walked back across the grounds to the Mansion where Stacey's office was. When I got to Stacey's outer office, her secretary said, 'You left your bag in Stacey's office.' She handed it to me.

I left the Mansion and went back to my office. I then spent the next hour sending emails and postponing appointments so that there was nothing requiring immediate attention. Jaswinder refused to leave me on my own and said that he would stay until I was ready to leave. I was so touched by what he had done for me. I left the college extremely grateful that I could finally get some rest.

The rest was short-lived, as two days later the Tribunal copied me in on the Prison Service response to my claim. I had gone downstairs at about 9.30am and picked up the mail. When I recognised the postmark from the Tribunal, I opened the envelope without even leaving the hallway. As I read, the blood drained from my body. In their response, the Service had cited grounds for resistance to my complaints. Their reasons included what I saw as lies, and the strength of their arguments was based on discrediting me. I flicked to the end of the document to find that they had denied each and every allegation I had made. My eyes flew to the end of the last page where in summary they said:

> 46. *In reliance on the relevant and material facts set out herein, the Respondent denies it discriminated against the Claimant (1) on grounds of her race in accordance with the Race Relations Act 1979, (2) by way of harassment, (3) by way of victimisation, or at all.*

> 48. *Save for that which is expressly admitted in the Response, the Respondent denies each and every allegation set out in the Claimant's Claim Form.*

It was the words 'or at all' in paragraph 46 that hurt the most. The investigation findings had neither proved nor disproved discrimination on racial grounds, yet there was acceptance that I had been harassed and victimised. And now, in the Tribunal response, not only was the Service saying that it had not discriminated against me on racial grounds by way of harassment or victimisation, there was this 'or at all' ultimate statement. I couldn't understand how the Service could blatantly contradict its own investigation findings. I felt that I had fought and put my health at risk for nothing.

It dawned on me that the Service response citing Susanne as the contact, was faxed to the Tribunal on 1st September. This meant that, during our meeting on the 4th, both Susanne and Stacey were trying so hard to convey their concern and the need to move forward, whilst knowing their response to the Tribunal rejected my allegations and essentially made me out to be an untrustworthy, unsociable and unreliable employee. The hypocrisy of it made me feel sick and angry. That they could both sit in a meeting with me, knowing I was hurting and broken, look me in the eyes telling me they wanted to resolve things whilst, at the same time, justifying their treatment of me to the Tribunal as not only necessary but well within the scope of managing an antisocial, dishonest, defective performer. I didn't know what I was supposed to do now. I was disgusted by them.

The two-facedness of the Service was overwhelmingly hurtful, as I realised that they had lied to me. I reeled with the pain. I considered that blatant racism, though cruel and dehumanising, at least left you with no illusions about how people saw you. However, subtle racism—like the serpent in 'The Beginning'— attracted you, reasoned with you and beguiled you. Subtle racism, like cancer, ate away at you long before you realised it was there and by the time it had a face or a name it had begun to kill you. As I stared at their arguments in my hands, written so unashamedly, I looked back to my recruitment and the reasons I joined. The Service had called for me. All the people that made their marketing machine fly, said that they wanted me. They wanted my skills, my experience, and the skin they came in. But they had lied. I had arrived thinking that I was a necessary part of the plan for transformation and that everything about me had value. But the Service had lied. My experiences shaped by my culture, faith, personality and education (both academic and social) meant I would naturally see things, and approach things differently from the average white, middle-class person. That was supposed to be part of the plan. That's what the richness of diversity is supposed to be about—the celebration of differences and the wealth added by the same. Yet all Sue wanted was for me to contact the other advisors to find out what *they* were doing in *their* areas. There was no question of them learning anything from me. There was no recognition that I had brought anything of substance to the fore or that I had enough internal resource to draw from to allow me to hit the ground running and deliver exceptional results. No! I needed to be watched. I needed to be told off. I needed to know my place.

My tears splashed onto this document that I felt was designed to deceive. Each tear held a piece of my soul. And as each tear soaked into the fibres of the paper, another piece of my soul was trapped behind layers of processed dried pulp. I had cried so much over the past months it was no wonder I was beginning to feel dead inside.

How foolish of me to think that the organisation, this *national treasure* was going to do right by me after I dared to challenge and expose its failings. The organisation had every right to defend itself, as long as it was the truth. But this wasn't the truth. I rebuked myself for ever thinking that, somewhere down the line, someone would have approached me and said, 'Olivea we got it wrong—how do we put things right?' Still staring at the paper—the poison in my hands—it was as if I could see unwritten arguments lifting themselves from the pages like a coded secret. As the words of this secret unfolded between the spaces of each line, I read, 'The law says we can defend ourselves, so we will. We *could* use your experience as a model to inform the way we handle complaints, or how we educate our managers about how to deal with people, both staff and prisoners from different ethnic backgrounds. We *could* do that, but instead we choose not to learn anything from your pain. Instead, we'll pour our energies, expertise and money into proving that we were right to treat you this way and you were wrong to take Goliath on!'

After some time, I'm not sure how long, my eyes returned to the actual words that were written and the specifics that made up their defence. As I read them, I wanted to curl up in a ball and pretend that my life hadn't just completely fallen apart. In it, with regards to my behaviour, Sue stated that, *'Olivea was working very much in isolation and that when in the* [LMD] *building she did not make her presence known in any way.'* She responded to the question of insisting that I report my arrival and departure times to Helen and her secretary Ros as *'not a form of official monitoring* [but] *more a case of saying 'hello' and 'goodbye' and taking a more proactive approach to building professional relationships with the rest of the team'*. With regard to my work practice, Sue stated that she *'had been informed by coincidence as she carried out her own duties that* [I] *was not at the prison or premises that* [I] *had detailed on* [my] *calendar.'* Furthermore, Sue contended that I was not authorised to work on a particular project that she described as *'a project* [Listen to Improve in HMP Lincoln] *that was taking place outside* [Olivea's] *area based work and outside her area…'* Then Sue went on to state that [I] *had been told and had agreed that* [my] *outputs in* [the East Midlands] *area were too low'*. And there you have it, I thought; according to Sue's version of events I was so rude I needed to be told to be courteous and say 'Good morning' to other people. Sue was not randomly scrutinising my work for no reason, she simply happened across me lying about my whereabouts and, having caught me in the lie, she had every right to raise it as a performance and conduct issue. And instead of getting on with the work I was given, I was difficult to control and busied myself with things that did not concern me. All this–despite being told that I didn't do enough actual work and my output wasn't just low, it was *'too low!'*

I didn't understand why this approach was necessary or why they needed to make so much effort to discredit me. I wondered where this overdependence on stereotypical argument emanated from: the lazy black, the antisocial and rebellious worker. How far back and how deep did this mess really go? Did it go as far back as the fear of black dominance in retribution for the crimes committed against us–the fear that we would be as brutal and deplorable as they were? I couldn't understand that, after centuries, no one could see that that's not who we are. Amid rape, sodomy and mutilation as exertions of lordship–kindness and forgiveness was still found among us. In the midst of mental torture and separation from loved ones, country and lands, we hoped for a time when we could live and work together *with* our oppressors. Didn't somebody have a dream…? I wondered why all this didn't say more about us, than the lie that we would be hell bent on revenge should we gain any semblance of promotion.

By this time, I was in my bedroom, although I don't remember climbing the stairs. I was still crying with a mix of hurt and confusion as I continued to try to make sense of how easy it was for this very white organisation to perceive me as a stereotypically black problem. Through the tears, I belligerently mulled over how easy it would have been for black people who were remotely obsessed with world domination or a separate black state to have achieved it. With our long-evidenced fortitude of spirit, our capacity to endure and thrive under extreme pressure and our willingness to die for faith, family and future, we would have pushed for it until we got it. I reasoned that, instead of *that*, what we *had* fought for was not supremacy of any kind but equality. Even after the horror, even after the unaccounted loss of millions of lives, today we simply fight for equal standing. And what of those who did not consider themselves our equals, what were they fighting for, I asked, throwing my arms about in the safety of my bedroom, my sanctuary? What were Stacey and Sue fighting for? What was the Service fighting for? For me to be treated as equal to any other member of the management team or to prove that I was wrong, that I had abused the freedom afforded me as a professional, that I had squandered the gift of autonomy and being able to work on my own initiative? Or perhaps they were fighting to help me to understand my place and that I had 'no business up in here making a fuss!' Perchance they elected to reinforce that I was a solitary black woman who had no right taking on a powerful, white, male, national institution. The Service had flexed its corporate muscles, making plain, as its managers gathered round the body that they had dismembered with lies, collusion and the sheer might of the organisation, that my imminent demise should serve as a stark warning to any other uppity black member of staff who dared to look at them the wrong way again. And, with my mostly rhetorical address, my soliloquy ended, I dramatically threw myself on my bed and cried myself to sleep.

I awoke a couple of hours later with a throbbing headache, to the voice of my Mum worriedly calling my name.

'Livie! Livie, are you all right? I made some lunch do you want some?'

'Yes Mum,' I shouted back. 'I'll be down in a minute.'

I got up and looked in the mirror. I looked awful and my eyes were all puffy. I went to the bathroom, washed my face with cold water and made my way downstairs to Mum. She took one look at me and said 'You don't look right. What's the matter?'

'I've...got a really...bad head,' I said evasively.

'I heard you come down this morning. Have you heard anything from them?'

'Yes. They're denying everything, which means I'll have to go to court. This is going to drag on forever and I don't know how much more I can take.'

The tears started to well up again.

'Oh Livie. Please don't cry. Don't cry. Look, see your favourite sausages—Herte Frankfurters. I had my carer pick them up special for me.'

Smiling through the tears as they stung my eyes I said, 'Oh Mum...I love you!'

'Well, I should hope so. Morrisons were doing a two for one deal. The opened pack is yours!'

The next day, I sent an email to Susanne to confirm the terms of my special leave and rang Stacey's secretary to say that I was unable to come in for the next week. I didn't know when I would be able to face them, knowing that they were content to pretend that they valued me, whilst discrediting me at the same time. My confidence in Stacey had been hanging by a thread since the first time I met her and now it was beyond gone. I felt they would contact me in due course and tell me when my special leave was over and I would have to deal with it then.

As I revisited their Tribunal response, I was devastated once more by the fact that their best defence was not the truth but lies about my performance and my integrity. I decided to send a letter to Paul Carroll, the Commissioning Officer to challenge the Service's approach. I conveyed that I felt that the corporate response made a mockery of the investigation.

In the meantime, I got a letter from the CRE. They were asking for documentation that related to my case. I had hoped that I would have had an answer from them as to whether they would handle my case. The Tribunal had written giving notice of a case management meeting I needed to attend in October. These meetings were designed to determine which parts of the claims I submitted were legally viable and would stand the test of law. I did not want to attend this meeting alone. I decided simultaneously to make a claim on my household insurance policy, which had a legal cover provision. I would get a lawyer just in case. Then, if the CRE assigned a representative in time for the case management discussion, I could dismiss the lawyer and use the CRE instead. Hopefully, once they read the documents they had asked for, they would see that my case had merit and choose to support me.

Paul Carroll responded to my challenge about the Service's response to the Tribunal on 22nd September. I was disappointed. He stated that he fully understood how I could be confused *'by what may appear to be differing views'*, but said that their approach was due to *'the differing requirements of the individual processes'*.

He said,

> *...internal investigations are able to be much broader and able to provide the investigator the freedom to express views that do not require tighter definition of evidence required by law.*

So, in other words, he was telling me that the investigators for the internal investigation had liberty to express views that they did not afterwards have to substantiate with evidence. I couldn't see the point of that and felt that surely, if their findings could be dismissed in this way, it made a travesty of the grievance process.

The same week I received a call from Susanne in personnel, to say that a letter they had sent me by special delivery from Stacey had been returned to them. I explained that I did get a 'tried to deliver a package' note from the Post Office; however, because I had become so depressed I couldn't leave the house. Consequently, I hadn't collected anything from the depot.

'So you won't be in on Monday then?' she asked.

I said I was still unable to return to work. She said she would resend the letter via the normal post.

I looked for the letter for the rest of that week; however, it didn't arrive until 26th September. I noted that the letter said special leave had been granted up to 22nd September–even though I didn't get the letter until the 26th. The whole thing was plainly ridiculous: I was expected simply to return to work even though nothing had been sorted out to prevent me from being exposed to further abuse. The letter briefly summarised the meeting I had had with Stacey on 4th September. She then went on to respond to my two outstanding grievances. Since the investigation report, I had asked for formal inquiries into the outstanding claims not covered by the first investigation's remit; I had hoped this would lead to formal explanations and recommendations. Instead, Stacey had chosen to respond in writing to the reminder note that Jaswinder had me compile for the last meeting. That note briefly reminded her that I was still awaiting a formal explanation regarding outstanding complaints and that she had ignored my previous requests for an investigation. I was annoyed she thought that, after all this time, and in view of the fact that a number of my issues had been upheld, she could simply comment on these grievances independently of the overall impact they would have on the investigation findings and the effect they had had on me and my career. I saw it as another attempt to subvert the course of effective resolution to my problems.

She had dismissed the very notion that race was involved in her decision to prevent me from working at REAG or that race featured in my not having an appraisal. I knew that I had raised a number of claims, maybe even too many, yet not without good reason. And I knew that some people don't do themselves any favours by crying foul every time something upset them. But for there to be this spontaneous denial that race could possibly play a part in any complaint was so uninformed and damaging. I couldn't get my head round the fact that there was simply no genuine acceptance that racism existed in the Service, apart from the racism displayed between the prisoners and the odd (bad apple) officer. This was why they dragged their feet when complaints were made.

This was why they were so insulted if one even suggested that their behaviour was racist and differential. And this was why they now saw fit to defend themselves at the Tribunal.

It was amazing to me that I had spent more time dealing with the affront I had caused, than actually having my claims sympathetically and honestly heard. Everything had been processed through this filter of justification and policy-driven validation and then, if any of my issues hadn't been refined to insignificance and remained, they were conceded as examples of poor management, as opposed to racist behaviour. Thus there were no breaches of prison service conduct, no breaking of the law, just unfortunate management styles for which, by and large, it now turned out that, according to their Tribunal response, I was responsible for stirring up as a poor performer in the first place!

Paulette, my good friend, came up to spend the weekend, like she often did. She is nearly six years younger and one inch shorter than me (although she regularly argues that we are the same height). Her skin is the deepest mahogany and almost pore-less to the naked eye. Paulette is forever being complimented on her Nubian and Ashanti good looks and glowing skin. She is quite simply unique: her right eye is hazel and her left eye is dark brown. She is always good company and, like sunshine in a bottle no matter how dull and dark the day, with her arrival comes unrestrained laughter often shortly followed by some chaos and more laughter! She is a little accident prone, a lot comical and deceptively insightful. Whenever the three of us are together, we have a good meal and invariably put the world to rights whilst eating. This weekend, the topic of conversation was the ethnic classification on application forms for jobs. Paulette was looking for work and had been filling in forms and having to disclose her ethnicity.

'I hate having to tick that box,' she said. 'Black British, Black Caribbean, Black Other.'

'I know,' I said. 'No matter the classification, from B1 to 01, Black British Caribbean to Chinese, we all fall into the same category—non-white, so why bother.'

'And when did I become a minority exactly, a black and minority ethnic—or a B *M* E?' she said emphasising the 'M'.

'Have you noticed that the ampersand gets conveniently dropped for ease of expression coupling us with the word minority?' I observed.

'But why Minority–smaller than, insignificant? That's what I'd like to know,' said Rudy powering up.

'Wow,' I said, 'even in our classification it's okay to refer to us as less than–and we take it. What's wrong with being of Black and Ethnic Origin or of African or Asian Ancestry?'

'Oooh, I like the sound of that,' Paulette said. 'Triple A! You've been thinking about this haven't you?'

'Sounds good, doesn't it?' I responded. 'Actually, on second thoughts, we couldn't use that because triple 'A' conjures up images of quality and star rating,' I said sarcastically.

The doorbell rang signalling that our food had arrived. Rudy leapt up to pay the delivery person and Paulette and I continued to talk.

'I mean, why do we need to be told daily that we're smaller than everyone else?' I queried. 'Every form that we fill in, we have to tick the appropriate BME box to affirm that we're less. Every job we go for, having evidenced ourselves as suitable applicants, in complete contradiction, we then have to confirm that we understand that even though we're often more than qualified, we're *minority* ethnics. We have to demonstrate that we accept that if we join a particular company, we will never be part of the majority. Even if the women outnumbered the men, we'd be subdivided again to reaffirm that we're still in the minority. How is it that a white man in Africa is a White Settler or a member of the White Elite, yet a black man in England is a minority?'

'But we are smaller in number, though, aren't we?' Paulette legitimately questioned.

'Of course. I understand the obvious intention, to recognise that we are smaller in number. But what of the unseen and negative effects of such labelling, that we are always seen as outsiders, immigrants or new arrivals and therefore never truly integrated. What about the constant reinforcement that I am not seen as British first but as a BME, part of a smaller group who settled in a country that we don't belong in. And, as such the government makes equally small measures to encourage tolerance as long as there aren't too many of us, as long as we don't ask for too much or overstep the mark.'

'Yep. I see your point,' she agreed.

'We may be fewer in number but, in terms of contributions and in terms of rights, are we less, are we smaller? The government has no right to call me a minority and label me as smaller than everyone else in Britain, for the rest of my life! I am not *a* minority! A statistical analysis is not the sum of who and what I am. It is not a prediction of what I will become. How can anyone quantify the weight of my contribution to this country, to this life the minute I am born, based on the colour of my skin? Can you imagine what it could have been like at my birth?

'Have you decided what you'll call her?' says the midwife.

'I'm going to... call her... Olivea–I need to push...'

'Yes...Push Bertha, push...nearly there...one more big push...yes...well done...you have a beautiful baby girl and she has your eyes and minority status, how lovely!'

Rudy walked in at this point with a plate of food for Paulette. 'Liv, do you want a bit of everything?'

'Yes please.'

'I mean, statistical analysis has its place,' I continued as Paulette ate, 'but to be relegated thereafter by this blanket terminology to the ranks of ever smaller than the majority in all else, I don't subscribe to. And the more I think about it the more incensed I become .'

'Where did this terminology come from anyway?' Paulette asked as she tucked into her Chilli Salt Crispy Chicken Wings.

'It's insidious, like devious conditioning that we've just accepted without question. How has it been with us so long without detection? Did we contribute to this classification? Did they ask us? *I don't think so!*' I said, embellished with an African-American wagging-neck and snapping-fingers attitude. 'And what about the other diversity strands the government busies itself with: religion, disability, age, sexual orientation? There's no juxtaposition with the word minority here. Just the ethnic groups–that's the only place we need a visual, aural and spoken reminder that we are subject to the ruling class. It seems that only in terms of colour do we need to be reminded that we are the smaller group–the ethnic *minority* group.'

'Why do you think that no one is challenging this?' Paulette asked, whilst licking her lips and her fingers.

'I wish I knew. And, more importantly—where's *my* chicken?'

On 4th October, I went to see my doctor. I had been at home for a month by this time and still didn't feel rested, less stressed or more relaxed. I explained what was happening at work and the impact it was having on me. I told him that I was feeling quite depressed and was having great difficulty sleeping and this was in turn making me very irritable and over-anxious. I also informed him about the dizzy spells when driving and that I was taking Kalms by day and Natursleep at night (these were herbal tablets), doing deep breathing exercises and so on. He assured me that I was doing everything that I could do without being medically prescribed something, and that all the symptoms I complained of were related to stress.

I confessed that sometimes I felt as if I was losing my mind. I related how I had wanted the investigation results to compel the Service to do right by me and treat me better, but it had made things invariably worse. I specifically mentioned how they had contradicted their investigation findings in their response to the Tribunal, leaving me more confused than ever. I left the surgery having decided that I didn't want to start taking antidepressants.

I maintained regular contact by phone with Paul, the Chair of RESPECT, since Jaswinder had been admitted to hospital the previous month, for an operation on his 'dodgy' knee. I conveyed my despair with what was going on, on many occasions. It was strangely comforting that Paul was equally bewildered by the Service's approach in its Tribunal response. He determined to speak to Phil Wheatley, the Director General.

On 25th October, I was due to attend a case management meeting at the Tribunal in Birmingham. According to the documentation I had received, these meetings were where they decided what was in and out of the scope of the case and timescales. I had never attended one before and I was sick with nerves. I arranged for Sam, a member of the church, to drive me to Birmingham. Just before she arrived, as I was about to put my shoes on and grab my jacket, I was overwhelmed with fear and panic. I started to cry and hyperventilate and became very unsteady on my feet. The suddenness of this attack caused me to panic all the more.

'Livie! Sam's here.' Mum shouted up the stairs.

'Coming.' I shouted back.

I knew that it would distress Mum to see me this frightened, so I had to calm myself down so that I could say goodbye whilst telling her I would be fine. I don't even know how I managed to compose myself. It was almost as if the panic hadn't happened or as if I had watched it happen to someone else. In an instant, I was perfectly fine. And then *that* scared me. Where did the tears go? Was I losing my mind? I finished dressing and walked down the stairs having left the crazy woman waiting in the shadows for my return.

Mum hugged me. 'Now,' she said, as though I was twelve again, 'you are going to be fine! God has not given you more than you can bear and he will be with you in this meeting. Amen?'

'Amen, Mum.'

As we drove to Birmingham, Sam made some polite conversation but she could see that I had a lot on my mind, so she turned up her music and had a little hum-along. Within twenty minutes, the town houses, mothers with prams and green countryside became stretches of concrete and beads of cars. I longed for the days when the only things I had to worry about was whether my un-permed hair was pinned tightly enough and which boys I liked the best. In those days, there was hopscotch, sky juice (tap water) and sugar sandwiches. *Arabian Knights* with their 'size of an Elephant' catchphrase, and home shopping catalogues we never ordered from, we just looked at the pictures and pretended we had everything that was available to order. Ice cream vans and corner shops. Seaside coach trips with 'Bun and cheese', fried chicken and bulk-buy crisps that weren't our favourite brand *Walkers*, but we ate them anyway because the pack size was smaller and we were allowed to eat them two packs at a time. The entertainment was mimicking church folk: the Pastor who preached so hard, his false teeth flew out of his mouth, over the lectern to rest on the podium like joke teeth; the missionary who would jump in the spirit, whilst holding on to her hat and wig. Occasionally, shoes would be danced off and jackets would be jumped off, but never the hat and the wig! There was an art to being 'in the spirit' and practice made perfect. Those were simpler times. Shielded times. Without effort or permission, I was automatically a part of something: family, friends, church. Now it seemed the older I got, the harder I had to fight to be accepted. I was about to make a business case for equal treatment as if I was new to the human race–a pitch for inclusion. I was an unseasoned soldier, waging war against invisible forces discriminating against me at will.

The case management meeting was easier than I had anticipated. There was no great war of words. In fact, the chairperson for the day seemed harder on the Prison Service barrister, for his lack of preparation. I was very relieved finally to get a date to go to a full hearing. Even though it wasn't until 14th May 2007, I was grateful that I would get the chance to tell my story and put an end to this torment.

At the beginning of November, not having heard from the CRE since September, I decided to phone them. After attending the case management discussion, I was given various instructions from the Tribunal to produce certain documents that needed drafting first. My household insurers had come through and I had a solicitor, but I really wanted to be represented by the CRE. I couldn't produce the required documentation without help, so I needed to make a decision about who would be representing me. When I called, I spoke to Ms Galler. I asked her for an update. She told me that my case had not yet been tabled for discussion by the panel that reviewed cases. When I asked when the next panel meeting was, she said that one had just been convened and as my case was not on that agenda, I would have to wait until December for the next meeting. I asked if my case would definitely be discussed at the next meeting, to which she replied, 'I don't know.' I ended the call knowing that I couldn't afford to wait for the CRE to review my details and I needed to stick with the solicitor that had been arranged through my household insurance policy. I was disappointed that they hadn't told me the wait was going to be so long. I would have made the decision to use a solicitor much earlier and saved myself some stress.

On 6th November, I sent my second claim into the tribunal. This was in relation to my complaint raised in August, having not had an appraisal of my performance for the reporting period 2005-06. I found Stacey's response to be inadequate and she hadn't formally investigated the complaint as requested. I very much felt that I hadn't been listened to and that Stacey had failed to properly determine if the decision to deny an appraisal was tantamount to victimisation. In the absence of an appraisal, issues of unacceptable performance and conduct were being cited as part of the Service's response to the Tribunal, with one incident never having been brought to my attention before. I didn't believe it was fair to send me a letter on 20th September, saying I hadn't been victimised, after having communicated matters of poor performance and conduct to the Tribunal on 1st September.

Since the investigation results and apology from Gareth Hadley, Director of Personnel, I was due to meet him to discuss the findings and recommendations. We had agreed to meet on 6th December, however, just before this date he resigned and left the Service almost immediately. Robin Wilkinson, his successor, stepped in.

Jaswinder accompanied me to this meeting. I didn't really want to go—I was anxious, scared and drained.

I didn't know much about Robin Wilkinson apart from the fact that he had taken over from Gareth Hadley. He had attended for part of a team meeting in August to tell us all that we shouldn't worry too much about the restructure and assure us that we would all be taken care of. He left the meeting after he had finished. To be honest, I barely heard a word he was saying because I knew that the next item on the agenda was to discuss the racist remarks that had been made by Di Watkins in March. And now I was sitting in front of him as he made a bid to remedy my situation.

He introduced himself and gave me a brief outline as to how he expected the meeting to run and what he hoped to achieve at the end of it. As he talked, I didn't get the sense that he cared about me. He didn't recognise that I had been hurt, nor did he acknowledge that the Service had been at fault. In fact, apart from a cursory mention that the investigation had taken place, his concern was squarely focused on getting me back to work. I could almost hear him saying, 'Now, let's put all this silliness behind us shall we?– you've made your point.'

Very early on, I got the impression that he wasn't going to cut his teeth on me or risk aligning himself with me in his newly promoted position. If he was to forge a name for himself, it wouldn't be with issues as precarious and uncertain as rooting out racism in the Service. It would be with organisational strategy, materialising as efficiency savings, a decline in staff sickness and headcount reductions. That's how he would move forward. As for me, the only thing on offer was a return to work in an organisation that hadn't changed.

'What's important is to get you back to work.' he said.

'What's important to me, is to come back to a safer and friendlier environment.' The meeting was to end without either of us getting what we wanted. After he had outlined his goal of returning me to work as the priority, he handed over to Stacey for her and Susanne to tell us about all the changes that had been made since the investigation.

Stacey talked at great length, confirming occasionally with Susanne about how the half-day diversity workshop had been rolled-out and how well it had been received, how they had put up Diwali lights (for the Indian festival of lights celebration) and how great people thought they were and that they had even included vegetarian meals on the menu at Newbold. What is more, an equal opportunities committee had been set up. I kept waiting for something that would indicate that they had addressed my problems, yet nothing was forthcoming. Jaswinder said that it was great that all these things were being done; however, what we needed to remember was that these were things that should already be in place. He asked if anything had been done specifically to address my needs.

Stacey said that Sue had already had a counselling session with one of the investigating officers and had attended the diversity workshop with the team.

I asked if anything else had been done to help Sue recognise the problems she had caused and show her how to avoid repeating her mistakes.

'Sue's SPDR also reflects the need to make sure that when she manages robustly, it won't be construed as harassment,' Stacey responded.

'Does Sue have any other Black and Minority Ethnic (BME) members of staff to look after, now that I'm out of the picture?'

'No.'

'If there is any doubt that Sue's unsatisfactory management of me was racially motivated and targets have now been set to consider this, how are you going to be able to measure the effectiveness of the said targets when Sue no longer has any BME staff to manage?'

There was silence. I continued. 'How will you be able to tell if Sue has satisfactorily met this particular target, to make sure that robust management doesn't become racial harassment, if that part of the target isn't measurable?

Now Stacey was looking at Robin.

I tried to strengthen my point. 'Isn't it possible that, in the next three months, this same target is likely to be written-off for the same reason and that a new SPDR will be opened in March 2007 as a matter of course, and that Sue will no longer be tied to this target?'

Again, there were no answers: nothing from Robin, the Director of Personnel, nothing from Stacey, the Head of the college; and nothing from Susanne, the Head of Personnel at the college. As I questioned them, I wondered if they thought I was being disrespectful, because I wasn't. I wasn't afraid of them—someone had to ask the tough questions. As I continued, they seemed put out that I dared challenge them. It was as if I should have been more grateful.

'It seems to me,' I said, 'that Sue has been given a target which hasn't been thought through properly. It's a target that is unenforceable and a target which will soon be off her records for the new financial year. I, on the other hand, will still be left with the legacy of discrimination and harassment along with the stigma of having raised complaints.'

I didn't think that I was being unreasonable. All I wanted to see was an approach that effectively communicated to Sue that she had managed me poorly, that the Service considered her approach inappropriate, and that they were committed to sustainable change and challenge to unacceptable behaviour. Anything less than that was worthless to me, because it essentially meant the abuse would continue.

As there were no answers coming forward, I decided to comment on the actions Stacey had outlined as progress since the investigation. I suggested that, overall, there didn't seem to be much that was measurable about the initiatives she had put forward and asked how both she and her team would know if something was achieving desired results or not. Stacey said they had done a 'forward-looking' exercise but she hadn't brought the results to the meeting. She couldn't outline any measurements in the meeting; however, she assured me they had done some. She asked me to look over the proposals and actions she had gone through and to make recommendations for after the meeting. I agreed to do this; however, I continued to protest I didn't feel any real advancement had been made in relation to me personally. I gave examples of how Di and Sue avoided speaking to me and even looking at me and that I couldn't see how any of the actions that were being discussed were going to deal with the way they were devaluing me. Robin then confidently remarked that that kind of specific behaviour was something they could do something about, now that they knew what else was distressing me. I went on to say that Sue and I had not had a professional or civil conversation since she claimed I was accusing her of racism last year.

'That's interesting,' said Robin. 'Are you saying that it was Sue who made the first reference to racism?'

'Yes, that's right. Sue put racism on the table, as all I was trying to do at that time was identify the rationale behind the differential treatment I had experienced. If you look at the first grievance dated 1st November 2005, you'll see that the only time racism was mentioned was when I repeated what Sue had said.'

'I didn't realise that,' he said, quite surprised.

'Actually, from that point onwards,' I continued, 'it was difficult for me to discount any racial prejudice in her actions, when comments about racism were her first response to difficulties with me. I'd also like to state at this juncture that, in all of the responses to date, no one has actually dealt with Sue's comments to me about racism. It's hard for me to move forward when issues like this are being ignored or avoided. Even the investigation recommendations didn't cover what needed to be done to restore good working relationships with my peers, and neither do Stacey's proposals which, ultimately, leaves me working in a hostile environment.'

I thought that, whilst I was there, it made sense to get everything off my chest, as I couldn't be sure when I would get to speak my mind again. I went on to explain that I shouldn't be left on my own to restore relationships and move past the awkwardness that I had experienced to date. Robin assured me that something would be done.

The meeting ended in approximately one and a half hours without resolution or even a date for the next meeting, and Robin had to go to another appointment. He had asked for another meeting before Christmas—however Jaswinder was unavailable. I therefore spent another Christmas fighting depression and illness.

Chapter Thirteen

A Merry Old Dance

In the New Year, a meeting was arranged for 16th January 2007. Jaswinder couldn't make it; however, Paul Haughton, the Chair of RESPECT, agreed to accompany me. Robin arranged this meeting so we could look at what I needed in order to move forward and return to work. I had prepared terms months ago, as directed by Jaswinder, who had told me to aim high and be ready to negotiate down from there; however, until this point I hadn't had an opportunity to present them. It was clear from the Service's response to the Tribunal–denying everything–and Stacey's take on what progress looked like, that they weren't ready to talk about me and my needs. Yet for this meeting, I was specifically asked to outline what I felt I needed to move on from the investigation.

Before I left the house, I had a brainwave–to do a direct comparison of the opportunities to progress in the Service between myself and Sue. I felt it would be useful in support of my terms for advancement and redress. I set about quickly compiling a basic working example of progression, comparing myself with her. As I didn't have Sue's Curriculum Vitae or anything like that, I based the comparison on what I had heard about her career and my experience of her rapid advancement since my arrival at the college. I felt the comparison would demonstrate how easy it was to progress, when you had got the backing of management–which was what I was going to ask for in the meeting.

Once I had completed the comparison, I instantly became quite depressed. There was such a stark difference in Sue's progress compared to my stagnation. I had expected to see differences but the impact of seeing it on paper, and so plainly, filled me with resentment and anger. I calmed myself down and reminded myself that I had done the comparison to demonstrate that significant progression through management grades in one year was possible. I believed I was now able to show this quite categorically, and that was what was important. Even if the dates were off by a few months, the comparison adequately showed that quick advancement was possible. I had been in the Service for nearly four years without any progression of any kind—and we needed to discuss this.

The comparison started in January 2001. From discussion with other advisors, I learned that, at that time, Sue was the education manager at HMP Onley. Having recruited and managed education managers in the Service, I had a good idea of what Sue's salary would have been in 2001, so I placed her on an equivalent Manager G grade. When I considered what I was earning at the same time, in my role as a European training manager for my previous company (and the extent of the role in terms of number of staff, number of countries managed and so on), I mapped the equivalent management grade to Manager A/B, which earned a higher salary than a Manager G.

I felt that it was important to start the comparison before we both joined the college in order to incorporate the level of skill and breadth of experience we both brought to Newbold. I then tracked, as best as I could, both my and Sue's progress in the Service from January 2005. I knew that, just before I had arrived in May 2005, she was a Manager E, because she spoke to me approximately two weeks before my arrival and offered me her area, the East Midlands. She had just secured temporary promotion as deputy of the team, which promoted her to Manager D grade. I could safely say then, that in January 2005 she was a Manager E, as an Area Advisor and I was a Manager E, at the top of the grade as the Head of Learning and Skills at HMP Leicester. I moved on with the comparison to May 2005, when she was temporarily promoted to Manager D as Deputy, and I arrived to take her role. Accepting the role of advisor did not change my grade. I remained a Manager E. The following month, Chris (Sue's predecessor) was permanently escorted off the premises and Sue became acting head of LMD. This put her at Manager C and, by April 2006, she became substantive at that grade with another pay rise. This meant that from approximately April 2005 to April 2006, Sue had moved two grades, from Manager E to Manager C, in just twelve months and enjoyed approximately four pay rises. I, on the other hand, had arrived as a Manager E and was still a Manager E after nearly four years.

When I arrived at Cleland House, I went to meet Paul, in the RESPECT office before the meeting with Robin. Although we had spoken on the phone many times, we had not met before. He greeted me like an old friend, with a warm handshake and a kiss on each cheek. He looked at me with deep concern and placing his hand on my arm he said, 'How are you?'

I said I was fine. Paul looked much like the photos I had seen of him in the RESPECT newsletters. He was dark, about 5' 8" with a slim build. His eyes were very kind and expressive. Although we had just met, we were well acquainted and I felt comfortable with him. I showed him the comparison sheet I drafted. He wasn't surprised and said he had seen this kind of progression in the Service many times. He said that management always said this kind of thing didn't happen, that they have to abide by policy, but they always find ways around the system to justify promotions whenever they wanted.

Paul then confirmed that he had sent my terms for discussion to Robin. We then had a quick conversation about what the sticking points might be, based on his experience of these kinds of meetings. Overall, Paul reckoned there wasn't anything on the list that couldn't be done either in part or full, if the Service had the will to do it. He encouraged me that we would get through it and that I was doing very well. We went to the meeting.

Once we were all seated in Robin's office (Stacey and Susanne were also in attendance), Robin asked me to outline the things I felt were necessary for me to move forward. I had eight terms designed to open dialogue about the things I felt would provide closure, redress and opportunities for advancement within the organisation. I also wanted to discuss steps that would help to rebuild professional relationships between me and my peers.

My first term for discussion was a return to work outside the college, in a new role as a Manager D at the top of the pay scale. I also requested relevant development in line with the new role, as appropriate. Robin asked me to explain the rationale behind this. I had documentation proving what I was earning before joining the Service and I explained that, since joining, I had never been so professionally or financially stagnant. I had a background of progressive achievement yet, having joined at the top of the pay scale for the Manager E grade, I was still there nearly four years later. I talked about how I had applied for the Head of Learning and Skills role in 2003, which had been advertised up to the Manager D level. I felt that I should be much closer to earning what I was used to earning by now, in line with my skills and experience, and have a proper career plan.

Robin questioned whether any Head of Learning and Skills roles were the Manager D grade—he thought they were all Manager E and not earning that much. Stacey also said that, according to her understanding, there were no Manager D Head of Learning and Skills roles. I wondered if they thought that I was making it up or was delusional. In any case, I explained that I had actually met Heads of Learning and Skills who were nevertheless at Manager D level. I named a couple of people, so that they could check their records. I knew what I was talking about because I still had the original recruitment paperwork, which confirmed the grades that were on offer at that time. I moved on to say that I was informed at my initial interview there was only one post that attracted the top salary in the region, and it had already been taken. I had therefore accepted the Manager E post, feeling confident that with my experience and potential I would soon progress. I was unaware that there wasn't an established promotion route for non-operational staff. I went on to explain that, after a couple of years, as I wanted to progress and stay in the Service, I had applied for a job with the college.

Robin asked what had contributed to my thinking that there would be better prospects at the college. He asked if I had seen a particular future job that piqued my interest. I said I hadn't but, having looked at the college's organisational chart, I could see more options because of the way the college was set up. Furthermore, because it was the training centre for the Service, my skills would be better matched. I explained that, had I not been treated less favourably than my peers, I would have secured advancement in line with my abilities and recovered the financial ground I had lost when I joined the Service.

I was quite put out with Robin's response to all of this. 'It's not likely that you would have secured a Manager D position or be at the top of the grade by now.'

'What is he saying?', I thought. Paul stepped in.

'Robin, I don't think you can necessarily make that kind of judgement. And because of what Olivea has endured, we can't say that her advancement wasn't likely. What's clear is that discrimination has prevented her from progressing and these terms are about redressing the balance.'

'Well I can't simply promote you,' Robin said looking at me and ignoring Paul's comments, 'on your assessment of yourself, Olivea. And as such you would need to be properly selected at board.'

Stacey piped up, 'Perhaps you could attend a development centre to see if you have Manager D potential.'

I hid my frustration and insult. 'I've already done that,' I reminded her. 'And out of 46 development areas measured by the assessment consultancy, they only found four areas that I needed to work on. Coincidentally, one of those areas was the Psychometric development that has been denied me to date, one was for Prince 2 training and the other two concerned exposure to different parts of the organisation—all very do-able. Passing at this level more than qualified me to apply for a Manager D role and when I did go for one, I failed at interview in August by five points. It seems to me that when my abilities are being measured by anyone *outside* the Service, I do quite well.'

Incredibly, Stacey said, 'Perhaps we could work on the four remaining needs identified, to see if you can do a Manager D job.'

As I sat 'gobsmacked' by how obtuse she was being, I wondered if *she* would have only had four areas needing development after a barrage of assessments at the height of being bullied. It troubled me that neither Robin nor Stacey could see potential sitting there in front of them—that they could only see deficits and a lack of ability. I was amazed even further that I was expected to be one hundred percent in terms of my capacity. Essentially, needing to be developed in the four remaining areas meant that I couldn't seek advancement until I was proficient against all 46 measures. Everyone has development needs, yet I was expected to ensure that I had none before they would even consider me promotion material.

'I've already jumped through enough hoops,' I continued. 'And the tests showed I have the relevant competencies, knowledge and experience to do a Manager D role right now. I don't see the point in doing another battery of tests.'

Robin was still stuck on protocol. He continued to reiterate that I would need to go through proper routes. At this point, Paul insisted that there were examples of individuals advancing without going through the routes Robin had identified.

Robin agreed. 'There are special circumstances where this does happen, but I still think that it is unlikely that Olivea would have progressed to Manager D in her two years at the college.

'Well,' I said, jumping in, 'I think it's only fair that you take my full service into consideration; I've been working at the top of the Manager E grade for nearly four years.'

Paul then decided to play our trump card. He outlined Sue's rapid advancement in comparison with my lack of movement.

Robin simply said that Sue's advancement was in keeping with her five years at the college. I protested, as I felt that, if he insisted on going back five years to justify Sue's progression, then he should also include my experience at that time which actually put me above Sue in role, responsibilities, experience and previous salary.

Robin then did the unimaginable. He said, 'A like-for-like comparison isn't appropriate here; we should do a survey across the organisation and then we can use the statistical evidence to form a judgement.'

This was beyond my comprehension. Sue had hopped through two grades in twelve months. On top of that, Val (as Sue's deputy) had moved up from Manager E to Manager D, twelve months after arrival in the Service. And within seven months of joining the Service, Di had secured a Manager D role, as national Fast Track manager. These people were not randomly dotted about the organisation, they were in my department–in plain view. Here were three examples that Stacey had signed off and Robin (or his predecessor) had endorsed. Yet still Robin was looking me in the eye and discounting my experience. He was dismissing my skill and four years' experience of the Service competencies and culture (including two years of documented client feedback about accomplishment at the college) as 'unlikely' to be enough to facilitate a move up a single grade! 'Unlikely'–the words were ringing in my ears.

'Robin,' said Paul, refusing to let it go, 'here is clear evidence that Sue, a member of the college staff, has succeeded in gaining the level of rapid promotion that you were just suggesting was unlikely.'

Robin changed tack slightly. 'What we need to be aware of is that there are issues with whether or not there are any suitable Manager D roles and also that, even if you were to return in a Manager D position,' he said, looking at me again, 'it would only attract a ten percent increase on your current salary.'

Paul was determined not to go down without a fight. 'Isn't it possible, Robin, that if a Manager D job was available and it carried the top of the scale salary, then the incremental ten percent wouldn't matter–Olivea would get a job valued at the top of the scale?'

Stacey then clumsily interjected, 'Can I just say that the Manager D positions that were available were openly advertised, and you could have freely applied for any of them.'

'I disagree. Since formally complaining in November 2005, I have been unable to compete fairly as I was already being treated less favourably than my peers, and *that* knowledge prevented me from applying. You now have the investigation findings that prove that I was not being treated fairly at the time these roles were being advertised.'

To my surprise and great annoyance, Stacey then said, 'The calibre of candidate was very high and competition stiff for both Sue's and Val's roles. Do you really believe that you would have been able to compete for either of them?'

I was incredibly insulted. I don't know how I got the words out.

'I believe I was more than competent. The assessments have proved that I was more than competent. And you're forgetting that I have previously worked at *above* these levels. The issue here is not competence–it is confidence. I lacked *confidence* that I would have been treated fairly. Open and fair competition goes way beyond simply advertising to everyone. You can't say that you have transparency or a fair system on the back of an advert. You have to have eliminated bias from all parts of your selection process and I knew you had not done this–hence my lack of confidence.'

Above the table where we were sitting, I was consciously trying to convey that I was relaxed and engaged. My tone remained measured, my head was nodding in the right places, my arms were open as I gestured with open palms; yet below the table line, my limbs were tight with fury and tension. I had everything clenched: stomach, buttocks, thighs, knees and toes. I could feel the tension rising up through my spine. I knew it would soon be in my voice. I had to stop that from happening. But I couldn't see how, as the insults kept coming.

Not content that she had made her point clearly enough, Stacey said again, 'Are you sure you could have competed?'

'Yes,' I said, 'I am sure.' The tension had reached my voice.

What a tremendous show of no confidence, I thought. And to think we were only on the first term for discussion: a job outside the college, a promotion and pay rise—not as some unfounded favour but actually commensurate with my experience. I anticipated some discussion about the promotion and the pay scale, yet a flat out refusal—I didn't see that coming.

The conversation was going round and round and I didn't have a sense of how much time had lapsed. Robin then moved the conversations on to question my refusal to return to the college. Before I could answer, Stacey, picking up from Robin's query, suggested I could work in a satellite unit and not have to come in to Newbold regularly. In response, I told her that I didn't feel safe at the college as I had been failed by them. I wondered if Stacey would have felt safe in a place that had abused her, if she would have been happy to go back, even though little to nothing had changed.

In an attempt to help them understand, I posed the scenario of encountering further difficulty in a new role at the college and then having to rely on the same structures and people who had already failed me. I tried to show them how unappealing that was. I reminded them that there were people there who were currently ignoring me, and how painful I found that to be. Paul supported me by saying that it wasn't unusual for a victim not to want to return to the place where they were abused, particularly when there hadn't been sufficient time to change the culture of the place in question.

We moved on, because Robin felt that we would not solve the issue of promotion or place of work at this meeting. We had only just begun and I was already very disappointed. I had been trying to secure promotion virtually from arrival in the Service. I had put my best foot forward in August the previous year, even though I felt bullied, victimised and harassed. No account of my situation had been taken into consideration, and now further attempts at securing promotion were being denied. It was apparent now that, whatever route I tried–merit, assessments, valid experience or career development–promotion wasn't available to me. I could only deduce that this was, first and foremost, because of my colour and then because I had raised grievances.

We moved on to the second term: outstanding training and development needs to be met, including MBTI. These were agreed to, virtually without any discussion. In fact, they were agreed so quickly, I wondered why we had had to labour so hard with no outcome with the first term, especially considering that promotion and development went hand in hand.

A little disoriented by the swiftness of the decision, I moved on to the third term.

'I would like us to determine and agree a course of action, clearly holding the negligent individuals accountable. Since the investigation, the three people who have caused me the most harm have secured promotion. Now I'm not against anyone being promoted on merit; however, I do take exception to individuals doing this level of professional wrong and remaining unaffected in terms of their career. Whilst they are moving onwards and upwards, my life and career are on hold. I'm sitting here right now trying to defend my capacity and potential, even though there is no evidence of poor performance or poor judgement on my part. Yet we have evidence of the same, as generated by the behaviour of Sue, Val and Di and it's almost as if it's of no consequence. Before I leave here today, I really need to know how people who were being investigated for poor management, poor conduct and racist comments, were able to secure advancement *during* the investigation.'

Stacey listened, and then she said, 'I'm sorry, Olivea, but I wasn't in a position to withhold promotion from someone, just because they were being investigated.'

I was so glad Paul stepped in because I was ready with my clown-sized feet! 'I understand that,' Paul said. 'But once the investigation concluded that certain individuals were clearly unsuitable as managers or failing in their responsibilities as managers, you should have had the necessary evidence to demote the said individuals, develop them and monitor them until such time as they demonstrate the appropriate competencies. Then once they do that, you can reinstate them or find them a suitable position elsewhere.'

He went on to say, 'This is one of the things that has always bothered me. It's regrettable that RESPECT has never had the resources to challenge the issue of managers who are found culpable during an investigation getting off with little or no sanctions, while the victim struggles to get recompense.'

I couldn't hold back any longer. 'These people were seeking promotion whilst their performance as managers at their current grades was in question. And we are not talking about a solitary complaint but several complaints about a group of people who worked closely together, accused of harassing the same person. Surely there was room to interview with the caveat that, pending the investigation outcome, any appointments made would be subject to review?'

'But we've met the recommendations that were outlined in the report and disciplinary action was not a recommendation,' Stacey said, with alarm. 'If there was a case to answer regarding disciplinary action, this would have been picked up by the investigating officers or the commissioning officer. No disciplinary action was recommended because those accused hadn't breached Prison Service rules of conduct.'

She spoke with an air of almost childlike innocence, except that she wasn't an innocent child unaware of the harsh realities of life, she was the Head of the Prison Service College. I found it impossible to believe that she had so completely failed to grasp that the investigation report would, in any event, only go so far and that she, as the Head of the college, had the capacity to move beyond the recommendations and deal with her staff in the most fitting way.

'Stacey, they *did* breach prison service rules of conduct, unless you're suggesting that it's okay to harass someone as long as it's not on grounds covered by legislation. The investigation report might not have definitively said that I was discriminated against on the grounds of my race, but it did say that I was harassed; it did say that I was victimised by these individuals. This means there was a breach.

'—and there were only four recommendations,' I argued. 'I don't believe them to be absolute or exhaustive in terms of next steps, but rather that they were the starting point to fix things. As the Head of the college you should be able to use the recommendations as a platform to do everything that's required, as opposed to simply actioning the four points in their most basic terms.'

I went on to explain that I hadn't raised a grievance about every single thing that had happened to me, which meant that things like being ignored by staff were not covered in the recommendations. It was for this reason I had felt we needed to have a discussion to make sure that sanctions and actions were appropriately designed to challenge the behaviour of the perpetrators on every level where they caused offence.

Stacey was quite resistant and reiterated that it was not within her gift to go against the recommendations and that neither she nor Robin had the wherewithal to add to them.

Robin then turned his attention to Paul and asked if he felt that the recommendations were wrong.

'In my experience,' Paul began, 'cases where racial discrimination and/or racial harassment were an issue, for reasons yet to be challenged by RESPECT, investigating officers have consistently shied away from recommending disciplinary action against the managers found to be complicit in the racism experienced by the victim. This could be for any number of reasons, but the fact remains that, even when discrimination is proven, disciplinary action is not recommended.'

Neither Stacey nor Robin would move from the standpoint that sanctions were unnecessary. This left me feeling that they were still protecting the perpetrators. They didn't seem to care that behaviours hadn't changed and I was still being abused.

We moved on to my fourth term: monetary compensation for the victimisation, bullying and harassment I had endured. I wanted to see a clear sign that the Service knew it was wrong and was truly sorry. As much as I knew that money couldn't eradicate the pain, I felt something tangible from them was a very necessary part of my being recompensed. It was not so much about punishment, it was about making amends and restoration. I felt that monetary compensation was an indication of good faith and a demonstration of my worth to the Service.

Robin refused even to discuss my rationale behind asking and said that the issue would be passed to ACAS (the independent mediation and conciliation service that tries to settle claims between the parties before the hearing of the case takes place).

'Why don't we have a look at your next term,' he said, smiling and nodding politely. And in that instant, I remembered my very first interview for a job which had ended with a smile masking true intent, as I was ushered out of the door because my skin was darker in person than my voice and my spoken English suggested.

My fifth term requested an agreed advancement strategy to include career progression from Manager D to Manager C in twelve months; then progression from Manager C to Manager A by 2010. At this stage in the negotiation, it seemed to be a nonsensical point considering we had arrived here without any agreement to my advancing even to Manager D level. Moving on to talk about how I was going to get from D to C was somewhat redundant, yet I persevered because I couldn't think of anything else to do.

'I think this is necessary,' I ventured, 'to ensure that there are no more halts to my capacity to progress. Assuming we resolve the outstanding discussions about me becoming a Manager D, I don't want to end up stuck in a broom cupboard somewhere and every time I apply for a job, I don't get it because of some seemingly innocuous reason. I think it is important that I am properly supported by a plan, development and coaching, to ensure that I cultivate the right skills within the Prison Service culture, to sustain my chances of promotion.'

In response to this, both Robin and Stacey continued to reiterate the lack of positions available throughout the Service at these levels. They batted the problem between them.

'How many positions are there at Manager C level?' asked Robin.

'Not many,' said Stacey.

'They don't come up very often, do they?'

'No, there's very little movement at those levels.'

'You see, that's the problem, Olivea,' Robin said, 'the higher you go up the organisation, the less movement there is.'

'Yes,' said Stacey confirming, 'Not much happens unless someone retires.'

They played like this, even though they knew that, out of over 4,000 operational and non-operational managers in the Service, only 228 Black and Minority Ethnic (BME) people had made it to a management grade. With seating for 342 passengers, more people would be boarding the Midland Mainline train I was to take home later! And incredibly, of this measure of ethnicity, an unknown quantity were white people. This is because not all white staff see themselves as *'White British'*, so when filling in the monitoring form, some of them tick the *'Ethnic Group Other'* box from the category options available and fall into the statistical collation of BME people. Finally, at the top of the management grades or Manager A, there were no BME staff, making that grade 100% white.

Robin then asked me to explain how my advancement plan could work. In response, I cited current Fast Track schemes for operational staff.

'Here we take groups of people with potential; we provide training and support under the proviso that, if they demonstrate competence within two years, they can be certain manager grades at the end of the programme. The Prison Service has called it many things over the years, APS, IDS, Fast Track—the principle is the same; if we make the investment in people with potential, they can advance quickly.'

'Yes,' said Robin, 'except the Service doesn't have the same provision for non-operational staff.'

'Well, don't you think that that in itself is discriminatory practice? I don't think that I should be held back because I have never worn a uniform. Perhaps it's time for a change,' I proposed.

'The Senior Prison Manager Programme is open to non-operational staff,' Stacey piped up.

'Yes, it is,' I acknowledged. 'However, the identified route for progression is still operational and only suited those who want to become governors or deputy governors of a prison. This means it isn't suitable for non-operational staff like me who want to progress through non-operational roles.'

Rather strangely, Robin then said that he couldn't *guarantee* advancement. Very quickly Paul jumped in.

'Robin, Olivea is not asking for a guarantee. She's asking for there to be a *plan* in place to ensure that she gets the relevant developmental support. If, for example, in two years' time she applied for a Manager C position, there should be no reason why she wouldn't be suitably skilled enough to be selected for the post, because she would have been developed in line with her potential. The same would apply for progression from Manager C to Manager A, three years afterwards.'

Even though Robin thanked Paul for this clarification, after a little more discussion, he still proceeded to reject the proposal on the grounds that he couldn't *guarantee* advancement.

In due course, we moved on to my sixth term: I asked to be allocated a senior manager to mentor and coach me as well as oversee and sign-off development actions in line with the advancement strategy. I explained that this was a necessary part of the advancement strategy to ensure my development was in line with the roles I was aiming for. Robin conditionally agreed to this term. He suggested that, in view of his inability to guarantee advancement, that I should consider returning to work, still as a Manager E. I should attend assessment centres and receive coaching in line with *possible* suitability for a Manager D role. I was too exhausted to explain again, that I had already done this to no avail.

My seventh term was to request a verbal apology followed by the same in writing from Sue, Stacey and Di. Robin suggested that Stacey had already expressed sorrow for the situation. I acknowledged that Stacey said that she was 'sorry things had come to this'. In my mind, that was not the same as apologising. As such, it was difficult to tell if Stacey was just sorry for the trouble I had caused her. I felt that there was no point in Stacey expressing sorrow and then doing nothing to change the conditions in the college. Sorrow and corresponding action went hand in hand. I didn't get a sense that she was sorry about what happened to me—or even understood it. If she had, the response to the Tribunal would have been different. I went on to talk about how I felt that, once agreements were reached and I had the confidence that real progress was being made, then the apologies would have more weight.

I found Robin's response quite remarkable. 'I'm not in a position to force anyone to apologise,' he said. 'And apologies need to be something each person is prepared to do for themselves.'

I sat incredulous. 'Well, first of all,' I thought, 'I shouldn't even have had to ask for an apology from anyone. And if these individuals, after nearly six months since the investigation report was circulated, hadn't worked out for themselves that they should apologise, then shouldn't someone say something? And having given them the benefit of the doubt, inasmuch as they didn't have the guts or the courage to find me and say sorry, who was to say that they didn't need a formal and structured arrangement, to encourage them to do the right thing.' I wasn't asking for anymore than that. 'And another thing,' I ranted on in my head, 'in the absence of any other strategy to rebuild professional relationships and reopen dialogue, how else was that going to happen, if not with a sincere apology?'

It was my view that, if Sue and Di were committed to making our relationships work, they both would need to appreciate that the recommendations in the report were not the end of the matter. They needed to know that more was required on a personal level. If they thought everything was over because the report was out, we would never restore congenial working arrangements. Whilst I justified my approach internally, Robin reminded me that Di had already apologised. I reminded him that she sent a quick emailed apology instead of meeting me, as I had asked. I wanted to explain properly why the comments she made were racist, so that she wouldn't be in that position again. Robin then stated, quite defensively, that any 'coaching' would be done officially and not by me. I couldn't understand why he was being so protective. Wearily, I explained that I wasn't offering to coach Di. She had personally offended me and I was perfectly within my rights to convey how I was affected. She would then have her own experience of the impact racism has, along with an experience of how properly to resolve the offence. Helpfully, Paul concluded that, although written apologies were welcome, verbal apologies were more personal and provided the opportunity for individuals to demonstrate their sincerity.

In essence, what I really wanted was some kind of platform to rebuild relationships and get past the awkwardness. My working environment was so hostile. And whilst my terms were being summarily rejected, no one was coming up with any alternatives. This meant that a return to work would mean a return to hostilities.

Robin's only concession was that he would *inform* Sue and Di that I would like an apology and that they could take it from there. I was still expected to work with them, even though they ignored me when I tried to engage them in simple pleasantries. It was also up to them, having done wrong and been found guilty of treating me poorly, disrespecting me and causing me great embarrassment and humiliation, to determine whether or not they wanted to express regret for how they were treating me.

My final term was to ask for a written apology from the Service. This was agreed.

Sadly, at the close of the meeting very little had been agreed and I left feeling that I was still being treated unfairly. It was clear that Robin and Stacey had decided what they were going to agree to before the meeting began. We revisited my terms over and over again and it seemed that we were going around in circles. Susanne, although she was Head of Personnel, with the capacity to comment on the proceedings, remained silent throughout, whilst taking notes. I was made to feel as if I was trying to secure advancement and privilege that ordinarily wouldn't have been available to me, but for the outstanding claims of discrimination. The meeting yielded little fruit. I was exhausted. I had battled with Robin and Stacey for nearly four hours and hadn't gained anything, bar a few conditional agreements. Training had been agreed, yet no way of facilitating it had been discussed; they had found another way to deny me promotion and I couldn't even get an apology from the main perpetrators.

Afterwards, Paul and I talked and compared notes. We were both bewildered by Robin and Stacey's intransigence. Paul also noticed that both of them had displayed a blatant lack of confidence in my ability to progress. I thanked him for his support and made my way home. I had been so tense all day that, by the time I got on to the train I had aches and pains all over, and felt as if a horse had trampled me.

I couldn't relax. Even the soothing motion of the train didn't help. My mind was in turmoil. I was angry at the way they just wanted me to move on and get back to normal. I wondered if, had my case been more spectacular and newsworthy, they would have tried harder to make things right, for fear of public outrage. It was as if somebody needed to die for anyone to take notice and, even then, there was no reason to be confident that they would. I face racism every day. Every day I have to consider if I will be judged purely because I'm black. Yet Robin and Stacey just wanted me to move on as if I get to leave my skin at home each morning. Everyday-pain, matters. You can only ignore it for so long until it consumes you, until you don't know anything else but the pain. I was working in an organisation that wouldn't say sorry for abusing me. I was living in a country that wouldn't say sorry for abusing us. No one wanted to say sorry for anything! There were always excuses. 'I'm not in a position to force anyone to apologise,' Robin says. 'You can't expect people who weren't there to apologise for slavery,' the country says. What should anyone be sorry for? The fact that English history records how we were viewed as copulating with and descending from apes, that we were seen as devils, rapists and thieves? Should someone say sorry about the debates that were held to determine whether or not we were teachable or intelligent and the legacy that still haunts us today? Should Britain say sorry for the laws they purposely crafted to actually uphold the belief that people of colour were mere chattels and property or that Queen Elizabeth I wanted to send blacks forth from her realm, because we were too many? Killing us was no different from squashing bugs. If we were viewed as human, then only psychopaths would have been able to sleep at night. But as abnormal, deformed and subhuman, the damage done to us was a necessary moral obligation, to prevent the world from being blighted and overrun by pests. And here I was–present day and still unable to get an apology for the way I was currently being treated, as if there was no legacy left by the poor treatment yesterday or a generation ago!

Did the Service need to apologise for readily accepting Sue's opinion that I was aggressive and workshy? After centuries of validating the perception that Africans, although apparently built for hard work, were inherently lazy, thus justifying brute and deadly force–we are being seen in the same way the minute there is a problem. And no one sees the link between how white people saw us then and how, when under pressure, some of them see us today? How could Robin look at my pain and tell me that it was up to my oppressors to decide if *they* wanted to say sorry? It was as if I was less than human with no feelings and no soul. But then, that's not the first time black people have been seen like this. In times past, there were ecumenical debates excluding black people from worship on the grounds that we had no souls and, furthermore, no Abrahamic relationship or inheritance. As mere beasts, we were beyond redemption. Maybe that's what Robin and Stacey saw in front of them–a mere beast. Not a human being who needed to be heard and understood. They saw something that needed to know its place in the world. Something they didn't have to negotiate with. Something they had to show who's boss. And that's why there was a dearth of black senior managers in the Prison Service and an all-white Manager 'A' grade! Who was I to ask for an advancement strategy to begin to change that? My dream to push the door of opportunity ajar, ever so slightly, had been thrown back into the pen with me!

When I got home, I went over everything again with Rudy. I tried not to get upset, yet the tears flowed. Having skipped through the centuries from slavery to today, in the time it took to get from Pimlico to Wellingborough, I couldn't help getting upset.

He kissed me on my forehead and held me for a very long time. 'They're just wasting your time, baby. I can't understand what they hope to gain from this. This is pointless. Is there anything I can do to help? I can't bear to see you like this. I hate it when you cry.'

On 31st January, I raised my tenth grievance in relation to the meeting with Robin, Stacey and, to a lesser extent Susanne, citing further victimisation. I had received correspondence from Robin summarising the meeting by this point, but the way it read, made me feel even more victimised and harassed. As I answered him, my thoughts were a little clearer than in the meeting. The issue that I felt I needed to respond to most strongly was how, during the meeting, Robin had discounted my private sector and prison experience as not accumulatively relevant. In his summary letter, he reiterated this point and said that it wasn't realistic to compare private and public sector experience. This made me angry because, in 2003, my private sector experience was relevant enough to secure a job for me in the public sector as the Head of Learning and Skills at HMP Leicester. My private sector experience, combined with experience at the prison, was relevant enough to secure a job for me at the college in 2005. Yet now, according to Robin in 2007, neither my private sector experience nor my public sector prison experience was relevant to draw on in my bid for advancement. In my view, I was still the subject of victimisation.

Robin responded to this complaint on 21st February and made things even worse, so within days I was filling in my third ET1 application to the Tribunal. In it, I referred to the January meeting where I had suggested that my inability to progress was compounded by the fact that the Service had recruited me under false pretences. I explained in my application that, at my interview in 2003, I was able to demonstrate consistent professional advancement throughout my career and conveyed how I had believed that working for the Service would have developed me further, allowing for more advancement. I said that the Service, at the very least, should have told me in 2003 that options for promotion wouldn't be as available to me as they had been in the private sector, so that I could have made an informed decision in terms of whether I wanted to take a job with limited progression routes. When I had made this point to Robin in January, he had written back to deny that I had been employed under false pretences, even though he stated in the same letter that *'the Service remains primarily an operationally focused organisation and this means that vertical career progression opportunities for non-operational staff are more limited, especially at more senior grades'*. He further stated, *'career progression for non-operational staff* [is] *limited and…I* [do] *not consider it a likelihood that you would have progressed to* [Manager D] *in the period between taking up your post at* [the college]'.

This had made me feel that, not only was I clearly disadvantaged as a non-operational member of staff, I was disadvantaged by not being formally appraised, along with the disadvantage associated with raising grievances and Tribunal claims against my employers and all the ensuing repercussions. I was frustrated that, with all this, Robin believed I didn't need help to overcome the barriers created by the Service, as an institution with a focus on operational staff, or my stagnant situation caused by unfair treatment and management failings. Rather, he stated, in another letter in February: *'I am not persuaded that it would be right to agree a managed promotion…I believe it is appropriate* [for you] *to do so through the normal rules of promotion.'*

I was extremely confused, because the normal rules of promotion were clearly not available to someone who was being victimised and who was, as yet, without resolution. He now expected me to secure advancement under my own steam as surplus staff. I had done everything that was humanly possible to advance in the Service, whilst under tremendous pressure, and without management support or endorsement. Yet still Robin remained unconvinced of my abilities and suitability or his need to get involved.

I had always suspected that the Service was playing games with me. Even as I held on, the suspicion was still there. Maybe they had done this in the hope that I would just disappear, like others before me. I couldn't understand what more they wanted from me: I had filled out appropriate forms, had had informal and formal talks, been through first stage mediation, written letters, compiled and supplied evidence. I had endured investigation interviews, been the subject of alleged poor performance with no investigation into those allegations. I had gone without annual performance appraisals and endured line management changes without consultation or agreement. I had the majority of my terms for moving forward systematically rejected–*all* this and I was still without resolution. Somebody was definitely playing games with me!

I considered that I was well within my rights to make my third claim to the Tribunal. I wanted them to see that I had tried everything, that I had subjected myself to every mechanism suggested by the Service. As I wrote, I was upset about how these grievances had consumed my professional and personal life. I very much felt that I was now without a job, and without a future in the Service.

As February merged into March, I maintained contact with Paul and the Tribunal. The pain in my heart about what was happening and how things had got so bad, deepened daily. I fought demons of resentment and bitterness and wrestled them to the ground in prayer, yet they proved resistant, as they rose up and overpowered me in the next bout. I was tired. I knew who I needed to be. I knew who I wanted to be, but my strength was failing. Every time I got a call or opened a letter, it was as if no progress had been made and I had to begin to explain myself again. I was so very tired. My brain was fatigued; my heart was breaking and my body was fading.

25th March 2007 marked the 200th anniversary of the abolition of the British transatlantic slave trade in 1807. I had watched the various documentaries over the weeks leading up to the anniversary: 'No Blacks, no Irish, no dogs.' But the 25th was the day history was made two hundred years ago. As I watched the news coverage of the various events commemorating the day, I paused to consider for a while the changes that had been made over the last two hundred years. Black people were 'free': free to own property, free to work, free to marry. Yet I wondered how far that freedom reigned. Legislation and politics said that I was free. The media said that I was free, yet my experience of late said differently. I was eternally grateful that we were no longer non-persons, property to be bought and sold, being beaten, brutalised and raped. And, of course, I was perpetually cognisant of the fact that we're no longer being hanged from trees or gallows, left for birds to pick at our flesh as a warning to other wannabe runaways. Yet, I felt deeply that all traces of the insanity and inhumanity of slavery had not gone and that Britain had merely exchanged tolerance of one form of slavery for tolerance of another.

As I thought, I determined that, although my freedom wasn't being restricted by physical shackles and chains, I was still manacled, still fettered, still bound—for what was talk of freedom if I couldn't be heard? What was the right to challenge, without legitimate avenues for recourse, if not empty rhetoric and cruel play?

Almost to the day, twelve months previously, I had raised five Race Incident Reporting Forms and since then, having endured further abuse, I had raised another four complaints. If I included the original complaint from November 2005, I had raised ten formal grievances. Ten! The physical shackles might no longer be visible, yet I was most certainly encumbered by procedures and protocols that were woefully inadequate and incapable of advancing my cause. And I was unquestionably burdened by the stigma of raising race claims. The shame and dishonour of 'turning' on my organisation whilst they were still paying me was perhaps no different from the 'ungrateful' slave running away after all the master had done for him!

Two hundred years ago, my ancestors were beaten with rods and whips until they couldn't stand or until they were dead. Today we are being beaten with complicated legislation that discourages complaints and glass ceilings that maintain racial disparity in organisations. We're beaten by the lie that racism no longer exists in civilised society, immediately branding those who say otherwise as mean-spirited activists, hell bent on destroying the harmony of our good and gracious country. I concluded that there had been many changes, though I found that the garb of the slave owner had changed little and the mantle had simply been passed from one generation to another. It was my view that they had refined their methods somewhat, yet their contempt for black people remained.

Later that day on the evening news, I watched the Prime Minister, Tony Blair, sitting with a group of young black teenagers. His response to their question, 'Why won't Britain say sorry for the slave trade?' was along the lines of, 'Would you apologise for something you didn't do?' As I watched, I thought that Mr Blair's response was quite a clever question to a fourteen-year-old and it was beautifully staged for the camera. Of course, the teenager said 'No'. What Mr Blair omitted to throw up for discussion for those enquiring minds was the question of advantage and disadvantage borne of slavery. He might not have held the whip, yet I was sure that centuries of being *'on the privileged side of the colour line'* [1] had yielded great illegitimate advantage. I wondered how many mornings Mr Blair had to wake up en route to becoming Prime Minister and repeat an empowerment mantra saying, 'I'm as good as any black man, yes I am!'? As far as I was concerned Mr Blair, and many others like him, had benefited from being regarded as the superior race by both black and white across the globe for centuries and had enjoyed the resultant deference paid to them because of it– whether they thought it was right or not. There was a time when what we might refer to today as extreme racialist or nationalist views, were once commonly and conveniently held beliefs. Not so long ago, pseudo-scientific and theological meanderings were offered as evidence to endorse the position that white was superior and black was inferior and legislation was drafted to enforce the said evidence. Consequently, today, the world does not look at the white man and instantly think 'idiot, criminal or lazy'–nor should it. In fact, to elicit any semblance of a generalisation about white people, one needs to be more specific about a particular group from a particular place or mention a particular person, before any generic labels get spat out–if any. But as soon as we start talking about black people, terms like aggressive, drug-addicted, gang-related, criminal element, mentally unstable and absent fathers, synonymously roll off the tongue. No different from two hundred years ago!

Again, even whilst celebrating the abolition of the slave trade, there was no authentic connecting of the past with the present. In my mind, an authentic connection would necessitate a determination of pure unadulterated regret and public contrition, evidenced as steps taken to make sure any semblance of the iniquity on which this country had grown rich and powerful was stamped out–both by government and a people committed to equity for all. It would be evidenced by a commitment to remember the pain and share the wealth. However, that's not what we have today. What we have is a nation with little to no history of their wrongs, as they use the distance of the colonies to separate themselves from the slavery they readily embraced, to feed their covetousness and nourish their avarice. We have a nation that is content to believe that the African added nothing of value to their country–at least nothing significant enough to inform the way we educate our children about history. We have a nation which, despite the fact that they traded in slaves, wrongly believes that black people only arrived a few decades ago on the 'Windrush'. We have a nation who feel justified to react as they do to the alleged recent explosion of blacks who have taken their jobs, their homes and their women. Instead of sorrow and regret, flush with an understanding of the disadvantage caused, we have white noise–'Why are our laws changing to protect the dark-skinned usurpers… why do we have to be the ones to watch our 'p's' and 'q's'… how is it *they* can use the 'N' word and *we* can't… why do we need so much diversity training?'

A whole day had been reserved to commemorate the abolition of slavery, yet I didn't see any discussion about the results of centuries of veneration for one part of humanity and centuries of irreverence for another. As a black woman in Britain, I couldn't deny the lingering effects of the racial dehumanising of the African peoples that still underlines my being seen as second class and not belonging, on sight. Throughout the evening as I watched the programming, I was saddened that the direct and indirect benefits of slavery had become a mere whisper because time has lapsed–because arguments prevailed that, even though millions of pounds were generated by slavery, we needed to move on. Yet it still mattered to me. Maybe my experiences of the Service had heightened my sensitivities, as I felt that it was all connected: the bitter–the sweet, the slavery–the wealth, the present.

Throughout the day I also noted the occasional mention of the African involvement in the slave trade as if to suggest equal accountability. It angered me that there was a desire to share the guilt, but not the wealth! I felt that the question of African involvement was more of a distraction than a genuine desire to understand the past. In the raising of this issue nothing was said of the millions of Africans who were kidnapped in order to fuel the voracious American and European appetite; nothing was said of the horror of forced breeding to increase the slave-holder's estates. I was sure, even though I did not have much knowledge about my heritage, that Africans were not equal partners in the trade; in its perpetuation or in the generational wealth generated. Each time I heard a comment from some politician (as an attempt to shift the guilt) about African chiefs, I wondered just how much sway African chiefs had over the conditions slaves had to endure in the middle passage. How much influence did they have over American and British legislation and religion in the classification of slaves as chattel and subhuman? How many shares did the African chiefs buy in the shipping, manufacturing and insurance conglomerates? I was fairly sure the answer would be a resounding 'zero'. I knew there was some involvement, but I was confident that it wasn't a collective, united African nation selling slaves in the same way that America and Europe banded together to meet the demand for forced labour. I was sure that the situation was more one of individual countries on the continent of Africa that did their own thing; making war and devaluing each other not unlike countries in Europe at that time. In the history of the world, country has overthrown country yet no one thought it strange when 'white' enslaved or terrorised 'white'. Even today the news is rarely short of a story about Eastern European trafficking of children and women for labour and sexual exploitation. Yet African involvement in the slave trade or rather black people selling black people gives rise to wonderment as if it is a phenomenon unlike anything white people have ever done to each other.

Over the days that followed, my need to move beyond speculative argument drove me to look into what had happened to the black man in Britain leading up to and since the abolition. I determined that his foot might not have been 'Kunta Kinte'd' [2] but that the Black Briton still had to hobble through hundreds of years of disadvantage. As I searched the internet and ordered books, I wondered how awful it must have been to begin life in a foreign country that despised your very presence and then to live with a people that resented the fact that the law had granted you equal status. I wondered what it must have been like to subsequently have no power to tip the balance, despite the changes; to be refused the right to buy or rent where you pleased; to find work only after every white person had been accommodated with a role and to be paid less than everyone else no matter your effort, skill, or aptitude. For generation after generation to be treated that way could only have served to keep the disadvantaged, disadvantaged.

When the books that I had ordered started to arrive, I ambitiously read them several at a time. I had been without knowledge for long enough, I needed to catch up. I alternated between the internet and the books. As I read, my suspicions were confirmed in that, after the transatlantic slave trade was abolished in

1807, those who had become rich from it did not, in recognition of their wrongs, share their wealth and advantage with the slaves. No white man surrendered his castle for the cause. No white man bequeathed his stocks and shares in tobacco or sugar. No one said, 'You helped to generate this wealth, here is your portion, let's go about ensuring that you are now on an equal footing with us—let's make sure your children go to Eton, Oxford or Cambridge.' There was no gentleman's handshake or restitution of any kind. Furthermore, I didn't realise that the abolition did not free all slaves it merely prevented the trading of slaves, which simply continued to happen illegally and with greater proliferation. British slaves effectively emancipated themselves after an act of Parliament in 1833, with a succession of resistance by either running away or refusing to work unless they got paid [3]. Conversely, the white man, who so graciously granted our freedom, continued to prosper as the British government compensated slave owners for their loss of human property to the tune of twenty million pounds. His children continued to learn about their great nation as they soaked up the influence of good role models; they thrived under national pride and the power of strong family creeds that had existed as such for generations.

As I absorbed all this information, I could see that, when the line was drawn in the sand in 1807, the new world for the white man was much the same: still rich, powerful and established the world over. The new world for the black man was also much the same: still alien, impoverished and destitute. He started without a penny in his pocket or a piece of land to his name. He started with fragmented family units, and a history of violence and powerlessness. He had to reconcile himself with a past where he endured a life of degradation and a bearing in the body of beatings, comforted only by a holding in the heart of visions of freedom, seasoned with a mouth saying 'thank you' to the Master with the whip, for the sparing of lives that day. Then he was simply expected to move forward from there. He, like generations before him had held his pain in, had done the work he was given to do, whilst looking beyond the inhumanity of his condition into the realms of a greater hope and, when it arrived, it was barely noticeable. (It all seemed strangely familiar.) I spent my time imagining what it must have been like to spend centuries watching our women and daughters raped and our men being put out to stud, decades of being told that we were less than nothing, years of being tortured for having spirit and then, one day, responding to someone saying something about freedom and apprenticeships without pay to help us through transition. There was no time to heal. No time to find the dignity that had been trodden underfoot. No time for the haze to clear, for strategies to form because, even though we were free, we were still (by the account of the ruling class) uneducable, still unclean, still less than everyone else. There weren't any psychologists on hand to help us deal with the trauma of systematic generational abuse of mammoth proportions.

As I searched and read, I started to bring my own experience of inequality in Britain to bear. I became even more despondent when I considered that the information I was soaking up was not just referring to eighteenth and nineteenth century disadvantage. I remembered the short-sightedness of the 'Sus Law', that whole stop-and-search business in the early 1980s that allowed police officers to arrest anyone they chose, purely on the basis of suspicion. I needed more facts, so I looked it up on the internet and found that it was a crime prevention tactic based upon Sections 4 and 6 of the 1824 Vagrancy Act, which made it *'illegal for a suspected person or reputed thief to frequent or loiter in a public place with intent to commit an arrestable offence'.* [4] Although I considered that that in itself seemed reasonable, I remembered the level of allegations of abuse that were levelled at the police. Furthermore, few people realised that, while the amended Race Relations Act had become law in 1976 making discrimination on the grounds of race unlawful, police forces were exempted from its provisions for national security reasons [5]. By the early 80's, under a Thatcherite government with strict monetarist policies and around three million people unemployed, the crime rate soaring and burglary rates high in inner-city areas, targeting black people as the criminal element was a natural development for the police. It didn't take long before many young black men were accusing the police of using the 'Sus Law' to discriminate against them. They didn't realise that the police were allowed to target certain racial groups; it was a matter of national security after all. I remember discussions at the time, where the 'Sus

Law' was invariably seen to be another way to legalise the nigger hunt. Before the law, the police were able to turn a blind eye to racial injustice because no race relations law was being broken. After the law in 1976, the police were empowered to discriminate in the interest of the crown.

My mind turned to the Brixton riots in 1981 and I began a search for the details. There were various accounts saying mostly the same things about 'Operation Swamp 81' where, in the space of just five days, plain-clothed police randomly stopped and searched one thousand black people, mostly young black men in Brixton. The searches were, to a large extent, unrecorded. The 'criminal element' targeted were burglars and robbers, yet out of a thousand stops, there was only one actual arrest for burglary and a few for theft. The rest of the charges were for the crimes that happened in situ, like obstructing the police and insulting behaviour, which naturally arose out of people resisting these unjustified and indiscriminate stops and searches. This ultimately sparked the riots that shocked the nation.

I continued to search, because I felt that today the story was not much different. I found that under the 1984 Police and Criminal Evidence Act (PACE), the latest published statistics for 2005-2006 recorded 878,153 stops and searches. 25% of those (or 219,538 people) were classified as stops of Black, Asian or people of Other Ethnic Origin, which was an increase on previous years of 3.4%. The publication 'Statistics on Race and the Criminal Justice System—2006' said:

> *Numerically, most of this rise was accounted for by an increase of 14,169 (11.8%) for Black people...increases for Asian people (14%), and* [an increase of] *people in the 'Other' minority ethnic group* [classification] *(16%), while stop and searches of White people rose by 0.4%*

I found that, for this period, only 12% of stop and searches of Black, Asian and other ethnic groups led to an actual arrest, which is a very small proportion of the total of 1.3 million arrests for that period. There were no figures available showing how many convictions had resulted from the arrests. Furthermore, according to the same report today, black people are seven times more likely than their white counterparts to be stopped and searched, three and a half times more likely to be arrested and five times more likely to be sent to prison for a first offence. Wow, I thought. And we wonder how it is that black youths are over-represented in prisons. It was no wonder that so many youths saw no future and lived for instant gratification at any and sometimes all costs, because tomorrow said nothing of promise to them. Tomorrow only spoke about harassment and unequal treatment, despite legislation.

As much as I knew that, against this backdrop of disadvantage and historical indifference, a black man or black woman could make it, I realised that there was little understanding or compassion for the over-representation of black youth in prison or the under-education of black youth in schools. In a lot of my research, there was not much advocating that the reasons went beyond criminogenic factors (a tendency to commit crime) or laziness. Those pro-slavery arguments, although no longer spoken publicly, seem to have sown seeds deep into the white British psyche that, two hundred years down the line, still cause them to see us in the same way.

In my search I was encouraged to see slave resistance at every turn. This was not a message that had been driven home to us as children. Although we had seen *Roots*, for the most part our sense was that the African was placid and docile and had given up any chance of freedom until a few white people who felt that slavery was wrong, had pushed for change. I was thankful to see that African countries had resisted the slave trade and we had indeed fought for freedom ourselves. Though as I read I couldn't imagine how hard it must have been to face the coordinated effort of countries banded together in a common cause, exploiting the weakness of separate African countries with separate identities, different cultures, languages and different resources.

Each night when Rudy came home, we would have a discussion about what I had learnt during the day. Sometimes I would send him excerpts, so that he could read it before he got home. Other times I was too impatient and too angry to wait for him to get home, so I would read bits of articles on the internet to him over the phone. We would sit over our evening meal and agree things like, 'You couldn't honestly tell a black man that the prejudice he is experiencing today is completely different from the prejudice his forefathers experienced hundreds of years ago!' We were clear that, because of this, when some of us were treated poorly, we were instantly and subconsciously transported back to a time that we never lived in—yet a time we fully identified with. Rudy and I discussed government knee-jerk reactions to an increase in crime or numbers of people migrating and the lack of well-thought-out long-term plans to rebuild lives and self-esteem; plans to fill in the gaps in our knowledge of self and origin; plans to secure a better future— for everyone.

Both Rudy and I had spoken to many disaffected youths over the years. We had seen the impact of years of being shown in a disparaging light and how that has left them with little of our ancestry to be proud of, their minds constantly corroded with images of poor, backward and hungry Africans. Ultimately, in the absence of pride in who we were or where we had come from, we could see how for many there was little optimism for the future. Instead, we had witnessed an experience akin to being in no-man's land, a kind of limbo, an inability to look back for shame carefully constructed by lies about our worth and value, coupled with a resultant incapacity to look forward for the same reasons. All that was left was a hollow existence, tortured by acutely inflamed senses resistant to soothing and an anger that flared up, seemingly without provocation. As diasporic Africans, our loss of self is all too apparent in the faces of our disempowered youth.

Britain had gorged herself on our blood and marrow, daily consuming us like the first meal of a starving man. Then, when her belly was bloated and her bones fat, her lust turned to the machines that would continue to generate wealth: machines to do the work of ten, 20, 30 slaves, machines that didn't need feeding or breeding. Then slaves, once an inconvenience because they were troublesome (needing to be housed and supervised), became an inconvenience, simply because they existed. Today, we evoke the same irritation in some, anger and scorn in others, just because we are here.

As the weeks unfolded, I had to deal with another request for postponement made by the Prison Service to the Tribunal. They cited reasons around needing to consider my last grievance under the Prison Service grievance procedure. Even though I understood grievance protocol, I knew that this was just another stalling tactic. They made out that they hadn't known from the outset that I wanted the matter pursued formally, which surprised me a great deal. Had they read their own grievance policy they would have seen that, due to the complexity of my case and the fact that informal resolution had already failed miserably, there was no other suitable route other than formal considerations. They had wasted time trying to deal with it informally with letters and now they were attempting to hold up proceedings because they wanted a chance to do things properly. In their request for postponement, they also talked about Robin's unavailability for the hearing dates. This all filled me with dread, because they were also asking for an extension of time for lodging a response to my claim, for some 28 days after concluding the second stage of the grievance procedure, which they considered wouldn't be until after the middle of May. If the extension was granted on these terms, there was a strong likelihood that the full hearing might be postponed. All of my energy and hope was being channelled into knowing that, by May 2007, this would be over–and now it was looking likely that my torment would be extended. I wasn't sure if I could cope for much longer.

Before I knew, it the month of April was under way. I received a letter from Robin asking for us to meet to discuss the January meeting, an email from Beverley Thompson asking if I'd be interested in a job as a Training Curriculum Development Manager D, and an email from Susanne in personnel offering me dates to meet with Val Woodcock to complete my appraisal for 2005. At the January meeting, I was caught off guard, right at the end, when I was asked if they could arrange dates for my appraisal to take place. Having not thought through the implications of sitting through my appraisal at this late stage and, after nearly four hours in a room with them, I was left without the capacity to evaluate the offer properly. Since the January meeting, the timeframe to do my 2006/7 appraisal had also expired, yet they were only offering to do the 2005/6 appraisal. There was also no mention of how they were going to evaluate my performance. Normally, I would have secured feedback and commendations for work done leading up to reviews, in order to be able to comment factually on my own performance. This is especially important as a mobile or remote worker in view of the fact that one was rarely shadowed by a manager. Yet I couldn't now ask clients to remember back to 2005 and specifically comment on the work I had done for them, the impact it had had on their prison and staff, the competencies that had been developed as a result of my input and so on. I was embarrassed just thinking about it. Since the previous year, many of my clients had moved on to different prisons and were no longer able to comment on the ongoing effects of the learning and development initiatives delivered at their previous prisons. A number of clients had left the Service altogether, and this was compounded by the fact that I hadn't been in touch with, nor had I done any work for my client base, for seven months. And, of course, not forgetting that in that period of 2005/6, because I had raised grievances, my reporting line had been changed twice—which meant that, for the reporting period in question I had three different managers, none of whom were able to comment on my performance for any significant period of time. Yet I was offered no concession to offset the possible negative impact of these disadvantages. As far as I was concerned, offering to do my appraisal for 2005 as normal was unfair. I also felt that, because there had been resistance to formally investigating why my appraisal had not been done, it had not yet been established if the rationale behind that action was indeed an act of victimisation—nor had any detriment to me been considered. Simply arranging the appraisal wouldn't answer any of those questions. Finally, this still left my performance for 2006/7 with exactly the same issues. I asked my solicitor to draft a letter with these points.

All this backwards and forwards was taking its toll on me. I had been carelessly thrown into a tumble dryer and left to spin this way, then that way, for hours—spinning in dry heat until every drop of life-sustaining water had been driven out of me, leaving me crisp, barren and impossible to straighten out. I hadn't slept properly for several months. I was at home, and presumably should have been coping much better, yet that was not the case at all. Every letter, every email, and every phone call increased my anxiety. I was still getting panic attacks and I could often hear my heart beating rapidly and loudly in my head. I was quite weepy generally and felt that I was just not coping.

With the solicitors dealing with Susanne's email, I set about responding to Beverley and Robin. First, I expressed an interest in the role mentioned by Beverley. Then I turned my attention to Robin's request to meet. I emailed him to let him know that Paul and Jaswinder were both unavailable for the dates he had offered me—he had given barely a week's notice. I made a point of explaining that I particularly wanted Paul to be present because he had his own recollection of the January meeting and could speak accurately about what had happened. I felt this was important, given the discrepancies cited in notes from Robin since that meeting occurred. I especially had in mind the occasion when Stacey asked if I thought I could compete for Sue's and Val's roles. Robin had said in his letter dated 21st February that '*This* [was] *not an accurate recollection of the conversation.*' Stacey's repeated questioning was actually something that Paul and I remembered vividly. This discrepancy, along with others, made it absolutely imperative for Paul to attend any meeting we were going to have to discuss what had happened in January.

When Rudy got home, I told him that I didn't know how much longer I could hold out.

'Sweetheart,' he said, 'you're the strongest person I know.'

'But I'm crying every day. You must be so sick of leaving me in the morning in my dressing gown and coming home to find me in my dressing gown. One day I'm focused and motivated and the next day I'm a mess! And I can't stop crying.'

'You are going to get through this. Tears don't mean you're weak—they mean you're human. Listen, I don't want you to worry about the house or the bills. I will take care of everything. All you need to do is focus on the case. You'll be fine—we'll be fine.'

Endnote

1 **Goulbourne, H**. (1998) *Race Relations in Britain since 1945* Hampshire, Palgrave Macmillan. p. ix

2 **Hayley, A** (1976) *Roots: The Saga of an American Family*

3 **Fryer, P** (1984) *Staying Power: The History of Black People in Britain.* London . Pluto Press

⁴ Vagrancy Act 1824. Office of Public Sector Information. Available online: http://www.opsi.gov.uk/RevisedStatutes/Acts/ukpga/1824/cukpga_18240083_en_1

Vagrancy Act 1824 Main Body c.83; "every suspected person or reputed thief, frequenting …any street, highway, or avenue leading thereto, or any place of public resort, or any avenue leading thereto, or any street…with intent to commit [an arrestable offence]; and every person apprehended as an idle and disorderly person, and violently resisting any constable, or other peace officer so apprehending him or her, and being subsequently convicted of the offence for which he or she shall have been so apprehended; shall be deemed a rogue and vagabond, within the true intent and meaning of this Act; and it shall be lawful for any justice of the peace to commit such offender (being thereof convicted before him by the confession of such offender, or by the evidence on oath of one or more credible witness or witnesses,) to the house of correction…"

⁵ PART VI. GENERAL EXCEPTIONS FROM PARTS II TO IV : **Section 42.** Acts safeguarding national security. —Nothing in Parts II to IV shall render unlawful an act done for the purpose of safeguarding national security.

⁶ Commonwealth Immigrants Act 1968 CHAPTER 9. An Act to amend sections 1 and 2 of the Commonwealth Immigrants Act 1962, and Schedule l to that Act, and to make further provision as to Commonwealth citizens landing in the United Kingdom, the Channel Islands or the Isle of Man; and for purposes connected with the matters aforesaid. [lst March 1968] "BE IT ENACTED by the Queen's most Excellent Majesty, by and with the advice and consent of the Lords Spiritual and Temporal, and Commons, in this present Parliament assembled, and by the authority of the same, as follows:- …(2A) The condition referred to in subsection (2)(b) of this section, in relation to a person, is that he, or at least one of his parents or grandparents,- (a) was born in the United Kingdom, or (b) is or was a person naturalised in the United Kingdom, or (c) became a citizen of the United Kingdom and Colonies by virtue of being adopted in the United Kingdom..."

The British Nationality Act 1948 was an Act of the British Parliament which conferred the status of British citizen on all Commonwealth subjects who resided in those places that were still British colonies on 1 January 1949, when the 1948 Act came into force. Any Citizen of the UK and Colonies had the right at any time to enter and live in the United Kingdom and to bring their families with them without a visa. Due to overwhelming hostility to the migration of mostly post-war Caribbeans to the UK the right to reside in the was restricted by the 1968 Commonwealth Immigration Act and 1971 Immigration Act. From then onwards the right of abode was limited to those who could demonstrate prior ancestral links to the UK, such as parents or grandparents who were born in Britain.

Chapter Fourteen

Crash and Burn

On 12th April, I woke up feeling at my lowest. I found myself brushing my teeth and weeping bitterly. I looked in the mirror and simply didn't recognise the broken person staring back at me. There were dark rings under my empty eyes. My skin was ashen and in need of exfoliating. My hair was limp and dirty. I couldn't stop crying. In a couple of years, I had gone from a well-balanced individual to this pathetic mess. There was a time, in what seemed like eons ago, when I went shopping, I liked meals out and had a good network of friends. I had faith in a higher power and loved being in a position where I could help others. I enjoyed cooking and walking. I was ordinary and like everyone else, give or take the odd idiosyncrasy. Yet I had gone from this person, who loved life, to someone who was unable to distinguish between racially and non-racially motivated actions. I had gone from someone who liked to hear both sides of the argument before making a decision, to someone who was viewing every encounter through glasses tinged with suspicion. I was in a place where paranoia reigned.

How had this happened? I asked myself. What had changed in a few years to bring me so thoroughly to my knees? I hadn't been kidnapped or displaced. I wasn't being denied food or drink. I wasn't being physically beaten. My circle of supportive friends hadn't changed; no one had been ripped out of my life. There had been no such trauma, yet still things had deteriorated to the point that I was unable to leave the house. I couldn't be around people without being drawn back to my bedroom, my sanctuary. I was spending hours crying every day. Anything would set me off. Crying until my strength left me; grieving as if somebody died. Falling asleep, hardly able to breath for the congestion in my nasal passages, only to wake up after scarcely any time at all to cry again. Although much of my life remained the same, something had changed. As far as I was concerned I was working in a racist organisation. This single factor was like a malignant cell that had taken over every other element of my being. It felt as if I was being hollowed out from the inside. I had underestimated the effects of working in an institutionally racist organisation. If you have any sense that human beings are more than flesh and bone—you can feel the oppression that comes from being in a place where you're not wanted. Even if you never hear a word spoken to confirm it—you know. It can be unbearable living in a house with *one* person who wishes you would leave—multiply that by twenty or thirty thousand people wishing the same and you get a sense of what it's like working for the Prison Service.

Unbeknown to me, I had spent months walking through corridors where, only moments before, an officer or manager had been breathing out his or her irritation with my presence—and others like me. I walked through the mists of resentment they had left hanging in the air. Discussions about my competence and suitability hung in the atmosphere like vapour for me breathe in. I filled my lungs. Comments like, 'It's not that she's unintelligent, it's her attitude I object to. The way she swans around as if she's better than anyone else,' were clandestinely shared. An advisor from my team once said with resentment, 'Oh Olivea, you always look so glamorous. It makes the rest of us feel like tramps!' And that was to my face. What was she saying out of earshot? I had been breathing in these noxious fumes of non-acceptance and negativity towards black people for the last few years and it had finally made me very sick.

I continued to stare at myself in the mirror, the tears streaming down, the uncontrollable sobs and convulsions, and the toothpaste foaming at the corners of my mouth. What a mournful sight!

I cleaned myself up and went to the study. I phoned my doctor for an emergency appointment. They gave me the next slot, which was 30 minutes away. I drove myself to the surgery.

Within minutes of arriving, I heard my name over the loudspeaker. When I got into my doctor's office, all he said was 'What can I do for you today?' and I was in floods of tears again.

'I'm…not…coping…anymore!' I had to wait a few seconds, just so I could get a few more words out. 'The situation at work'—I blew my nose—'is worse than before, even though I'm still at home. They won't give me a minute's peace, so that I can think.' I took my glasses off because I could no longer see through them and the tears.

'I'm still getting dizzy spells, I can't eat, and the palpitations are so frightening—I can hear my heart in my head beating frantically. Every time the phone rings or I get a letter or I'm expected to meet with them, a sheer dread and anxiety envelops me. And all I want to do is run in the opposite direction. I can't sleep. If my mind isn't racing and obsessing, then my skin is itching or my legs are jumping involuntarily like…like a cat having a bad dream. It's *so* irritating. Sometimes my legs twitch and kick so much I want to cut them off, just so that I can get some sleep! I'm not doing anything in the house, my husband…' (more tears) 'my husband doesn't have a wife anymore. He's married to this mess in front of you…and sometimes my heart hurts…I get pains in my chest…' The list of concerns was very long as I told him how incredibly harassed I felt. Then I told him something I'd never told another soul: that I was preoccupied with my own mortality. I thought I was dying!

I tried to put things into context. I explained how my eldest sister, Dell, had died from cancer four years earlier and that we hadn't known she was ill until three weeks before she died. She only ever complained of feeling tired. I told him that I couldn't stop thinking about how exhausted I was and couldn't help wondering if I would soon die, like my sister. I just couldn't shake the feeling that the Service had damaged the quality of my life to the extent that I was dying and didn't know it. Hearing myself talk out loud made me realise how pathetic I sounded. Like an old Southern Belle from a black-and-white movie, swooning from the heat, with the back of one hand on my forehead and the other hand holding a fan furiously and ineffectively trying to disperse the heat: *Oh doctor I think I'm dying, can you give me something for the pain!* I was a complete mess. I was crying and shaking. My voice was cracking and trembling. Even when my beautiful sister died, I had coped better than this. I didn't have to seek out a physician then.

My doctor was remarkably accommodating and very patient with me. He checked my breathing, my heart and felt for swollen or enlarged organs. He explained it was only natural for someone under this kind of stress to respond in this way. He also had me complete a questionnaire to determine my levels of stress anxiety and depression. Then he explained that, with treatment on antidepressant tablets, I might feel less anxious; they would also help me sleep, which in turn would help with the other symptoms. He did a little more explaining and encouraging. When we had spoken the previous October, I had refused antidepressants, yet this time I was without strength. I was empty and he had diagnosed that I was suffering from depression. I agreed to take them.

I left the surgery, filled the prescription and went home, defeated. I went straight back to bed in tears. I had never taken antidepressants before. I felt like a failure. I dreaded Rudy coming home to find me like this, all pathetic and wilted. He had been amazing while I was going through this. He was dealing with everything: the ministry, the bills, the food, the housekeeping, everything. He said it was his way of supporting me. He was doing so much, but it didn't matter, because the Service had broken me anyway. What would Rudy say when he got home? Would he smell the wretchedness dripping from my pores? Would he still love me, if he truly knew that I was losing my mind, that I was unstable? That I might not get better? What would I see in his telling eyes; unconditional love, disappointment, time for a quick exit? I knew I had lost myself—I couldn't bare to lose him too!

When Rudy came home from work he found me in bed. He asked what had happened. I broke down yet again. I told him how defeated I felt because I had been prescribed antidepressants. He just held me, prayed for me and said everything was going to be alright.

For weeks, I continued to feel incredibly detached and heavily depressed. It was as if the me I used to know and the real world were outside a glass dome looking in on the me I had become: the one taking the pills, the one spending all day in bed and the one I didn't recognise. Whilst inside the dome, I could only see distorted images and hear distorted voices outside and, because they were outside, they couldn't make me do anything I didn't want to. I didn't have the energy to do anything, so I didn't do anything. I felt especially resentful towards the Prison Service and, despite what I knew about what happens when you focus on negative things, I didn't care anymore. I fluctuated between anger and brokenness, clarity and confusion. I was so sad, and the sadness was oppressive—like a great weighted blanket of sorrow smothering me—I could barely breathe. I had told my immediate family that I was taking antidepressants and they were checking on me on a daily basis. Although I was very touched by their concern and their support, I also felt irritated each time the phone rang or if Mum or Rudy asked how I was doing. My emotions were out of control and I just wanted to be left alone. To make matters worse, my solicitors advised me that the likelihood of the full hearing being postponed was increased, and that left me feeling entirely hopeless.

As the days blurred into one amorphous continuation of numbness, I was in utter darkness. I could hardly lift my head off my pillow each morning. I hated what I had become: lost, feeble and wretched. Where is your faith, Olivea? I challenged myself. I called to it. There was no answer. My faith is at the core of my identity; if I had lost it, then I was nothing and no one! Is this what nothing felt like? I called to God. I knew he was there yet it was as if there was something between us, something interrupting the flow of our relationship. I needed him so much—where was he?

Well, Pastor Olivea, I patronised myself, a fine leader you're turning out to be. I hope you're not going to stand in front of your flock and preach faith and resilience on Sunday. Look at you—you hypocrite! Look at what you've allowed this little trial to do to you. Who are you going to encourage? Who are you going to counsel? If you can't cope with this, God forbid that anything really difficult should come your way.

I had sunk into this deep pit of despair, self-mortification and loneliness and I couldn't see how I was ever going to climb out. Why couldn't I hear God's voice anymore? Could it be because I had inadvertently found a new god? Had the Service become the new deity in my life? I knew that I was not a willing or adoring worshipper, yet did I not fill my waking and sleeping hours with thoughts about the Service? The Service dominated every conversation and each email. It was the focus of almost every prayer, as I sought solace and escape. I had spoken more about it and its power to hurt me than I had about the greatness of Jehovah the provider, Jehovah my banner and champion. I had become their slave. Before I had been granted the special leave of absence, I toiled by day to avoid the whip and planned my getaway by night, whilst singing songs of freedom.

I am not sure how much time had passed, but one morning I picked up my Bible. I sat on the edge of my bed staring at it in my hands, unopened. I looked at the frayed edges of the cover and along the spine, where the leather was worn and patchy from constant opening and closing, mirroring my own shabbiness. I looked up to the ceiling as if, by doing this, God would know more pointedly that I was talking to him.

'If I open this today,' I said, 'will you help me? Will you heal me?'

As I listened, I heard cars passing outside my window and the idle chatter of children on their way to school. I looked again at the Bible in my hands. I'll read a psalm, I thought—psalms always speak to me. I opened my Bible and flicked through, scanning the chapters. As I read the first verse of Psalm 102, I settled there. David the Psalmist, had entitled it, *'A prayer of one overwhelmed with trouble, pouring out problems before the LORD.'* 'How fitting,' I thought. 'Well, let's see where this takes me,' I said aloud with a tinge of insolence.

'LORD, hear my prayer!' I read quickly and dispassionately. *'Listen to my plea! Don't turn away from me in my time of distress. Bend down your ear and answer me quickly when I call to you, for my days disappear like smoke, and my bones burn like red-hot coals.'* I spoke as if I had entitlement that he had overlooked! *'My heart is sick, withered like grass, and I have lost my appetite.'* 'Oh,' I thought, 'this is just like me!' I read on. *'Because of my groaning, I am reduced to skin and bones. I am like an owl in the desert, like a lonely owl in a far-off wilderness. I lie awake, lonely as a solitary bird on the roof.'*

The words had a power all their own, as my temperament started to change. My reading aloud slowed. The words, no longer angry and petulant, became heavy with reflective emotion and revelation. How could this be so apt? How could David know how to encapsulate my mood and my woe so completely? I read on with mounting astonishment. *'My enemies taunt me day after day. They mock and curse me. I eat ashes instead of my food. My tears run down into my drink because of your anger and wrath. For you have picked me up and thrown me out. My life passes as swiftly as the evening shadows. I am withering like grass. But you, O LORD, will rule forever. Your fame will endure to every generation. You will arise and have mercy on Jerusalem—and now is the time to pity her, now is the time you promised to help.'*

As my tears flowed, it was not because the psalm spoke to me—it was because it spoke *for* me. Millennia ago, someone articulated my trouble in a way I could not, for the pain. God was going to pity me. He would show me compassion and help me. It was time.

Over the days that followed I started to spend time reading the psalms aloud, willing myself to connect with God, willing myself to find peace and joy, believing that, as I spoke, the life in those words would permeate the darkness I felt like shards of light, breaking through dampening clouds. I spoke loudly and in defiance of what I was feeling. I listened to praise and worship CDs and reached out to the heavens. 'Away' by Israel Houghton played for hours every day, non-stop. As he confessed that it had been a while since he had spoken to God, so did I. My voice joined his solitary and melodic request to get away from everyday life, to be alone with God, because nothing else mattered. As his yearning unfolded, so did mine; as his desire to worship rose, so did mine. Every day for four or five hours, I read the Bible and listened to the music. I let my soul groan and I poured out my complaint to the Lord of Hosts and, once emptied out, I asked him to fill me with the love I so desperately needed. Still more hours and still more tears…until I started…to feel something. Even then, the tears flowed, but this time they were not a complete witness to despair. This time, my tears were imbued with an unusual mixture of anguish and gratitude. I felt something, a flutter in my heart. There was the tiniest notion that something was changing, that hope and peace were returning. Somewhere in the distance, they were calling my name. With everything I was going through, I had to believe that God was taking care of me. I was surrounded by loved ones who cared about me too. A spectre of faith, a mustard seed, was all I needed for hope to eventually manifest itself as substance. The smallest seed had been planted and I knew it would grow. I knew that, in its season, it would outgrow and dominate all doubt and fear and I would be able to rest in its shade once more.

With this tiny and most precious hope, daily I chose to give God thanks. Daily I praised him; daily I prayed for his comfort and assurance. By the end of the month, I was reluctantly forgiving Sue, Stacey, Robin and everyone again. I didn't feel like doing it, and I didn't think that they deserved it, but I knew that I would not be forgiven if I didn't do it. And I needed forgiveness for not trusting God enough, for not believing (even if it was for a moment) that this would work out. I was still very delicate, but I told myself that I was going to make it, even though I didn't know how. What I did know was that I had to cling to that glimmer of hope in the midst of the darkness, like a shipwrecked survivor in the middle of the sea. In my exhaustion, all I had to do was cling. This was a strange place, an ethereal place. It was one of absurdity and conflict, shame and hope; to declare and believe that I was okay whilst knowing and seeing that I wasn't, made insanity look like a progressive step! If I was mad, would I know it?

On 8th May, I was waiting for a call from my solicitors for the outcome of the case management discussion that was going to be held that day. I was told that I didn't need to attend. My solicitors called me around 4.00pm. I was relieved to hear that all of my claims were consolidated to be heard at the same time. I was, however, horrified to learn that the full hearing was now postponed to January 2008. It had also gone from a five-day hearing to fifteen days!

It had taken everything I had to last this long. Now I had to face the reality that, not only was this going to drag on another eight months and into the New Year, but I was going to run out of funds before the hearing–meaning I would have to represent myself. I was convinced this was another ploy from the Service's arsenal of delaying tactics, used to make sure that either my health failed or my funds ran out–and now they had achieved both. I was numb again. How was I supposed to represent myself in court for three weeks? How was I supposed to prepare? I wondered if I would be doing myself a disservice.

I don't know whether I was too preoccupied with this mess, but at the weekend I fell down some steps to my basement. I was in a lot of pain. I don't even know how it happened. One minute I was going to fetch some curtains for Mum and the next I was immobilised on the basement floor, watching both of my ankles balloon. Mum heard me fall. Then she started screaming my name and asking if I wanted her to come down to help me. I was in so much pain; I could barely catch my breath to say 'No! Send Rudy.' As much as she wanted to, she couldn't help me. She didn't have the strength. I could hear her panicking. 'Rudy! Rudy, Livie's hurt.'

Rudy ran down the steps to find me sitting up with my legs in front of me, and tears streaming down. 'Can you move?'

'No.'

'What do I do?'

'Pray.'

After he prayed, Rudy ran back upstairs and wet two towels with cold water. When he returned, he wrapped both my ankles. It was about 20 minutes later when I felt able to hop upstairs, with Rudy assisting me. 'They look pretty bad. I should take you to casualty,' Rudy said.

'I think they're just badly sprained,' I replied.

'So you're a medic now are you?' he challenged.

'No,' I said. 'But I've just been walking, albeit with your assistance. It can't be that bad, can it?'

I bandaged my ankles, took some painkillers and rested. The days that followed found me keeping still and surfing the net for guidance on what to expect at a Tribunal. After a few days, the toes on my right foot were turning blue and the swelling, although reduced was not dissipating as quickly as I expected. I thought perhaps that I had bandaged my foot too tightly. I made an appointment to see the nurse at my doctor's surgery and drove there in the hope that she would bandage my ankles correctly.

The nurse told me that the discolouration was because of bruising. But the swelling suggested that I may have chipped a bone. She said I should get it x-rayed at Kettering Hospital. She filled out a form and told me to hand it in when I arrived there and the consultant would see me quicker than if I turned up without an appointment.

'You'll need someone to take you because you can't drive. Do you have someone who can give you a lift?'

'Yes,' I said. 'I can call someone.' I daren't tell her that I had driven there and would drive home. Once home I called Norma, one of the Elders of the church and asked for a lift to the hospital. She said she was happy to, but would have to go to work straight afterwards. I told her that would be fine as I would probably get the bus home anyway. Norma is in charge of hospitality at church and always charms everyone with her Wilma Flintstone laugh. Nothing is ever too much to ask. It is a joy to have such people in my life. Norma dropped me off, I walked in to the hospital, and had an x-ray done on both ankles. After about 20 minutes, a consultant came into the cubical where I was waiting, examined my ankles, and left without a word. Then he came back with a nurse who watched him examine my ankles.

Then the consultant spoke. 'You do realise that you've broken your ankle, don't you?'

'No,' I said, somewhat surprised.

'You've torn ligaments in your left foot and broken your right. How long ago did you do this?'

I counted back in my head. 'Er…ten days ago?'

'You have been walking around for ten days on a broken ankle?' he said in disbelief.

'Yes…I mean no. Well, I didn't know it was broken. I thought I had sprained both ankles.'

'Didn't you feel any pain,' he queried, as if I had made medical history.

'Yes, but I took painkillers,' I replied.

'Which painkillers did you take?' he questioned.

'Ibuprofen.'

'How many? he asked it as if I was going to say a box every half-hour with a shot of brandy to wash them down!

'No more than the recommended dosage–between four and six a day. I only came in because my toes were turning blue.'

'Come,' he said. 'Let me show you.' The nurse helped me off the gurney so that I could see my x-rays. We drew the curtain that had screened me off from the other cubicles. 'Look at this. This is your right foot. Can you see this break?' he said pointing at what looked like a deep crease in the bone. 'And you see this?' he said pointing at a lighter crease. That's what happened when the bone broke and bent backwards, away from the ankle. And you've been walking on *this* for ten days?' he asked again.

'Yes,' I said, as I started to feel quite irresponsible.

'Somebody's watching over you, that's for sure. Your bone has repositioned itself and has started to heal. It looks good, so we don't have to break the bone again to reset it. You're very lucky,' he said. 'I don't see how you could have walked on it for so long. You must have a very high threshold of pain,' he concluded.

'Oh I do–I live with my mother!' I joked. They both laughed. 'No, but seriously she's a great woman. What happens now?' I asked not quite ready to give up the day job.

'We can't allow you to leave without putting that leg in plaster! Six to eight weeks, maybe. You are a strong lady!'

A strong lady? His words resonated. That's not how I saw myself of late. As I waited for a wheelchair so that I could get my leg plastered (I was no longer allowed to walk unaided), I wondered why I had resisted Rudy's advice to go to the hospital in the first place. On reflection, when I fell in the basement, the pain was quite excruciating, yet I took pleasure in hushing everyone up and demonstrating that I was fine, having only needed to take a couple of pain killers and then watching the telly. I suppose I was trying to be strong, trying to be who I used to be. I had grown tired of being this pathetic creature consumed by afflictions. Every day Rudy left for work and every day he came home, something was wrong with me: I was in pain in my heart, my head, my back. I had been spending quality time with God and I was earnestly striving to dispel this image of a woeful and wilted Olivea. Rudy deserved to come home to someone who was smiling from time to time, to someone who could genuinely say, 'I had a good day, how about you?' Dismissing the pain of my ankles, watching my toes change colour and making nothing of it, then driving to the doctor's surgery made me look more as if I was coping and that was a much better message to send. I didn't want to admit to another injury or more discomfort, because I needed to believe that I was back on the road to becoming the woman he married–the one who could cope. And even though I was in denial, it felt better than embracing yet still another ailment. But now my cover was blown and everyone would know that something *else* was wrong with Olivea.

I had to call Sam from church to pick me up, as I negotiated with two crutches and plaster from the knee down to my blue toes. Sam is a student (she had driven me to Birmingham Tribunal in October). She is tall and pear-shaped, with red hair, very fair sun-shy skin and freckles. When she saw me she squeaked, as she often did in youthful effervescence and surprise, as she gave me a big hug that nearly toppled me over and kiss once I was steadied. 'Pastor Livie! What's happened now?' She thought that I had sustained another injury. I got the same reaction from Rudy, Mum and the church on Sunday. All reactions were promptly followed by a good telling-off for not going to the hospital earlier and for thinking I always know best. And I had to take each telling-off because it was better than the alternative. If I had had to admit that, on some level, I had always known that I should have gone to casualty but I didn't want to show any more weakness, it would have invited a level of additional analysis and enquiry from them that I was not ready for yet. I was not ready to discuss openly how long it was taking me to feel well, consistently. I was not ready to share that I sometimes thought I would never get better, despite my faith. Although, since spending more time with God, my temperament was improving, yet I was still being haunted by shade and shadow.

On 15th May, my solicitor forwarded me a settlement offer they had received from the Prison Service solicitors–(Treasury Solicitors or TSol). TSol were offering me the Training and Curriculum Development Manager role I had been made aware of by Beverley Thompson in April! It was still a Manager D grade; however, the promotion to that grade was now a temporary one for 18 months. After this period, there was a possibility that I would revert to my present grade, with no job to go to. I was stunned that they were conditionally offering me the role as part of a settlement to my claims against the Service! This was making less and less sense to me. I couldn't understand how the role had become entwined into the court case. Equally, I couldn't understand why they felt a temporary promotion was going to offer me the stability and confidence I needed to return to work. I rejected the offer, as there didn't seem to be any real incentive to take it. In fact, it seemed somewhat detrimental.

By the end of the week, I managed to reach Paul to tell him that I was in plaster and could not meet with Robin as planned. He said that he would postpone the meeting on my behalf. The call should have ended there, but I was still reeling from the change of tack regarding the REAG role. I had a good old moan.

The weeks that followed found me struggling with depression and the frustration of not being able to move about without a lot of pain. Since being told that my ankle was broken, incredibly, I was suffering more pain than when I thought I had simply sprained it. And the itching inside the cast was just unbearable! I wished everything were at an end: the court case, my illness. I wanted to look back and say, this is what happened, but I'm better now, I'm not there anymore. I resigned myself to taking each day as it came–as to dwell on how I was going to last until January 2008 increased my anxiety and sadness.

Yet, in the midst of this torment, there was the most contrastingly good news. On 30th May, my tutor sent me an email to congratulate me as I had passed my Masters with *distinction* and not only that, I had won *The Aston Prize* for outstanding academic achievement and best overall student performance. As I read the email for the third time, I shouted an emphatic 'Thank you, Jesus!' How amazing, I thought! Me, a Masters with Distinction. And a prize! 'It could only be God!' I exclaimed.

I hopped downstairs on a single crutch to share the news immediately with Mum. She was more excited than I was.

'You see,' she said 'I told you, you would kick hell!' She didn't normally use language like this but she made an exception. 'You can't listen to those people, you know,' she said referring to the Service, 'they will make you feel that you can't do anything, when really they are afraid of you passing them and leaving them behind. Oh, praise God. Oh, thank you, Jesus!'

'It's true–according to them I am lazy, aggressive and not promotion material and on the other hand I am an outstanding Masters graduate,' I gloated. 'Whose perspective am I going to take? Mmmm…I think I'll take the university's, thank you very much.' We were both heady with laughter.

Afterwards, I hopped back upstairs and emailed Rudy. He responded by phone. His joy lifted my heart.

'You deserve it, sweetheart! You've worked so hard. I'm so proud of you.'

He was laughing and talking and laughing.

'Now,' he said, 'all you have to do is rest. Just take it easy and get better. That's all that matters. I love you.'

I was crying again, but it was okay.

In a couple of days it was June, and I realised that I had not heard from Beverley regarding the REAG role. I had sent her an email explaining the offer from TSol, the Prison Service solicitors, and I asked her to explain how the role had become temporary, as that was not what we had originally discussed. I also told her that my results had come through and, along with my distinction grade in a Masters degree, I was to receive another award. I wanted her to know that, in spite of all the controversy surrounding my ability to perform, that I was still achieving to a high standard. I was hoping that she would take that into account, when clarifying the details of the role.

Throughout June, I went through a cycle of resting, rejoicing, relapsing and recovering. I took some steps forward and some back, but I kept stepping. I was starting to feel human again. There was still a high degree of detachment, as if I was somewhere else watching myself go through this, yet I could feel myself improving– or at the very least I was willing myself to.

Beverley responded on 28th June, with an apology for the misunderstanding about the role within her department. She reiterated the terms and conditions in line with the settlement offer, except that the salary that she was referring to was now different from the one in the TSol settlement letter. When I queried it, she replied by telling me that she could not account for where the salary that the solicitors were talking about had come from. It was impossible to know how anything was to be resolved in this atmosphere of chaos.

July came and, with it, the excitement of graduating. On the 11th day, I went to Leicester University with my leg still in plaster accompanied by Mum, Rudy and Paulette. My sister Suzie was due to come but had to pull out at the last minute. Everyone was so proud of me. When they called my name, I hobbled across the stage on one crutch to applause from the crowd and shook hands with the dignitaries. It was an amazing day and immensely gratifying. Damon Buffini received an honorary degree and made an inspirational address. He was introduced as one of the most important men in Britain that you've probably never heard of! In my graduation brochure, he was described as the Managing Partner of Permira, a London-based private equity firm, who also sat on the Prime Minister's National Council for Educational Excellence. The write-up said that he was expected to serve on a new Business Council for Britain, advising the government on all policies affecting business. As a black man, born in Leicester in 1962 to an African American serviceman (who was never a part of his life) and a white British woman, he struck a chord with me as he spoke. And from where I was sitting, I watched his stories about his childhood, his trials and triumphs of life, stir Rudy too. Damon had lived on a council estate; his mother had worked hard in a local hotel and then later on in a pub to make sure he excelled. He went to the Boys' Grammar School in Leicester and did very well academically. This opened doors to St John's College in Cambridge and then onwards to Harvard. Here was a black man who was in our age group, was brought up by his Mum, and didn't have the best of starts. Yet he had made it. Even though he stood out, he never stood down! He was a family man and loved God. This could be us, one day!

After we got home, Mum went for a lie down as it had been a full day for her. Rudy, Paulette and I were still buzzing and a little hungry. We ordered some food and decided to have our own party. We talked about Damon a lot: about the dedication of his mother and how their combined efforts and hard work had paid off, to make him an incredibly powerful man. We wondered, contrary to how he was introduced in the ceremony, if Damon's name would soon be on everyone's lips as champion, leader, the next PM? It wasn't long however, before our discussions turned back to the Prison Service and life in general in Britain.

'Today was brilliant, but it's heartbreaking to think how hard we have to work for things,' said Paulette.

'And even then we're still not accepted.' I said. 'Inclusion and acceptance are interesting concepts in a country that had a national debate about whether or not the next *007* could be blond! BLOND!' I emphasised. 'With *blue* eyes! Imagine that.'

'Oh yeh, didn't they set up websites for and against Daniel Craig as the next James Bond?' Rudy chipped in.

'Yep,' I said. 'If the country was split over a fictional character being blond then what chance for a black man…what chance for a woman? Oh and what about *Doctor Who*?' I added. At this point, both Rudy and Paulette were looking at me as if I had lost my marbles.

'Don't look at me like that. We've been watching *Doctor Who* since we were children, right?'

'R-i-g-h-t.' they both drew out in unison whilst looking at each other as if to confirm that I had really lost it.

'Dr Who has changed faces something like ten times on the BBC across 40 years, yet out of all the faces they could have chosen they have never chosen a black face to play the Doctor. Haven't you ever noticed that? Did you know that, since its debut in 1963 it is the longest running sci-fi TV show in the world?' I could see the realisation dawn on their faces. 'Hmmm—not so crazy after all, am I?'

'Has it been running longer than Star Trek, then?' Rudy asked, as a complete aside to the point I was making.

'Yes,' I said and threw him a look that said, I can't believe you just did that. *'Anyway,'* I emphasised, 'the point I'm making is that the regenerated Doctor has been old, young, short, tall, grey-haired or with a thick, dark brown, curly mop, ever quirky and eccentric but always, always white! Just think,' I continued 'here we have two fantastical stories where the lead character could be whatever was imagined in the mind of the writer, director or producer—yet no one has dared imagine something as simple as another colour. Where do we fit if our colour can't even be imagined in the minds of the…imaginators?'

'Is that even a real word?' Rudy queried in retaliation for the many times I had told him not to make words up.

'It doesn't matter if it is or not…you *know* what I mean. And by the way, how dare you question me…I've got a Masters you know. You don't want to be correcting me,' I said with theatrical airs and graces and a posh English accent.

'TV doesn't reflect us or our history,' said Paulette. 'Everything I know I've had to learn for myself.'

'That's true,' I said. 'The national education curriculum said nothing of our history when we were at school and I don't think much has changed for the kids coming up. The parts we played in two great wars—we don't know who the black veterans are or if they're being looked after. I have never seen them lay a wreath on Remembrance Day, yet thousands died for King, Queen and country. Where are their stories of patriotism and heroism?'

'The historians didn't record much about the sacrifices made by black men and women,' said Rudy. 'We were everywhere, in every time, yet no one would know.'

'They didn't die for medals and ceremony though, did they?' Paulette countered.

'No, but I am certain that they didn't expect to be expunged from our records and forgotten altogether' I replied.

'When I was at school,' said Rudy 'there was no mention of our contribution to the rebuilding of this country after the wars nor was there any word on our positive influence on the culture of the nation over centuries of change. There weren't any references to black literature, black art or black invention.'

'Yeh,' I said in confirmation. 'I think I must have been in my twenties before I found out that a black man working for Thomas Edison invented an electric lamp and the carbon filament for light bulbs. His name was Lewis…Lewis…ah come on, brain…Lewis…Howard Latimer!' I said in triumph. 'There was no mention of him at school. Our white counterparts,' I continued, 'had many an inspiration to shape their fragile futures. And who were we supposed to aspire to be: Shakespeare, Winston Churchill, Florence Nightingale?'

'I found history so boring. There was nothing of us in it.' Rudy said.

'Oh, me too!' I said in agreed reminiscent tedium. 'That *and* geography. They were the first lessons I got myself excused from to do a play or dance production instead. All that heroic storytelling about intrepid explorers like Sir Walter Raleigh, John Hawkins and Francis Drake. Ugh! Now, what would have generated interest and engagement was their involvement in the slave trade.'

'Sir Francis Drake was involved in the slave trade?' Rudy said in total disbelief.

'Oh, I'm sorry, was he a personal friend?' I said mischievously.

'No,' he replied in good humour. 'I just didn't know that.'

'Actually, neither did I until recently,' I admitted.

'We learnt something about it at school, but not much' Paulette offered. 'It was mentioned incidentally, more like a one-liner and very quickly skimmed.'

'Well, you are younger than us,' I reasoned, 'so maybe there was some improvement in your day. I'm learning these things now. It pains me to know that our Eurocentric education left us without a clue as to who we were, where we came from, and what we could be. And the result for many of us is a form of psychological and spiritual genocide. It's like the deliberate and...oh, I don't know um...systematic extermination of our national, political, and...cultural consciousness. And this failure—which looks innocent enough—to mention our many and substantial contributions has resulted in the careful erasure of our collective experiences. '

'Okay...somebody needs a chill pill' Rudy said, lightening the mood.

'I've taken my medication, thank you very much,' I said, with a wry smile, 'but doesn't it make you wonder how long we've been asleep?' They were both nodding.

'I remember my careers advice to this day,' I persisted. 'I had decided that I was going to be a speech therapist. When I told the careers counsellor, she told me that I would be better suited to auxiliary nursing (meaning emptying bedpans) or secretarial work—just like that. She was careful to point out that I was not on the appropriate educational route to facilitate access to my dreams because I hadn't taken biology as a subject. And even when I determined to take the necessary study options the following year, she told me that I was far too late to start a new discipline—and I believed her. It took more than a decade for me to have any semblance of a plan for my life because I couldn't see what there was for me to do.'

'Well, I was told I should be a PE teacher,' Paulette said.

'Please tell me that it wasn't just because you're black!' I replied.

'A PE teacher...you?' Rudy questioned cheekily.

'Shut up you—I wasn't always this size and shape!' Paulette was now a glorious and generous size 18 and equally stunning with every pound she had put on since leaving school. 'And I'll have you know that I was *very* good at sports. I did netball and hockey to county standard. And I had the opportunity to go for England trials for hockey. I ran 100 and 200 metre sprints and I played basketball. So there!' She announced.

'You...' he was laughing hard by this point...'ran?' Rudy said, almost in tears.

'Get lost, you!' Paulette said, having given up on getting anything sensible from Rudy.

Since breaking my ankle, I had not heard much from anyone at work and I was thankful. Robin had proposed to come up to see me; however, I had refused his offer, preferring to meet when I could get about and was in much less pain. Apart from that and the odd call from Paul to check on my well-being, there were no phone calls or emails, no badgering or harassment. This left me with only myself to battle with.

By the time it was August, I at least felt that I had finally had a break from work—nearly a year since being put on special leave. I considered that, perhaps, breaking my ankle had worked in my favour because I experienced some peace for the first time in two years. Perhaps if I had continued in the vein that I was going and the Service continued with its weekly assaults, I might have had a much worse breakdown. It had been four months since I had succumbed to the weight of this ordeal and started taking antidepressants. Most days I woke with thanksgiving to God for blessing me with another day to get well. Most days I then climbed awkwardly out of bed still feeling nothing, my emotions cauterised by the drugs. Without a cup of tea or a glass of juice, I would make my way to the computer to work on my witness statement: version 1, version 2...version 5. It was ever longer and more detailed, as directed by my solicitors. 'You need to explain more fully what happened on the 10th, Olivea,' the solicitor would say. 'You need to explain why the incident on the 25th was so devastating. You need to cross-reference the evidence supporting the incident on the 8th, Olivea.' I revisited the pain and the shame day after day, trying to convey the injustice, the indignity; trying to link incidents to demonstrate an ongoing campaign of harassment. Every glimmer of light from morning prayers was snuffed out by evening. No matter the peace or commitment to do better, by the time I had rehearsed the hurt, line by line, paragraph by desperate paragraph, I was trapped again under thick ice, listlessly floating out to a shore-less sea, immobilised by glacial cold. Depression is a curious thing: a sickness without conscience, defying one's intelligence. It smothers hope and wraps you in shame that has no basis. It makes you watch yourself decline as punishment for crimes unknown: torture for the hell of it. The worst thing is that it is a sickness unshared, though many suffer with it. I find that people will more readily talk about loss of limb than loss of mind. After all, you can't go around telling people that you're mental!

Most days I felt like this, but some days I didn't. Some days, after giving God thanks, I was able to embrace the day. Some days I would open my bedroom door and face the snarling dogs of paranoia and acute anxiety. I would silence their intimidating frenzied barking with an incredibly authoritative, 'Shut up and back off!' I would meet their frothing mouths and densely demonic stares with eyes that were not afraid for a day: eyes that remembered the dogs were not in charge; eyes that knew what it meant to be loved and have direction. Those were good days. It was days like this that I left the ranks of the un-dead and did the most ordinary of things without fear. I would open the mail and pay the bills our funds would allow. I would ring those we owed, yet had no funds to pay, and explain our circumstances. I would venture into town on my crutches, buy a few perishables and face people who had no idea of the turmoil in my life, all without consuming panic. Those were good days, like a solitary full moon in a universe of darkness.

Snarling dogs or not, I spent a lot more quality time with Mum than I had done for a long while. I would get into her electronically adjustable bed, press the button to elevate my head and my legs and then press the massage button. Now this was living! Mum and I spent hours talking and, for the first time ever, we talked at length about her experiences of living in Britain. My Mum is an amazing woman. She brought six of us up virtually on her own, even though she was chronically ill for most of my childhood. We grew up in constant fear of her dying, and so did she. This meant that she had neither the time nor the strength to socialise us or prepare us for a life of racial intolerance. She had barely made peace with the racism she had encountered herself in this country, let alone processed it in a way that would allow her to extrapolate coping strategies for us. As we talked, she shared some of her most vivid memories on arrival as a domestic worker, related to when she saw white people actually looking after their own babies and doing their own shopping. She remembered what they looked like and even how they smelt. She said that white people would wear the same one or two outfits for the whole week without washing them and, by the end of the working week, most of them were 'frownsy!' smelling of sweat, cigarettes and fried food. She couldn't believe that each household didn't have a black person to do their housekeeping for them. She maintained that 'back home' white people didn't do anything for themselves! She recalled how bread was sold without being in a bag and how white people would put the naked loaf under their armpits and walk home. And fish and chips were served in newspapers! All this was very distasteful to Mum. She was at a loss as to how black people were considered dirty when the white people she worked with were not embarrassed to talk about how they would wake up and get dressed in the morning without having a wash! It was a different world.

She recalled a few incidents that never left her. One such account happened a few days after arriving in Britain, when she had become very ill and had to go to hospital. Two nurses were giving her a bed bath and one of them said, 'The way this one (referring to Mum) is looking at me is making my skin crawl.' She said this as if Mum didn't speak English.

Another memory was when she was looking for work. She went to a factory that had just advertised for unskilled labour. Mum said she was the first applicant to arrive the next morning. She was directed to a front office with a hatch for a window. She rapped on it and waited. She heard voices and one, in particular, grow louder on approach to the hatch.

A woman opened it and Mum said, 'She took one look at me and I could see the fright on her face. She just slammed the shutter closed without a word. It was as if she had seen a beast in front of her. I just waited and after a little while, the woman opened the shutter again and said that the position was filled and closed the shutter back. I walked away. Later that day, the friend who told me about the job in the first place before they even advertised it, said that they took a white person on after me.'

Mum eventually found a job working in a laundry where white employees would make jibes about her skin colour or treat her like an idiot by over-pronouncing words to 'help' her understand or make out that they couldn't understand her when she spoke. Once, whilst washing their hands before a break because they handled chemicals, one of the women said. 'At least we can tell when *our* hands are clean–not like Bertha's!' Another time, a group of the same women decided to have a loud discussion in earshot about how Mum ate Kitekat (cat food) for lunch.

One of the most painful memories for her, and now for me, was when Mum was heavily pregnant with me. 'When we used to live at Newcomen Road,' she began, 'and I was pregnant with you, I was coming back from town after picking up a few things and I started to feel very poorly, very bad, and I felt I needed some water. I made it to Winstanley Road and I couldn't go any further. There was a Chemist there then so I went in and asked for a glass of water. You know they told me that they didn't have any! You could see I was heavily pregnant. You could see that I was unwell. I could hardly speak for sickness. They said I could buy some pop. Can you imagine that? A Chemist with no water? Where did they wash their hands after going to the toilet? And everybody knew the English loved their cups of tea–tea that we died to sweeten. But dem feget 'bout dat. They stood there watching me. No one offered me a chair and it wasn't like now when you can buy bottled water. After I caught my breath, I left there. It was hard to think that they would rather let me be ill than let me drink a sip of water out of one of their cups! For me, if I had felt so strongly about a person, I would have given them the water and dashed out the cup afterwards. But I would never, you know...not give them something to drink. That really hurt.'

When I asked her why she didn't fight back or stand up for herself she said that having scarcely arrived that she didn't want to make matters worse and as I considered that the Race Relations Act wasn't enforced until 1976, I was sure that she probably had good reason to feel that way.

Over the days that followed her storytelling, I surfed the net on and off, to see if there was anything in place to protect Mum had she chosen to make a stand. It was an interesting paradigm to see the interplay between authority and subservience that seemed to blight my mother's life. At home, when it came to managing the house and us as children, she was without doubt the boss. Yet when it came to Dad and work, she was quiet and yielding. In between bouts of writing my witness statement and looking for case law to build my case, I would take a break and hobble downstairs to see Mum with whatever interesting stuff I found out about her times. Whatever I found, I would share it and we would talk about it for hours. We were both astonished at how little we knew about the country we were living in. For example, in 1954, I found that the government had sent questionnaires out to labour exchanges because they wanted to find out if it was true that 'coloured' people were unsuitable to work in England due to them being work-shy or poor workers in general. Then, a year later, a working party concluded that, due to 'coloured' people being unsuitable to the rigours of work and employers subsequently being less willing to employ them, that this would most likely result in 'coloured' workers becoming a burden on national assistance (Goulbourne, 1998). As I looked at my current situation as well as all the fuss about immigration, it would seem that in over fifty years not much had changed.

'If they didn't want us to come, then why did they advertise after the war that the streets of England were paved with gold?' Mum said. 'They invited us here to work and do work that they didn't want to do.'

'Well, I think it's a pretty poor show to invite a particular people as workers and then, once they arrive and start contributing, to get nervous about numbers. Then to rationalise that 'coloureds' have become a threat to national resources so that they could rush through immigration legislation which restricted entry is the height of double standards! Plus they flouted the legislation that gave rights of citizenship in the first place.'

'When we came here, we were on our own—there was no one to help and no one cared.'

'Mum, do you remember Enoch Powell?'

'Oh he was a brute of a man, a terrible man. He wanted us all to go home. Oh, that was a terrible time. We weren't safe at all. Those days you just went to work and came straight home. You feared for your life. For the man in the street to hate you was bad, but for government to hate you…no, no—that was very bad.'

I was only four years old when the conservative MP Enoch Powell called for the forced return of all immigrants to their countries of origin and delivered his infamous 'Rivers of Blood' speech. Even though he was sacked, the law continued to evolve in a way that changed our status from citizens to migrants and from migrants to immigrants, whilst offering little protection. As Mum and I talked, we agreed that it was a wonder that she survived and managed to bring us up in such an intimidating and repressive environment. Everything was so uncertain: hardly a place to live, nowhere to worship and no one to trust in the new world, especially the government, their laws and their officials.

I considered that it would be so much easier to move past centuries of injustice, if the dregs of that era were not used as platforms for legislation and policy today. Like the 1968 Commonwealth Immigration Act [6] that I read about, which drew an important distinction between citizens who were 'patrials' i.e. those who possessed identifiable ancestors (parents or grandparents) in the British Isles and were therefore not subject to immigration control, and those who were unable to demonstrate ancestral links. Effectively, this exceptionalist or selective legislation meant that people from Australia, Canada, New Zealand and South Africa or the Old Commonwealth, were allowed to settle in Britain, whilst most citizens from the Caribbean and South Asia, from that point on, were not, thus making the 'patrials' almost exclusively white. I genuinely believe that every person of colour would be in a different place today (emotionally and socially) if elements of disadvantage purely because they are black or brown were not replicated and presented to them daily on a plate.

Mum said she was shocked when she arrived in Britain. She had thought that as a commonwealth *citizen* she'd be accepted with open arms, having responded to national invitations to come and work for queen and country. She didn't know that no one really wanted her here or that they wanted to exploit her for a while and then send her packing! She was unprepared for the racism and, by the time my younger brother and I were born, she hadn't thought through how to prepare us, especially not having been taught herself. She didn't know how to articulate her experiences until we were grown up. As we talked, she expressed sorrow and considered that if she had prepared me better maybe I might have had better skills to avert what was happening to me in the Prison Service.

'Mum,' I said 'you don't have anything to be sorry for. This isn't your fault.' Mum taught us what she knew about, what she understood–hard work. She taught us all to cook, clean and look after ourselves. She showed us how to make ends meet. She taught us to be kind, generous and loving. She taught us to honour God, respect our elders and speak well of others and, most of all, she encouraged us to forgive. Thus, in all matters practical, we were adept. In all matters spiritual, we were informed but in all matters social, we were only partly equipped. We had not learned on our mother's lap that we were living in an unfair and unequal society. Our experiences of racism were not buffered by pre-emptive approaches, crafting skills of stoic resistance and noble purpose. We did not learn, in the privacy and safety of our home, how to deal with taunting and dismissal. When we experienced racism as children and young people, we didn't quite know what it was. What we experienced didn't have a name. We didn't know things were happening to us because we were black–we were just hurt; and when we couldn't make peace with or validate the pain, we got angry. Unlike our parents, we refused to accept the poor treatment that had been formally dished out and, as youth, we were largely unsophisticated and uncoordinated in our resistance.

I suspected that my family was not alone in this. I supposed many young people then, and many now, were never taught how to deal with racism or how to project worth. Instead, they simply got angry and frittered away their future, responding to the ignorance of a few. Mum and I did wonder, though, if things would have been different for many of us, if we had been helped to understand how to cope, how to wait for our moment, how to pursue our goals instead of reacting to the pain inflicted by disadvantage. How many more of us would have made it? How many more of us would have broken the mould?

When I asked Mum what she knew about slavery, she said that she didn't know anything, and this surprised me a great deal.

'But Mum,' I said, 'your grandmother or great grandmother must have been a slave. Didn't anyone talk about it?'

'If they did, it was never in front of us as children. Things were different then. We were not allowed to be in the same room with big people. Adults would not talk about their business in front of us and we wouldn't dare ask them such forward questions. Even when I was big people, I could never ask my mother anything—not even my age! Slavery was never spoken of.'

On 7th August, I was anxious about having to attend a 'Without Prejudice' Counsel-to-Counsel mediation meeting in London. In this meeting, a barrister (who had been instructed by my solicitor) would meet with the TSol barrister to outline my terms. I would have to wait in a separate room for him to come back to me and my solicitor with the outcome of that discussion, and then he would go back to the TSol barrister with my response. This bizarre practice was to go on until we reached agreement about the way forward. That was the 'Counsel-to-Counsel' bit. The 'Without Prejudice' part, despite my solicitor's explanation, had me searching the internet for a better understanding. I found that employers, who are contemplating dismissal of an employee they are in dispute with, will hold meetings on a 'without prejudice' basis, so that they can entertain discussions about dismissal whilst offering to pay a sum of money, if the employee signs a compromise agreement. Essentially, this means that the subject matter of any discussions, and any correspondence resulting from them, cannot then be used as evidence in any ensuing legal proceedings. The whole point is to give both parties the freedom to negotiate without fear that anything that is said might subsequently be used against them.

Rudy was ironing his shirt whilst I put together the papers I thought I might need. 'What outcome are you looking for tomorrow?' he asked.

'Well, it looks as if they want to dismiss me. I'm thinking maybe I should settle,' I replied.

'Why?'

'I am so tired of this. I hate what it's doing to my health and to us. If they offer me a settlement to leave, I will get another job. I could do a PhD. We could use the money to fix the roof. That would be one worry out of the way.'

'But you're not doing this for the money,' he challenged. 'What about proving that racism is operating from the top down? Isn't this what you wanted to do...to help the prisoners?'

'Yes, I know,' I said, slightly irritated that he had to remind me of my cause. 'I'm not as strong as I thought I was. I just want to leave!' I said, defeated.

'Okay, sweetheart. You know I'll stand by you, whatever you decide.'

The following day I was in London and trying to make the best of this insane third-party barrister-to-barrister arrangement. I found the process particularly frustrating as I had difficulty making myself understood to a barrister I had just met and adding sufficient weight to arguments that only he could present. It made for a very long day. The TSol barrister repeatedly offered a package deal comprised of the 18-month REAG role (that I had rejected previously) along with a payment as a final settlement to end my claims. This was difficult because the role was of interest, but not as part of the settlement.

I was torn. Should I push to leave the Service? Should I stay and settle? Should I fight on? I knew God wanted me to stay, but I wanted to leave. Rudy's challenge the night before surfaced in my mind–what about the staff who were experiencing the same sort of treatment? What about the prisoners? Who would speak for them? It was what I had been preaching about for many years–a life beyond self. It was easy for me to give money or open my home to the homeless–something I had watched Mum do and something Rudy and I had done several times in ministry. We had clothed the naked and fed the poor, but this was different. What God was asking of me could not be answered with a second-hand suit or a cup of chicken soup. He wanted me to endure with faith to believe that a judgement in my favour was possible and more important than the money. There needed to be an outcome from this that would genuinely encourage others. It was time for real honesty. Why did I want so badly to settle? Was I thinking purely about myself and the things I could do with the little extra cash, plus a promotion (however fleeting)?

It was lunchtime. I left the room to call Rudy. 'How's it going?' he asked.

I updated him on where we were in the process.

'Have you decided what you are going to do yet?'

'My strongest impulse is still to settle. People *do* settle–sometimes settling is the right thing to do,' I said, as if Rudy needed convincing.

'Isn't that when the terms address the issues though, babes? You know, set the record straight, and provide appropriate redress?' he offered. 'What will *you* get if you settle–what will change for you or anyone?'

There was silence. He broke it with another question. 'Will you be better off if you settle?'

'We'll be able to fix the roof,' I said, rather inadequately.

'Anything else?' I could hear him smiling.

'I guess not–I'd still be vulnerable here; perhaps even more so because their fallback position in the future will always be that my claims were never substantiated and remained as unproven allegations. I wouldn't be able to press for change for me or anyone from that position.'

'Sweetheart, you know I'll stand by you whatever you decide–I've got to go now, babes. I've got a meeting. I'm praying for you.'

I stood in the corridor for the duration of the lunch break. I hardly noticed my surroundings as I made and unmade my mind. When I went back into the room, the Counsel-to-Counsel process began again. I continued to negotiate, because I still needed time to think. The afternoon dragged. Eventually it was 5 pm. We were waiting for the barrister to return with an increased offer, probably the last for the day. That was when I realised that the reason I was wrestling so much was because I had always known what I needed to do. I was just tired and afraid–which in the grand scheme of things was okay. What wasn't okay was if I allowed the fear to stop me from completing my mission to prove that racism was a problem in the Service. After all, something done in fear is no less done! If they had offered me anything that demonstrated an acceptance of the problem and a desire to tackle racism head on, then I could have settled first thing this morning. But they were not interested in fixing the problems, they just wanted this to go away. I couldn't let that happen. I *was* afraid and still wanted to run, but I had to stand my ground, even if the fear never left me.

When the barrister came back, it was with an offer that had increased fourfold since the negotiations began. I turned it down. The barrister cautioned that it was not likely I would get anything similar to the final sum offered by the Prison Service when I got to court, assuming my claims were successful. I told him that a judgement was of more value to me than the settlement offer. I needed a platform for change and the judgement would give me that. I needed to return to a safe working environment and to have confidence that prisoners were being treated fairly. That meant fundamental changes to the way the Service did business—and it only changed when it was proven wrong. So, that's what I needed to do. He then advised that my insurers would be informed that I had rejected a reasonable offer and that this would most likely result in them withdrawing funds to support legal representation. Simply put, from that point onwards, I would be representing myself in court.

I found peace throughout August. By this point in my journey, as much as having to represent myself was not what I wanted, the brief respite facilitated by my broken ankle had given me time to regain some strength. I had got over my little blip of wanting to settle and run for the hills. I was now confident that the Prison Service had discriminated against me on the grounds of my race and that there was sufficient evidence to support that. Whether or not I had enough skill to argue my case was questionable: the experience certainly was not there, yet the will to do it was. I had to do my best and I determined that I would ask no more of myself.

Surprisingly, on 20th August, I received a letter from Robin Wilkinson stating that, during the 'Without Prejudice', meeting I had confirmed that I felt able to return to work. As a result, he summarily decided that my place of work was to change from the college in Rugby to London in the REAG role, temporarily promoted to Manager D. He confirmed that this would be for up to 18 months, after which time I would have to apply for the role through open and fair competition; then, if I was not successful, or the role was not substantiated (no longer funded) that I would revert back to my Manager E grade and salary. I was most put out by his highhanded behaviour. I was still awaiting clarification of the role. Beverley had since agreed to talk to me about it outside of the court case action, acknowledging that she had originally presented it to me as separate to my ongoing concerns with the Service. I hadn't yet met with her, despite attempts on both sides to do so. In the meantime, Robin was using the output from this 'Without Prejudice' meeting to change my base, my reporting line and my role. I wrote to Beverley, copied to Robin, and stated that I felt this move to be insensitive and premature. I wasn't supposed to suffer detriment as a result of anything I said in that meeting–that was the whole point of it being 'without prejudice'!

The next day, 21st August, I received an email from Robin's staff officer to set up a meeting to progress the outstanding grievance dated 31st January and suggesting some dates. As I read the email, I thought, 'It's my birthday, my plaster has not long been taken off (though I was still on crutches) and Rudy is going to take me out for a meal later on.' Determined to not let Robin spoil my day, I switched off my computer and refused to think about anything that wasn't fun. Even though it was just one day–it was *my* day–and I wasn't going to spend it worrying about what Robin wanted.

I spoke to Paul the following day and we talked about the tremendous stress I was under in these meetings. I explained that, apart from the Service being 'seen to be doing', I didn't have any confidence that the proposed meeting with Robin would culminate in anything except more humiliation and harassment for me. He agreed and shared his own misgivings with me, saying that he would respond on my behalf. I was truly grateful for his level of involvement. Paul was unable to make the proposed date in any case, and I made it very clear that I did not want to meet with Robin unrepresented. I wanted Paul there and he was happy to support me.

Paul contacted Robin within the next couple of days and conveyed our conversation. Having attended the meeting in January where agreement couldn't be reached, Paul said that, unless the meeting was going to put my needs above those of the Service, he felt he would be playing a part in victimising me further and didn't want to be party to that. He said that he didn't feel comfortable attending a meeting that was designed purely to seek to change my mind about what I felt I needed to regain my confidence. He then confirmed his next available date as 13th September as an alternative. I was very happy with his response, because I had grown weary of these meetings, as they left me physically and emotionally drained and no farther forward. I was especially thankful, because someone was speaking up for me in a way that I was sure they would take notice of.

On 23rd August, I received a call from an old friend to wish me a belated happy birthday. Lascelles and I had known each other since childhood. He is not unlike the late Luther Vandross in many ways. He plays the keyboards, writes music and has the most incredible velvet voice. He is now the headmaster at a school in London. I was out in the town centre when my mobile rang.

'Where are you?' he said without a greeting.

'Lascelles?' I queried.

'Why aren't you at home?'

'Where are you?' I asked in return.

'I'm outside your house!' he announced.

'Really? Don't move. Well, I'm still on crutches, but I'll be there as soon as I can!'

It was lovely to see him; it had been at least two years since we had seen each other and a year since we had last talked. After he had congratulated me on achieving my Masters degree (and telling me that he had no doubts whatsoever that I would pass), it wasn't long before we were talking about the court case.

'Is that still going on?' he asked with surprise.

'Yes, it's really dragging on.'

'I know we talked about it a little the last time, but what specifically happened that led to this?'

I went into detail about my expenses, waiting for MBTI training, the 'Are you accusing me of racism' comment from Sue, together with what I was now calling the 'Mmm factor' as comments made by Di–Medicine, Magic and Marijuana–and so I elaborated.

'I knew you said it was bad,' he began referring to Sue's and Di's comments, 'but this is unbelievable. I cannot believe that in this time and era that kind of mentality still exists–that people still think like that and *say* what they're thinking, without concern that it is inappropriate. And that it goes unchallenged in a society that has supposedly moved on. *And* that she felt the freedom to say that in front of you and be totally at ease that it wouldn't be challenged.'

'This is what I've had to deal with all these months. Incredible isn't it?'

'From what you're telling me, these people were meant to model and demonstrate the inappropriateness of stereotypes?' he shrewdly queried and answered at the same time. 'And as to her reference about you being aggressive, if she had any inkling as to who you are as a person, she would know that you would never have dignified her expectations with a show of anything remotely stereotypical. You would never have given her that kind of satisfaction. In fact, even if she didn't know you well, on meeting you, anyone can instantly tell that you're not the kind of person to lose it and shame yourself or give people that type of ammunition to use against you.'

'Yes, that's what I'd like to think,' I countered. 'But because of her, that's how I'm being seen. Certainly, I don't know that anyone has challenged her perception with a "We've never seen Olivea behave like that" or "What you're describing, Sue, is uncharacteristic of Olivea." Her comments have been allowed to define who I am and every meeting I attend I get this feeling that they're just waiting for me to kick off!'

'I'm disappointed,' he continued, 'but not surprised because we know–as black people–that racism hasn't been eradicated; it hasn't diminished; it's gone underground; it's extremely subtle. But because we are more astute, we recognise it for what it is. It's more venomous because of the crafty way they cover it up.'

'Well, I've had real difficulty even raising my grievances, because the forms designed by the Service prompt you to record a single incident as if that's the only way racism occurs. There was no way to group a series of experiences or events together that you felt were tantamount to racism. The law is the same. It kind of herds you towards recording a single event and then that event is measured as either discriminatory or not. And we know that, especially when racism is subtle, it's most likely a number of things that you connect that form the overall picture of discrimination.'

'So what are you going to do?'

'My best,' I said, shrugging my shoulders.

'It's everywhere and it's happening all the time,' he said. 'Not long ago an inspector came to my school. She had called to arrange the inspection, she was warm on the phone, and her emails were warm and friendly. When I met her–I can't explain it. When I introduced myself, I got *that* look. You know...the one that says "Oh I didn't realise you were black!" Her perception of my school and me changed immediately. I'll never forget it; she made this really inappropriate comment as the inspection got under way. "You've got to make sure that the Indians know what they're doing!" And when I asked her what she meant, she said, "You can't have too many chiefs and not enough Indians." Then, during the feedback regarding one of the initiatives that we had not long started, her assessment of that was, "Oh, that's a bit Irish!" Livie, I thought this woman can't know what she is doing!'

As I listened, my mouth fell open. I closed it and then it fell open again.

'Then the parents. That's another ballgame altogether,' he said on a roll. 'You work twice as hard as any white person to get where you are and then no one wants you to tell them anything about their kids. White parents treat you as if you got where you are by token. Whenever I meet them for the first time, again there's this look as if to say "you can't be the Head–what are you doing in this meeting; where's the real headmaster?"'

'Where do you think we fit then–as black professionals in Britain?' I asked.

'Well, my immediate reaction is why "black professionals"? Why do we talk about white middleclass and black professionals as if we don't belong anywhere? You might as well say black with money! Personally, I know I don't fit. I've broken all the rules, so it's harder to accept me. I'm not a black man who got involved with drugs and crime and then made good. I don't have a past that they can drag up in the tabloids when I make it to the top. I'm not a black man that some white person had mercy on and as I climb I'm forever in their debt. I made my own way.'

'Don't you think that makes you a good role model then?'

'That depends on who you talk to. Although black people have a good sense of community, sometimes the cohesion is better in some places than others.'

'You mean some black groups work better together than others?' I qualified.

'Yes…and no. Well, maybe not groups but types.'

I scrunched up my face as a way of conveying that I didn't understand.

'How can I explain it?' he said, standing up and walking towards the window in the lounge. 'Okay, let me give you an example. I had to deal with a black parent who was on the verge of having his kids taken into care. He was so incensed by the advice I gave him that he said that I was just "a nigga in position!" It was as if…because I didn't agree with him and tell him to "tump de social workers dem down when dem com fe de pickney dem,"'–he switched to Patois for greater effect and then back to his virtually accent-free English enunciation–'because I saw another point of view, he felt that I had betrayed him and sided with the white institution.'

'So you get it from both sides?' I said.

'Each side presents its own challenges and you have to fluctuate between the two as well as try to get where you're going. It's hard, because you and I both know that wanting to achieve something in life, wanting to own a house or drive a nice car, does not make you less black. You want to stay true to your roots, because the higher you climb the less acceptance there is up there. In fact, the higher you go, the more obvious your blackness is. You find increasing rejection from white people because their club wasn't created for the likes of you and you're abandoned by your own because they think you've become a white black man. It's difficult…and lonely. Actually now that I think about it, your question about black professionals makes a little more sense now. We are in a league of our own and not by choice.'

As the complexity and impossibility of our situation settled on us both, there was silence for a few seconds. 'Overall,' he concluded, 'I know that I would have less challenge to my decisions from *both* sides if I were a white man. And the darker you are as a black man—the harder you have to work!'

'You think even your complexion plays a part?' I asked tongue in cheek, knowing full well it did.

'Girl, you know that the darker you are, the further away you are from being white. If you're a little black man with brown skin they simply decide from the outset that you won't fit in and they can take you down without too much trouble. But if you're a big blacker man they are instantly threatened and that's when they start colluding and conspiring, looking for anything that will discredit you.'

'And what about if you are a little black woman?' I said.

'Well then—you've got no chance! You likkle,' he returned to the patois vernacular, 'you shart and you black, in a tall white man's world...might has well, head fe de kitchen and fix some yard food fe de master?'

'Yeh...well tanks fe de vote of confidence bredrin!' It was my turn to play with the language. 'But seriously, though, how do you deal with prejudice of this magnitude?'

'Where it directly affects me,' he answered, 'I will directly challenge it. It's not about being aggressive—it's about a firm challenge. For a long time I just used to dismiss the ignorance and I was always conscious about not making people feel uncomfortable. But it's as if that level of accommodation has made them increasingly insensitive around us. Now I think, I'll challenge it—if they're uncomfortable, they might learn something!'

'This is exactly what I have tried to do. But because we are not talking about a single incident, and because it's gone on for so long, it has worn me down,' I confessed. 'I think more deeply about everything, making connections where formally in my mind there were none. I think about slavery and the legacy left to us. I think about what kind of future our children will have and about what we should be doing to help them.'

'I worry too,' he said. 'It's as if our generation of black parents have gone the other way. There was a lot of discipline for us when we were growing up. Now everyone has decided that their parents were too strict and they're not going to inflict the same levels of discipline on their children. There are barely any extended families to speak of; the kids have no boundaries. They have a lot more opportunities than we had. They live in a technologically advanced society, and they are embedded in it, but their emotional well-being and social skills are severely lacking. Most of them are so far removed from their parents' and grandparents' struggles, they can't identify with the need for restraint or sacrifice. Their vision of the world is warped, and the parents hardly recognise the damage caused by the media and allow them to watch anything. I'm not saying parents shouldn't let their kids watch what they want. I'm saying that parents should be *aware* of what their children are watching and listening to. They should be on hand to provide their children with balance and challenge—to say when they see the many stereotypical depictions of black people, that that's not who we really are.'

'Is this what you see in school? That's really depressing.' I said.

'You think I'm exaggerating? Listen, as part of a drug-awareness programme, the children had to draw a picture of what a drug dealer looked like. The learning outcome should have been that a drug dealer could be anyone, so choose your friends wisely—they all without exception, drew a black man! Livie, they see me every day— a black headmaster—and they still think a black man and drugs are synonymous! I genuinely despair.'

We talked for hours, going back and forth about work, church and relationships. We alternated between English and Patois, because sometimes there isn't enough Queen's English to say what we want. Patois (or Patwa) is not bad English. It is connection to places we have never been and history we've never known. It allows for limitless possibilities of liquid poetry and expression. Patois celebrates uniqueness and encourages soul-centred communication. When new words are formed, rounded and full-bodied, lapping at the ears like sea on sand, we have no need of etymologists to identify root and meaning. Our words are universally understood in context, in tone, in emotion. Sometimes they are immediately adopted by all, at other times not used for a generation, then reborn. With island-to-island dialects they are neither pidgin nor broken. Mosaic and buoyant, our language is remembrance and legacy. I have known some resist its use as if it demeans them, exposing a lack of intelligence and breeding. Or worse still, some don't like to use it because they think it confirms that our loyalties and possibly even our identities are split. I don't see why–in the pursuit of wholeness and belonging–I have to choose loyalty to one language or another. Surely I am whole when all the constituent parts of me come together without shame or apology. I think that it is not Patois or Jamic or Creole that demeans us, but rather it is the abandonment of it as something to be ashamed of that shows us as lacking in resolve to preserve what started out as linguistic protest to enslavement. Enough of our history has been buried and lost! As such I will never be ashamed to 'drap two lyrics fe emphasis an' clarity sake!' or even just for fun.

Paulette turned up just when Lascelles was about to make a move to go.

'Bwoy y'goin' live long y'nuh! I was thinking about you the other day and wondering if anyone had heard from you lately.'

As she hadn't seen him for ages, he stayed for another hour. Since he was up for the bank holiday, I invited him back for the weekend because Rudy's family was coming up from London for a barbecue–and to celebrate my degree, my birthday and our July wedding anniversary. He agreed to swing by.

Two days later and we were preparing for the barbecue and the arrival of Rudy's very large and loving family. Although I still fluctuated between feeling good and feeling like a regurgitated breakfast, I was coping better because I had a lot of help around me. The catering team in our church–Emmanuel Ministries–had agreed to do the food. The members of the church had been incredibly supportive. They had helped with the housework, cooked meals and the Eldership took on many of my pastoral responsibilities so that I could rest and get happy. I was very blessed to be surrounded by people who cared so much about me, Rudy and Mum. For the most part, all I had to do was get dressed, which took ages because I didn't feel right in anything.

The barbecue, the weather, the company was fantastic. Everyone had a great time. Lascelles swung by as he had promised and stayed for a short while. Members of the church popped in and out throughout the day. There were party games and dancing. I mostly watched from the sidelines but I enjoyed myself, even though the old me would have been at the centre of all activity—I was just glad to be there and everybody else's enjoyment was enjoyment enough for me.

As the daylight started to give way to the approaching blanket of night, so the exuberance of the family gave way to reflection and deeper thought. Throughout the house and in the garden, small groups had formed deep in conversation about careers, increased gas and electricity prices, church and sport. Karryn, one of Rudy's cousins pulled up a chair next to me on the patio as I sat happily observing everyone. Karryn is a very attractive, tall and graceful woman. Her complexion is a rich caramel colour and I have never seen her without her hazel contact lenses in. They make her look even more exotic. She is what I wanted to be when I was a little girl—striking! She is the Head of Human Resources for a company that runs hostels for young people.

'It's been a great day, hasn't it?' she said, with satisfaction. 'This was just what we needed. I haven't caught up with you all day. How are you coping? Rudy's been keeping us all up to speed. But you know what he's like, it's mostly headlines and I like the details.'

Well rehearsed by now, I shared the details with her and watched the all too familiar responses of shock and disbelief. I know a lot of people from many different backgrounds, faiths and cultures. No matter what we talk about there is always a variation of thought and expression about any given topic—except for when I talk about what has been happening to me in the Prison Service.

'She's mismanaged this situation completely,' Karryn said, referring to Sue. 'She's got issues with you, but where is it coming from? And where the hell did the comment about racism come from? It's evident that she's demonstrating a sensitivity to your colour. The level of unprofessionalism isn't even funny. You have to close meetings off. You can't just get up and walk off. Even if one of you needed a time-out, it should be done respectfully.'

I smiled and nodded and watched the dawning of my situation unfold across her face.

'She…what's her name?' she asked mid-flow.

'Sue,' I responded.

'Sue sowed the seed. You never recover from something like that. Even if you thought her treatment of you had nothing to do with race, her comment pushed you into a corner. Your HR department aren't getting it either. From that point on you should never have been expected to meet with her alone. Even if she wanted to talk about Dolce & Gabbana—someone should be there with you!'

Then she said something that struck a nerve.

'Mind you, you probably make things hard for yourself!'

What did she mean? Was she going to tell me that I had made a rod for my own back? I had asked myself many times if I had brought this on myself. Maybe she was going to show me something about myself that I had not seen before. I braced myself for her comments.

'You're a high-functioning individual. If you were white and high-functioning you would have been an asset. They would have embraced you. But because you are black and high-functioning, you're a threat. They will always think that you're there to expose them. You will always have to prove yourself, and in your bid to do so they will feel threatened with every step you take.'

'You must have the same kind of difficulty?' I questioned.

'Sort of. I think maybe it's a little different in London. Because the population of black people is higher than it is here—maybe that forces them to behave a little better. Although...' she said reflectively, 'people are invariably surprised when I meet them for the first time as the Head of HR. Once I was due to meet this woman I had spoken to on the phone. I came down the stairs leading to our reception area and saw a woman waiting and assumed she was my appointment. She looked up at me and then looked passed me as if she was expecting someone else to walk down behind me. She kept her gaze looking behind me even though I was clearly walking towards her and I knew it was because she was thinking "That can't be Karryn—she's black!"'

'Oh my gosh!' I exclaimed. 'A friend of mine has just told me the same kind of story. The parallels are uncanny.'

The evening drew to a very successful close. Rudy's family took food for the trip home and Rudy was very happy. He has missed his family since moving out of London to live with his country wife and whenever he is able to spend time with them, he always radiates pride at their achievements and growth as individuals. They are a loving and supportive family and Karryn *was* right–this was just what we all needed. Members of the church stayed behind and did the clearing up. They are a faithful crew. As I watched them vacuuming and straightening up the house, I thought a little more about the other things that Karryn had said about my situation. She was also right about me making things hard for myself. I realised that there were periods in my life when I hadn't experienced any difficulties to speak of. The times when I wasn't visibly aspiring turned out to be the most peaceful times in my life: like when I was at secondary school doing CSE exams. Apart from the disparaging comment made by Mr Rowley about the cornflakes box, my school life went without a hitch for as long as I was prepared to coast and leave school unqualified. But the minute I decided to take responsibility for my education–there was trouble.

At 15 years old, after I got my exam results, I was affected enough by failing virtually everything to spur myself into action. I knew that as long as I had gained a CSE 'Grade 1' in any subject that it was equivalent to a 'Grade C' at 'O' Level, which meant I was eligible to take the same subject at 'A' Level. Seeing as I had only secured three subjects at Grade 1–in English Literature, English Language and Drama–I decided to go back to school in September, enrol in the sixth form and do an 'A' level in English. I didn't know it at the time, but this was to be the first fight of my young adult life. On my return to school, Mr Rowley refused my application for the 'A' level English course stating that, educationally, it was too big a leap to make. I understood his reservations. After all, I had made little effort in five years. Yet I did have a flair for and a joy of English, I had reached the minimum standards and I was now committing myself to working harder than I had ever worked before. I had to make an appeal to the Deputy Headmistress, who overturned his decision. But he wasn't finished yet. Mr Rowley convinced the Deputy that I should demonstrate my competence and commitment by sitting the 'O' level English Language retake exam in November. She agreed. This meant that as well as getting to grips with the 'A' level syllabus for English Literature and English Language (and by the time this decision was made, my workload also included 'A' Levels in Sociology and Art), I additionally had to prepare to do an English exam in approximately six weeks! I wasn't given any extra tutelage–no past exam papers so that I would know what to expect. Nor was I able to sit in the classes where others who had narrowly missed passing the exam earlier on in the year were preparing. I was on my own. But it didn't matter because I was sure I could do it. November came and I sat the exam. The results came early the following year and I had achieved a 'Grade B'. I was elated. 'You can put *that* in your pipe and smoke it, Mr Rowley,' I thought (because that's how we used to talk back then). Extremely chuffed, I continued with my studies. Within a few weeks of getting my results, Mr Rowley decided that I now needed to sit the 'O' Level English Literature exam twelve weeks away, in June! When I protested that there wasn't enough time for me to read and understand all the books on the reading list that he smarmily handed to me, as well as all the books I had to read for 'A' Level English Literature, he suggested I attend the after-school exam prep group. They met once a week for extra tutorial sessions that he ran. I didn't have any choice. The same week, I joined a group of approximately ten students who had been reading and studying the books on my list for the last two years. As Mr Rowley posed questions and scenarios from book to book, I struggled to get a sense of what was going on, having only just started to read them. After this first tutorial, I asked the girl I sat next to where she got the study aid booklet I had seen her refer to in session. She directed me to WH Smiths. I went straight there to find out prices and when I got home, I asked Mum for the money to buy them. When June came, I sat the exam. In August, my results came and I had achieved another 'Grade B'. I decided that I wouldn't go back to school in September, because it was evident that they were not going to take my attempts at improving myself seriously. I enrolled at the local college instead, where I successfully continued my studies in English, Sociology and, additionally, Psychology.

 As I sat thinking, I realised that problems had only started to surface in my life the minute I decided I wanted to progress. When I worked in a factory picking and packing items for fashion catalogue order fulfilments or when I worked in a library stacking shelves, I experienced very little difficulty. I was their best girl, acquiescent and loved working overtime. However, the moment I said I wanted a career and advancement, my work life changed and I have had to fight for every step forward from that point on. It seems that when I was stacking shelves, I didn't experience any opposition because I was where I was supposed to be—at the bottom. But, as soon as I started to climb, there were problems that very soon materialised in recognisable patterns. Either I wasn't quite suited to where I was heading—and needed to be told as much to spare me the embarrassment of rejection and failure—or 'issues' about my current performance would mysteriously surface, thus confirming that I wasn't management or senior management material.

All of this thinking triggered something in my head. I remembered reading something and I needed to find it again. I made my way upstairs to the pile of books in the study and started to flick through the pages. Rudy came up shortly afterwards. 'Everybody's gone now. Today was fantastic!' he said beaming with pride. 'What are you doing? You're not going to study now are you?'

'No, no' I said reassuringly. 'Karryn said some stuff downstairs and it reminded me of something...and if I don't find it...it'll bug me all night. Ahh, here it is. I knew I'd seen it!' I briefly summarised the conversation I had had with Karryn about high functioning black people and showed him a passage in Peter Fryer's *Staying Power: The History of Black People in Britain*.

'—read the last paragraph on page 186—the bit highlighted in yellow' I said, eager for his reaction.

He read aloud.

> *...From* [Sir Charles] *Eliot* [Commissioner for East Africa from 1901 to 1904] *came an interesting admission that 'the average Englishman...tolerates a black man who admits his inferiority, and even those who show a good fight and give in; but he cannot tolerate dark colour combined with an intelligence in any way equal to his own.'*

'Well,' Rudy said, 'that about sums everything up doesn't it?'

For the Bank Holiday Monday, Rudy took me to Pitsford reservoir. It was beautiful. We watched people fish, boat and cycle as we took in the breathtaking views. We sat and walked for a couple of hours holding hands and occasionally talking, mostly about the weekend and how much he enjoyed having his family around him. I wanted the court case over for Rudy as much as I wanted it over for myself. The Prison Service had affected the quality of all our lives. We were all being held captive.

Rudy used to come home to a cooked meal, set bath, ironed shirts and a warm bed. Now he rarely came home to any of these things. These were never standards that he insisted were in place: they were my standards. This meant that, when he married me, they were intrinsically part of the package. His dreams were on hold because of me. He had supported me through job changes whilst he stayed where he was so that we had some stability. He never once moaned about the hours and late nights I spent studying for my degree. He had supported me through the internal investigation and preparation for court. He continued to love me through the persecution by the Service and depression. And I knew he would be there for the court hearing, the judgement and a return to work– if there was one. Each step of this journey required my time, energy and focus, leaving him with a shell of a wife and a relationship where the goal posts kept moving. All he wanted was a good wife– and I used to be one. Rudy never complained, yet I could regularly see the strain on his face. Everything Rudy has ever thought about anything is always on his face. He missed his wife. I knew he missed her, yet I was without strength to return her to him. Among everything else I was accused of being, I had now become selfish and self-absorbed.

And of course there was Mum. There was a time when I thought she wouldn't live to see my eighteenth birthday. By God's grace, she was soon to see her eightieth year. My plan had been to spend more time with her, but I had wasted days locked in my study. Even on a good day when I felt well, I had used that time to drive myself to find the information I needed for the degree or the case. Now that my leg was out of plaster, the old pressures had returned; Rudy would be back at work the next day and I would be back in the study. He had lost his wife and Mum had lost another daughter.

Unlike Rudy, she *did* protest, although not directly to me. Her way was to talk about me whilst I was in earshot. For instance, after church on a Sunday in response to someone suggesting that it must be great to live with her daughter, I would hear her say, 'Yes, we live in the same house, but sometimes I don't see her for days.' And she was right. Wrestling with depression and the compulsion to be alone, along with the mania of court case preparation, barely left me a moment to watch *Diagnosis Murder* with her. Neither Rudy nor Mum had signed up to this. I was not the easiest person to live with at best. I was fussy, critical and particular, outspoken, opinionated and never satisfied with less than perfection. The things they loved about me also drove them crazy. My mind was active and my outlook positive and I always had big, big dreams. Now I was in need of constant encouragement, holding and consoling. I was a drain on the people I loved the most.

I stopped dead in my tracks. I turned to Rudy and looked straight into his eyes. They are the deepest pools of delight I have ever seen. I reached up on my toes to mitigate the difference in height and kissed him deeply. Then I held him tightly. As I let go, he said, 'What was that for?'

'Because you're the best and I'm a pain. I appreciate everything you have done and are doing for me. Even though I feel consumed by this mess, I've got to find time to tell you that I love you and that I think you're amazing!'

When we got home, I went to Mum's room and told her the same things.

Paul and I were to meet with Robin on 13th September; but just two days before that was supposed to happen Robin sent a letter to say that he couldn't make it. He reiterated that the purpose of the meeting when we next agreed a date would be to discuss the grievance dated 31st January. He went on to offer a further two dates to meet. Overall, I was quite disturbed by this letter. In it, he had suggested that, instead of waiting for Paul's availability for the newly proposed dates, I found either a union rep or a colleague to accompany me. That was when I noticed that Paul had not been copied in on the letter. I left messages for Paul to call me urgently as I set about drafting a response to Robin.

Robin had opened his letter by cataloguing all the steps he had taken to meet me from the time he realised that I wanted a formal response to the grievance. It read as if he was implying that *I* was avoiding him. I was upset by his tone and the way he listed and dated all his efforts as if it had cost him something. I knew that I was not one of his priorities, yet he felt this need to draw attention to his superficial engagement with my case. I had made my complaint to him in January. He hadn't made himself available to meet until April and then he hadn't given me enough time to find someone to accompany me. *He* was the one who had wasted the time. And now he was trying to make out that he had made a concerted effort to help me, and was additionally implying that there was resistance on my part. What he had failed to recognise was that any resistance was in relation to having another *pointless* meeting and that, if the format or rationale to meet hadn't changed, then we would be doing the same dance around the issues. I couldn't understand how he couldn't see why I wouldn't want another meeting like the one I had had in January.

As I wrote, I made him aware that I had spoken to Paul since our last correspondence and that he had expressed deep concerns about the purpose of the proposed meeting, along with the impact it might have on me. I explained that, as much as both Paul and I were aware that the proposed meeting was to progress the grievance raised in January, it very much seemed to me that the real purpose didn't go much beyond the need to observe the protocol of having the meeting. I raised a number of points to include my dissatisfaction with his refusal to formally investigate and consolidate my outstanding complaints.

As I took time to construct my response, I wondered when the political posturing was going to end. I was so tired of this pretence, this constant chipping away at my resolve. It was as if each communication and meeting was designed to redefine me, sculpting fear, suspicion, sanctioning paranoia and stripping away my individuality. Every encounter was trying to stamp me down and crush me until I no longer resembled Olivea the optimist, Olivea the secure—their goal being to make me more palatable to the Service. They didn't want the character and depth that had been forged by being black, making my mark and resisting oppression.

They didn't want the inevitability of varied viewpoints and different approaches. They wanted to pestle-and-mortar me down until I was nothing under the skin– just black enough to tick the boxes and meet the quotas with nothing underneath but the colour of drones. The colour of see nothing, say nothing–have nothing, be nothing! In retrospect, I should have known how this was going to turn out from my earliest days at Leicester prison. In my first senior management meeting, the governor had welcomed me and remarked that he was especially pleased about my arrival because it brought the prison that much closer to the BME staff recruitment target!

I went on to remind Robin that I had been tormented by insensitive and short-sighted treatment for over two years, all compounded by delay tactics and red tape, and that I had tried to convey my distress and distrust in meeting after meeting. I argued that, whilst I didn't advocate breaching protocol, I thought something should be said about the number of times I had had to meet without resolution and about how traumatic it had been for me each time.

I tried to be as thorough as possible, because I was tired of the games. My letter continued with reference to Paul's concerns. I registered surprise and disappointment at what seemed to be a very blatant discounting of Paul's several years of expertise specifically dealing with BME staff complaints. I reminded Robin that Paul was employed by the Service as the interface between BME staff and management and had key responsibilities to give advice and guide management through the minefield of equal opportunity policy, discrimination legislation and employee relations. Furthermore, he was able to contribute expertly to policy, negotiate proposals and worked at the highest levels in the Service. I said that I found it inconceivable that Robin was content simply to sidestep Paul by ignoring his concerns, whilst suggesting that somebody else could accompany me. In fact, I went as far as to ask him if he was suggesting I draw from the pool of staff who sat in our team meeting and allowed racist comments to go unchallenged and who, to this day, have never spoken to me about it or contacted me in over a year! I told him that I could not imagine trying to re-explain to someone new everything I had encountered over the last two years, so that they were sufficiently up to speed to be able to support me in a meeting where I would be outnumbered by him, Stacey and Susanne in terms of recollecting issues from the January meeting. I explained that, were I to exercise this option it would clearly leave me unsupported and that I was saddened he thought this was even viable.

By the time I had reached this point in my letter, I was finding it difficult to disguise my anger and cynicism. As I drew my letter to a close, I expressed that it would have been so refreshing to see that he was willing to broaden his understanding of the debilitating effects of discrimination and to know that he would reflect that understanding in any subsequent meetings.

There! I had emptied myself out. I knew my pain was evident and my letter was raw and without finesse, but I had deduced that the softly, softly approach and diplomacy weren't working. I needed to be understood, and maybe after this letter I would be.

On the same day, I received an email from Paul. He had sent me copies of communications between himself and Robin concerning the proposed grievance meeting. I was quite upset and disheartened by the contents. Robin had reacted to Paul's concerns about endless meetings causing me more harm by saying that he was very disappointed with Paul's views and closed by curtly saying that it was a matter for me who I wished to have accompanying me. It was clear to me that even my representative had become a source of irritation to Robin and he was now being as rude and dismissive with Paul as he was being with me.

In the meantime, I was earnestly preparing for the court case. There were so many terms and phrases to get my head around: prima facie (at first sight), burden of proof, vicarious liability, Vento guidelines, uplifts, actual and hypothetical comparators, tribunal discretion to draw inference, primary facts, the balance of probabilities and overriding objectives! I searched the internet for documents to help me prepare and understand my role and that of the Tribunal. I read the *Employment Tribunal (Constitution and Rule of Procedure) Regulations 2004*. This was a huge file outlining the legal framework Tribunals were to operate within. It covered every aspect of a Tribunal hearing, from the role of the Judge to general powers to manage proceedings. I found the mass of legal terminologies, citations and references to other related acts of legislation overwhelming. Then I tried *Tribunals for Users One System, One Service*, by Sir Andrew Leggatt. Again a large file, this was more of an academic review of the Tribunal system and its effectiveness. Although much easier to read because the English was plainer, it didn't further my understanding of what I needed to do to prepare for my case. Finally, like Goldilocks, I read *Research Series No. 64 Review of Judgments in Race Discrimination Employment Tribunal Cases* by Alison Brown and others. I was relieved to find something that I understood and it helped me prepare—what is more, it was current, having been published in 2006. This report gave me insight to the factors Tribunal Judges considered when they were managing a case and the basis they used for decisions; it explained the different types of discrimination, when and how the law changed, as well as directing me to relevant case law. I had found the right chair to sit on, had eaten my porridge, and was ready to sleep in baby bear's bed!

There were a number of other publications and thematic reports, and I read numerous websites about racial discrimination, all saying the same things, yet few telling me what I needed to know. I often had to read across several sites just to understand a single terminology. I read as much case law as I could get my hands on—which actually was not very much, as many of the cases were only privy to the legal profession and I was often denied access. Repeatedly, I read the case law I could find, trying to understand the language and the contexts. It was a different world and, despite the suggestion that a lay person can do this, I would have fallen foul had I not been able to get a few months support from a solicitor and confer with a solicitor friend called Wayne. His advice was invaluable. I was able to ring him or drop him an email asking him to explain some of the terms and tell me if the case law I intended to rely on was relevant; often it wasn't, so he saved me making a fool of myself. As I searched, I found that there was very little that actually reflected my circumstances and the law seemed incredibly rigid and parochial. Then there were principles that I never quite got to grips with, even by the time I eventually got to the full hearing in January 2008. For example, direct racial discrimination is when a person has been treated less favourably on racial grounds than others in similar circumstances. Although this sounds straightforward enough, I found it very difficult. In order to determine if I had endured less favourable treatment, I needed a comparator. In my naivety, I thought all I needed to do was compare myself with the white people in my team. But it was more complex than that. I didn't understand until I was in court (at the full hearing) that I needed to compare myself with someone who was in the exact same position (or 'thereabouts') if I was to use them as a comparator. So, when I wanted to complain that my allegations were not taken seriously by the Service, I needed to compare myself with another person who had also made similar allegations and who was treated better in that process because they were white! As it happened, in January 2008, I had arrived at court with my simplistic model, and each time I tried to compare myself, the reality was that no one was in a similar situation to me except for when Sue and Stacey had allowed Di Watkins to work on a shared-resource basis and I was not. This then left me with the most confusing part of this process–the use of the hypothetical comparator. When the complainant–that's me–can't find an actual comparator, the Tribunal can use a hypothetical one. I never fully understood this before, during or after the court case. I couldn't see how the panel could look at any one of my scenarios and use a pretend character to test the law without it being completely subjective– like when Sue moved upstairs in our building at Newbold and left me as the only member of staff and the only black person in the building on the ground floor. The panel had to imagine a white person being left on the ground floor alone and the repercussions of that and any comparative treatment, in order to test the law. To this day, I still don't understand this principle.

Thus, September was fraught with episodes of complete bafflement, with brief visitations of clarity, as I continued to build my case. My solicitors had handed everything over to me (since the insurers would no longer pay to retain them) and even though they had done a lot of work, there was much I needed to do and just as much that I didn't understand.

On 8th October, I had to go to see a Prison Service Occupational Health doctor. This appointment had been made by my interim manager, Steve, to assess my capacity to return to work. Once I was seated in front of the doctor, he seemed to think that the appointment had been made because my role had been absorbed by the restructure—I had broken my ankle and he needed to determine if my ankle was fit for the REAG role. I cut straight to the chase. I told him that I was actually not at work due to the stress, anxiety and associated illnesses I was experiencing as a direct result of being a victim of racial discrimination and disadvantage at work. After some discussion, he concluded that my reaction to such a high level of stress was normal and a return to the same environment would result in a relapse.

The next day I sent an email to Steve. I asked him to send me a copy of the Occupational Health report as soon as it was ready. Approximately two weeks later, I got a call from him to say that he had received a faxed copy of the Occupational Health report, which he read to me over the phone. He said they would need to query a comment made in the report about my situation being a 'management' one and not a 'medical' one and that the doctor hadn't answered the question as to whether or not I could return to work between now and the hearing next year. Steve then said that he would send me a copy as soon as the hard copy arrived in the post from the doctor.

After I put the phone down, I looked around my study to see files and paper in piles all around the room. There was so much to do and the Service was trying to bog me down further by getting me back into work so that I couldn't prepare. I decided to leave Steve with his endeavours and set about working more systematically to try to alleviate the ever-present confusion I felt. I had to do a better job with all the paper and requests from TSol, the orders from the Tribunal and the things my solicitor had told me to do at our final handover meeting. I needed to be better organised, so I made an up-to-date to-do list of the main activities that would take me up to Christmas. I recorded things as they came to mind and from the notes that I had made in my final meeting with my solicitors and the directions they had given me.

1. make sure my witness statement answers all points in grounds for resistance expressed by Prison Service

2. produce cast list (main characters and roles of people involved) to court and TSol by 10 Oct 07
3. letter to TSol stating that my solicitors are no longer instructed and that I will be representing myself
4. adhere to new timetable of Case Management Discussion (CMD) instructions
5. include compensation required in witness statement (check with Wayne) Suggestions:
- injury to feelings
- injury to health
- aggravated damages (use Prison Service response to investigation as basis)
- uplift to compensation re: 2004 new regulations @50%? (ask Wayne to explain this bit)
- include difference between salary 2006 & promoted role (had I secured it)
- make references to other test cases e.g. Vento and ???

6. check that the 'list of issues' from solicitors covers all complaints
7. make sure my witness statement is aligned to 'list of issues'
8. do 'schedule of loss' in same format as 'list of issues'(will need this at next CMD 12 Oct)
9. expand on 'ring-fenced' issue when I made application for job (see para. 159 in my witness statement)
10. include GP & Occ. Health reports in witness statement
11. include GP & Occ. Health reports in bundle to TSol
12. draft a list of major events chronologically
13. make sure my witness statement is aligned with list of major events
14. bring witness statement up to date to Oct 07
15. sequentially number all supplementary evidence (emails/letters)
- send to TSol to be paginated & inserted into bundle
- insert own copies into home bundle
16. put full hearing timetable proposal together
17. summing up–check internet for tips
18. witness statement from Paul needed by Nov 23

19. by Christmas prepare list of questions in relation to witness statements for cross examination

STRATEGY FOR CROSS-EXAMINATION OF WITNESSES!

✓ Gain agreement ('You say in your statement that 'x' happened on Tuesday... Is that correct?')

✓ Point out discrepancies ('Yet you say later on in your statement blah blah blah...Doesn't that mean that 'x' couldn't have happened on Tuesday?!')

✓ Then ask why discrepancies exist and pursue a line of questioning that exposes the truth!

20. At next Case Management Discussion, ask for the following:

- witness statements to be taken 'as read' (for the Tribunal to take a couple of days to read the statements first before giving evidence begins)

- permission for me to sum up in writing (explain to Chair that I have never done it before and don't know what it looks like. Ask for TSol to go first. Then ask for a copy of theirs and follow that example the following day?)–contact solicitors to explain this bit again!!! Alternatively speak to Wayne.

- confirmation that all respondents will be attending hearing in Jan 08

All this was in addition to the research that I was doing.

On 12th October, I had to attend another case management discussion at Birmingham Tribunal. The coincidence did not go unnoticed in that it was on 12th October 2005 that I had had that meeting with Sue when she asked me if I was accusing her of racism. That meeting had become the catalyst to this whole nightmare. I wasn't looking forward to this case management discussion because I still didn't understand the process that I was, by now, heavily committed to. During the final meeting with my solicitors, they had talked me through a number of documents, but I was still unclear about several things. I had since rung them back to raise my queries but they had not got back to me, no doubt because they were no longer being paid by the insurers. Can't say I blame them. But this left me with a case management discussion that I was not fully prepared for. I had spoken to Wayne and he seemed to think that I was on the right tracks with regards to the things we talked about. But there were things that I couldn't articulate, and the whole 'you don't know what you don't know' situation really applied to me at this time. This case management meeting was to revolve around the 'list of issues' that had been partially completed by the barrister hired in August for the Counsel-to-Counsel meeting I had attended then. It was all very complex with, to me, the most incoherent legal jargon.

On arrival, and within minutes of beginning the meeting, I was right to be nervous. The TSol barrister started going through my 'list of issues' asking for the Chairperson to strike each item off because they were not 'pleaded issues.' Of course, I had no idea what he meant and had to stop the meeting to disclose my ignorance. The Chairperson for the day decided to check my level of understanding by questioning me about some of the issues listed and when I couldn't explain them even though they supposedly related to my case, she decided to postpone the meeting. I was so grateful when she explained that the 'list of issues' was the document where I was to summarise key events that I felt breached the law. She further explained that it was the document that they (the Tribunal panel) would ultimately refer to when they made their judgements. I had no idea how important the document was until that point. She kindly gave me an extension to revisit the items listed and to make sure they picked up on points that were listed in my original applications. It was then that I realised that, if I had not written something in my application, I could not refer to it as an incident in the 'list of issues'. This was something I did not know. When I had filled in my applications to the Tribunal (June 2005), I had written for the most part what I considered to be the gist of my complaints, expecting that during the hearing I could bring the specifics of my claims out in more detail. I did not realise that if I had not cited a particular incident, I could not then refer to it later, as it would be classed as presenting new information. The horror began to settle as the Chairperson wrapped up the meeting. I had taken care when making my applications, yet it was without this specific knowledge. It was now a distinct possibility that, when I reviewed each of the three applications in order to lift a series of issues on which to base my entire case, that there were pertinent events and information that were never explicitly detailed in any of the applications. As I journeyed home, I began to realise that, with all my preparation and reading and interactions with friends and family for advice, I might have let myself down in the first instance when I originally made my claims. And here is the learning for anyone who might be going through this: anything that you later want to rely on as evidence—every slight, every encounter or comment that you think has breached the law—needs to be in your originating application (ET1). There were things that I had planned to raise once the full hearing was under way in January 2008, like Sue's description of me as aggressive. I had wanted to ask Sue to demonstrate what was aggressive about my behaviour so that I could show how easy it was for her embellish her account. I had hoped to demonstrate that she was not a credible witness and part of the institutional barriers I had to face was that she, as a manager, could say anything and it was taken on face value as the truth. That *was* my plan for 2008. But, because I did not mention her descriptions of me as stereotypical and therefore detrimental in the originating applications, when I finally got to court I was not allowed to ask the questions I had drafted that related to the matter of aggression.

On 25th October, I received an emailed letter from Robin. He apologised that he had not responded sooner to the letter I had sent six weeks ago. His tone was more considered than in his last letter. In this letter he revisited how well he felt previous meetings had gone, but also noted my dissatisfaction with them. He said that that would be sufficient to warrant a simple investigation into the four outstanding issues, in line with *PSO 1300 Investigations*. I wasn't quite sure what he meant and I couldn't understand his preoccupation with the term 'simple investigation' which he had cited some three times. I decided to look up the said PSO on the internet. When I found it, it said under *1.5 Simple Investigation section 1.5.1*:

> *'Managers are encouraged to make greater use of simple investigations where there is no need for a formal investigation or the need is uncertain.'* Under the

section *'Formal Investigation' section 1.6.1* it said, *'A formal investigation will be necessary if, from the findings of a simple investigation or <u>from the outset</u>,* (emphasis added) *it appears that any of the following apply:-*

It is likely that misconduct has occurred which may require formal action under PSO 8460 Conduct and Discipline.

Where there is a specialist element to the investigation...for example, financial impropriety/fraud and sexual or racial harassment or discrimination.

It is for the Commissioning Authority [in this case Robin Wilkinson] *to make a judgment of the seriousness and nature of the incident or allegation in all cases, having examined the information available at the time.'*

My complaints clearly met the criteria for a formal investigation, yet Robin was attempting to deal with them as a simple investigation. I viewed it as another attempt at making the right noises without doing what I had asked for and a breach of policy. I decided to wait to see who the investigating officer would be and whether or not he or she would realise that a simple investigation would not suffice and would indeed be detrimental to me.

By Monday 29th October, I had spent the weekend going over and over Robin's proposal to have a simple investigation. I was really distressed and angry that, after all this time, I was still complaining to people who were pretending to be doing right by me. I called Paul and couldn't hold back my misery. I told him everything I was upset about: from Robin's approach, his proposed content, the number of issues he put forward, to his breach of *PSO 1300*.

On 2nd November, I received another letter from Robin giving me details of the simple investigation. He formally outlined the terms of reference. I called Paul on 6th November to discuss the terms in more detail and I could not help but to complain again. I felt sorry for him having to listen to me moaning, though he was always telling me that it was not a problem. I always felt better afterwards.

When I went through my mail later that day, I noticed the occupational report. I opened it and I took note of the main comments, namely *'she remains vulnerable to relapse of her symptoms'* and *'I think that her psychological symptoms would relapse and prevent a sustained return to work whatever adjustments were offered or made'*.

I was grateful for it because it meant that I didn't have to go back to work until the hearing in January—not that I was getting any peace, with the emails, calls and letters, but at least I was home until then. Or so I thought. Whilst I was doing my admin, I had missed a call from Steve. He wanted me to call him back and when I did, right out of the blue, he asked me if I felt fit enough to return to work. I explained that it was not simply a matter of fitness and that it was a matter of the kind of environment I would be returning to. I told him that I didn't feel comfortable flying in the face of two independent reports by returning to work before my situation had been resolved.

I read him excepts of the report from my doctor, dated 10th May: *'...the most obvious precipitating factor seems to be the ongoing stress at work...I am afraid it would probably be best to obtain an appropriately qualified Occupational Health Physician's assessment...but my own opinion from the GP point of view is that, once the current difficulties have been put behind her I would expect Mrs Ebanks to be able to return to and be able to perform the duties of her post.'*

Steve pressed me again for a response to the question of returning to work.

'I understand that,' he said 'but Shared Services have a duty of care to get you back to work.' Since the restructure, Shared Services were dealing with virtually all human resources activity centrally, as opposed to being dealt with by a personnel manager (like Susanne) on individual sites.

'Shared Services have a duty of care to eliminate the problems that are keeping me at home and remove the things that are causing me harm,' I argued. 'A simple return to work is not a full execution of their duty of care.'

He said he understood my point, but continued to press for an answer.

I went back to the Occupational Health report and read the line, *'her psychological symptoms would relapse and prevent a sustained return to work whatever adjustments were offered or made'*.

'You see…it's clear even to the doctor that adjustments and knee-jerk reactions are not the answer and that substantial change has to be committed to in order to eradicate the abuse I have been exposed to and to put things right.'

We went around in circles until I said plainly that, in light of two independent reports into my health at two different points in time, one in May and one in October, I felt unable to return to work until my circumstances had changed.

His response was, 'That's all I needed to know. Now in view of this particular aspect of the report and your refusal to return to work you need to think carefully about your future and options in the Service. The report hasn't left you in a very good position. You can't be retired medically, there's no provision for you under the DDA (Disability Discrimination Act) and no recommendations to return to work. The report hasn't left you with any real options.'

'Well, I think that what the report has done is to place the responsibility to fix things firmly on the shoulders of the Service and that you should stop looking for a way out of this by trying to secure reports about my mental health. You should put things right.'

'Yes, I'm sure. In any case, the most likely option that will be pursued by Shared Services will be to take you off special leave and put you on sick leave where you'll get up to six months' full pay, and then six months' half pay.'

He closed the conversation by wishing me luck and telling me that he might see me in January at the full hearing.

I was fairly bewildered after the call and shared it with Paul who was equally puzzled.

'Olivea, nothing the Service does surprises me anymore.'

On 23rd November, I received a letter from the consultant appointed to do the simple investigation, requesting a date and time to meet with me and my representative, so I called him to make an appointment.

I continued to busy myself with preparation for the court case. I had to prepare legal papers–further and better particulars–various lists and chronologies and attend further case management discussions, all of which I found incredibly stressful. Half the time I wasn't sure if I was helping or hurting my own cause.

The Prison Service lawyers (Treasury Solicitors or TSol) were sending me stuff, the Tribunal was sending me stuff, and there were papers and files everywhere as I struggled to build my case. On 4th December, TSol sent two boxes by courier of all of the documents they were going to rely on in the hearing. When I opened them, I found reams of paper. They had sent a copy of every email that concerned me over the last few years, dating back to when I worked at HMP Leicester! I made myself a cup of tea and decided to read the papers. Very quickly, I began to come across little notes, contradictions and handwritten sarcastic comments that had been independently recorded or scribbled onto my monthly activity reports and emails since joining the college. I became especially affected when I realised that these notes had then been placed on my file without my knowledge. Had I not been taking the Service to court I would have never known that this information was on my file. From what I could see, this had been happening since 2005 and in each case bar one (failure to make an appointment to see Governor Taylor at HMP Lincoln), the suspicions recorded were never brought to my attention, giving me an opportunity to defend myself or correct any misunderstandings. I felt sure that these comments were evidence of a prevailing perception of me that I was stereotypically untrustworthy and lazy, yet I did not know how to use them as evidence in my case, especially as they were not part of my originating applications. If I wanted to use these comments, they would be seen as new evidence and rejected. Furthermore, the comments did not mention my race, making it a moot point if I wanted to use them as evidence of racial abuse. In addition, I would not be able to prove that Sue or Val did not deface the activity reports of other members of the team, no matter how much I believed that they didn't. I was appalled that, over the years, my managers had formed these opinions and had held them against me and this had subsequently informed the way the college had treated me.

There were notes about the times I had rung in, reasons I had given for being in a certain place at a certain time, recorded suspicions about where I was on certain days, evidence of calls made to individuals to check if I had made particular appointments and contradictions to what I had actually said physically handwritten on the activity reports that I had sent in to Val. For example, where I had listed meetings attended for a given month, Sue or Val had written 'guesstimates' of how long they thought each meeting had lasted, saying things like *'2 hrs* [at] *most'* followed by question marks and exclamation marks. These calculations and attempts at summarising how long each meeting took suggested that either I had not spent that time well or they raised questions as to what I had done with the rest of my time. They wrote comments contradicting my activities. Where I had written on a report under 'Ongoing activities: Profiling and contacting Glen Parva delegates for MBTI & PDP (Personal Development Plans)', they had written *'OE didn't do it–Fran did.'* Where I had recorded the extent of work I had done for a Heads of Personnel programme, citing that I was heavily involved in designing Train the Trainer notes, scenarios, presentation tips, case studies and handouts, they had written that my involvement was only *'as part of* [a] *working party. OE only did* [a] *small part.'* And for all the training that I had delivered at HMP Foston Hall/HMP Sudbury from June to September 2005, they had written '[OE only] *observed! Foston Hall* [was] *set up by SB (Sue Brookes)* [and] *commenced before OE started.* [Delivered by] *SB.'* And, of course, there was a note about Nigel (the Newbold trainer who wanted to skip a promotion grade), where I had cited that I had had a personal development discussion with him and reviewed his application forms to make sure he was presenting himself in the best light, they had written *'following several requests'.* There was even a note about when I had rung in to say that I couldn't attend the Middle Managers meeting in December 2005 because of a fatal accident on the M1 and a note about when I had taken Mum to the Wafarin clinic. I was upset that no real attempt had been made to address these suspicions, assumptions and contradictions and that no one had given me a chance to clear my name. There were no attempts to find rigorous proof of my failings, just an all too familiar acceptance that I was at fault. Moreover, the culprits sought to embarrass me further by revealing these discrepancies in the first instance to the Tribunal, in order to justify treating me unfairly.

It was now painfully apparent to me that I could have never competed with these prevailing stereotypical and negative opinions of me captured on my file. It would have been impossible for any manager reading my file for the first time to see anything positive about me as a person or an employee. It would have taken a very insightful manager to see that there weren't any notes detailing challenge and resolution of suspicions, and I was not blessed to have one of those. It was evident to me that I wasn't paranoid after all, and that I had been harassed and persecuted from the outset.

I was deeply saddened to know that, every time I had dismissed feelings of acute insecurity and distrust of people at the college, I *was* actually being watched to the extent that phone calls into the admin department were recorded and placed on my file without being followed up with me. There had been an undercurrent of falsehood and hypocrisy flowing unchecked from Sue, infecting everyone she encountered concerning me. Even the admin staff were empowered to comment on my whereabouts, my plans and my intentions. It was my belief that this behaviour proved that there was never any intention on the part of my managers to monitor my performance in line with development and advancement: their intention had always been to collate enough evidence to try to discredit me at the appointed time.

As I both looked ahead to the hearing and looked back to the beginning, it was painful to see the deterioration of a decent working environment; I hadn't been treated like a valued member of the team for such a long time. Since joining the college, I had known members of my team to have been off work for any number of reasons—ranging from boyfriends leaving a relationship and emotional breakdowns leading to absences of up to two months. In most cases, I had seen well-wishing emails and had been asked to sign well-wishing cards or contribute to collections for gifts and flowers for team members, which I did willingly. I had been at home for over a year and I hadn't received a single call from a member of my team, or an email from anyone expressing best wishes for a speedy return to work, or a single card or text message. I had been forgotten and I didn't know what I had done to make myself deserving of such negligence and rejection. I hadn't offended anyone to my knowledge; I hadn't been rude or hostile to anyone and I hadn't let anyone down professionally or embarrassed or hurt them. Yet I was the pariah and not even worth a simple phone call from my team to say, 'Hello, we haven't seen you for a while, how are you?'

I had spent most of this journey normalising the things that had happened to me, slow to react, slow to challenge for fear of making too much of nothing. I had expended so much effort to see another point of view and spent an inordinate amount of time trying to see my bosses, my peers and this organisation from different perspectives other than racist. Why? Why did I try so hard to see a different truth when no one thought twice about the stereotypical 'truths' they held about me wedded to what they saw as stereotypical behaviour? As I looked at each box containing over one thousand pages sent to me by TSol, I recalled how Sue's first response to me when challenged was to consider me manipulative enough to use racism as my 'get out of jail card'. Stacey compounded this by denying me my rights because she considered me unreasonable and unrealistic. Then, after being publicly shamed by Di, the team's response was to abandon me.

By the time Rudy came home, I was a wreck again. He came in and took one look at me trying to make up files and sort paper and said, 'What's wrong?'

'I don't think I can do this! I…I don't know what I'm doing!'

'Did something happen today?'

'Look at all this stuff they've sent me. Look at what they *really* think about me. It's one thing having them panic and talk about poor performance when they're faced with court action, but look at these.' I handed him some of the notes and the activity reports that they had defaced. As he read them his countenance fell, and I could see the hurt on his face too and that hurt me even more.

'See? How am I supposed to fight this? This is proof that they have never accepted me. I have spent months looking for case law that can help me and there is little to nothing there. I thought the law was supposed to help me, but it doesn't. It's like using an old vacuum cleaner that makes a lot of noise without picking anything up bar a few obvious bits of dirt which clank loudly as they are sucked up the tubing. Everything else, even though it's visible to the naked eye, is left on the carpet for you to follow on afterwards, picking it up manually. It's just wasted effort!' My arms were flailing and I was talking to him as if he was the enemy.

'Babes, I know this is hard and I wish I could do more to help you, but you need to calm down.'

'Can we just go somewhere?' I said, defeated. 'It's not as if we belong here. No matter how hard we try, we'll never be accepted. There'll always be some plan, some scheme to get us out. We'll only ever be almost British.'

'You're not almost anything!' Rudy said firmly. 'The Bible tells us that we are more than conquerors—*more* than! You weren't put on this planet to be British—almost or otherwise. You're here for far greater than that!'

His clarity was both a reprimand and a release. Rudy often didn't have much to say, preferring to listen, yet when he did speak he was full of profound insight.

Looking at the empty cup beside me, he said, 'Shall I make you another cup of tea?'

'Yes please,' I said, somewhat embarrassed.

As I waited for his return, I knew he was right. Being more British was never a goal of mine, but I suppose when the reality that I'd never be British enough hit me, that's when it became a consideration. The call on my life is far greater. From the time I invited Christ into my life, I had an expectation to be all he wanted me to be, all that I could be—*that* is my goal. I had no control over where I was born but to be the best, wherever I am, *is* my choice. Before this ordeal, I had never considered just how British I was and now I never will again, because what matters is just how 'Olivea' I am.

I tried to rest over the Christmas period, though it was difficult to put the court case out of my mind completely. I had prepared as much as I could. I also decided to wean myself off the antidepressants. They had helped inasmuch as they stopped me from feeling, but that's no way to live. I had been taking them for eight months and my doctor had wanted to wean me off earlier, but I was too afraid of relapsing. Yet I had to consider the long-term effects and I didn't want to become dependent on them. It was time to stop. I was grateful that God had prevented me from completely crossing over to the darkness that few return from whole. Though depression and self-loathing still beckoned, their siren song was more distant and less compelling. It was through listening to them in the first place that I had crashed and burned in April, and the wreckage had smouldered for many months. I went to church from Sunday to Sunday, feeling nothing. After some wallowing in self-pity, God's words touched my heart and moved me to pray and talk to him constantly. He showed me that I could not trust my feelings—they were too erratic, and being subject to them made me unstable. As much as I wanted to be temperate in the midst of adversity, to offer a perfect example of how to cope when faced with the racist behaviour of others, giving in to my feelings of insecurity made me the opposite. For months, I was more like a child lost in the dark and was sick with fear—heart pounding, breathing shallow, hands grasping and feet shuffling. I was repeatedly afraid of what I might do, afraid of what might be done to me and, most of all, angry that any of this was happening at all. As much as I understood that anyone who has encountered any form of racism in Britain would experience a range of negative emotion, I was nonetheless disarmed and disappointed by the intensity and force of the emotion that I felt. I was also dismayed at the speed with which I went from someone who was balanced, resilient and objective, to someone who felt rage with no outlet: a rage that caught me off guard and caused me to implode. I felt emotions so hot over the tiniest things that they made me ashamed to have entertained them even for a moment. I watched myself free-fall from the height of being able to confidently give any terrain in life a reasonable challenge—empowered by the word of God to wrestle principalities and powers—plummeting to depths of unpredictable thought processes and depression, with disabling pain and a diminished capacity to cope with daily life. This was a very new place for me. Unable to pray and unable to sleep, I even found myself considering John Calhoun's argument that like every slave—and by *slave* I know he meant African and black, for in their minds slavery and blackness were intertwined—I was 'incapable of self-care and [had indeed sunk] into lunacy under the burden of freedom'. Was he, and others like him, right? Was it 'a mercy to give [me]…guardianship and protection from mental death' by forcing me to accept a paradigm built on exploitation and baseness, disguised as help? Should I have recognised attempts to keep me in my place, as rescue? If so, then I had brought this madness on myself by resisting the outstretched arm of my managers, whose only crime was to save me from the burden of freedom to chart my own course. Like the prisoners I had cared for, who were 'excused' from the encumbrances of looking after their families and the stress of paying mortgages or holding down a job, I was being similarly 'excused' from the perils of promotion and the yoke of aspiration. Had I failed to understand that my managers' concerted resolve to find evidence of poor performance as I did my job and devalue me in the process, was actually for my own good—cruel to be kind as the saying goes?

I had spent nearly two years resisting the compulsion to surrender fully to depression, and then in April a tornado had swept me up like Dorothy from the *Wizard of Oz* and abandoned me in a strange world of contradictions. And, like those characters, I lived a double life for a while, one where I was still counselling and singing and one where I was in tears and without counsel for myself. The rescue for me was not in ruby slippers but rough knees and carpet time on my face before God. I could not allow my double life to judge me, for I was coping in the only way I knew how. Amidst the doubt and burden, I replaced the internal taunts of hypocrisy with the promises, signs and wonders of God: the people around me who never lost faith; the fact that Rudy and I were still afloat and employed in the middle of a deep recession; Mum was still with us; and I was functioning. Some days I got out of bed, some days I didn't, but I had not ceased to function on all levels. I had passed my Masters degree, I was preparing for court (and that took guts and intelligence)—these were signs and wonders confirming that I had not been abandoned by God or the people who loved me. So, each day I gave myself permission to be human, permission to fail and the opportunity to rise again. I continued to pray, often feeling as if nothing was changing. Even so, like only time-lapse filming can reveal on replay, that's when I saw the changes. When I played my life back, I could see the progress, the triumphs and the courage. And this gave me the confidence to walk away from the antidepressants.

The New Year began with the simple investigation. I met the consultant with Paul on 9th January and, after a torturous six hours, the interview was over. Yet, to what end? I thought, as the investigation outcome wouldn't be ready until after the Tribunal hearing had concluded.

Chapter Fifteen

The Awakening

It was Sunday, the day before the court case. I went to church—everyone was energised and confident that God would bring me out of this victoriously. We sang and worshipped with great joy and exuberance. Ronnie, one of the ministers, called me forward during the service. He read Luke 12: 11-12 over me:

> *Now when they bring you to the synagogues and magistrates and authorities, do not worry about how or what you should answer, or what you should say. For the Holy Spirit will teach you in that very hour what you ought to say.*

Then he said a prayer of protection, discernment and wisdom over me. And the church said 'Amen'.

After the service ended, the members came to hug me and tell me that they would be praying for me throughout. Though nervous about what awaited me, I was greatly encouraged and emotionally bolstered.

Paulette, Ronnie and his family stayed for lunch. Mum made a special effort to cook. She had insisted. She put on such a spread–it was like Christmas. There was seasoned chicken, spare ribs and Curry Goat; rice and peas, plantain, potato salad, green salad, roast potatoes, sweet potatoes, Yorkshire puddings and desert! She had been cooking from the night before and had asked the catering team at church to help her. As we tucked into this wonderful meal, I was grateful for her effort and sacrifice. The conversations around the table varied from the faithfulness of God and how he never lets us down even though we fail him constantly, to the court case. Mum decided to share another one of her stories of life in Britain in the 60s.

'One time,' she said, 'I was working at Weetabix. We weren't allowed to eat anything on the factory floor. This woman was chewing gum and when she saw the supervisor coming, she took the gum out of her mouth and put it under the lapel of her overall.

Now, we couldn't take our overalls home; when they were dirty we would throw them into a basket, they would be washed and returned to us. The next week we were all putting our clean overalls on and this same woman, while she was fixing up herself, ran her fingers under her collar and found the chewing gum from the week before! The woman said "Oh! I forgot about that" and threw it into her mouth!'

'Eeewww!' chorused everyone around the table.

Mum was holding her Santa-Clause belly and laughing. She was clearly very satisfied with the reactions generated by her story. She continued, still laughing, 'I thought..."Woman, you naaasty!" He, he, he...whoy!' she exclaimed, holding her head with both hands as if to keep it on her shoulders. 'De ting mek me toes curl up. Imagine! All those dirty overalls together? Then they get cleaned with all kinds of chemicals, and she still tink it was okay fe eat? Whoy...Oh me belly hurtin'!' Her laughter and inability to contain herself was infectious, and before long we were all in tears with her.

As the boisterous laughter subsided, and napkins that had been used to dab watering eyes were returned to their rightful positions on each lap, Mum spoke again. 'The reason I shared this was because, these people thought they were better than me. And for a time you know, I thought they were right. But when I saw who they really were, I thought to myself, "dem nuh betta dan me!"'

'Did you start to think you were better than them? I asked.

'No,' Mum replied contemplatively. 'It made me realise who I was. It took many years to understand that God made me in *his* image. But b'woy wen de knowledge lick me, it sweet me. It made me think, "You're not in a position to devalue me! God didn't make me less than you." It gave me strength. Maybe I didn't fight in the way you are fighting now. But my fight was to resist...feeling less. So when they called me names like "Monkey" and so forth, I knew it wasn't the truth. Instead of looking at the ground in shame or fraid, I would look in their face as if to say, "Yu nuh betta dan me–*you* eat dirty chewing gum!"' Then whilst looking at me, steadfastly she said, 'When you go into that courtroom tomorrow, jus remember, we are equal–nobody in dere is betta dan you...*nobody*!'

After lunch, a few more stories and the washing up, Paulette, Ronnie and his family went home. I made sure an exhausted and satisfied Mum was settled for the evening, then I went upstairs to the study. I checked that I had all my paperwork and then I decided what I was going to wear. Rudy pottered about as he often did when he had a lot on his mind. We would take the train to Birmingham early in the morning. He had wanted to come with me almost every day but I had discouraged him. It didn't make sense to use all his annual leave sitting in a courtroom. I knew his heart was for me and that was enough. Besides, other members of the church had agreed a rota between themselves so that I would have support for as many days as they could manage. I was truly blessed.

Whilst sat on my bed, I read Luke 12 again. I was still very conscious that, not having been through this experience of legal battles and lawyers before, I would need to respond quickly in session. I was therefore very grateful that God was going to teach me 'in that very hour' the things I needed to say.

As I lay on my bed, I wondered why I was doing this, what I had lost and what I hoped to gain. Enduring the process had caused me to question everything I knew to be true. I questioned my God and my faith. Why wouldn't he let me leave the Service? Once I understood that he was building my character, did I epitomise God's love? When cornered and hurt, did I forgive quickly enough? I claimed Jesus to be the centre of my joy but, with the pre-eminence that I had given the Service, could I still legitimately make that claim?

I had questioned my worth. Maybe all these years I'd thought too highly of myself. Maybe this was exactly the coming down to earth I needed. I was aggressive, I was lazy, I was untrustworthy. Maybe *that* was the truth!

I had questioned my sanity. Did every encounter with Sue have racial overtones? How well had I coped? One minute I was rejoicing in the joy of the Lord, the next I was crushed with despair because the Most High God had abandoned me. One day I could make it: that day I was strong. The next day, I didn't even know why I was on this planet or why God loved me, because I had failed and I was a fraud and everybody would soon see me for what I was.

I even questioned where I belonged. I was born here. I love it here. Having travelled to Europe, America and the West Indies, I'm always glad to be home. But if this wasn't home, then where? I hardly see myself reflected in magazines or the media. I have to go to special shops to buy my food, make-up and products for my hair. Then I have to pay special prices for them all because of the special effort it took to get them here. By omission, TV advertisements portray that I don't wash my hair or have turkey at Christmas; I don't wear expensive perfume or drive luxury cars; I don't eat ice cream and don't use sun-care products. It's fascinating to watch a nation loathe my skin yet spend millions and risk cancer to be me for a summer!

It grieved me to look back at my original reasons for joining the Service to see what looked like a complete failure to meet any of my objectives. Yet now, all things considered, it was hardly surprising. When I joined, I was naively colour-blind. I knew I was black and a woman. But I didn't expect to be treated as either. I expected to be treated as a professional, even though my professionalism is informed by everything that I am and have been exposed to in life. My skills were what I expected the Service to respond to. But they didn't respond to my skills, knowledge or experience. They responded to my race and my gender. To them, I was either a black radical or a feminist and actually, I was neither. If I wasn't black or a woman, I would have still wanted to be treated fairly and respectfully. It's not a 'black' thing–it's a 'human being' thing! I had thought the Service wanted to change. I was going to be a part of their endeavours to help prisoners rehabilitate and lead purposeful lives back in their communities. I had failed miserably. My role at the college should have been a pivotal one. I should have been able to influence change at the highest levels to bring innovative approaches to staff development and tackle unjust treatment of others. I couldn't even achieve that for myself! Mum has many old West Indian idioms, but this is one of my favourites: *'You de invite duck fe swim an you nuh have water to wash you back!'* The anglicised version being, 'How are you going to invite a duck to swim when you don't even have enough water to wash yourself with?' And there you have it: with the youthful passion of a forty-something, I thought I could change the world, when I couldn't even secure a meagre morsel of fair treatment for myself! I laughed aloud sardonically. Rudy popped his head round the door.

What are you laughing at? Still amused by Mum's stories?'

'Oh I'm just thinking out loud.' I replied.

Yet my will to do well had not been broken–frayed in places, but still intact. I was still fighting. Tomorrow was my first day and I would get through it, then the next day and the next.

We were up quite early. Neither of us had slept very well. We drove to Northampton, paid and displayed, and waited on the cold dark platform for the train. The commute each day (excluding the drive to Northampton) would take an hour, followed by a 10-minute walk to the court.

We were quiet for most of the journey. I was still in reflective mood and I'm not sure what Rudy was thinking. I didn't ask. The train was quite full and noisy and I didn't want to compete with all the chatter. By the time we reached the first station en route, there was standing room only. It was going to be like this every day for the next three weeks. I didn't relish it at all, but at least boarding at Northampton pretty much guaranteed me a seat.

We arrived in good time and Paulette met us there. We were directed to the claimants' waiting rooms. As we entered, it was already full of very nervous looking people. We found seats and sat down. Again, we were quiet. After nearly an hour, around 9.30, my name was called and we were shown into a small courtroom. It was quite bare: three rows of seats, with a table for me to sit at, and one for the barrister just forward of the rows. There was a small platform where the Tribunal panel would sit raised above us, and on either side of the platform there was a desk for the witness with a Bible on it, and the desk opposite was for the court clerk. The room was cold.

As we waited for the judge, I looked round the room to see senior managers from the Service, out in number to support themselves; there was even a couple brought out of retirement to make up the numbers, plus a barrister and solicitor; then there was me. How much was this costing the taxpayer? I wondered. Then I thought, 'am I really going to take on a qualified legal professional?' But then, what choice did I have? I had to try my best and, no matter the outcome, I had to know that I had done all I knew to do to fix this.

I was amazed that we had arrived at this point. In reality, I never thought we'd get here. Somewhere down the line, I genuinely thought we would settle this; someone would see sense; someone would admit wrongdoing. But here we were–Birmingham Tribunal, 21st January 2008, day one of the hearing. I had so much information to carry I had to buy a new suitcase the day before to haul it all around: four lever-arch files, my list of questions, supplementary information, diary and my Bible.

I was grateful for both Rudy's and Paulette's presence. I knew I wouldn't have the benefit of good company every day, as three weeks is a long time to expect support from working people–yet I was thankful for those who had promised a day here and there. As we sat in the courtroom, the clerk came in and asked us all to rise. Three panel members made up of women (two white and one black) came in and sat down to face us. I immediately wondered which of them would understand my issues. Would the black woman empathise? If she understood something a little better from a cultural perspective, would the judge and the other panel member take her word or would she be overruled? Could they overrule each other? How would the panel see me? They will only get a snapshot of my life and who I am; will it be enough to decide who's telling the truth? I had three weeks to make my case, to share my story and cross-examine my peers and my bosses. I had prepared as best as I could, yet it was hard not to entertain thoughts of failure, having never done this before. I was painfully aware that my ability to articulate successfully this particular brand of racism was in question–and most undoubtedly lacking. After all, racism is carefully woven into the very fabric of British society, forming an overall picture of tolerance and intricate normative patterns that adorn policies and practices, to demonstrate acceptance of us under the pretence of equal and fair treatment. Our eyes are constantly being drawn towards the minority of white people who shockingly practice overt racism, yet little to nothing is shown of the majority who practice covertly. They are often oblivious to the part they play in discrimination, whilst simultaneously being offended by and indignant to the notion that their behaviour is remotely racist. Unlike the law, in many respects racism has changed–rarely blatant, it has mutated into a strain of behaviour resistant to identification and treatment. Then, when the majority are infected and have reconciled themselves with the mutation, the few uninfected become the hunted, the abnormal, the different.

Having spent the last year preparing for this day, I was all too aware of the dearth of test cases for racism and its many forms. There was so little case law that I could draw upon to help me confidently shift the burden of proof from me to the Prison Service and build a comprehensive argument. Yet I had to use this law and say something, however clumsy and unsophisticated: the need to speak out had overshot my insecurities about how I might be perceived or, indeed, misunderstood or whether or not I would succeed.

'Remember the Word, Olivea' I told myself, '...*do not worry about how or what you should answer, or what you should say. For the Holy Spirit will teach you in that very hour what you ought to say.*' I rehearsed the verse in my head over and over. I determined to take each day as it came, to learn and keep learning on a daily basis, and to apply everything I saw. The friends who were coming to court to support me were primed to take notes about what was being said by either the judge or the witnesses. I knew that, during the hearing, the pressure on me would be great and I would miss things. Furthermore, I couldn't cross-examine the witnesses and write down their responses at the same time. I had to focus on listening to what they were saying so that I could follow relevant lines of questioning.

I breathed deeply as Mum's words also resonated in me. Nobody was better than me, I had value, I had worth–and I deserved better than what I was getting. And not only me, but everyone deserved to be treated as if they were worth something. Therefore, my opinion and my experience did count, and I wasn't about to let a few narrow-minded, fearful and unenlightened individuals diminish me. I mattered. It's not right to treat me differently because I'm not white. And it's not right to expect me to keep quiet about it when it happens. That's why I was here.

The morning was going very quickly. The judge outlined her role and the roles of the other panel members. She told me that, because I was unrepresented, she would do her best to enable me and facilitate without taking sides. She said that it was important to help me in order to ensure that I was not at a disadvantage, but was very clear that she would not in turn become my representation. We all went on to agree who would be giving evidence, when and for how long. It had begun; we had officially started the full hearing. How was this going to end? Would I be able to demonstrate that the differential treatment I had experienced was because of my race? Would I survive the fifteen days without breaking down and running away and, if I did survive, what fruit would it yield? I had lasted from 12th October 2005, when Sue unconscionably revealed that she had factored my race into decisions that she made concerning me. I had fought emotional impulses to retaliate in order to behave myself wisely. I had endured the slow death of watching others judge me and withdraw themselves from me, either as a show of support for Sue or as a form of their own survival. What was going to help me go the distance? Was it the hope of that elusive, age-old apology, the simplest and sincerest sorry that will reach all the way back through time to heal wounds centuries old? If the court found that I had been discriminated against on racial grounds and the judgement prompted an apology from Sue—would it be enough? In all this time up until this moment, I had not seen any sign of real understanding on Sue, Val or Stacey's part that I had been treated poorly. And of course I was here because there had been no acceptance from the Service of any wrongdoing on racial grounds or any grounds 'at all'.

For a large chunk of the morning, most of the talking was between the judge, her panel members and the TSol barrister. I started to feel excluded. I did not feel that *they* were excluding me, but it was a combination of my lack of knowledge and the discomfort of being in court that was preventing me from staying connected. Hence, even though they spoke English, I found their language foreign and intimidating. Everything was being filtered through my amplified emotions. I heard the words, but only after fear, apprehension and gut-twisting nerves had taken a big bite, leaving me very little to make sense of. My calm exterior contradicted the internal panic as my eyes flashed between them in ignorance and bewilderment. To stay engaged, I wrote down the terminologies I heard them using with a view to looking them up when I got home. The judge told me not to worry and that she would explain anything that required a response or action from me.

As I watched them talk, the hours passed and I slowly disappeared into my personal amphitheatre where I was both the orator and the audience: empowering to be empowered. I needed a distraction to calm and encourage myself. I stood on my internal soapbox and built my nerve with reason and passion. 'The enmity between black and white is neither original nor eternal. The cycle can be broken.' Wow, that's a good line. Write it down, I instructed myself, you never know, it could come in handy! I continued speechifying. 'I am here make the way ahead clearer for those who follow and at least carve out a shackle-free future for myself—a future with dignity and the confidence to exercise my right to say that what the Service did to me was wrong, it broke the law, and I utilised my right to prove it. I need to live in a future where steps forward are possible...'

As I sat there, speech-making aside, I knew that I *was* representing myself—and others. God's words came back to me: 'This is bigger than you.' I was standing in the gap and I was sure that this was what we all needed to do when our turns came, or else the shackles would remain. 'We must remember,' I continued to write, 'who we were and know who we are. We must rate ourselves first and know that we are capable, and not wait for someone else to do it for us.' (I was feeling better already!) 'We were not enslaved because we were worthless, despite what we've been told. The slave trade lasted as long as it did because it was profitable—*we* were profitable! We were enslaved because we had value, we were productive even under extreme duress, and *we* generated wealth. We were enslaved because we were feared. Slavery is the offspring of fear and a work of cowardice. Slavery removes the risk inherent in any partnership that one party might grow stronger than the other and shift the balance of power to the detriment of the newly overtaken. The beatings and killings, the division and suspicion sown amongst us were to corrupt and break our spirit. They were to ensure that we were never in a position to challenge the established rule. Yet our strength and our power live on. It needs to be declared that we have a great power—to accommodate the infirmities of the weak, to love our enemies and to do good to those who would despitefully use us. All these are signs of a deep and enduring strength. The Service needs to see this strength. I am in court because I have this strength. I am no longer their slave. And I am not afraid. To fight for love, to die for love and to last for love takes a power that we have seen evidence of in black people of old. I am determined that my very presence in the courtroom is to serve as a call for us to return to this indisputable knowledge and stir up the principles that make us a strong and cohesive people. We need to wake up a faith, a vision and community, and remain connected by bonds of fellowship that cannot be broken—no matter the weapon forged; no longer divided by the craftiness of cruel hearts, but looking out for one another and truly becoming our brother's keeper...'

'Mrs Ebanks...Mrs Ebanks?'

'Yes. I'm sorry. Yes?'

'Will you need a full day for your closing argument?'

'Erm...I don't know—I've never done one before. I'm happy to take direction on that.'

'One day should be enough,' the judge offered.

'One day it is then.'

And, with that, it was time for lunch.

Chapter Sixteen

Limits of the Law

On 14th April 2008, with regard to Case No 1304048/2006, Case No 1307055/2006, Case No 1301543/2007, Mrs Olivea Ebanks vs. Her Majesty's Prison Service, the Tribunal's unanimous judgement was that,

1. *the claim of harassment on racial grounds in respect of the incident on 28 March 2006* [where Diane Watkins stated in a team meeting that 'white woman bring medicine' along with references to magic and marijuana in Barbados] *is upheld* [against both Diane Watkins and the Service]

2. *the claim of direct racial discrimination and victimisation arising from the refusal by* [Stacey Tasker and the Service] *to let the claimant work part-time in her post and in a REAG secondment are upheld*

3. *the claim of racial harassment in respect of a comment made by* [Sue Brookes in that she asked the claimant 'are you accusing me of racism?'] *succeeds against Sue Brookes and the Service*

4. *the claim of victimisation on racial grounds in relation to* [Diane Watkins] *ignoring the claimant on 15 Aug 2006 is upheld.*

When I read the judgement, I was pleased that I had won. I was, however, immediately conscious that many of the instances that I had cited in my 'list of issues' (34 in all) in order to demonstrate that the abuse was continual, had been reduced to four rulings. The panel had concluded that I was exposed to a few discrete incidents (where they made findings in my favour) as opposed to an ongoing campaign of harassment. In the final paragraph of the judgement the panel said:

> *Ms Brookes had reasons which were untainted by race, and which we have found were justified, to feel she had to closely performance manage the claimant. The breakdown in the relationship between them occurred because Mrs Ebanks could not see the basis for this type of management and was not able to accept such management*

from somebody for whom she clearly had little personal respect...It came down to a matter of management style. The claimant clearly resented Ms Brookes' way of managing her and came to perceive that this was on the grounds of her race because in her understanding of events, there was no other plausible explanation for such treatment. (Reserved Judgment. Date 14 April 2008 paragraph 302)

Very soon, the questions abounded as to what I had won and even what I had lost.

I returned to work in the disputed REAG role on 28th April 2008, in Pimlico, London. Not much had changed about the offer. In an earlier meeting with Robin Wilkinson and Beverley Thompson (2nd April), I had outlined my reservations about the permanence of the role again. The core component of the job offered, revolved around the inquiry into the murder of Zahid Mubarek and the subsequent recommendations. Most of the work outlined was in relation to an action plan devised to improve prisoner treatment in light of the Mubarek inquiry findings. The resultant action plan was due to be concluded in December (2008). I raised concerns about the legitimacy and shelf-life of a role so intrinsically linked to an action plan that was due to end shortly. I wanted to know what I would be doing when the core components of the job finished along with the Mubarek action plan. I was assured that, although the promotion to Manager D was temporary, the role itself was permanent, as there would be on-going work to improve prisoner treatment after the action plan activity concluded. And so I came back to work knowing that the role would be advertised within 18 months, after which time I would get the opportunity to apply for it, along with others. If I was successful at interview, I would be able to dispense with my temporary status and become a substantive Manager D. I asked the Lord to give me 12 months' safety without any issues in the role so that I could build my skills and confidence again, having been out of work for so long. Going back wasn't ideal, but the country had just entered recession and I needed to make wise choices, not emotional ones. In any case, I felt I was in a stronger position. I would no longer be talking about *allegations* or unproven perceptions—I had a judgement! Even if I had only managed to secure a single ruling, the law had been broken and the Tribunal had recognised as much, so the Service would have to take notice: they would have to make changes.

On my second day back at work, I wrote to Robin. I asked what he would do in light of the judgement against the Service and the senior managers that were implicated. I made specific enquiries as to what steps would be taken to restore me to a congenial working relationship with those members of staff who were found to be culpable.

Robin responded on 6th June 2008:

...I think it is important to confirm...that where the Tribunal have made a finding against the Service, those findings have been accepted and the appropriate action taken...I have already discussed...the lessons to be learnt with Stacey...Stacey has already met with Sue and discussed, in some detail, the findings and criticisms of the Tribunal with her...[and] *Di left the Service some time ago.*

The investigation...into your original complaints [in 2006] *recommended one-to-one discussions with all the people present at the meeting on 28 March. Those meetings took place and...a theatre-based workshop was set up to deliver an awareness session...*

Whilst I understand your concerns about coming into contact with those staff that **you have made complaints against,** *I am very clear that you should be treated as any other employee, irrespective of* **the fact that you have brought claims against the Service.** (Emphasis added) *I expect that any dealings you may have with staff in the HR Directorate to be courteous and professional...*

Nothing had changed! I felt that Robin was getting ready to play games all over again. Apart from a chat with Stacey and a chat with Sue—nothing more was to be done. I struggled with the hypocrisy of working for an organisation that is in the business of enforcing sanctions against offenders, yet refuses to do the same when its own managers break the law. I believe their failure to sanction the perpetrators actually promotes discrimination and sends entirely the wrong message throughout an organisation that principally exists to punish and rehabilitate.

In the beginning, I was, as the saying goes 'bright eyed and bushy tailed'. Then, as a direct result of this ordeal, I lost my trust in the Service, and their response to the judgement did not restore my faith in their will or capacity to care or treat people fairly. As such, returning to work in a different location didn't stop me from feeling pretty vulnerable.

One year on, Beverley Thompson moved on from REAG on secondment. Matt Wotton, her deputy, acted up as Head of group. When this happened, he immediately told me that the core components of my job as Training and Curriculum Development Manager needed to change (under the guise of broadening my skills). I knew my role was to be advertised to allow for open and fair competition, but Matt was talking about changing the role before advertising it, to make it more generic and increase its appeal to a wider recruitment trawl. It was at least another six months before I drafted a new job description that satisfied Matt. He returned it to me several times to broaden. During that time, I busied myself with the varying bits of work he'd given me–bits of work that even he referred to as 'a bit of a hodgepodge'. I felt I knew where all this was heading because Matt had told me at a senior management team 'awayday' (3rd April 2009) that the training and development elements of my role–which equated to approximately 80%–sat better at Newbold Revel, my old haunt. He also told me that, should someone apply for my role (generically redrafted) with 80% policy and ministerial experience and only 20% training acumen, that that person would be a strong candidate, based on the new direction he intended to take the group in. From that point onwards, I came in to work each day wondering if it would be the day that he would tell me that my skills, though suited for where the group was previously heading under Beverley, now failed to match the new programme of work.

It was incredibly hard, watching what I considered to be the cycle of preference begin again in Matt's reign. I remember the Tribunal hearing when Robin was under oath, and how emphatic he was that what I had experienced was limited only to Newbold, an isolated episode and the court had believed him—that's why moving me was supposed to be such a good idea. Yet here I was, with some 100 miles between me and Newbold and, since Beverley's departure, the subtleties in differential treatment were once again prominent in my mind. What I saw looked like my new manager only grooming certain white members of the team, whilst I was being told when I presented the same piece of work repeatedly for inspection, 'Don't worry, Olivea—you'll get there; this is not difficult, it's just a bit tricksy!'

Throughout 2009, Matt continued to find fault in me and cast doubts on my approach to projects, whilst he seemed to be fashioning others in his own likeness. I was so uneasy with what I was experiencing, that I mustered up the courage to ask, as diplomatically as possible, why the major projects were not being shared equally between the SMT and why he spent more time with Chris and Claire in extra one-to-one meetings. I explained that my skills and experience were not being fully utilised in the group and that I felt he viewed my capacity too narrowly. I told him that I was having to source additional work for myself outside of REAG, just to make sure I had enough key projects at the appropriate level to stretch me and demonstrate competence as a Manager D. I outlined my experience and shared the type and scope of projects I had worked on in the past. (The last thing I wanted was to get to the end of the reporting period and find that he did not have enough quality work to appraise because of the way the work had been shared out—I couldn't afford to wait for that to happen!) Matt's response was that it was natural for him to gravitate to people who thought like him and spoke his language. He said that people were more comfortable with people like themselves and confessed that work did sometimes get distributed according to those comfort levels and familiarity [1]. He went on to say that he would consider what other work he could give me to do.

Whilst I don't have an issue with people liking people like themselves—I take exception to people who apportion work in line with those preferences. I believe this to be an abuse of power and discriminatory practice. Matt went on to repeat these sentiments later on in the New Year at the RESPECT conference for BME staff. In response to questions from them about why black staff were consistently unable to secure an 'Exceeded Expectations' appraisal marking (as compared to their white counterparts), he said,

> ...*I think that staff who are doing the marking whether they be white or otherwise are giving out unfair marks. I think that is almost certainly the case...I think my only point is that certainly not all 93% or 94% of those staff have got up in the morning intending to do that...You might take a different view, but my judgement is that we are not setting out as a Service, and white people per se, where they are in positions of line management—are not setting out to do that. It is happening and it is happening for different reasons* [to them being racist]. *One of the reasons I think it is happening is very mundane:* **I think we like people who are like us, and I think as managers, we tend to give out pieces of work to people who are almost like us.** *(emphasis added) So I think a white manager will tend to find that easier and more straightforward—to* [deal] *with white members of staff.* [So] *you'll get to the end of the year and somebody* [will have] *done a lot of high profile work* [whilst] *somebody* [else] *hasn't...* (Transcript of 8th RESPECT Annual National Conference held at Newbold Revel on 27th January 2010. Paragraph 122)

And so, loath to repeat my past experiences of grievances, court cases and depression, I continued to watch Matt pour his experience and praise for 'thinking outside the box' into those he naturally gravitated towards, like fine wine into a carafe. I watched him create platforms for them to excel and raise their profile with the Board. Key pieces of work seemed to be passed automatically to these individuals without appraising team competence or willingness, and this practice ensured that only these like-faced individuals matured and thrived, whilst the rest of us were pushed out of the nest to fend for ourselves!

Sometimes, when the team was discussing new initiatives to take REAG forward or if we were analysing problems as a think tank, when I made suggestions that Matt wasn't comfortable with, he'd respond *to* me whilst looking *at* Chris, one of his chosen, for agreement or confirmation. Matt's blue eyes would lock with another set of blue eyes and the defensive pistons would fire up to reject my contribution. It was the strangest thing to make a point and to have him respond whilst looking squarely at someone else across the table, as if fascinated by his own reflection. I wasn't expecting validation or agreement with everything I had to say, but I was expecting to be treated as if I was still in the room. Except for deliberately leaning into his line of vision, waving and saying 'Hey, I'm over here!', I never quite knew what to do about this bizarre behaviour. In the end, I just took it. After everything I'd been through–I took it! And each time I did this, I felt layers of newly formed confidence being stripped away. He had made it abundantly clear that I didn't think or sound like him. I was a mild irritant. He could tune me out by simply shifting his gaze to another. It is extraordinarily invalidating to work for someone who can hang on every word certain others say and outline the heavens as a career path for them, yet, when they look at you, the very question of the need for your existence is written all over their face. I knew I couldn't stay for much longer.

By the autumn (2009), Matt had reduced REAG in size, like several other departments, to accommodate the efficiency savings the Prison Service needed to make. Yet REAG seemed to suffer in a very blatant way, in that the diversity had visibly been stripped out of the group. It seemed to me that Matt had achieved his dream. He was now able to come into REAG and work predominately with people who looked like him and spoke his language. Some of those affected by the restructure shared their perception about what they saw as very obvious unfair treatment, but they were reluctant to complain formally, believing that it would sound like sour grapes because they were the ones selected for redeployment. Richie and I fought for these individuals during the restructure, even though decisions to redeploy staff had already been agreed within Matt's inner circle. As members of the SMT, Richie and I should have been part of the decision-making process from the outset–but we weren't. When challenged, Matt suggested that it was an oversight and unintentional. I struggled with his explanation. I couldn't understand how the Head of Group, with a core team of only four (office-bound) senior managers could allow the two black managers to be forgotten in discussions about major restructuring in the group—resulting in proposals being sent to the Director General before the forgotten two had had a chance to comment. Not surprisingly, raising the question of fair selection after the fact made us somewhat of an inconvenience. The pair of us fought, knowing full well that we would not be able to influence the decisions that were already in flow, but did so anyway because it was the right thing to do.

On 21st December 2009, I asked Matt why my role had still not been advertised, leaving the year to close without me being able to apply for it. I explained that I didn't understand how he had managed to confirm Claire in post in the summer, as a Prison Service employee and a substantive manager D, whilst I was still waiting. Matt had created a new role for Claire, who was on temporary promotion and on loan to REAG from the Equality and Human Rights Commission (EHRC). Claire had joined REAG a matter of weeks before my arrival in the department. Where she should have returned to her permanent job at the EHRC on completion of the Mubarek action plan, Matt put a business case forward to create an additional and permanent role on the REAG SMT and got permission to recruit for the role from the Director General. When I had read the job description, in my view the role was so specifically tailored that Claire was the only person truly eligible to apply for it. Matt advertised the role and, after a two-tier sift process left Claire as the last applicant standing, he confirmed her in post as a substantive Manager D without an interview. She then resigned from the EHRC and became a Prison Service senior manager. I suppose I shouldn't have cared one way or the other considering I was after all, desperate to put an end to what I felt was renewed differential treatment, but common sense prevailed. I needed to secure my status and salary as a substantive Manager D, even if that meant applying for my current role. Being only temporarily promoted to the grade meant that I could be returned to Manager E at a moment's notice, for any number of reasons. I had seen it done before. If it happened to me now, I would have to start climbing all over again and I couldn't face that. Better to endure the current discomfort, I thought, than to risk walking out in reaction to it, and losing everything I had worked so hard for. At least if I secured my status, I could move on from a permanent senior grade to another job as soon as something better came along. So, despite my feeling that Matt's prejudice was disguised as preference, his regular criticisms and how demeaned I felt, I had worked very hard. My work and projects were on target or were completed ahead of time, with commendations from partners and stakeholders alike, including the college at Newbold! I was doing extra work across departments that I had sourced myself as a consultant on projects that had relevance to the equality agenda. So it was hard for me to understand how Claire's position could be secured whilst I remained vulnerable to demotion. Once I had made Matt aware that he was in breach of the original agreement to advertise the role within 18 months, he was unable to tell me what was taking so long. He was unable to tell me when it would be advertised, and suggested that the delay was due to 'ordinary, everyday mundane things'.

In February 2010, Matt appraised my performance for the year 2009/2010. By this time, I had been told by senior staff at Newbold that the support I had given them was invaluable and had been formally thanked for my guidance on a number of projects. I was especially pleased, because this demonstrated that I had succeeded in the very difficult task of rebuilding damaged relationships. What is more, I had received formal thanks for the support I had given on a project to launch a new qualification for probation officers. And, finally, I was in receipt of a commendation from the EHRC for a national project I had led on for the probation areas. Matt had given it to me as a low-level, short-term piece of work that he had expected to be completed within a matter of weeks. However, once I had begun, unforeseen complexities came to light which made it a sizeable project that created opportunities for me to shine. I produced and followed through on a number of quality measures and national intensive support initiatives that Matt showed some irritation with, because he had never intended the brief to become a project spanning a number of months. Yet I believed that my diligence had paid off when in response to my efforts and that of my small team, the EHRC sent me a personal letter saying,

> ...*Following disappointing progress on this matter from 2005 by* [the National Probation Service] *and then* [the Prison Service], *your work since early last year to ensure effective* [Single Equality] *Schemes across now virtually all of the probation service is a significant achievement.*

This letter drew formal praise from the Director General, the Director of Operations and the Director of Personnel because the Prison Service could now claim national compliance with the regulator in this area. With all this, Matt took the view that he couldn't give me 'Exceeded Expectations' as the top mark for my final year-end assessment. He felt that in the course of the year I could have made more effort to appreciate the way he thought as my manager, to better understand how to handle the Board and the EHRC, as our regulators. To paraphrase, he said that had I emulated him more closely or adopted his thinking style, he would have been less involved in the letter writing and he would have been better able to give me the top marking in recognition that I had fully led on the project. On hearing this I smiled as Matt's words from the RESPECT conference played out in my life. Despite my best efforts, despite others recognising the quality of my work, I had became yet still another example of a black member of staff in the Prison Service who was unable to secure this coveted award of 'Exceeding Expectations'. I was eternally grateful that, by this point, I was working my notice and very excited about starting a new job!

Even though I had competently worked in the REAG role for two years, Matt never advertised it, so I never got an opportunity to apply for it. My last official day with the Prison Service was 4th April 2010. A week later Matt moved on to another government agency, and Claire took his place as Acting Head of REAG.

With all the pain and torment I have experienced in the Prison Service, I have gained much. Rudy and I have learned how to care more for each other, love deeply, and hold to our faith. My dear friends have become dearer still. They have shown themselves to be true and loyal. My Mum, determined as ever to see this through with me, has been an inspiration and my church, Emmanuel Ministries, have been constant in their support and belief that God is faithful. I have made new friends and, of course, God has blessed me with the opportunity to write this book and share my journey.

I have, in addition to all these blessings, learned more fully the power of forgiveness for those who remain unrepentant and for those who escape justice. The Service never apologised for exposing me to racist treatment despite being cited in each ruling as liable. Stacey and Sue never apologised and, as far as I know, Stacey at least remains in a senior and key position within the Service, still heading up the college. I am not sure where Sue went; it is probable that she moved on to another government agency, as it is common practice to recycle managers with 'issues' in this way. Even though they broke the law, no sanctions were imposed as a result of the judgement, and both women initially continued to do their highly paid jobs with impunity. If anything, I was the one viewed with suspicion when I returned to work and suffered disadvantage.

It's fair to say that I was expecting an apology and when I didn't get it my mind ran to thoughts of age-old apologies still not spoken. The power of saying 'sorry' is unprecedented. No legislation and no sanctions can pick the barbs from a heart full of resentment, bitterness and unbridled anger quite so thoroughly as genuinely spoken words of regret to the hurting. True sorrow, true repentance, releases both the victim and the perpetrator. It reaches into the heart and spirit; it allows opposing forces the most coveted of opportunities—to start afresh. Yet no one had the intelligence, courage or humility to say it.

I believe that the power of the apology can have a most incredible disarming quality, yet there is another power—the aforementioned power of forgiveness and the will to forgive the unrepentant! There are those who think that forgiveness is weakness or that it can only be bestowed when sorrow for misdeeds is apparent, but I have learned another way. When we refuse to forgive, we actually surrender *our* power to those who have hurt us. They cause us continued pain without lifting a finger. All they have to do is show up at a party or pass us in the supermarket and we hurt all over again. In January 2007, the thing that hurt me most during the meeting with Robin, Stacey and the ever-silent Susanne, was that no one saw the need to say sorry. It was the principle! I shouldn't have had to even ask for apologies. If you cause people pain—you say sorry: 'them's the rules'! But I heard a saying once: 'hurt people, *hurt* people—whole people, *help* people! If I am to help others—I need to be whole. Whilst I angrily waited for apologies, the Service became more and more intolerant at my carping. Where I was becoming increasingly disillusioned about the time it had taken for the few disingenuous steps towards fair treatment, the Service maintained it didn't know what else I wanted—at least, that was the sense I got from Robin's letter in April 2008. Someone needed to get off this carousel and, in the absence of any other willing parties, it needed to be me, since I was the one most affected.

Waiting for apologies can make us weary; waiting for justice can make us despondent. Though indispensable substances of civilised society, sometimes the wait for both builds unrealistic expectations in us. If they come and are sufficient, we are translated to a place of liberty and healing, but if they do not, the light grows ever dim and our hearts grow slowly cold, manacled by disappointment and unabashed resentment for the unanswered wrong that has been done to us. The right that was once ours becomes engulfed, ultimately in stubborn hate. Apologies and justice make us dependent, and leave us at the mercy of our tormentors. My Dad has never said sorry. He has hurt our family in ways I tell myself he couldn't possibly have known that's what he was doing because if he had, it would have made him inhuman. He left Mum on the day she returned home from hospital after she had had her third heart attack; he left, having gambled us out of our first home and having put us in chronic debt in our new council home, awaiting bailiffs; he left Mum for *several* other women that he was bedding at the same time; he left us fatherless whilst he fathered more children; he left when I was only thirteen and so in need of a Dad. What a waste of my life, my energy and my future to have never got past the pain! I had two choices. Either I could let his abandonment destroy any hope I had of becoming a whole person—I could allow the long bony fingers of rejection to form a chokehold around my neck, squeezing ever tighter until I was dead inside, leaving me as a puppet corpse whose strings were being pulled by bitterness and hatred for the apportioned three score and ten years—or I could let the pain go. I chose the latter. I forgave him. I released him. I put myself out of reach of infection, for I dared not become him. And even though, today, he doesn't have a kind word to say about me, because he has acrimoniously allowed selfishness and the unjustified blame of others to press the life out of his heart—I can say that I bear him no ill will. I love my Dad because hate costs too much! Dad is not an awful person, he's just broken and is only comfortable around brokenness. I don't know who broke him or when, but I do know that he has never forgiven and he has never healed. All this I have learned, not because I am a great person—it's because I understand much better now how forgiveness lends me a positive power to move on. It means that, even if you have hurt me—you don't then get to keep hold of me. I don't have to stick around to see if you get your just deserts and my life isn't burdened by that wait. I do not forgive because I think the Service ignorant of its continuing crimes against black people. As much as its most senior people herald equality for all from the turrets of medieval structure, their inward, bourgeois, guilty pleasure is that they are not prepared to walk away from the privilege of their positions to pay the price for rebalancing the scales. So, I forgive but I do not forget. I remember, with all my strength, the injustice, so that I can recognise it in whatever form it takes as I fight on. For I know it will not simply fade or die a sacrificial, willing death. Those who practice racism in all its forms will not easily give up the power and advantage it grants them. Racism as a symbiotic entity will resist and will cry foul; it will slither on its belly along the dirt floor of politics and climb the whitewashed walls of economic reason, looking for opportunities to remain and justification to exist.

I have grown in other ways. I have discovered, that belief is the most resistant part of me. If I believe that I can do something, even when there are days when insecurities threaten the extremities of that belief, and have me contradicting it with contrary speech and tears, as long as the core remains wrapped in God's words, the belief remains untarnished. It might take me some time to determine a course of action. I may veritably falter whilst I construct my stance, but once formed, I hold fast.

As much as I hated what I went through, I now thank God that some hard knocks, including this one, have honed a realism in me— not to fit, but to do; to prefer and pursue achievement rather than inclusion. Robin's responses on my return in 2008 made it clear the

Service didn't want me to be secure and a part of its elite—which was fine by me. I didn't need polite or tokenistic inclusion, as I have no desire to fit what is already well established and crafted for others and not me. What I wanted was my own path.

I have developed strength enough to make sure I no longer spend myself in the pursuit of assimilation. I have no desire to be 'Matt-like'. I can just as easily direct my energies to simply reaching my potential, furthering my knowledge and investing in my children. I am not about to be limited by the scared and the foolish, seeking approval from the blind and unlearned who for so long have been convinced by their own lies that they do good and are better than anyone who isn't like them. I am not grateful that I was allowed to eke out a predetermined existence, whilst living in fear that if I made too much noise, the little I had would be taken away. I am not afraid anymore. As 2010 unfolds, I absolutely refuse to be satisfied with the crumbs thrown to me by those who would prefer to give me nothing. Rather, I am disposed to reach for the things that are mine, without the guilt that has been conferred on us of old for wanting more. This guilt and fear of speaking up is not mine. It was a passive, aggressive transference projected on me by those who subjugate and rule on the premise that they are divinely entitled to have more than anyone else.

I have grown. I won my court case and, even though I didn't initially get everything I wanted, I won. I took on a major institution and, when it flexed its muscles, I stood my ground. I won! The prize at first seemed small, yet when I consider who I have become and the things I have learned, I am richer this side of the experience. I am no longer silent. I want to remember. I want to talk about the past, today and the future, because there are modern-day implications that need to be discussed. Stepping back is not about dwelling in the past or recrimination, it is about gaining momentum; creating the space necessary for the long-jump into the future. I want to do more because there are others who are hurting, and they have nowhere to turn, and I want to help. Some directly share my experience. My hope is that they will understand the extent of preparation that is necessary if they are to go to Tribunal stage and recognise where the law does not help, especially where white-collar, sophisticated racism plays a major part. The temptation to walk out of a hostile environment never to return, especially when encouraged by family and friends, who say things like, 'Just leave and sue the company!', can be overwhelming. I say exercise some caution and remember that the system, though designed with you in mind, can prove cumbersome and fall short of satisfactory remedy. I do not advise wholehearted adoption of law as sufficient for our needs. It was designed to expose loud-mouthed and uncouth racists—'patriots' who would deny you goods or services because you are black. But for the ones who think themselves liberal, the ones who talk about preference when discharging their professional duties, there is no law, because everything they do has a base note of reasonableness. As a victim, when you get to court and you prove that you have received differential treatment, it is the top note in the proceedings smelling like racism. Your company provides the reasonable explanations for the differential treatment, like middle notes in this courtroom fragrance acting to mask the often unpalatable, first impression of base notes about you being unreliable and not a team player. They cite business needs and financial constraints as justification for treating you a certain way. But then, over time, this defence cleverly leaves an enduring impression of you as a non-achieving, inflexible and ungrateful individual. Thus, you must be blameless in all things! And this is hard: never to be late to a meeting or miss a project deadline. It is human to be imperfect. Yet, as near as perfection as you can be is what is necessary to show this 'reasonable explanation' for what it really is—prejudice—the end of which is unlawful discrimination.

My other concerns still rest with the prisoners. Black men are over represented in the criminal justice system (relative to the general population) [3] and suffer a disproportionate level of unequal treatment. They do not commit more crime than white people do, yet it has been statistically proven that young black people are more likely to be given a custodial sentence, and be sentenced at the higher end of the tariff. [4] Their white equivalents on the other hand, are more likely to get bail, community orders and avoid prison altogether. Although an established fact, outside of statistical measurement in the Prison Service, little is being done to address this effectively and purposefully. Use of force by prison officers in particular on black prisoners is unacceptably disproportionate. The number of racial-incident prisoner complaints has risen by over 50% to 13,323 in 2007-8 (Race Review 2008 p. 69). This number continues to rise each year.[5] The 'reasonable explanation', as quoted in *The Guardian* on 7th February 2010 is that 'reported incidents [have] increased as a result of complaint forms becoming more accessible and confidential.' In the Race Review carried out as a response to the Mubarek Inquiry, black prisoners were reported as 30% more likely than their white counterparts to be on basic regime (the lowest level of privileges), 50% more likely to be in segregation for breaches of good order and 60% more likely to have force used against them (p. 37). These disproportionate outcomes are also on the increase for no known good reason, and all this is happening without the organisation fully accepting that it is institutionally racist and that racism is flowing unimpeded from the highest levels in the organisation. The last figures I was able to obtain showed that, for the period of January 2009 to the reporting period of January 2010, black prisoners were 53% more likely than their white counterparts to be on the basic regime. This is a rise of 23% in just two years. Furthermore, black prisoners are now 55% more likely to be in segregation (a rise of 2%). And, rather horrifyingly, black prisoners when compared to white prisoners are currently 80% more likely to have force used against them for any number of reasons, ranging from failure to comply with instructions to simply 'appearing' threatening! (SMART figures, January 2010) I additionally remain concerned that, despite being reported nationally every year, employees from an ethnic background are still less likely to be promoted to senior grades. With too few black and ethnic staff able to progress to be representative at every level of the organisation, and with black prisoners overwhelmingly likely to be treated unfairly, this imbalance poses a pernicious and dangerous problem. I am raising the alarm. I believe that poor treatment of staff and prisoners is destructive and can only end in tragedy. Someone has to listen, someone has to take note, and I will continue to sound the alarm until someone does. As much as I want to put this behind me, to say that I have done my bit–I can't, because the injustices are ever-present and constantly insisting that something must be done. Change is possible and must come.

I wasn't supposed to make it this far—everything about my education and work-life testifies as much—but I did! And I will continue to defy the odds. I have found that the best retaliation to prejudice and discrimination is success. I must succeed at whatever I do. It is now that I understand why I have to work twice as hard as any white person I know; because I cannot take comfort in the hope I will be treated fairly as a matter of course—there will always be somebody grabbing at my heels. But if I climb higher, I'm harder to reach and, whether they think me British enough or not, they will never be able to doubt my intelligence or discount my contributions.

I am holding to the belief that together as black people in Britain, we can be better than we are right now if we take the blinkers off and wholeheartedly climb out of the mire of disadvantage. We need to expect less from those who should know better and expect more from ourselves. If we would stop looking for rescue, and start looking for opportunities to excel whilst working hard, we would progress further. Entrepreneurialism is like the melanin in our skin: abundant, deliberate, and enduring! When we are successful they will come to us (like they did before), they will seek us out—our votes, our knowledge, our enterprise—and when they arrive we will be better prepared than before, because history has taught us. She has taught us about the ones who will come as soon as we excel—the ones who will brand us inexperienced or unable to sustain momentum in order to justify abuse, theft and nefarious rule. Under the pretext of a higher intelligence, advanced technology and with their deification of money, they will assume the right to divide, dispossess and dominate, leading to carnage that will be hailed as needful and exact—the darkness of their souls never questioned. But today, even though no one wants to talk about how it was even possible (and still is) for such an 'advanced ruling class' to believe that pigmentation or varying levels of melanin in the skin can make a people distinct from the human race, we know the truth! In times past they were too arrogant and deluded to admit that they preferred to steal rather than trade fairly, to kill rather than live alongside and to 'discover' and lay claim to lands rather than visit and respect. We know that the truth is that the supposedly scientific thinkers and great philosophical minds, who continue to peddle their lies, seek only to perpetuate a racist society to their own advantage as the privileged. Therefore, we have learnt—and continue to learn—that we cannot allow or be party to the raping and looting of our ideas and endeavours and the stripping of our people.

I call to remembrance that although we were deliberately scattered all over the world to keep us disoriented and weak, we still resisted the oppression of slavery, the power of the whip, the law and organised religion across continents and centuries—as one people! We rose up in songs that crossed oceans and blood that stained the earth, preferring to die free, than to live bound. Slave owners thought that they had all the power with the might of the government, the military and private enterprise behind them—and yet *we* won! The Prison Service thought they had all the power with the might of the institution, a corporate legal firm and public money at their disposal—and yet *I* won! How did this happen? These things happened because though despised and dismissed, we had faith to believe that there was greatness in us and greatness waiting for us.

We must never again allow ourselves to be tricked and conquered, only to wait for centuries to have the carefully guarded facility to fight for equal rights graciously bestowed upon us. We must succeed in our ventures, with the learning securely engrafted to our spirits. We need to share our experiences, share our tears and share our resolve with our children. We must pool our resources and open our homes in the way we used to and get the young people off the streets to teach them about who they really are; show them what love and belonging truly looks like and take the lid off the future. We need to stop waiting for the various local councils to find money for a youth club or the government to build Titan prisons. Our children are our responsibility and their future is our today. Together we will do more and go further. Soon our voices will be too reverberant to ignore, our love and excellence will be too brilliant to be obscured behind grievance procedures, statistical interpretations, courtroom doors or prison bars.

Endnotes

1   *Transcript of 8th RESPECT Annual National Conference* held at Newbold Revel on 27th January 2010. Comments by Matt Wotton during a Q&A session in response to comments from the floor that black staff consistently get poorer appraisal markings than their white counterparts because of racism in the Service: '...I think there is power and usefulness in terms of the diagnosis [being racism]. I just don't think it moves us on in terms of the solution...I think there is an issue about tactics, I think there is an issue about labelling. I think to say that white people are more comfortable–anybody is more comfortable with people who are like them–is an uncontroversial statement, and I don't regard that as racism. We have a difference of opinion and I have a difference of opinion with most of the audience on that.' (Paragraph 127)

2   *The Word.* RESPECT Newsletter Spring 2010 Matt Wotton's Message: 'I am grateful to have the chance to clarify some of the comments I made at the recent [RESPECT] annual national conference which seemed to have generated some potential for misunderstanding. A number of members have approached me since the event to discuss the issue and I am glad to have the opportunity to do so with our wider audience.

At the event I talked about the progress we have made in largely eliminating the most blatant forms of racism. I spoke also about what more there is to do and part of that was understanding and resolving the disproportion in SPDR [appraisal] markings. I suggested that what's driving that disproportion is not simply blatant racism and I stand by that. Because I am eager to find a solution to this I think I failed to acknowledge the real disadvantaged (*sic*) that comes with any form of discrimination–whether it's intended or otherwise. During the Q&A session I put forward a view that there is evidence that sometimes we tend to be more comfortable with people who we see as being like us, less comfortable with difference, and therefore sometimes work gets distributed according to those patterns of comfort, habit and familiarity. What happens then at the end of the year is likely to reflect who got given what work. I still maintain that this is a possible explanation but what was missing from my Q&A response was that such behaviour leads to discrimination and disproportion and clearly that situation needs to be tackled.'

3   Prison Reform Trust. Experiences of Minority Ethnic Employees in Prison: A briefing on a PRT survey of the views of black and minority ethnic prison staff. People from BME groups make up about 9% of the general population, 25% of the prison population, and less than 6% of those employed in prisons. Available online: http://www.prisonreformtrust.org.uk/subsection.asp?id=640

[4] 1 NATURE AND EXTENT OF YOUNG BLACK PEOPLE'S OVERREPRESENTATION Prepared 15 June 2007. 23. Once they have been charged with an offence, black young offenders are significantly less likely to be given unconditional bail compared to white young offenders and black young offenders are more likely to be remanded in custody compared to white re-offenders. [38] In 2004/05, 8.1% of black people under 18 were remanded in custody, compared to 5.1% for Asian and 4.4% for white people of the same age-group. [39]

24. We know that young black people and young people of 'mixed' ethnicity, when sentenced, are more likely to receive more punitive sentences than young white people. Whereas black young offenders accounted for 6% of total offences in 2004-05, they received 11.6% of total custodial sentences. Available online http://www.parliament.the-stationery-office.co.uk/pa/cm200607/cmselect/cmhaff/181/18105.htm

[5] *The Guardian.* Sunday 7 February 2010 'COMPLAINTS OF PRISON RACISM RISE AMONG STAFF AND INMATES' by Rowenna Davis and Paul Lewis. 'Ministry of Justice complaints data reveals a steady rise in alleged racist incidents at the 139 prisons in England and Wales. The figures, released under the Freedom of Information Act, are likely to add to concern over extremism in prisons. They come as prison staff express concern over growing sympathy for the British National party among colleagues.

The figures show there have been 46,000 complaints by staff and prisoners that were categorised as racist since 2006. By 2008 there were 14,191 complaints about alleged racism in prisons, a 25% increase on 2006, when there were 11,389.

A spokesperson for the justice department said reported incidents had increased as a result of complaint forms becoming more accessible and confidential, and stressed that few of the reported incidents consisted of serious allegations. However, the improvement in availability in complaints forms began nine years ago, long before the recent surge in complaints.

[The] latest figures will raise concern over racial tensions in prison. They show that while alleged racism between prisoners has actually decreased between 2006 and 2008, so-called alleged racism by prisoners against staff–the most common complaint–increased by 39%. Similarly, "staff on staff" racism has increased by 37% in the same period, while "staff on prisoner" racism also increased, by 13%.'

PART THREE

Setting the Record Straight...

'[Egypt was] a great civilised power during the period in which Europe was being overrun by savage tribes. Arithmetic, architecture, geometry, astrology, all the arts and nearly all of today's industries and sciences were known while the Greeks lived in caves. The pattern of our thinking originated in Africa.'
Eilesee Reclus (1893) *The Earth and Its Inhabitants*, **Vol 1 New York: D. Appleton and Co., p.207**

'The African Continent is no recent discovery, it is not a new world like America or Australia. While yet Europe was the home of wandering Barbarians, one of the most wonderful civilizations on record had began to work out its destiny on the banks of the Nile.'
History of Nations **(1906) Volume 18 1.**

'Modern canons, flying missiles, ship propellers, automatic hammers, gas motors, meat cleavers and even the upholstery tack hammers were developed in Africa's early use of power.'
John W Weatherwax (1962) *Ancient Africa: The African Contribution*

'Architects, artists, merchants, mechanics, operatives, sailors, agriculturists and shepherds of ancient Egypt were undoubtedly of Negro stock.'
Adam Gurowski (2005) *Slavery in History*, **Univ. of Michigan Library: Scholarly Publishing Office.**

'Many important models which have been developed to explain the cumulative process of economic development from Smith (1776), Marx (1967)...to Barro and Sala-i-Martin (1991) and Parente and Prescott (1994 and 1999) have not acknowledged Ibn Khaldun's analysis of economic development...due to their ignorance of the African literature. What is fascinating about Ibn Khaldun's analysis of economic development is his concentration on human capital...their skills and decisions, capital accumulation, the free movement of economic resources between nations, technology, the relevant institutions of development, and the optimal rate of taxation imposed on business enterprises. In fact, some of the dominant growth models which have been recently developed by very well known economists are essentially similar to the development model introduced by Ibn Khaldun in 1380.'
Adil H. Mouhammed (2009) *Early African contributions to economic development, the business cycle, and globalization* **International Journal of Business Research**

Most textbooks credit Europeans with the origin of mathematics and omit the contributions of non-Europeans. The resulting bias creates a distorted version of history...(p2) Our current method of multiplication, [was] brought to Europe by Arabic-speaking Africans (p17). The main body of elementary and high school mathematics was developed in Africa and Asia. The later European development of mathematics rests on an African and Asian base (p49).
Beatrice Lumpkin (1987) *African and African-American Contributions to Mathematics*. Portland Public Schools Geocultural Baseline Essay Series.

The 70th anniversary of World War II is being commemorated around the world, but the contribution of one group of soldiers is almost universally ignored. 1,355,347 African soldiers [fought] in the Second World War.'
Martin Plaut (2009) *The Africans who fought in WWII* BBC Africa analyst

To say that the Negro cannot develop sufficiently in the business world...is to deny actual facts, refute history, and discredit the Negro as a capable competitor in the economic battle of life...Properly awakened, the Negro can do the so-called impossible in the business world and thus help to govern rather than merely be governed.'
Carter G. Woodson (1933) *The Mis-Education of the Negro*. African American Images. Chicago, Illinois

Don't you know who I am? I am an African Queen, stolen and traded a million times over. Attempts at systematically erasing my memory—have failed! Trying to breed the black out of me has failed. Refusing to educate me, has failed. Even the glass ceiling cannot keep this black woman back, as my spirit simply passes through it. I am not beautiful because you have decided which shade of my skin, is in. I am beautiful because I choose to believe I am. Go back to your history books and see, that you have never truly diminished me. Resistant and rising; persistent and climbing, ever upwards. And there's nothing you can do about it! How you like me now!
Olivea Ebanks (2010) 'Defiant' in *Chronicles of Colour*. An anthology of poems. Unpublished Collection

I will praise You, [Lord God] for I am fearfully [and] wonderfully made; Marvellous are Your works, And [that] my soul knows very well.
Psalms 139:14

References & Bibliography

Batty, David. (2004) *Feltham Officers 'Racially Abused Inmates'*. Society Guardian. Available online: http://www.guardian.co.uk/society/2004/dec/17/youthjustice.prisons

Best, J. W. & Khan, J.V. (1998b) *Research in Education*. 8th Edition. Needham Heights MA: Allyn & Bacon. p.30

Brown, Alison, Erskine, Angus and Littlejohn, Doris (2006) *Research Series No. 64 Review of Judgments in Race Discrimination Employment Tribunal Cases*. University of Stirling & Law at Work. The Department of Trade and Industry. Available online: http://www.berr.gov.uk/files/file34687.pdf

BSM Consulting (1998) *Portrait of an ENTJ: The Executive*. Available online: http://www.personalitypage.com/ENTJ.html

Calhoun, John C. (1844) *Secretary of State arguing for the extension of slavery*. Available online: http://en.wikipedia.org/wiki/Stereotype

Colfax, Richard H. *(1833) An Excerpt from:* Evidence Against the Views of the Abolitionists, Consisting of Physical and Moral Proofs, of the Natural Inferiority of the Negroes. *New York: James T. M. Bleakley Publishers*

Commission for Racial Equality (2003a) *The Murder of Zahid Mubarek: A formal investigation by the Commission for Racial Equality into HM Prison Service of England and Wales*. London: Commission for Racial Equality p.3

Commission for Racial Equality (2003b) *The Murder of Zahid Mubarek: A formal investigation by the Commission for Racial Equality into HM Prison Service of England and Wales*. London: Commission for Racial Equality p.12

Crown copyright (2004), *Employment Tribunal (Constitution and Rule of Procedure) Regulations* Statutory Instrument 2004 No. 1861. Available online: http://www.opsi.gov.uk/SI/si2004/20041861.htm

Davis, Rowenna and Lewis, Paul (2010) *Complaints of prison racism rise among staff and inmates*. Available online:

http://www.guardian.co.uk/society/2010/feb/07/complaints-prison-racisim-staff-inmates

Dew, Thomas (1832) *An Essay in Favor of Slavery*. Available online: http://www.wwnorton.com/college/history/archive/resources/documents/ch15_03.htm

Ebanks, Olivea (2010) 'Defiant' in *Chronicles of Colour*. An anthology of poems. Unpublished Collection

Ferguson, G.O. (1916). *The Psychology of the Negro*. Wesport, CN: Negro Universities Press, p.124.

Fryer, Peter (1984) *Staying Power: The History of Black People in Britain*. London: Pluto Press

Goulbourne, Harry (1998) *Race Relations in Britain Since 1945*. Hampshire: Palgrave MacMillan

Gurowski, Adam (2005) *Slavery in History*. Univ. of Michigan Library: Scholarly Publishing Office.

History of Nations (1906) Volume 18 1.

House of Commons (2006) *Report of the Zahid Mubarek Inquiry*. London: The Stationery Office. p. 329 Available online http://report.zahidmubarekinquiry.org.uk/volume_one.pdf

House of Commons Home Affairs (2007) Select Committee on Home Affairs. *1 Nature and Extent of Young Black People's Overrepresentation*. Available online http://www.parliament.the-stationery-office.co.uk/pa/cm200607/cmselect/cmhaff/181/18105.htm

Howe, Darcus (2006) *Darcus Howe remembers the "insohreckshan" The New Statesman*. Available online http://www.newstatesman.com/200604030015

Jones, A. & Singer, L. (2007) *Statistics on Race and the Criminal Justice System–2006: A Ministry of Justice Publication under Section 95 of the Criminal Justice Act 1991*. Available online: http://www.justice.gov.uk/publications/statistics.htm

Kirby, Maurice (2000) *Slavery, Atlantic Trade and the British Economy, 1660-1800. New Studies in Economic and Social History.* Cambridge: Cambridge University Press

Krebs-Hirsch, Sandra and Kummerow, Jean. (2006) *ENTJ-The Leader.* Available online: http://www.geocities.com/lifexplore/entj.htm

Leggatt, Andrew (2001) *Tribunals for Users One System, One Service.* Available online: http://www.tribunals-review.org.uk/leggatthtm/leg-00.htm

Lumpkin, Beatrice (1987) *African and African-American Contributions to Mathematics. Portland Public Schools Geocultural Baseline Essay Series.* Available online:
http://www.pps.k12.or.us/depts-c/mc-me/be-af-ma.pdf

Ministry of Justice (2006) *Statistics on Race and the Criminal Justice System–2006*
A Ministry of Justice Publication under Section 95 of the Criminal Justice Act 1991. Available online: http://www.justice.gov.uk/publications/statistics.htm

Ministry of Justice (2010) *Matt Wotton's Message.* RESPECT Newsletter spring edition no.32 p.14

Mouhammed, Adil H. (2009) *Early African contributions to economic development, the business cycle, and globalization.* International Journal of Business Research. FindArticles.com. 30 Nov, 2009. Available online: http://findarticles.com/p/articles/mi_6773/is_3_9/ai_n39236693/

Plaut, Martin (2009) *The Africans who fought in WWII BBC Africa analyst.* Available online:
http://news.bbc.co.uk/1/hi/world/africa/8344170.stm

Reclus, Eilesee (1893) *The Earth and Its Inhabitants, Vol 1.* New York: D. Appleton and Co., p.207

Scarman, Leslie (1982) *The Scarman Report: The Brixton Disorders, 10-12 April, 1981.* London: Penguin Books

Shakespeare, William. *King John.* Act 5 scene 7

Shyllon, F.O. (1974) *Black Slaves in Britain*. London: Oxford University Press

SMART (2010) *Identifying and Tackling Disproportion*. REAG presentation on SMART data 9 February 2010. Available on request: REAG@noms.gsi.gov.uk

Terman, Lewis. (1916) *The Measurement of Intelligence, in Nobles, W.W. (1986). African psychology: Toward its reclamation, reascension, and revitalization.* Oakland: The Institute for the Advanced Study of Black Family Life and Culture.

Weatherwax, John W. (1963) *Ancient Africa: The African Contribution*. Pamphlet, Los Angeles: Bryant Foundation.

Woodson, Carter G. (1933) *The Mis-Education of the Negro*. Chicago, Illinois: African American Images. p187

Also by Olivea M. Ebanks

Chronicles of Colour

An anthology of poetry.

This collection will feature a range of poetry styles from Patois to prose poetry. The subjects covered will be wide ranging to include politics, relationships and faith as they relate to growing up in Britain with a West Indian heritage.

Coming Soon